COMMENTARIES

ON

THE FOUR LAST BOOKS OF MOSES

ARRANGED

IN THE FORM OF A HARMONY

BY JOHN CALVIN

TRANSLATED FROM THE ORIGINAL LATIN, AND COMPARED WITH THE FRENCH EDITION; WITH ANNOTATIONS, ETC.,

BY THE REV. CHARLES WILLIAM BINGHAM, M.A.

RECTOR OF MELCOMBE-HORSEY, DORSET, AND FORMERLY FELLOW OF NEW COLLEGE, OXFORD

VOLUME FOURTH

WIPF & STOCK · Eugene, Oregon

Wipf and Stock Publishers
199 W 8th Ave, Suite 3
Eugene, OR 97401

Commentaries on the Four Last Books of Moses Arranged in the Form of a Harmony, Volume 4
Translated from the Original Latin, and Compared with the French Edition;
with Annotations, etc.
By Calvin, John and Bingham, Charles William
Softcover ISBN-13: 979-8-3852-0990-3
Hardcover ISBN-13: 979-8-3852-0991-0
eBook ISBN-13: 979-8-3852-0992-7
Publication date 12/11/2023
Previously published by Baker Book House, 1852

This edition is a scanned facsimile of the original edition published in 1852.

THE FOUR LAST BOOKS OF MOSES

ARRANGED IN THE FORM OF

A HARMONY, WITH COMMENTARIES.

DEUTERONOMY, CHAPTER I.

6. The Lord our God spake unto us in Horeb, saying, Ye have dwelt long enough in this mount:

7. Turn you, and take your journey, and go to the mount of the Amorites, and unto all *the places* nigh thereunto, in the plain, in the hills, and in the vale, and in the south, and by the sea-side, to the land of the Canaanites, and unto Lebanon, unto the great river, the river Euphrates.

8. Behold, I have set the land before you: go in and possess the land which the Lord sware unto your fathers, Abraham, Isaac, and Jacob, to give unto them, and to their seed after them.

6. Jehova Deus noster loquutus est nobis in Horeb, dicendo: Sat vobis est habitasse in monte isto.

7. Vertite vos, et proficiscimini, et ite ad montem Amorrhæorum, et ad omnes vicinos ejus, in solitudine, in monte, et planitie, et meridie, et in littore maris, terram Chenanæi à Lebanon usque ad flumen magnum flumen Euphraten.

8. Vide, dedi coram vobis terram, ingredimini, et possidete terram illam quam juravit Jehova patribus vestris, Abraham, Isaac et Jacob, se daturum eis, et semini eorum post ipsos.

6. *The Lord our God spake to us in Horeb.* In this Second Narration, Moses expressly declares that God not only gave them a visible sign, by uplifting the cloud, but that He also verbally commanded the people to leave Mount Sinai, and to set about the performance of the rest of their journey. God says, then, that enough time had been spent in one place;[1] for, before they left it, an entire year had passed

[1] "Et non sans cause;" and not without reason.—*Fr.*

away there. Although there were eleven days' journey before them before they would arrive at Kadesh-barnea, nevertheless, lest anything should delay the people, who were naturally but too indolent, He stimulates them by setting before them the ease with which it might be accomplished, telling them that they had but to lift up their feet and advance, in order to attain the promised rest.

NUMBERS, CHAPTER IX.

17. And when the cloud was taken up from the tabernacle, then after that the children of Israel journeyed: and in the place where the cloud abode, there the children of Israel pitched their tents.

18. At the commandment of the Lord the children of Israel journeyed, and at the commandment of the Lord they pitched: as long as the cloud abode upon the tabernacle they rested in their tents.

19. And when the cloud tarried long upon the tabernacle many days, then the children of Israel kept the charge of the Lord, and journeyed not.

20. And *so* it was, when the cloud was a few days upon the tabernacle; according to the commandment of the Lord they abode in their tents, and according to the commandment of the Lord they journeyed.

21. And *so* it was, when the cloud abode from even unto the morning, and *that* the cloud was taken up in the morning, then they journeyed: whether *it was* by day or by night that the cloud was taken up, they journeyed.

22. Or *whether it were* two days, or a month, or a year, that the cloud tarried upon the tabernacle, remaining thereon, the children of Israel abode in their tents, and journeyed not: but when it was taken up, they journeyed.

23. At the commandment of the Lord they rested in the tents, and

17. Quum discederet nubes à tabernaculo, postea proficiscebantur filii Israel: atque in loco ubi manebat nubes, illic castrametabantur filii Israel.

18. Ad os Jehovæ proficiscebantur filii Israel, et ad os Jehovæ castrametabantur: cunctis diebus quibus stabat nubes supra tabernaculum, manebant.

19. Quum autem moram trahebat nubes supra tabernaculum diebus multis, tunc observabant filii Israel custodiam Jehovæ, et non proficiscebantur.

20. Quando autem nubes paucis diebus erat super tabernaculum, ad os Jehovæ manebant, et ad os Jehovæ proficiscebantur.

21. Quando igitur erat nubes a vespera usque mane, ascendebat autem nubes mane, tunc proficiscebantur: aut si nocte et die, et postea ascendebat nubes, tunc proficiscebantur.

22. Aut duobus diebus, aut mense, aut anno, quando moram trahebat nubes super tabernaculum, manendo super illud, in castris manebant filii Israel, nec proficiscebantur: si autem illa ascendebat, tunc proficiscebantur.

23. Ad os Jehovæ castrametabantur, et ad os Jehovæ proficisce-

at the commandment of the Lord they journeyed: they kept the charge of the Lord, at the commandment of the Lord by the hand of Moses.

bantur: custodiam Jehovæ servabant ad os Jehovæ per manum Mosis.

EXOD. xl. 36. And when the cloud was taken up from over the tabernacle, the children of Israel went onward in all their journeys:

37. But if the cloud were not taken up, then they journeyed not till the day that it was taken up.

38. For the cloud of the Lord *was* upon the tabernacle by day, and fire was on it by night, in the sight of all the house of Israel, throughout all their journeys.

36. Quum recederet nubes a tabernaculo, proficiscebantur filii Israel in cunctis profectionibus suis:

37. Quòd si non recederet nubes, non proficiscebantur usque ad diem qua recedebat.

38. Quia nubes Jehovæ erat super tabernaculum interdiu, ignis vero noctu in eo, coram oculis totius domus Israel, in cunctis profectionibus eorum.

17. *And when the cloud was taken up from the tabernacle.* Moses before informed us that the tabernacle was so distinguished by a visible miracle, that God made it manifest that He dwelt there: not that He left heaven and removed to that earthly house, but in order to be nigh to His people by the presence of His power and grace, whenever He was invoked by them. He now reports another miracle, that God, by uplifting the cloud, gave a sign, as it were, by which He commanded them to strike the camp; and when the cloud rested on the tabernacle, it was a sign that they should abide where they were. Here, however, a question arises; since it has been already said that, immediately after their departure from Egypt, the cloud was like a banner to direct the march of the people, it follows that they were not now for the first time admonished by its being lifted up to collect their baggage, and ordered as it were to advance. The answer is easy, that the people were indeed previously directed by the sight of the cloud, as we have seen; but that here a new fact is related, viz., that since the tabernacle was set up, the cloud, which hitherto was suspended in the air and went before the camp, now settled on the sanctuary: for a fresh acquisition of grace is here proclaimed by the more certain and conspicuous sign, as if God shewed Himself more closely and familiarly as the leader of the people. Although, therefore, the cloud had been the director of their march from its very commencement, yet it more fully illus-

trated the glory of the tabernacle when it proceeded from thence.

18. *At the commandment of the Lord.*[1] The *mouth* is here used by metonymy for the speech; nor does there appear to me to be so much harshness in the Hebraism, but that it may be appropriately retained. But it is asked whether God actually spoke or not; for the word *mouth* is often repeated. It is indeed likely that Moses was instructed but once what was meant by the removal or remaining of the cloud; yet I doubt not but that the name of *word*, or *commandment*, was given to the sign, inasmuch as God speaks as much to the eyes by outward signs as He does to the ears by His voice. Still, from this mode of expression we may gather that the use of signs[2] is perverted and nullified, unless they are taken to be visible doctrine, as Augustin writes. The repetition, which certainly has no little force, shews how worthy this is of observation.

19. *Then the children kept the charge of the Lord.* Some,[3] in my opinion, extend this too far, thinking that when the cloud tarried, the children of Israel, being as it were at leisure, employed themselves in the worship of God; but I restrict it rather to that heedfulness which is then praised at some length. To keep the charge (*custodiam,*) then, is equivalent to regarding the will of God with the greatest earnestness and care. For, when the cloud had begun to rest in any place, the people knew that they were to remain there; but if on the next day they were not

[1] "At the mouth of the Lord."—*Lat.*

[2] "Des sacremens."—*Fr.* I cannot find that Augustin anywhere uses the exact words which *C.* here attributes to him. In his *Tract. in Evang. Johan.*, lxxx. § 3, however, he says, "Detrahe verbum, et quid est aqua nisi aqua? Accedit verbum ad elementum, et fit sacramentum, etiam ipsum tanquam *visibile verbum.*" (Edit. Bened. vol. iii. part. 2, p. 703.) And again, *Contra Faustum, lib.* xix. *cap.* xvi.: "Quid enim sunt aliud quæque corporalia sacramenta, nisi quædam quasi *verba visibilia?*" &c. Vol. viii. 321. Both these passages are quoted by *C. Inst.* iv., xiv. § 6.

[3] Dathe agrees with Malvenda and other ancient commentators in adopting the opinion here rejected by *C.* "The sense of the passage (he says) is, that the Israelites set up the holy tabernacle, and observed the holy rites, if they were detained for many days in one place; but if for a short time only, the tabernacle was not set up. Whether this was to be the case or not was indicated to them by Moses, according to ver. 23."

attentive, the cloud might vanish, and thus their neglect and carelessness might deprive them of this incomparable advantage.

To this end it is said immediately afterwards that, If for one day, or more, or even for a month, or a year, the cloud stood still, the people was, as it were, tied to the spot. The old interpreter[1] has not badly rendered it, "The children of Israel were upon the watch;" since day and night they anxiously expected the time when God would command them to move forward. The last verse of the chapter confirms this sense, where it is again added, that "they kept the charge of the Lord at His mouth by the hand of Moses:" whence it appears that Moses was God's interpreter, so that they might set forth on their march whenever the cloud being lifted up pointed out to them the way. Nor can it be doubted but that it preceded them; so that they might know in what direction God would have them proceed, and whither they were to go. Moreover, it must be observed that in both respects it is counted worthy of praise in the people, that they should either journey, or continue where they were, at God's command. Thus is that absurd activity condemned which engages itself in endless work; as if men could only obey God by turmoil. Whereas it is sometimes no less a virtue to rest, when it so pleases God.[2]

EXOD. XL. 38. *For the cloud of the Lord was on the tabernacle.* Moses more distinctly explains what he had said generally respecting the cloud, viz., that by night a fiery column appeared, because the cloud would not have been visible amidst the darkness. A second explanation is also added, that this did not happen once or twice only, but "in all their journeys;" so that they were never without a sight of the cloud, which might be a witness of God's presence, whether, being settled on the tabernacle, it commanded them to rest, or, by its ascension, gave them the sign for removing the camp. Now, the equability of this proceeding, in all the variety of times and marches, did not a little conduce to

[1] *I.e.*, the Vulgate: "Erant filii Israel in excubiis Domini."

[2] "They also serve, who only stand, and wait."—Milton; Sonnet on his blindness.

certainty; for, if the cloud had daily accomplished the same course, this very regularity would have obscured the power of God; but when for a whole year it did not move, and then frequently proceeded to a new place, and now by its guidance pointed out a longer journey, now a shorter one, by this very diversity the paternal care of God, who was never unmindful of His people, more conspicuously manifested itself.

NUMBERS, CHAPTER X.

29. And Moses said unto Hobab, the son of Raguel the Midianite, Moses' father-in-law, We are journeying unto the place of which the Lord said, I will give it you: come thou with us, and we will do thee good; for the Lord hath spoken good concerning Israel.

30. And he said unto him, I will not go; but I will depart to mine own land, and to my kindred.

31. And he said, Leave us not, I pray thee; forasmuch as thou knowest how we are to encamp in the wilderness, and thou mayest be to us instead of eyes.

32. And it shall be, if thou go with us, yea, it shall be, that what goodness the Lord shall do unto us, the same will we do unto thee.

33. And they departed from the mount of the Lord three days' journey: and the ark of the covenant of the Lord went before them in the three days' journey, to search out a resting-place for them.

34. And the cloud of the Lord *was* upon them by day, when they went out of the camp.

35. And it came to pass, when the ark set forward, that Moses said, Rise up, Lord, and let thine enemies be scattered; and let them that hate thee flee before thee.

36. And when it rested, he said, Return, O Lord, unto the many thousands of Israel.

29. Dixit autem Moses ad Hobab filium Reuel Madianitæ soceri sui, Nos proficiscimur ad locum de quo dixit Jehova, Illum dabo vobis: veni nobiscum, et benefaciemus tibi: quia Jehova loquutus est beneficentiam super Israelem.

30. Respondit autem ei, Non veniam: sed ad terram meam, et ad natale solum meum ibo.

31. Tunc dixit, Ne derelinquas nos: quia propterea nosti mansiones nostras in deserto, et fuisti nobis pro oculis.

32. Quum autem veneris nobiscum, et evenerit nobis bonum illud quod benefacturus est Jehova nobis, tum benefaciemus tibi.

33. Profecti sunt itaque a monte Jehovæ via trium dierum: et arca fœderis Jehovæ proficiscebatur ante eos via trium dierum illorum, ad explorandam illis requiem.

34. Et nubes Jehovæ erat super eos interdiu, dum proficiscerentur è castris.

35. Quum autem cœpit proficisci arca, dicebat Moses, Surge Jehova, et despergantur inimici tui, et fugiant odio habentes te a facie tua:

36. Quando vero requiescebat, dicebat, Revertere Jehova ad decem millia millium Israelis.

29. *And Moses said unto Hobab the son of Raguel* Very

grossly are those mistaken who have supposed Hobab[1] to be Jethro, the father-in-law of Moses, whom we have already seen to have returned a few days after he had come to see him. Now, old age almost in a state of decrepitude would have been but little suited for, or equal to, such difficult labours. Moses was now eighty years old, and still far short of the age of his father-in-law. But all doubt is removed by the fourth chapter of Judges, where we read that the descendants of Hobab were still surviving in the land of Canaan. When, therefore, the good old man went home, he left Hobab his son—still in the vigour of life, and to whom on account of his neighbourhood, the desert-country was well known—as a companion for his son-in-law, that might be useful to him in the performance of many services. Here, however, whether wearied by delay and difficulties, or offended by the malignant and perverse spirit of the people, or preferring his home and a stationary life to those protracted wanderings, he desired to follow his father. In order, however, that we might know that he had not sought his dismissal as a mere feint, (as is often the case,[2]) Moses expressly states that he could not immediately prevail upon him to stay by his prayers; nay, that he was not attracted by the promises whereby Moses endeavoured to tempt him, until he had been perseveringly entreated. Although the expectation of the promised land is set before him, yet, since mention is only made of temporal and transient prosperity, it may thence be probably conjectured that he had not profited by his advantages as he should. He had seen and heard the tokens of God's awful power when the Law was given; yet Moses urges him to come on by no other argument than that he would enjoy the riches of the land. Unless perhaps Moses desired to give him some taste of the graciousness and fatherly love of God as manifested in the temporal blessing, in order to lift up his mind to higher things. Still he merely refers to the promise of God, and

[1] So De Lyra, *S.M.*, Fagius, Tostatus, the *LXX.*, &c. See note on Exod. ii. 18, *ante*, vol. i. p. 54.

[2] " (Comme il adviendra souventes fois que les hommes font des rencheris);" as it will often happen that people want to be pressed to stay.—*Fr.*

then engages that he shall share in all their good things. Nevertheless, this alone is no trifle, that he should be attracted by no uncertain hope, but by the sure enjoyment of those good things which God, who cannot lie, had promised: for deceptive allurements often invite men to undergo labours, and to encounter perils; but Moses brings forward God, as it were, as his surety, inasmuch as He had promised that He would give the people a fertile land, full of an abundance of all good things. At any rate, Hobab represents to us, as in a mirror, the innate disposition of the whole human race, to long for that which it apprehends by the carnal sense. It is natural to prefer our country, however barren and wretched, to other lands the most fertile and delightful: thus the Ithaca of Ulysses has passed into a proverb.[1] But let me now reprove another fault, viz., that, generally speaking, all set their affections on this present life: thus Hobab despises the promise of God, and holds fast to the love of his native land.

31. *And he said, Leave us not, I pray thee.* Moses perseveres and urges what he had just said, that Hobab should be a sharer in the prosperity which God had given his people reason to expect. "*To this end*" (he says) "thou hast known all our stations in the desert," which words commentators do not appear to have observed or understood; for they translate them simply, "*for* thou hast known," as if Moses desired to retain Hobab to be of use to himself, whereas there is more than one causal particle here;[2] and thus it is literally, "*Since, for this cause,* thou hast known all our resting-places," &c. Its meaning, then, is as follows, that Hobab was ill-advised for his own interest; for he had borne many inconveniences, for this reason, that he might at some time or other receive his recompense; as if it were said, Wherefore hast thou hitherto endured so many inconveniences whilst directing

[1] "Comme l'isle en laquelle Ulysses estoit né, n'estant qu'une poure isle, voire quasi semblable à un rocher, est venue en un proverbe;" thus the island in which Ulysses was born, being but a poor island, indeed almost like a rock, has passed into a proverb.—*Fr.* See Cicero *De Orat.*, i. 44, and *De Legg.*, ii. 1.

[2] כי על־כן. Translated in *A. V.*, Gen. xviii. 5, *for therefore;* Judges vi. 22, *for because;* Jer. xxxviii. 4, *for thus;* and here, *forasmuch as.*

our course, unless that thou mightest enjoy with us the blessings of our repose? In a word, Moses signifies that the labours of Hobab would be vain and fruitless, unless he should endure them a little while longer, until, together with the children of Israel, he should enjoy the promised inheritance. What is here said, then, does not relate to the future, as if Moses had said, Be to us instead of eyes, as thou hast been heretofore; but by reminding him that the reward of his labours was at hand, he urges and encourages him to proceed.

33. *And they departed from the mount of the Lord.* He calls Sinai "the mount of the Lord," because in no other place had God's glory been so conspicuously manifested. This, I admit, it had been called by anticipation (κατὰ πρόληψιν) before the promulgation of the law; but this name was imposed upon it afterwards to inspire eternal reverence for the law. By "three days' journey," we must understand a continuous march of three days, for they did not pitch their tents until they reached the desert of Paran, but slept in the open air. When it is said that the ark went before them in the three days' journey, there is no reference to its distance, as if it was sent forward three days ahead; but that it was so placed in their van that, when the cloud settled upon it, they halted as at a station prescribed to them by God. This was the searching for a resting-place of which he speaks.

35. *And it came to pass, when the ark set forward.* Since their journey was by no means a peaceful one, but the attack of enemies was constantly to be dreaded, it was needful to beseech God that He would go forth as if prepared for battle. Thus, too, did Moses support their courage, lest any more immediate cause for terror should render them sluggish and inert. It is, then, as if he had prayed thus: O Lord, not only shew us the way, but open it to us also by the power of thy hand in the destruction of the enemies. He calls them not the enemies of *the people* but of *God*, in order that the Israelites might be assured that they fought under His auspices; for thus might both a more certain victory be expected, since the righteous God, who avenges

iniquity, was defending His own cause; and also, it was no slight matter of consolation and rejoicing, when the people heard, that whosoever should arise to harass them unjustly were also the enemies of God, since He will protect His people as the apple of His eye. Therefore has the Prophet borrowed this passage, in order to arm the Church with confidence, and to maintain it in cheerfulness under the violent assaults of its enemies. (Ps. lxviii. 1.) Further, the analogy and similitude between the visible sign, and the thing signified, must be observed; for Moses was not so foolish as to address the Ark in these words; he only asked God to prove effectually that the Ark was a lively image of His power and glory.

36. *And when it rested, he said, Return, O Lord.* By thus praying he also exhorts the people to be patient, lest the weariness which arose from the delay should beget indignation. Otherwise it would have been annoying that the time of their journeying should be protracted, so that they would arrive the later at their rest. And we see, indeed, how their minds were exasperated, as if a slower progress was a kind of disappointment. In order, therefore, to correct this impatience, Moses reminds them that their halts were advantageous to them, so that God, dwelling at home like the father of a family, might manifest His care of them; for the allusion is to men who take advantage of a time of repose and release from other business, to occupy themselves more unrestrainedly in paying attention to their own family.

NUMBERS, CHAPTER XI.

1. And *when* the people complained, it displeased the Lord: and the Lord heard *it;* and his anger was kindled; and the fire of the Lord burnt among them, and consumed *them that were* in the uttermost parts of the camp.

2. And the people cried unto Moses; and when Moses prayed unto the Lord, the fire was quenched.

3. And he called the name of the place Taberah; because the fire of the Lord burnt among them.

1. Et fuit populus quasi fatiscentes, displicuit in auribus Jehovæ. Audivit enim Jehova, et iratus est furor ejus, exarsitque ignis ipsius contra eos, consumpsitque extremum castrorum.

2. Tunc clamavit populus ad Mosen, et oravit Moses Jehovam, et concidit ignis.

3. Vocavitque nomen illius loci Taberah: quia accensus fuerat in eos ignis Jehovæ.

1. *And when the people complained, it displeased the Lord.*[1] The ambiguous signification of the participle[2] causes the translators to twist this passage into a variety of meanings. Since the Hebrew root און, *aven,* is sometimes trouble and labour, sometimes fatigue, sometimes iniquity, sometimes falsehood, some translate it, "The people were, as it were, complaining or murmuring." Others (though this seems to be more beside the mark) insert the adverb *unjustly;* as if Moses said, that their complaint was unjust, when they expostulated with God. Others render it, "being sick, (*nauseantes,*") but this savours too much of affectation; others, "lying, or dealing treacherously." Some derive it from the root תואנה, *thonah,* and thus explain it, "seeking occasion," which I reject as far fetched. To me the word fainting (*fatiscendi*) seems to suit best; for they failed, as if broken down with weariness. It is probable that no other crime is alleged against them than that, abandoning the desire to proceed, they fell into supineness and inactivity, which was to turn their back upon God, and repudiate the promised inheritance. This sense will suit very well, and thus the proper meaning of the word will be retained. Thus, Ezekiel calls by the name תאנים, *theunim,* those fatigues, whereby men destroy and overwhelm themselves through undertaking too much work. Still, I do not deny that, when they lay in a state of despondency, they uttered words of reproach against God; especially since Moses says that this displeased the ears of God, and not His eyes; yet the origin of the evil was, as I have stated, that they fainted with weariness, so as to refuse to follow God any further.

And the Lord heard it. He more plainly declares that

[1] *Lat.*, "And the people was, as it were, fainting (*fatiscentes,*) it was displeasing in the ears of Jehovah." *Fr.* "Apres il adveint que le peuple fut comme gens discouragez, (*margin,* despitez,) ce que despleut aux aureilles de l'Eternel;" afterwards it came to pass that the people were as persons discouraged (or fretted) which displeased the ears of God.

[2] מתאננים. Prof. Robertson and Simon agree in referring this participle Hithpahel to the root אנן, *he groaned heavily,* rather than to און. *C.*, as usual, has given some of the Rabbinical expositions which he saw in *S.M.* תאנה occurs in Judges xiv. 4., where *A. V.* has *occasion;* תאנים in Ezek. xxiv. 12., where Simon's Lexicon notices it as meaning *wearinesses,* placing this word under the root און.—*W.*

the people broke forth into open complaints; and it is probable that they even cast reproaches upon God, as we infer from the heaviness of this punishment. Although some understand the word *fire* metaphorically for vengeance, it is more correct to take it simply according to the natural meaning of the word, *i.e.*, that a part of the camp burnt with a conflagration sent from God. Still a question arises, what was that part or extremity of the camp which the fire seized upon? for some think that the punishment began with the leaders themselves, whose crime was the more atrocious. Others suppose that the fire raged among the common people, from the midst of whom the murmuring arose. But I rather conjecture, as in a matter of uncertainty, that God kindled the fire in some extreme part, so as to awaken their terror, in order that there might be room for pardon; since it is presently added, that He was content with the punishment of a few. It must, however, be remarked, that because the people were conscious of their sin, the door was shut against their prayers. Hence it is, that they cry to Moses rather than to God; and we may infer that, being devoid of repentance and faith, they dreaded to look upon God. This is the reward of a bad conscience, to seek for rest in our disquietude, and still to fly from God, who alone can allay our trouble and alarm. From the fact that God is appeased at the intercession of Moses, we gather that temporal punishment is often remitted to the wicked, although they still remain exposed to the judgment of God. When he says that the fire of the Lord was sunk down,[1] for this is the proper signification of the word שקע, *shakang*, he designates the way in which it was put out, and in which God's mercy openly manifested itself; as also, on the other hand, it is called the fire of God, as having been plainly kindled by Him, lest any should suppose that it was an accidental conflagration. A name also was imposed on the place, which might be a memorial to posterity both of the crime and its punishment; for *Tabera* is a burning, or combustion.

[1] *Lat.*, "fuisse demersum." *A. V.* "quenched." *Margin*, "*Heb.* sunk." "שקע, *Submergi; In profundum deprimi, comprimi, reprimi.*" —*Buxtorf.*

4. And the mixed multitude that *was* among them fell a lusting; and the children of Israel also wept again, and said, Who shall give us flesh to eat?

5. We remember the fish which we did eat in Egypt freely; the cucumbers, and the melons, and the leeks, and the onions, and the garlic:

6. But now our soul is dried away: *there is* nothing at all, beside this manna, *before* our eyes.

7. And the manna *was* as coriander seed, and the colour thereof as the colour of bdellium.

8. *And* the people went about, and gathered *it*, and ground *it* in mills, or beat *it* in a mortar, and baked *it* in pans, and made cakes of it: and the taste of it was as the taste of fresh oil.

9. And when the dew fell upon the camp in the night, the manna fell upon it.

10. Then Moses heard the people weep throughout their families, every man in the door of his tent: and the anger of the Lord was kindled greatly; Moses was also displeased.

11. And Moses said unto the Lord, Wherefore hast thou afflicted thy servant? and wherefore have I not found favour in thy sight, that thou layest the burden of all this people upon me?

12. Have I conceived all this people? have I begotten them, that thou shouldest say unto me, Carry them in thy bosom (as a nursing-father beareth the sucking child) unto the land which thou swarest unto their fathers?

13. Whence should I have flesh to give unto all this people? for they weep unto me, saying, Give us flesh, that we may eat.

14. I am not able to bear all this people alone, because *it is* too heavy for me.

15. And if thou deal thus with me, kill me, I pray thee, out of hand; if I have found favour in thy sight; and let me not see my wretchedness.

4. Et collectio quæ erat in medio ejus, concupiverunt concupiscentia, et aversi sunt: quinetiam fleverunt filii Israel, dicentes, Quis pascet nos carnibus?

5. Recordamur piscium quos comedebamus in Ægypto gratis, cucumerum, et peponum, et porrorum, et ceparum et alliorum.

6. At nunc anima nostra arida est, nec quicquam est nisi man in oculis nostris.

7. Man autem sicut coriandri semen erat, et color ejus sicut color bdellii.

8. Diffundebant autem se populus, et colligebant, et molebant in mola aut terebant in mortario, coquebantque in olla, faciebantque ex eo placentas, quarum sapor erat sicut sapor recentis olei:

9. Quum verò descenderat ros super castra, descendebat man super ipsum.

10. Audivit itaque Moses populum flentem per familias: quemque ad ostium tabernaculi sui: unde iratus est furor Jehovæ valdè, ipsi quoque Mosi displicuit.

11. Et dixit Moses ad Jehovam, Ut quid malefecisti servo tuo? et quare non inveni gratiam in oculis tuis, ut imponeres onus universi populi hujus super me?

12. An ego concepi universum populum istum? et an ego genui eum, quòd dicis mihi, Porta eum in sinu tuo, quemadmodum ferre solet nutritius infantem, in terram de qua jurasti patribus ejus?

13. Unde mihi caro ut dem universo populo huic? Flent enim adversum me, dicendo, Da nobis carnes, ut comedamus.

14. Non possem ego solus ferre universum populum hunc: quia supra vires meas est.

15. Quòd si ita tu facis mihi, occide me quæso occidendo, si inveni gratiam in oculis tuis, et ne videam malum meum.

4. *And the mixed multitude that was among them.* A new murmuring of the people is here recorded: for we gather from many circumstances that this relation is different from that which precedes: although, as evil begets evil, it is probable that after they had begun to be affected by the disease of impatience, they spitefully invented grounds for increased tedium and annoyance. Yet there was something monstrous in this madness, that, when they had just been so severely chastised, and part of the camp was even yet almost smoking, and when God was hardly appeased, they should have given way to the indulgence of lust, whereby they brought upon themselves a still more severe punishment. Unquestionably, when they again provoked God by their iniquity, the remains of the fire were still before their eyes; whence it appears how greatly they were blinded by their obstinate wickedness. He states, indeed, that the murmuring first began among the strangers, or mixed multitude, who had mingled themselves with the Israelites, as we have seen elsewhere; but he adds that the whole people also were led into imitation of their ungodly complainings. Hence we are taught, that the wicked and sinful should be avoided, lest they should corrupt us by their bad example; since the contagion of vice easily spreads. At the same time also, we are warned, that it does not at all avail to excuse us, that others are the instigators of our sin; since it by no means profited the Israelites, that they fell through the influence of others, inasmuch as it was their own lust which carried them away. In the first place, therefore, we must beware that our corrupt desires do not tempt us, and we must put a restraint upon ourselves; and then that the profane despisers of God do not add fuel to the fire.

A question here occurs, whether it is sinful to long for flesh; for if so, all our appetites must likewise be condemned. I answer, that God was not wroth because the desire of flesh affected the Israelites; but, first, their disobedience displeased Him, because they longed to eat flesh, as it were, against His will, when He would have them content with the manna alone; and then their intemperance and violent passion. For this reason Moses says that they "lusted a lust,"[1] indicating that they abandoned all self-control, so as to go beyond all bounds. In the third place, their ingratitude displeased Him, which is here adverted to, but openly condemned in the Psalm, where the Prophet reproves them, for that God "had commanded the clouds from above, and opened the doors of heaven," so as to supply them with the "corn of heaven," and the bread "of angels," (Ps. lxxviii. 23-25;) and yet, even so they were not restrained from despising so excellent a benefit, and abandoning themselves to lawless intemperance. The rule of moderation, and of a sober and frugal life, which Paul prescribes, is well known; that we should "know both how to be full and to be hungry, both to abound and to suffer need." (Phil. iv. 12.) Well known, too, is his admonition, that we should "make not provision for the flesh, to fulfil the lusts thereof." (Rom. xiii. 14.) All improper longing is, therefore, to be repressed, so that we should desire nothing which is not lawful; and, secondly, that our appetites should not be excessive. Hence, when he refers elsewhere to this occurrence, (1 Cor. x. 6,) he warns us to fear the judgment of God; "to the intent we should not lust after evil things," thus distinguishing wild and uncontrolled appetites from such as are moderate and well regulated.

When they ask, "Who shall give us flesh to eat?" they seek to have it elsewhere than from God, who abundantly supplied them with food, though it was of a different kind. We see, then, that they rebelled with a brutal and blind impetuosity; for necessity was laid upon them by God, that they should eat nothing but manna; against this they struggled like fierce and stubborn beasts, as if they would make God the servant of their lust.

5. *We remember the fish which we did eat in Egypt.* By this comparison with the former mode of living, they depreciate the present grace of God: and yet they enumerate no delicacies, when they speak of leeks, and onions, and garlic. Some, therefore, thus explain it, When such great abundance and variety was commonly to be met with, how painful and grievous must it be to us to be deprived of greater delicacies!

[1] See Margin *A.V.*

My own opinion is, that these lowly people, who had been used to live on humble fare, praised their accustomed food, as if they had been the greatest luxuries. Surely rustics and artisans value as much their pork and beef, their cheese and curds, their onions and cabbage, as most of the rich do their sumptuous fare. Scornfully, therefore, do the Israelites magnify things which, in themselves, are but of little value, in order the more to stimulate their depraved appetite, already sufficiently excited. Still there is no doubt but that those who had been accustomed to a diet of herbs and fish, would think themselves happy with that kind of food. Moreover, to make the matter more invidious, they say in general, that they ate *gratis*[1] of that, which cost them but little: although such a phrase is common in all languages. For even profane writers testify that all that sea-shore abounds with fish.[2] The fisheries of the Nile also are very productive, and a part of the wealth of Egypt: whilst the country is so well watered, that it produces abundance of vegetables and fruits.[3]

6. *But now our soul is dried away.* They complain that they are almost wasted away with famine and hunger, whilst they are abundantly supplied with manna; in the same way as they had just been loudly declaring that they had lived in Egypt for a very little money; as if they were affected by a great dearth of provisions, when, by the pure

[1] *A. V.*, "freely." Ainsworth, "for nought;" "this (he adds) may be referred to the fish which they had for nought, without price, getting them out of the rivers freely; or for nought, that is, for very little, very cheap. It may also have reference to the former, *We remember for nought, i.e.*, in vain; so the Hebrew *Chinnam*, and the Greek δωρεὰν, sometimes signifieth a thing done or spoken in vain, and without effect; as Prov. i. 17; Ezek. vi. 10; Gal. ii. 21." Geneva Version, "for nought, *i.e.*, for a small price, or good cheepe."

[2] Herod., ii. 93, describes the abundance of the fish in Egypt, and their migrations for the deposition of their spawn: and states that the inhabitants of the marshes, some of them, "live on nothing but fish."—*Ibid.* 92.

[3] Raphelius has a striking note on this passage from Herod. "The herbs (onions and garlic) were ordinarily given to labourers in Egypt. Whence also this was the food of the Israelites, whose labours the Egyptians used, or rather abused, in making bricks. Herod. ii. 125. "It is declared by certain Egyptian inscriptions on the Pyramid itself, how much was paid to the workmen, ἔς τε συρμαίην, καὶ κρόμμυα καὶ σκόροδα, for radishes, onions, and garlic."—Raphel., *in loco.*

liberality of God, a kind of food was provided for them, more easy to prepare than any other, and so actually prepared without trouble or cost. But such is the malignity and ingratitude of men, that they count all God's bounty for nothing, whilst they are brooding over their own importunate lusts. Many in their gluttony consume, and bring to nought whatever God bestows upon them: others, in their avarice, dry up the fountain of His liberality, which else would be inexhaustible. But these, in the midst of their abundance, say that they are dry, because insatiable cupidity inflames them, so that God's blessing, however ample, cannot satisfy them. Thus the rain, washing the hard rock, wets it not within, neither tempers its dryness by its moisture. Since, therefore, a contempt of God's blessings withers them all, like a hot blast, let us learn to assign them their due honour, that they may be supplied to us in sufficiency. Thus will be fulfilled in our case: "The righteous shall flourish like the palm-tree: he shall grow like a cedar in Lebanon. Those that be planted in the house of the Lord shall flourish in the courts of our God. They shall still bring forth fruit in old age; they shall be fat and flourishing." (Ps. xcii. 12-14.) For Scripture does not so often declare in vain that God satisfies the longing souls, and filleth the hungry with food. They complain that there is nothing before their eyes but manna: as if their loathing of this one excellent and abundant kind of food was actual famine.

7. *And the manna was as coriander seed.* Moses had already adverted to this in Exod. xvi.;[1] but he now repeats it, in order more fully to condemn their perverse desire; for what could be more unseemly and intolerable than thus to eschew a food delightful both in appearance and taste? For the same reason the Prophet, in Psalm lxxviii., records that men were not satisfied with "angels' food," and "corn from heaven." Here, instead of saying that it was white, he calls it the colour of *Bedola*,[2] a precious stone, whether a pearl,

[1] See *antè*, vol. i. 275.

[2] *A. V.*, "bdellium;" Hebr. בדלח *bedolach*. "The bdellium of the sacred writer was in all probability the pearl, as the Arabic version has rendered it."—Illustr. Comment. on Gen. ii. 12.

or some other kind. Its very appearance, then, was calculated to give them pleasure; and, since without much labour, either by grinding or crushing it, they might make it into various sorts of food, and all of a sweet and pleasant taste, the baser was their ingratitude in complaining, as if God treated them with but little liberality as to their food.

10. *Then Moses heard the people weep.* Wonderful indeed, and almost prodigious was the madness of the people, thus all of them to mourn as if reduced to the extremity of despair. What would they have done in actual famine? what if they had to gnaw bitter roots, almost without any juice in them? What if they had had to live on tasteless and unwholesome bread? We see, therefore, how by the indulgence of their depraved lusts men make themselves wretched in the very midst of prosperity. Let us, then, learn to bridle our excessive passions, that we may not bring upon ourselves troubles and inconveniences, and all sorts of painful feelings; for if the cause be duly weighed, when men afflict themselves with sorrow and lamentation, we shall generally find that, whereas the evil might be lightened by endurance, its pain is increased by preposterous imaginations. But here a gross instance of luxury is set before us, when, in their satiety, they weep as if long abstinence threatened them with death. It was an effect of holy and praiseworthy zeal, that this great perverseness should displease Moses; but he was not without error in carrying it to excess; for he unjustly expostulates with God, complaining that He had laid too heavy a burden upon him, when he knew all the time that he was sustained by His power. His charge was indeed difficult and laborious; but in that he had experienced God's wondrous aid, whenever he had groaned beneath his burden, there was no room for complaint; besides, since he had been dignified by a peculiar honour, it was ungrateful to brand with disgrace the good gift of God. He reputes it his greatest evil that the charge of governing the people had been intrusted to him; whereas all his senses ought rather to have been ravished with astonishment, that God had condescended to choose him to be the redeemer of His people, and the minister of His wondrous power. This, too,

was very inconsiderate, to ask whether he had begotten or brought forth the people; as if his calling by God did not lay him sufficiently under obligation, or as if there were no other ties than those of nature. God, indeed, has inspired parents with such love towards their offspring, that they willingly undergo incredible troubles on their account; but Moses was bound by another kind of piety, for by God's command he was father of the people. Wherefore he ought not to have only regarded nature, but the obligation of his office also.

13. *Whence should I have flesh to give to all this people?* Justly, indeed, does he accuse the people, and deny that he is possessed of flesh wherewith to satisfy so great a multitude; but he is wrong in expostulating with God, as if he were burdened beyond his strength; for, since God knew that he was unequal to so many difficulties, He supported him by the influence of His Spirit. But he sinned most grossly in the conclusion of his complaint, requesting God to kill him. In these words we see how far even the best of God's servants may be carried, when they give too great indulgence to their passions. For it is the longing of despair to seek that we may be removed from the world, so that death may bring our troubles to an end. Since the impetuosity of his grief hurried away Moses God's most chosen servant to this, what might not happen to us, if impatience should hold dominion over our hearts? Let us, then, learn to put a stop to this disease in good time.

16. And the Lord said unto Moses, Gather unto me seventy men of the elders of Israel, whom thou knowest to be the elders of the people, and officers over them; and bring them unto the tabernacle of the congregation, that they may stand there with thee.	16. Tunc dixit Jehova ad Mosen, Congrega mihi septuaginta viros è senioribus Israel, quos nosti seniores esse populi et principes ejus, adducasque eos ad ostium tabernaculi conventionis, ut adstent ibi tecum.
17. And I will come down and talk with thee there: and I will take of the spirit which *is* upon thee, and will put *it* upon them; and they shall bear the burden of the people with thee, that thou bear *it* not thyself alone.	17. Tunc descendam, et loquar tecum ibi, et separabo de spiritu qui est in te, et ponam in eis: ut sustineant tecum onus populi: et non sustineas tu solus.
18. And say thou unto the people,	18. Ad populum autem dices,

Sanctify yourselves against to-morrow, and ye shall eat flesh: (for ye have wept in the ears of the Lord, saying, Who shall give us flesh to eat? for *it was* well with us in Egypt;) therefore the Lord will give you flesh, and ye shall eat.

19. Ye shall not eat one day, nor two days, nor five days, neither ten days, nor twenty days:

20. *But* even a whole month, until it come out at your nostrils, and it be loathsome unto you: because that ye have despised the Lord which *is* among you, and have wept before him, saying, Why came we forth out of Egypt?

21. And Moses said, The people, among whom I *am*, *are* six hundred thousand footmen; and thou hast said, I will give them flesh, that they may eat a whole month.

22. Shall the flocks and the herds be slain for them, to suffice them? or shall all the fish of the sea be gathered together for them, to suffice them?

23. And the Lord said unto Moses, Is the Lord's hand waxed short? thou shalt see now whether my word shall come to pass unto thee, or not.

Sanctificamini in crastinum, et comedetis carnes: flevistis enim in auribus Jehovæ, dicendo, Quis comedere faciet nos carnes? certe melius erat nobis in Ægypto: dedit enim Jehova vobis carnes, et comedetis.

19. Non una die comedetis, neque duobus diebus, neque quinque diebus, neque decem diebus, neque viginti diebus tantum:

20. Sed usque ad mensem dierum, donec egrediatur è naribus vestris, et sit vobis in abominationem: propterea quod contempsistis Jehovam, qui est in medio vestri, et flevistis coram eo, dicendo, Ut quid egressi sumus ex Ægypto?

21. Et dixit Moses, Sexcentorum millium peditum est populus in cujus medio ego sum: et tu dicis, Carnem dabo eis: et comedent mensem dierum.

22. Nunquid oves et boves ingulabuntur eis, et sufficient illis? an omnes pisces maris congregabuntur illis, et sufficient eis?

23. Tum dixit Jehova ad Mosen, Nunquid manus Jehovæ abbreviabitur? nunc videbis utrum eveniat tibi verbum meum, annon.

16. *And the Lord said unto Moses, Gather unto me seventy men.* God complies with the request of Moses, by associating with him seventy companions, by whose care and assistance he may be relieved from some part of his labour; yet not without some signs of indignation, for, by taking from him some portion of His Spirit to distribute amongst the others, He inflicts upon him that mark of disgrace which he deserved. I know that some[1] regard it differently, and think

[1] Thus, De Lyra; "It is not to be understood that anything was taken away from Moses and given to the others, but they were illuminated without any diminution of the grace of Moses; thus, by the light of one candle others are lighted, without any diminution of its own light." Ainsworth thus traces the gloss of De Lyra to its source: "Neither was Moses' spirit hereby diminished; for as Sol. Jarchi says, 'Moses in that hour was like unto the lamp that was left (burning) in the candlestick (in the Sanctuary) from which all the other lamps were lighted, yet the light thereof was not lessened any whit.'" So also St. Augustine, "We understand that God would signify nothing more than that they also would have assistance from

that nothing was taken away from Moses, but that the others were endued with new grace, such as Moses had been pre-eminent for possessing alone before. But, since the words expressly declare that God will make them partakers of that grace which He will take from Moses himself, I by no means admit the truth of this subtle exposition. The passage in Gen. xxvii. 36 is quoted, in which it is said, "Hast thou not reserved a blessing for me?" but, when God expressly says, "I will separate[1] of the Spirit which is upon thee," there can be no question but that a diminution is indicated. For, as long as Moses alone was appointed to rule the people, he was so supplied with the necessary gifts of the Spirit, as that his ability should not be inferior to the greatness of the labour. God now promises that the others shall be his companions in such sort, as that He divides His gifts among them all. I have no doubt, then, but that this division comprehends punishment in it; and from hence we may gather a useful piece of instruction, viz., that the greater the difficulty is which God imposes upon any one, the greater is the liberality with which He treats him, in order that he may be sufficient for his charge. Thus it is in His power to work with equal efficiency by one man, as by a hundred, or a thousand; for He has no need of a multitude (of agents,) but, as He pleases, He executes His works sometimes without the aid of men, sometimes by their hands. In sum, God indirectly reproves the gross ingratitude of Moses, whereby he depreciated that marvellous grace which had hitherto shone forth in him; and He declares that he shall not be hereafter so great as he was, in regard to the excellency he derived from the Spirit; inas-

the same Spirit of grace, as Moses had; that they also should have as much as God pleased, not that Moses would therefore have less. Quest. in Num. xviii. *Edit. Bened., tom.* iii. P. i. p. 535. *C.*, indeed, here, seems to have but few followers. The gloss in the Geneva version is; "I will distribute my Spirit among them, as I have done to thee;" and Attersoll says, "It it true he doth sometimes punish in this manner, sometimes by lessening, and sometimes by taking away, what he had formerly bestowed. Zech. xi. 17; Matt. xxv. 27. But we do not read or find that he dealt so with Moses, or that he was less fit for government than he was before," &c.

[1] *A. V.*, "I will take;" or "will separate."—Ainsworth.

much as he had in a manner thrown away the gifts of the Spirit, by refusing to bear the trouble imposed upon him. Our modesty, indeed, is praiseworthy, if through consciousness of our own weakness we recoil from arduous charges; but it is too absurd for us to withdraw ourselves under this pretext from our duty, and, despising the calling of God, to shake off the yoke.

The word Spirit is here, as frequently elsewhere, applied to the gifts themselves; as if He had said, I had deposited with thee gifts sufficing for the government of the people; but now, since thou refusest, I will distribute his due measure to each of the seventy, so that the grace of the Spirit, which dwelt in thee alone, shall be manifestly dispersed among many. It is now asked how Moses separated the seventy, whether according to his own judgment only, or by the election of the people. It is generally agreed that six were chosen from each tribe, and thus that they were seventy-two; but that for the sake of brevity two were omitted, as amongst the Romans,[1] they spoke of the *Centumviri*, although they were a hundred and five; for they appointed three for each of the thirty-five tribes. Since the opinion is probable, I leave it undecided; but at the same time I retain the conjecture which I have elsewhere made,[2] viz., that, since the race of Abraham had been increased in an incredible manner in two hundred and twenty years, lest so astonishing a miracle should ever be forgotten, the seventy were elected in accordance with the number of the fathers who had gone down into Egypt with Jacob. And, in fact, this seems to have been with them, as it were, a sacred number; as recalling to their memory that little band from which they had derived their origin. For, before the Law was promulgated, Moses was commanded to take with him seventy to accompany him to the mount, and to be eyewitnesses of God's glory. Meanwhile, I do not deny that there were two more than the number seventy; but I only

[1] "*Centumviri* were judges chosen from the thirty-five tribes, three from each, so that properly there were 105, but they were always named by a round number, Centumviri. *Festus.*"—Adam's Rom. Antiq.

[2] See *antè*, on Exod. xxiv. 1, vol. iii. p. 316.

point out why God fixed upon this number, viz., to equalize the leaders and heads of the people with the family of Jacob, which was the source of their race and name. In truth, from the fact that, when Moses went up into Mount Sinai to receive the Tables from the hand of God, he took with him seventy officers, we infer that the number of those who should excel in honour, was already fixed at this, although the charge of governing, which is here spoken of, was not yet committed to them. And it is probable that these same persons who had been appointed leaders, were called to this new and unwonted office, as the words themselves imply. It is indeed certain, that when the Jews returned from the Babylonish captivity, because they were not permitted to appoint a king, they followed the example here set them in the establishment of their Sanhedrim; only this honour was paid to the memory of David and their kings, that from their race they chose their seventy rulers in whom the supreme power was vested. And this form of government continued down to Herod,[1] who abolished the whole council by which he had been condemned, and destroyed the lives of them all. Still, I think that he was not impelled to commit the massacre only out of vengeance, but also lest the dignity of the royal race should be an obstacle to his tyranny.

It must, however, be observed that, although God promises new grace to the seventy men, he would not have them taken indiscriminately from the people in general, but expressly commands them to be chosen from the order of the elders, and heads of the people, being such as were already possessed of authority, and had given proofs of their diligence and virtue. Thus, also, now-a-days, when he calls both the pastors of the Church and magistrates to their office, although He furnishes them with new gifts, still He would not have them raised to their honourable stations promiscuously as they may come first, but chooses rather with reference to their spiritual endowments, wherewith He distinguishes, and commends those whom He has destined to any exalted office. In short, He commands the most fit-

[1] Josephus, Antiq., xiv. 9. § 4.

ting to be chosen; but, after they have been elected, He promises that He will add what is wanting. For this reason He commands that they should station themselves at the door of the tabernacle, that He may there display His grace. Although I think that two other reasons were likewise taken into consideration, viz., that they might know that the office was intrusted to them by God, and might always be mindful of the heavenly tribunal, before which they must be accountable: and also that they might be held in additional reverence by the very associations of the place, and that the people might submit to them as the ministers of God. Now, although God does not at present dwell in a visible tabernacle, yet are we reminded by this example that pastors and magistrates are not duly ordained, unless they are placed in the presence of God; nor rightly inaugurated in their offices, unless when they consecrate themselves to God Himself, and when His majesty, on the other hand, acquires their reverence. Cyprian[1] twists this passage further, but I know not whether on sufficiently firm grounds, to prove that bishops are not to be elected, except with the consent of the whole people.

[1] "Wherefore a people which obeyeth the precepts of the Lord, and feareth God, ought to separate itself from a Prelate who is a sinner, nor mingle itself up with the sacrifices of a sacrilegious priest, especially since it has itself the power either of choosing worthy priests, or rejecting the unworthy. This, too, we see to be derived from divine authority, that a priest should be chosen in presence of the people, in sight of all, and be approved worthy and fit by public sentence and testimony; as in Numbers, the Lord commanded Moses, saying, *Take Aaron thy brother, and Eleazar his son, and bring them up into the mount, before all the congregation: and strip Aaron of his garments, and put them upon Eleazar his son, and Aaron shall be gathered unto his people, and shall die there.* (Num. xx. 25, 26.) God commands a priest to be appointed before all the congregation, that is, He instructs and shews us, that the ordinations of priests ought only to be solemnized with the knowledge of the people standing by, that so by their presence either the crimes of the wicked may be detected, or the merits of the good proclaimed, and so the ordination be right and lawful, as having been examined with the suffrage and judgment of all."—Epistles of S. Cyprian. Oxford Transl. 1844, pp. 211, 212.

The above quotation is from a letter written in the names of Cyprian and thirty-six of his brethren, as a reply to inquiries made by the presbyter and people of Leon and Astorga, and the deacons and faithful people in Merida. Cyprian has not cited Numb. xi. 16, in any of the works now acknowledged as his, though the argument thus drawn from Numb. xx. 25, 28, would have been more reasonably collected from the text, to which *Calvin* has assumed that he referred.

18. *And say thou unto the people, Sanctify yourselves.* This is another part of the answer, which is given respecting the matter in consideration, viz., that the people should prepare themselves to satiate their greediness. Although the word קדש,[1] *kadesh,* signifies to *prepare,* yet its literal meaning seems to be most appropriate here; I have therefore retained the word *sanctify,* which is, however, here used ironically, for Moses does not exhort them to purge themselves from all defilements, and piously and sincerely to receive the grace of God, but he chastises their profane and brutal gluttony. Others translate it simply, as if it were said, Whet your teeth, and make ready your bellies: but, in my judgment, there is a reproof implied, because they are polluted by a foul and wicked desire, so as to be incapable of receiving God's paternal favour: for "ye shall eat flesh" follows, "because your weeping and complaining has reached the ears of God;" by which words he signifies that by their importunate cries they had provoked God's anger, so that they should devour none but deadly food. And soon afterwards it is stated more clearly that by their insolence they had deserved to be destroyed by the bounty of God. For "a whole month," he says, ye shall gormandize, "till it come out of your nostrils, and it be loathsome unto you." Thus he compares them to those guttlers who so overwhelm themselves with gluttony, that they are obliged soon afterwards to vomit what they have eaten too greedily, or who abominate the taste of their superfluous luxuries, as if they were something filthy. This is what is meant by to "come out," or to be blown out, "at the nostrils." זרא,[2] *tzara,* which we have translated *abomination,* properly means *dispersion;* but Moses indicates by it that they shall vomit, or spit it out, like something unfit to be swallowed. If any should object that it is said in Ps. lxxviii. 30, "They were not *yet* estranged from their lust:" this is easily solved by understanding that

[1] If קדש may be said to signify to *prepare,* it can only be so rendered when the preparation is by sanctifying.—*W.*

[2] זרא (loathsomeness) is said by *S. M.* to be an irregular form of זרה; and he renders it dispersion, agreeably with the acknowledged meaning of the root זרה. This account of the word has the sanction of modern lexicographers.—*W.*

their unrestrained gluttony is there rebuked,[1] as if he called them guttlers (*gurgites,*) whom no abundance can suffice to satisfy. Therefore the Prophet says, that although they were bursting with excess, they were not satiated ; but were so inflamed by their boundless voracity, that God's vengeance could alone repress it. But the reason alleged for this is especially to be observed, " because they had rejected God, who was in the midst of them." By these words, the excuse of error or inadvertency is barred ; for if, for the purpose of proving their patience God had withdrawn His power, the terror which they conceived at His absence might, perhaps, have been excusable ; but now, when they knew by sure experience that their means of subsistence were supplied by Him, they betray their deliberate wickedness by despising His present beneficence. For that God was in the midst of them is equivalent to His giving manifest tokens both of His infinite power and His paternal favour. These words shew us that the more immediately God manifests His grace to us, the more inexcusable we are, if we disparage it when it is thus liberally offered to us. What follows might appear not to deserve severe reproof, viz., that they " wept before God ;" but the enormity of the sin is specified directly afterwards, *i.e,* that they were vexed by their departure from Egypt : for this was not merely to repudiate the deliverance, which they had so greatly longed for, but to quarrel with God, because He had listened to their cry, and had condescended to redeem them from their wretched and lost estate.

21. *And Moses said, The people among whom I am, are six hundred thousand.* Although Moses' object was right, yet he fell into unbelief, and thus stumbled at the very threshold. His pious solicitude indeed impelled him to doubt ; because he feared that God's holy name would be exposed to derision and contumely, if he should send away empty those to whom he had promised food. But it seemed to him incredible that so mighty a multitude should be suf-

[1] Que là le Sainct Esprit deteste leur gourmandise desbordee ;" that there the Holy Spirit marks His detestation of their unbridled gluttony. —*Fr.*

ficiently supplied with flesh. When he calls them "six hundred thousand," he either does not calculate their numbers exactly, or indicates that some had died since their departure, when he had numbered the people. (Exod. xiv.) Yet it is probable that he referred to the recent *census*, in which they were found to be 603,550, (Numb. i. 46;) but for the sake of brevity he put the sum in the gross, as he does elsewhere, omitting the 3550. (Exod. xii. 37.) By speaking of *footmen*, he means the men, and thus excepts the women and children. Assuredly such a multitude might astonish him, or, at any rate, might inspire him with alarm, so that he should mistrust the promise. His doubt, however, was wrong in two respects; first, because he did not simply trust, as if he were not assured that God was true in all His words; and, secondly, because he improperly allowed his mind to measure God's inestimable power by his own senses. Let us learn, therefore, that, as soon as God has spoken, we should embrace, without discussion, whatever has proceeded out of His mouth; and so likewise let us learn to humble ourselves, and our own minds, and at the same time to rise by faith above the world, and our natural reason; so that no absurdity, which the flesh may suggest to us, should prevent us from certainly concluding that whatever God has promised He will, by His might, perform. For it is a most incorrect calculation to bind down God's doings to ordinary standards; as if His power were not more extensive than our minds can reach. We must, therefore, carefully take notice of the rebuke, whereby God so corrected Moses at once, that it ought to prevent and to cure all diseases of distrust in us. For the immensity of God's hand convicts the folly of those who would subject it to their own imaginations and rules. For, even although God should not stretch forth His hand, He holds heaven and earth in its "hollow," as it is said in Isa. xl. 12. What madness, then, is it to seek to grasp by our own senses, and, as it were, to imprison that hand which is greater than a hundred worlds! As soon, therefore, as distrust on the score of difficulties begins to take possession of our minds, let this conclusion be remembered, that the promises of God do not exceed the measure of His power to accomplish effectually whatever He has declared. This question, however, " Is the Lord's hand waxed short?" may be explained in two ways: for the old interpreter[1] has rendered it, " Is God's hand weak?" But God seems to adduce the proof, whereby He had borne witness to His power, not only in the creation of heaven and earth, but also in so many recent miracles; as if to rebuke the ingratitude of Moses, who had profited so little by these most striking lessons: for Isaiah uses the same word in this sense, where he says: " Behold, the Lord's hand is not shortened." (Isa. lix. 1.) Moses is unquestionably exalting the blessings received on former occasions, wherein the people had experienced the saving power of God. I have retained the future tense of the verb,[2] since it does not injure the sense. What is said amounts to this, Will God's hand be weaker than usual, so as not to put forth its power already known?

24. And Moses went out, and told the people the words of the Lord, and gathered the seventy men of the elders of the people, and set them round about the tabernacle.

25. And the Lord came down in a cloud, and spake unto him, and took of the spirit that *was* upon him, and gave *it* unto the seventy elders: and it came to pass, *that*, when the spirit rested upon them, they prophesied and did not cease.

26. But there remained two *of the* men in the camp, the name of the one *was* Eldad, and the name of the other Medad: and the spirit rested upon them, (and they *were* of them that were written, but went not out unto the tabernacle,) and they prophesied in the camp.

27. And there ran a young man, and told Moses, and said, Eldad and Medad do prophesy in the camp.

28. And Joshua the son of Nun, the servant of Moses, *one* of his young men, answered and said, My lord Moses, forbid them.

24. Egressus est autem Moses, et retulit ad populum verba Jehovæ: congregavitque septuaginta viros è senioribus populi, quos statuit in circuitu tabernaculi.

25. Tunc descendit Jehova in nube, et loquutus est ad eum: et seorsum accepit de Spiritu qui erat super eum, posuitque super septuaginta viros seniores: et fuit ut requiescente in eis Spiritu prophetaverint: et non addiderunt.

26. Remanserunt autem duo viri in castris, nomen unius Eldad, et nomen alterius Medad: super quos etiam requievit Spiritus (erant vero inter scriptos, sed non egressi fuerant ad tabernaculum) et prophetare cœperunt in castris.

27. Et cucurrit puer quidam, et nuntiavit Mosi, dixitque: Eldad et Medad prophetant in castris.

28. Tunc respondit Jehosua filius Nun minister Mosis ex juvenibus ejus, et dixit, Domine mi Moses probibe eos.

[1] That is, the *V.* " Numquid manus Domini invalida est?"

[2] In this *C.* follows the *LXX.* Μὴ χεὶρ Κυρίου οὐκ ἐξαρκέσει; " Shall not the Lord's hand suffice?" and most of the versions, according to Poole, in which it is rendered " abbreviabitur?"

29. And Moses said unto him, Enviest thou for my sake? Would God that all the Lord's people were prophets, *and* that the Lord would put his Spirit upon them!

29. Cui respondit Moses, Nunquid æmularis tu propter me? et utinam universus populus Jehovæ prophetæ essent! atque ut daret Jehova Spiritum suum super eos.

24. *And Moses went out and told the people the words.* We here see how greatly Moses profited by his brief rebuke, for he now actively sets about what he was commanded. Doubt had given him a check, so that he stopped in the middle of his course; whereas he now testifies by the promptitude of his obedience that his distrust is overcome. For just as unbelief discourages men, so that they sink down into inactivity, so faith inspires both body and mind with vigour for the effectual discharge of their duties.

Although the narrative does not expressly state that he spoke to them respecting the flesh, it declares in general terms that he omitted nothing; and, indeed, it would have been very inappropriate to speak only of the Seventy Elders, when the origin of all the evil had been the craving for flesh. Briefly stating, then, that he had reported the commands of God to the people, he includes both parts of the matter, the second of which he then follows up. And, first, he says that the elders were called to the Tabernacle, that they might there be appointed rulers and officers. When he states that they were "set round about," I do not interpret the words so precisely as to suppose that eighteen were ranged on each side, and, of the rest, half were placed before the court, and half behind the Tabernacle; but that they were so arranged, as to surround some part of the Tabernacle. Now, this was equivalent to their being set before God, so that they might hereafter exercise their office with more authority, as being sent by Him; and at the same time that they might devote themselves to God, and dedicate themselves to His service; and also, that being invested with the necessary endowments, they might bear the tokens of their calling. For this reason, it is soon afterwards added, that enough of the spirit of Moses was given them for the discharge of their official duties; for, although Moses by God's command had chosen men of approved virtue and experience, yet He would have them prepared anew, in order that their call might be effectual. When they are said to have "prophesied," this was a visible sign of the gift of the Spirit, which, nevertheless, had reference to a different object; for they were not appointed to be prophets, though God would testify by this outward mark that they were new men, in order that the people might receive them with greater reverence. In my opinion, however, prophecy here is equivalent to a special faculty of discoursing magnificently of secret things or mysteries. We know that poets were called prophets by profane writers,[1] because poetry itself savours of inspiration (ἐνθουσιασμὸν); in the same way that extraordinary ability,[2] in which the *afflatus* of the Spirit shone forth, obtained the name of prophecy. Thus, the gift of prophecy in Saul was a kind of mark of royalty; so that he might not ascend the throne without credentials. (1 Sam. x. 10.) Thus, then, this Spirit of Prophecy was only accorded to these persons for a short time; since it was sufficient that they should be once marked out by God: for so I understand what Moses says afterwards, "and they added not."[3] It is too forced an interpretation to refer it, as some do, to the past. I confess, indeed, that they were not previously prophets; but I have no doubt but that Moses here indicates that the gift was a

[1] *Vates* is a name commonly applied by classical writers to poets. "Quare suo jure noster ille Ennius *sanctos* appellat poëtas, quod quasi deorum aliquo dono, atque munere commendati nobis videantur."—Cicero pro Archiâ Poetâ, 8. "De versibus, quos tibi a me scribi vis, deest mihi quidem opera, quæ non modo tempus, sed etiam animum vacuum ab omni curâ desiderat; sed abest etiam ἐνθουσιασμὸς."—*Ibid.* Epist. ad Quint. Frat. iii. 4.

[2] *Fr.* "La grace de parler authentiquement de choses hautes;" the grace to speak authentically of high things.

[3] "These words are commonly rendered, 'and did not cease (to prophesy,)' as in our public version; or, 'and did not add,' as they are rendered by Ainsworth and Purver, neither of which renderings is to me intelligible. By adopting the Sam. reading with Houbigant, Dathe, and Rosenmüller, and placing ולא יאספי at the head of ver. 26, the text will be rectified, and the sense clear: At non congregati sunt, sed remanserant in castris viri duo, quorum nomen unius Eldad, et nomen alterius Medad, tamen requievit super eos spiritus ille (nam ipsi ex conscriptis, atsi non egressi erant ad tentorium) et prophetabant in castris."—Boothroyd *in loco*. Thus, Eldad and Medad will be the nominative case to the verb, and its meaning "were not assembled."

temporary one: as we are also told in the case of Saul: for, as soon as this token of God's grace had manifested itself in him,[1] he ceased to prophesy. The meaning, therefore, is that their call was thus substantiated for a short period, so that this unusual circumstance should awaken the more admiration.

26. *But there remained two of the men in the camp.* It is not certain why they had not appeared amongst the others. I do not at all doubt but that they were called for by Moses; nor would they have been endued with the same grace of the Spirit as the others, if through idleness or contempt they had not come at the time appointed. We may, therefore, probably infer that they did not actually receive the invitation, because they could not be found; and hence it arose that God excused their ignorance. Still, however, it must be observed that they were kept back by the secret counsel of God, that His grace might be made known by this illustrious proof amongst the common people in general, when they were not all eye-witnesses of it: for the greater portion of them had not assembled at the Tabernacle. In order, therefore, that its fame might spread more widely, and might reach even to the most lowly, God chose that this new and extraordinary gift of His Spirit should be conspicuous in the midst of the camp, lest any of the dullest and grossest among them should pretend to be ignorant of it. In fact, it is plain that they were all aroused by the miracle; for the "young man," who is spoken of, would not have run to bear the incredible news to Moses, unless struck by the novelty of the case.

28. *And Joshua the son of Nun, the servant of Moses.* It is obvious that this foolish and preposterous jealousy arose from a good source. Joshua saw that Moses was so preeminent above all others, as to be justly deemed, after God, the head of the people; he feared, therefore, lest, if any portion of his superiority should be withdrawn, the grace of God would be dispelled and lost. We know, too, that almost every change is injurious, and apt to give a shock to

[1] The *Fr.* applies this sentence to the elders, "ils ont cessé de prophetizer;" *they* ceased to prophesy.

public affairs. In asserting, then, the rights of Moses, he desired, as far as he could, to consult the welfare of all; but the excess of his zeal had some alloy in it, in consequence of the immoderate affection and love which he bore to Moses; just as it often happens to ourselves, that although our desires have a right object, they still go astray into erroneous feelings. So, then, let us learn to revere the most illustrious servants of Christ, as that God alone should be supreme; and that He, who is far above all, should still maintain His pre-eminence. And this will be the case, if we hold fast to the principle, that although "there are diversities of gifts," yet there is but one Spirit from whom they flow; and although there are "differences of administrations," yet but one Lord who must be served, (1 Cor. xii. 4, 5;) which also Paul confirms elsewhere, where he teaches us that the gifts are so distributed as that no individual should have all, but each "according to the measure of the gift of Christ." (Eph. iv. 7.)

29. *And Moses said unto him, Enviest thou for my sake?* This may be understood in two different ways. Some take it, as if Moses had said, It is no business of yours, if I have suffered any loss: and if anything is taken from me, it would be mine and not yours to grieve and grudge; but I think Moses spoke more simply, as if he had said, Behold, how differently I feel from you; for I, whose cause you suppose yourselves to be promoting, should desire that all were endowed with the spirit of prophecy. So was that foolish jealousy admirably rebuked, which would put a restraint upon God's blessing, so greatly to be desired by every pious mind. At the same time, we fully perceive the gentleness and humility of Moses, whom no ambition, nor consideration of his personal dignity, prevents from willingly admitting the very lowliest into companionship with himself. If any should object that it is God's pleasure, in order to enhance the excellency of the gift, that there should be but few prophets in the Church, and consequently that Moses inconsiderately sought for that, which is in repugnance to God's counsel in this matter, the reply is easy, that, although the saints acquiesce in His ordinary dispensations,

and are persuaded that the arrangement, which He makes, is the best, yet that it is an act of piety in them to desire to communicate with all others what is given to themselves, so as to be anxious rather to be last of all, than to begrudge perfection to their brethren. In sum, Moses declares that nothing would be more gratifying to him, than that God should diffuse the grace of the spirit of prophecy amongst the whole people, so that all should be partakers of it, from the least to the greatest.

30. And Moses gat him into the camp, he and the elders of Israel.

31. And there went forth a wind from the Lord, and brought quails from the sea, and let *them* fall by the camp, as it were a day's journey on this side, and as it were a day's journey on the other side, round about the camp, and as it were two cubits *high* upon the face of the earth.

32. And the people stood up all that day, and all *that* night, and all the next day, and they gathered the quails: he that gathered least gathered ten homers; and they spread *them* all abroad for themselves round about the camp.

33. And while the flesh *was* yet between their teeth, ere it was chewed, the wrath of the Lord was kindled against the people; and the Lord smote the people with a very great plague.

34. And he called the name of that place Kibroth-hattaavah: because there they buried the people that lusted.

35. *And* the people journeyed from Kibroth-hattaavah unto Hazeroth; and abode at Hazeroth.

30. Recepit autem se Moses ad castra, ipse et seniores Israel.

31. Et ventus egressus est à Jehova, adduxitque coturnices è mari, et demisit ad castra: quasi itinere diei hinc, et itinere diei illinc, per circuitum castrorum, et fere ad duos cubitos per faciem terræ.

32. Tunc surrexit populus toto die illo, et tota nocte, totoque die sequenti, et collegerunt sibi coturnices: qui pauciores collegit, collegit decem cumulos: et expanderunt sibi expandendo per circuitus castrorum.

33. Caro adhuc erat inter dentes eorum antequam concisa esset: tum furor Jehovæ exarsit in populum, percussitque Jehova populum plaga magna admodum.

34. Et vocatum est nomen loci illius Cibroth-hathaavah: quia ibi sepelierunt populum concupiscentem.

35. De Cibroth-hathaavah profecti sunt populus in Haseroth, et substiterunt in eo loco.

30. *And Moses gat him into the camp.* Although, after the appointment of the Seventy, all betook themselves to their own stations and dwelling-places, yet there is no doubt but that they were all forewarned of the approaching miracle, so as to be universally attentive to the event, which is presently related. When it is said that it was "a wind of the Lord" which brought the quails, there was no other

reason for this than that God might openly manifest that all things under heaven are subject to His dominion, and are ready to obey Him. He might, indeed, have created the quails at will (*nutu*,) just as He rained the manna from heaven; nor was it natural that by the force of the winds such an abundance of birds should be cast, and heaped together in one place; but by using the aid of the wind He confirmed what is written in Psalm civ. 3, 4, that "He maketh the winds his messengers,[1] and they bear him on their wings;" because in their swiftness they rapidly bear His commandments from the east to the west. Now, although it is true in the abstract that the winds come from Him, so that they are only His breath, and that the air cannot be stirred in the slightest degree except at His will, still an extraordinary miracle is here specified, as before in the passage of the Red Sea. The Prophet in the Psalm goes further: "He caused an east wind to blow in the heaven; and by his power he brought in the south wind," (Ps. lxxviii. 26,) in which words He signifies that the whole air was shaken, since the winds suddenly arose from different quarters, which covered the earth in all directions with an immense multitude of the birds.

When he says that the earth was filled "as it were a day's journey," I do not understand it as if the dead birds lay at so great a distance, but that they occupied such a space of ground in thick heaps, and, in fact, continuously. And this also we gather from the Psalm, where the Prophet says, that they fell "in the midst of their camp," and were carried to their tents round about. (Ps. lxxviii. 28.) What is added, as to their being "two cubits high," I do not interpret, as some do,[2] that they did not fly above two cubits from the ground, so as to be more easily taken with the hand; but that there was such a mass of them, that every one might carry away as much as he would. For to this also do

[1] *A. V.*, "Who maketh his angels spirits." See *C.'s* own translation and comment.—Cal. Soc. Edit., vol. iv. 144, and 147.

[2] So the *V.*, "Volabantque in aëre duobus cubitis altitudine super terram." "Sol. Jarchi saith, They flew so high as a man's heart, that he was not toiled in getting them, either by reaching high, or by stooping low."—Ainsworth *in loco*. Kitto, Illustr. Com. *in loco*, prefers this view.

those magnificent descriptions in the Psalm relate, whereby the miracle is extolled: "He rained flesh also upon them as dust, and feathered fowls, like as the sand of the sea." (Ps. lxxviii. 27.) But how "they spread them abroad—round about,"[1] is not very clear to me; unless, perhaps, they were placed in cages or coops, and daily taken out for food.

33. *And while the flesh was yet between their teeth.* Moses does not specify any particular day; but only that God did not wait till satiety had produced disgust, but inflicted the punishment in the midst of their greediness. We may, however, conjecture from what precedes, that time was given them to gorge themselves. From whence their insatiable voracity may be gathered, which prevailed for so many continuous days, and could not be appeased by any quantity of food. God, therefore, allowed them time abundantly sufficient for them to gorge themselves, unless their gluttony was prodigious: and yet punished their intemperance, while the meat was yet in their mouths. They were, then, suddenly surprised in the midst of their guttling; and hence it is said in the Psalm, (lxxviii. 30,) "they were not *yet* estranged from their lust;" just as any glutton might choke himself, by devouring more than his throat could hold. Nor is that at variance with their repletion, of which mention was lately made; for, however the belly may swell with the quantity of its contents, the furious lust of eating is never appeased. But, in order that their punishment might be more manifest, God inflicted it in the very act; nor could any better opportunity have been chosen.

34. *And he called the name of that place Kibroth-hattaavah.* It was requisite that some memorial of so great a sin should exist, that the sons might not imitate their fathers. Heretofore God had sustained them with a food both agreeable and wholesome: by longing for unlawful nourishment they

[1] "We are disposed to conclude with Calmet (in his note on this place) that the Hebrews salted their quails before they dried them. We have here, then, the earliest indication of processes, the benefits resulting from which have become so diffused and familiar, that it costs an effort of recollection to recognise them as benefits. Yet many centuries have not elapsed since the Emperor Charles V. thought it became him to erect a statue to the man (G. Bukel) who found the secret of salting and barrelling herrings."—Illustr. Com. *in loco.*

were their own poisoners and murderers. Now, such ingratitude was deservedly to be detested by their posterity ; and therefore the name was given to the place, not without the inspiration of the Spirit of God. So Paul reminds us, that in this narrative God's judgment against corrupt and vicious lusts was portrayed, that we might ourselves learn not to lust. (1 Cor. x. 6.) I have already briefly explained how far our appetites are to be restrained, and what intemperance, properly speaking, is.

NUMBERS, CHAPTER XII.

1. And Miriam and Aaron spake against Moses because of the Ethiopian woman whom he had married: for he had married an Ethiopian woman.	1. Et loquuta est Maria et Aharon contra Mosen propter uxorem Æthiopissam quam acceperat: uxorem enim Æthiopissam acceperat.
2. And they said, Hath the Lord indeed spoken only by Moses? hath he not spoken also by us? And the Lord heard *it*.	2. Et dixerunt, Nunquid solummodo per Mosen loquutus est Jehova? nonne etiam per nos loquutus est? Et audivit Jehova.
3. (Now the man Moses *was* very meek, above all the men which *were* upon the face of the earth.)	3. Vir autem ille Moses mansuetissimus fuit præ cunctis hominibus qui erant super faciem terræ.
4. And the Lord spake suddenly unto Moses, and unto Aaron, and unto Miriam, Come out ye three unto the tabernacle of the congregation. And they three came out.	4. Ergo extemplò dixit Jehova ad Mosen, Aharon et Mariam, Egredimini vos tres ad tabernaculum conventionis. Et egressi sunt ipsi tres.
5. And the Lord came down in the pillar of the cloud, and stood *in* the door of the tabernacle, and called Aaron and Miriam: and they both came forth.	5. Et descendit Jehova in columna nubis, et stetit ad ostium tabernaculi: vocavitque Aharon et Mariam, et egressi sunt ambo ipsi.
6. And he said, Hear now my words: If there be a prophet among you, *I* the Lord will make myself known unto him in a vision, *and* will speak unto him in a dream.	6. Quibus dixit, Audite nunc verba mea, Si fuerit propheta vobis, ego Jehova in visione apparebo ei, in somnio loquar cum eo.
7. My servant Moses *is* not so, who *is* faithful in all mine house.	7. Non sic servus meus Moses, qui in tota domo mea fidelis est.
8. With him will I speak mouth to mouth, even apparently, and not in dark speeches; and the similitude of the Lord shall he behold: wherefore then were ye not afraid to speak against my servant Moses?	8. Ore ad os loquor cum eo, atque in visione: non autem per ænigmata, neque (*vel*, sed) per similitudinem Jehovæ aspiciet: quare ergo non timuistis loqui adversus servum meum Mosen?

1. *And Miriam and Aaron spake against Moses.* This

relation is especially worthy of observation for many reasons. If Aaron and Miriam had always quietly and cordially supported the honour of their brother, and had not been carried away by perverse and ungodly jealousy, their harmony, however holy it was, would have been perverted by the injustice of many, and alleged against them as a deceitful and insidious conspiracy. It came to pass, then, in the wonderful providence of God, that his own brother and sister set on foot a contention with respect to the supremacy, and endeavoured to degrade Moses from the position in which God had placed him: for thus all suspicion of family favour was removed, and it was clearly shewn that Moses, being opposed by his own belongings, was sustained by the power of God alone. At the same time it may be perceived how natural is ambition to the minds of almost all men, and also how blind and furious is the lust of dominion. Aaron and Miriam contend with their own brother for the supremacy; and yet they had received the most abundant proofs, that he, whom they desire to overthrow, had been elevated by the hand of God, and was thus maintained in his position. For Moses had arrogated nothing to himself; and, therefore, it was not allowable that man should attempt to undermine the dignity of that high office, which God had conferred upon him. Besides, God had ennobled their own house and name in the person of Moses, and out of favour to him they had also been endued with peculiar gifts of their own. For by what right had Miriam obtained the gift of prophecy, except for the fuller ratification of her brother's power? But the arrogance and ingratitude of Aaron was still more disgraceful. He had been by his brother associated with himself: Moses had allowed the high-priesthood to be transferred to him and his descendants, and thus had placed his own in subjection to them. What, then, was there for Aaron to begrudge his brother; when so exalted a dignity was vested in his own sons, whilst all the race of Moses was degraded? Still he was so blinded as to deem the honour of his brother a reproach to himself; at any rate, he could not endure to be second to him in dignity, although he was his superior in right of the priesthood. By this example, then, we are taught how anxiously we should beware of so baneful a plague (as ambition). The wicked brother[1] in the tragic Poet says :—

> "For, if injustice must at all be done,
> 'Tis best to do it for dominion ;"

that, under this pretext, he might through treachery and murder proceed against his own blood with impunity. Now, although we all hold this sentiment in detestation, still it plainly shews that, when the lust for rule takes possession of men's hearts, not only do they abandon the love of justice, but that humanity becomes altogether extinct in them, since brothers thus contend with each other, and rage, as it were, against their own bowels. Indeed it is astonishing that, when this vice has been so often and so severely condemned in the opinion of all ages, the human race has not been ever freed from it ; nay, that the Church of God has always been infested by this disease, than which none is worse : for ambition has been, and still is, the mother of all errors, of all disturbances and sects. Since Aaron and his sister were infected by it, how easily may it overspread the multitude ! But I now proceed to examine the words.

Miriam is here put before Aaron, not by way of honourable distinction, but because she stirred up the strife, and persuaded her brother to take her side ; for the ambition of the female sex is wonderful ; and often have women, more high-spirited than men, been the instigators not merely of squabbles, but of mighty wars, so that great cities and countries have been shaken by their violent conduct. Still, however, this does not diminish the guilt of Aaron, who, at the instance of his foolish sister, engaged in an unjust and wicked contest with his brother, and even declared himself an enemy to God's grace. Further, because they were unable to allege any grounds, upon which Moses in himself was not far their superior, they seek to bring disgrace upon

[1] They are the words of Eteocles in the Phœnissæ of Euripides :—

> Εἴπερ γὰρ ἀδικεῖν χρὴ. τυραννίδος πέρι
> Κάλλιστον ἀδικεῖν· τἄλλα δ' εὐσεβεῖν χρεών.—538.9.

Cicero refers to them, De Off. iii. xxi.

> Nam, si violandum est jus, regnandi gratia
> Violandum est : aliis rebus pietatem colas.

him on account of his wife; as if in half of himself he was inferior to them, because he had married a woman who was not of their own race, but a foreigner. They, therefore, cast ignominous aspersions upon him in the person of his wife, as if it were not at all becoming that he should be accounted the prince and head of the people, since his wife, and the companion of his bed, was a Gentile woman. I do not by any means agree with those who think that she was any other than Zipporah,[1] since we hear nothing of the death of Zipporah, nay, she had been brought back by Jethro, her father, only a little while before the delivery of the Law; whilst it is too absurd to charge the holy Prophet with the reproach of polygamy. Besides, as an octogenarian, he would have been but little suited for a second marriage. Again, how would such a marriage have been practicable in the desert? It is, therefore, sufficiently clear that they refer to Zipporah, who is called an Ethiopian woman, because the Scripture comprehends the Midianites under this name: although I have no doubt but that they maliciously selected this name, for the purpose of awakening greater odium against Moses. I designedly forbear from adducing the frivolous glosses in which some indulge.[2] Moses, however, acknowledges that it[3] was not accorded to him to have a wife of the holy race of Abraham.

2. *And they said, Hath the Lord indeed spoken only by Moses?* They pride themselves on their gift of prophecy, which ought rather to have schooled them to humility. But

[1] Josephus (Antiq. ii. 10) has led some to suppose that she was Tharbis, daughter of the king of Ethiopia. Augustin, however, (*Quæst. in Numb.* xx.,) and the great majority of commentators, agree with *C.* in believing that she was Zipporah, and not a second wife, as contended by Rosenmüller, Michaelis, and others. The main difficulty arises from her being called a *Cushite*, which our translators have followed *LXX.* and *V.* in rendering "the Ethiopian." Bochart endeavours to prove that the Cushites and Midianites were the same people; and Shuckford (vol. i. p. 166, edit. 1743) states his opinion that "by the land of Cush is always meant some part of Arabia." Habakkuk iii. 7, in which "the tents of Cushan," and "the land of Midian," are mentioned together, seems to corroborate this view.

[2] "The Hebrew doctors make his not companying with his wife to be the occasion," &c.—Ainsworth. So also De Lyra.

[3] "Qu'il n'a pas eu ce bien et honneur;" that he had not the advantage and honour.—*Fr.*

such is the natural depravity of men, not only to abuse the gifts of God unto contempt of their brethren, but so to magnify them by their ungodly and sacrilegious boasting, as to obscure the glory of their Author. Miriam and Aaron had received the spirit of prophecy, in order that the grace of God might shine forth in them; but from thence they raise up clouds to throw darkness upon the light, which was far brighter in Moses. They boast themselves to be prophets; why, then, do they not consider that there was no ground for glorying in this, inasmuch as that, which had been gratuitously bestowed upon them by God, was not their own? Again, why do they not correctly estimate their own insignificance in comparison with the excellency of Moses, so as, by willingly yielding to him, to shew that they set at its proper value what God had respectively conferred upon them? Lest, then, the knowledge of those graces which God has intrusted to us, should puff us up with pride and presumption, let us remember that the more each of us has received, the greater obligations are we under to God and our brethren; and let us also reflect how much is wanting in us, and how much, too, God has conferred on others, so as to prefer to ourselves those whom God has designed to honour.

3. *Now the man Moses was very meek.* This parenthesis is inserted, in order that we might perceive that God was not moved by any complaint of Moses, to be so greatly wroth with Aaron and Miriam. It is said that "the Lord heard," that is to say, to undertake the cause in His character of Judge: and it is now added, that He spontaneously summoned the criminals to His tribunal, though no accuser requested that justice should be done him. For this is the tendency of the eulogium of his meekness, as if Moses had said that he submitted in silence to the wrong, because, in his meekness, he imposed patience on himself. Moreover, he does not praise his own virtue for the sake of boasting, but in order to exhort us by his example, and, if it should be our lot to be treated with indignity, quietly and calmly to wait for the judgment of God. For whence does it come that, when any one has injured us, our indignation carries

away our feelings in all directions, and our pain boils up without measure, except because we do not think that our ills are regarded by God until we have made loud and boisterous complaints? This passage, then, teaches us that although the good and gentle refrain from reproaches and accusations, God nevertheless keeps watch for them, and, whilst they are silent, the wickedness of the ungodly cries out to, and is heard by, God. Again, the silence of long-suffering itself is more effectual before God than any cries, however loud. But if God does not immediately proceed to execute vengeance, we must bear in mind what is written elsewhere, that *the blood* of Abel *cried out* after his death, that the murder which Cain had committed might not be unpunished. (Gen. iv. 10.)

4. *Come out ye three unto the tabernacle.* God calls Aaron and Miriam to the tabernacle, that the very sanctity of the place may cast down their haughtiness; for forgetfulness of God had overspread their minds, when they began to be so insolent before men. They are, therefore, brought back to the presence of God, from which all their senses had turned away, in order that they at length might learn to revere Moses, whose cause is upheld by God. God commands them to "hear His words," because they would never have dared to murmur against Moses if they had reflected on the account they would have to give. God, therefore, claims their attention, that they may learn to recollect themselves, and to awaken from the senselessness of their presumption. Moreover, they are separated from Moses, that they may confess their inferiority, and be ashamed of their temerity in daring to compare themselves with him.

6. *If there be a prophet among you.* He makes mention of two methods by which the will of God was wont to be revealed to the prophets, viz., visions and dreams. He does not, however, here use the word חזון, *chazon*,[1] which signifies a prophecy as well as a vision, but מראה, *marah*, expressive of some visible appearance, which confirms and ratifies the

[1] חזון, a vision, from חזה, to see, to look upon. מראה, either the act of sight, or the object of sight; a seeing, or an appearance, from ראה, to see, to perceive.—*W.*

truth of His word (*oraculi*) to the eyes and all the senses. Thus has God often appeared to His servants, so that His majesty might be inscribed upon His addresses to them. Before the giving of the Law such visions were frequently vouchsafed to the Patriarchs; whilst sometimes they were instructed by dreams. Thus Joel, when he promises that under the kingdom of Christ there shall be a complete fulness of all revelations, also enumerates these two forms of them, "Your sons (he says) and your daughters shall prophesy: your old men shall dream dreams, your young men shall see visions." (Joel ii. 28.) But we know that the prophets described the kingdom of Christ under the likeness of their own times: when, therefore, God sets forth these two ordinary modes of revelation, He withdraws Moses from the condition of others, as if to exalt him by a special privilege. Now, since Aaron and Miriam were not superior to others, they were thus reminded that they were far behind Moses in rank. With this view he is said to be "faithful in all God's house;" in quoting which passage in order to prove his inferiority to Christ, the Apostle says he was *a servant*, and a member of the Church, whereas Christ was its Lord and builder, or creator. (Heb. iii. 2-6.) But the difference between them is more clearly specified immediately afterwards, viz., that God speaks to him "mouth to mouth," by which expression, as I have said elsewhere,[1] more intimate and familiar communication is denoted. Still God does not thus deprive the prophets of anything which is requisite for the discharge of their office; but merely establishes Moses as the chief of them all. It is true, indeed, that the Patriarchs are so ranked, as Abraham was called a prophet by the mouth of God, (Gen. xx. 7;) and the Prophet thus names him together with Isaac and Jacob in Ps. cv. 15; but still God at the same time includes the whole dispensation, which He afterwards chose to employ under the Law; and so prefers Moses to all who were hereafter to arise.

Further, the word *vision* is used in a different sense from that which it had just above; for God, distinguishing Moses from others, says that He speaks with him *in vision*,[2]

[1] On Exod. xxxiii. 11, *ante*, vol. iii. p. 372. [2] *A. V.* "apparently."

which it would be absurd to explain as meaning an ordinary or common vision. It therefore here signifies actual sight,[1] which He contrasts with "dark speeches (*ænigmata*) and similitude," which word is equivalent to a representation (*figura*,) if the negative be referred to both. For there are some who take similitude for a lively and express image; as if God should assert that He reveals His face to Moses; and therefore read the clause *adversatively*, as I have given it in the margin. But the former reading is the most natural.

I have elsewhere treated of dreams and visions. It will then be sufficient to give the sum in one word, namely, that they were seals for the confirmation of prophecies; so that the Prophets, as if sent from heaven, might with full confidence declare themselves to be God's lawful interpreters. For visions had their own peculiar marks, to distinguish them from phantoms and false imaginations; and dreams also were accompanied by their signs, in order to remove all doubt of their authenticity. The prophets, therefore, were fully conscious of their vocation, so that nothing was wanting to the assurance of faith. Meanwhile, the false prophets dressed themselves up in these masks to deceive. Thus Jeremiah, in refutation of their ungodly pretences, says, "The prophet that hath a dream, let him tell a dream; and he that hath my word, let him speak my word faithfully. What is the chaff to the wheat, saith the Lord?" (Jer. xxiii. 28.)

9. And the anger of the Lord was kindled against them; and he departed.	9. Exarsit ergo furor Jehovæ in eos, et discessit.
10. And the cloud departed from off the tabernacle; and, behold, Miriam *became* leprous, *white* as snow: and Aaron looked upon Miriam, and, behold, *she was* leprous.	10. Nubesque recessit à tabernaculo: et ecce Maria erat leprosa sicut nix, respexitque Aharon Mariam, et ecce erat leprosa.
11. And Aaron said unto Moses, Alas! my Lord, I beseech thee, lay not the sin upon us, wherein we have done foolishly, and wherein we have sinned.	11. Tunc dixit Aharon ad Mosen, Quæso domine mi, ne nunc nobis imputes peccatum: quia stultè egimus, et quia peccavimus.
12. Let her not be as one dead, of whom the flesh is half consumed when he cometh out of his mother's womb.	12. Ne, quæso, sit quasi abortivus fœtus, qui dum egreditur ex utero matris suæ consumptus est dimidio suæ carnis.

[1] "Veuë, ou regard de quelque figure visible;" the view or look of some visible figure.—*Fr.*

13. And Moses cried unto the Lord, saying, Heal her now, O God, I beseech thee.

14. And the Lord said unto Moses, If her father had but spit in her face, should she not be ashamed seven days? let her be shut out from the camp seven days, and after that let her be received in *again*.

15. And Miriam was shut out from the camp seven days; and the people journeyed not till Miriam was brought in *again*.

13. Clamavit itaque Moses ad Jehovam, dicendo, Deus, quæso, sana nunc illam:

14. Respondit Jehova ad Mosen, Quod si pater ejus spuendo spuisset in faciem ejus, nonne erubesceret septem diebus? Excludatur septem diebus extra castra, et deinde recipietur.

15. Itaque reclusa est Maria extra castra septem diebus: neque populus progressus est, donec reciperetur Maria.

9. *And the anger of the Lord was kindled against them.* The expostulation is succeeded by punishment. God's departure was a sign of immediate condemnation; because there was no need of any further questioning, as concerning some matter of obscurity. After God, then, had convicted them of their sin, and had inveighed in a severe and stern reprehension against the ingratitude of Miriam and Aaron, He first pronounced their sentence, and then suddenly withdrew. What follows, that "the cloud departed," is added in explanation; for God, who fills all things, never moves from His place; but His name is applied metaphorically to the cloud, which was the symbol of His absence or presence.

The nature of the punishment which was inflicted upon Miriam was very appropriate to the offence. The foolish woman, puffed up with pride, had coveted more than was lawful; and her ignominy was the just reward of her arrogance, according to the declaration of Christ, "Every one that exalteth himself shall be abased." (Luke xviii. 14.) Let us understand, then, that in proportion as the proud are led away by their ambition to long for unlawful honours, they bring upon themselves nothing but disgrace; and although they may gloriously triumph for a season, still, it cannot be but that their glory will at length be turned into disgrace. For inasmuch as all who exalt themselves wage war with God, He must needs encounter them with the awful power of His hand, in order to restrain their madness. Now, whosoever are moved by envy to enter into contention with His servants, endeavour, as far as in them lies, to overthrow His glory by obscuring the gifts of the Spirit. No wonder, then, that God should avenge the insult offered to Himself, and should repay them with the infamy they deserve; as it is written, "Them that honour me I will honour, and they that despise me shall be lightly esteemed." (1 Sam. ii. 30.) Miriam desired to be equal with her brother, whom God had exalted above all others; what she attains is, that she should not occupy the extremest corner of the people, but be cut off from companionship with mankind. A similar instance occurred in the case of king Uzziah, who, not contented with the royal dignity, when he had unlawfully attempted to make an incense-offering, was also smitten with leprosy, so as to be no longer suffered to continue in association even with the common people. (2 Chron. xxvi. 16-21.)

Here, however, the question arises, why, when Aaron participated in the guilt, he was exempted from the punishment? If no reason existed, still we should have to adore the judgment of God; for it is not our business to complain, when He has mercy upon whom He will have mercy. Nevertheless, it appears probable that God's wrath was more exceedingly kindled against Miriam, because she had applied the torch to the ungodly contention, and had inflamed her brother's mind, as we see at the beginning of the chapter. It was just, then, that the blame should rest on her, since she had been the origin of the evil. I imagine, however, that in sparing Aaron, He had regard to the priesthood, inasmuch as, in his person, it would have been subjected almost to eternal disgrace. Since, therefore, Aaron was an image of God's only-begotten Son and our only Mediator, and this great dignity had recently had its commencement in him, it was of exceeding importance that he should be exempted from such infamy, lest any diminution of the reverence due to religion should arise.

11. *And Aaron said unto Moses, Alas! my lord.* Although Aaron was aware that, through God's indulgence, his own punishment was remitted, still he does not cease to consider what he had deserved. For we ought not to wait until God smites ourselves, but since in chastising others He invites us to repentance, although He may spare ourselves, we should profit betimes by their punishments. The disfigure-

ment, therefore, of his sister, alarmed and terrified Aaron, so that, examining his own condition, he acknowledged himself to be deserving of a similar judgment. His humble prayer manifests that those high aspirations were subdued, which had carried him away into unholy jealousy. Moses, who was younger than himself, and whose superiority he just before could not endure, he now calls his *lord*, and confesses himself to be subject to his authority and power. Thus the dread of punishment was the best medicine to cure his disease of ambition. In beseeching Moses not to impute his sin to him, he does not usurp for mortal man a right which God by Isaiah claims for Himself alone;[1] but inasmuch as Moses had been injured, he asks his pardon, lest by his accusation he should be brought before the divine tribunal. Where he confesses his own and his sister's foolishness, he does not extenuate the grossness of his crime, as most people do, when they generally seek to cover their transgressions under the plea of error or thoughtlessness; but it is precisely as if he had said that they were senseless, and out of their minds, as we gather from the next clause, in which he plainly acknowledges their criminality.

By the comparison which he introduces, it is evident that the leprosy of Miriam was of no ordinary kind, for nothing can be more disgusting than the dead body of any abortive *fœtus*, corrupt with purulence and decay.

13. *And Moses cried unto the Lord.* The event now proves, what was recently asserted, that Moses was of a meek and gentle disposition beyond all other men; for he is not only ready at once to forgive, but also intercedes with God for them. And thus the presumption of Miriam is best reproved; for the only hope of safety that remains to her is in the dignity of Moses, which of late she could not endure.

From the reply of God, it is manifest that the punishment which she alone had received was intended for the instruction of all. The pride and temerity of Miriam were sufficiently chastised, but God wished it to be a lesson for all, that every one should confine himself to his own bounds.

[1] No reference is here given by *C.* He probably alludes to Isaiah xliii. 25.

Meanwhile, let us learn from this passage to pay due honour to the judgments of God, so that they may suffice us as the rule of supreme equity. For if such power over their children is accorded to earthly parents, as that they may put them to shame at their will, how much more reverence is due to our heavenly Father, when He brands us with any mark of disgrace? This was the reason why Miriam was shut out for seven days, not only that she might mourn apart by herself, but also that her chastisement might be profitable to all. It is likewise addressed to us, that we may learn to blush whensoever God is angry with our sins, and thus that shame may produce in us a dislike of sin. This special example afterwards passed into a law, as we have already seen, (Deut. xxiv. 9);[1] for when God commands lepers to be separated, He recalls to the recollection of the people what He had appointed with respect to Miriam, lest, if internal impurity be cherished, its infection may spread beyond ourselves.

16. And afterward the people removed from Hazeroth, and pitched in the wilderness of Paran.

NUMB. XIII. 1. And the Lord spake unto Moses, saying,

2. Send thou men, that they may search the land of Canaan, which I give unto the children of Israel: of every tribe of their fathers shall ye send a man, every one a ruler among them.

3 And Moses, by the commandment of the Lord, sent them from the wilderness of Paran: all those men *were* heads of the children of Israel.

4. And these *were* their names: Of the tribe of Reuben: Shammua the son of Zaccur.

5. Of the tribe of Simeon; Shaphat the son of Hori.

6. Of the tribe of Judah; Caleb the son of Jephunneh.

7. Of the tribe of Issachar; Igal the son of Joseph.

8. Of the tribe of Ephraim; Oshea the son of Nun.

9. Of the tribe of Benjamin; Palti the son of Raphu.

16. Postea autem profectus est populus de Haseroth, et castrametati sunt in deserto Paran.

1. Et loquutus est Jehova ad Mosen, dicendo:

2. Mitte tibi viros qui explorent terram Chanaan, quam ego daturus sum filiis Israel, singulos viros de singulis tribubus patrum suorum mittetis, unumquenque principem inter eos.

3. Misit ergo illos Moses è deserto Paran, juxta sermonem Jehovæ: et universi ipsi viri principes filiorum Israel erant.

4. Hæc autem sunt nomina eorum. De tribu Ruben, Sammua filius Zachur.

5. De tribu Simeon, Saphat filius Hori.

6. De tribu Jehuda, Caleb filius Jephuneh.

7. De tribu Issachar, Igal, filius Joseph.

8. De tribu Ephraim, Hosea filius Nun.

9. De tribu Benjamin, Palti filius Raphu.

[1] *Ante*, vol. ii. p. 12.

10. Of the tribe of Zebulun; Gaddiel the son of Sodi.

11. Of the tribe of Joseph, *namely*, of the tribe of Manasseh; Gaddi the son of Susi.

12. Of the tribe of Dan; Ammiel the son of Gemalli.

13. Of the tribe of Asher; Sether the son of Michael.

14. Of the tribe of Naphtali; Nahbi the son of Vophsi.

15. Of the tribe of Gad; Geuel the son of Machi.

16. These *are* the names of the men which Moses sent to spy out the land. And Moses called Oshea the son of Nun, Jehoshua.

17. And Moses sent them to spy out the land of Canaan, and said unto them, Get you up this *way* southward, and go up into the mountain;

18. And see the land, what it *is;* and the people that dwelleth therein, whether they *be* strong or weak, few or many;

19. And what the land *is* that they dwell in, whether it *be* good or bad; and what cities *they be* that they dwell in, whether in tents, or in strong holds;

20. And what the land *is*, whether it *be* fat or lean, whether there be wood therein, or not: and be ye of good courage, and bring of the fruit of the land. (Now the time *was* the time of the first-ripe grapes.)

21. So they went up, and searched the land, from the wilderness of Zin unto Rehob, as men come to Hamath.

22. And they ascended by the south, and came unto Hebron; where Ahiman, Sheshai, and Talmai, the children of Anak, *were*. (Now Hebron was built seven years before Zoan in Egypt.)

23. And they came unto the brook of Eshcol, and cut down from thence a branch with one cluster of grapes, and they bare it between two upon a staff; and *they brought* of the pomegranates, and of the figs.

24. The place was called the

10. De tribu Zebulon, Gaddiel filius Sodi.

11. De tribu Joseph, de tribu Menasseh, Gaddi filius Susi.

12. De tribu Dan, Ammiel filius Gemalli.

13. De tribu Aser, Sethur filius Michael.

14. De tribu Nephthali, Nahbi filius Vophsi.

15. De tribu Gad, Guel filius Machi.

16. Hæc sunt nomina virorum quos misit Moses ad explorandam terram: et appellavit Moses Hosea filium Nun, Jehosua.

17. Misit igitur eos Moses ad explorandam terram Chanaan, dicens illis, Ascendite hac per meridiem, et conscendatis montes;

18. Et consideretis terram ipsam qualis sit, et populum qui habitat in ea, utrum fortis sit an debilis, utrum paucus sit an multus.

19. Qualis, inquam, sit terra in qua sit habitator, utrum bona sit an mala: et quales urbes in quibus sit habitator, utrum in castris an in munitionibus.

20. Qualis rursum terra, utrum pinguis sit an macra: utrum sint in ea arbores an non: et estote forti animo, atque decerpite è fructu terræ. (Dies autem illi erant dies primitiarum uvarum.)

21. Ascenderunt igitur, et exploraverunt terram, à deserto Sin usque ad Rehob, ingrediendo Hamath.

22. Et ascenderunt per meridiem, et venerunt usque ad Hebron, ibi autem erat Ahiman, Sesai, et Thalmai, filii Anac. Hebron verò septem annis ædificata fuit ante Soan Ægypti.

23. Pervenerunt itaque usque ad vallem Eschol, et absciderunt illinc palmitem et botrum uvarum unum, et portaverunt illum vecte bini, et de malogranatis et de ficubus.

24. Locus ille vocatus est Nahal

brook Eshcol, because of the cluster of grapes which the children of Israel cut down from thence.

Eschol propter botrum quem absciderunt inde filii Israel.

The Repetition of the same Narrative.

DEUT. I. 19. And when we departed from Horeb, we went through all that great and terrible wilderness, which ye saw by the way of the mountain of the Amorites, as the Lord our God commanded us; and we came to Kadesh-barnea.

20. And I said unto you, Ye are come unto the mountain of the Amorites, which the Lord our God doth give unto us.

21. Behold, the Lord thy God hath set the land before thee; go up *and* possess *it*, as the Lord God of thy fathers hath said unto thee; fear not, neither be discouraged.

22. And ye came near unto me every one of you, and said, We will send men before us, and they shall search us out the land, and bring us word again by what way we must go up, and into what cities we shall come.

23. And the saying pleased me well; and I took twelve men of you, one of a tribe:

24. And they turned, and went up into the mountain, and came unto the valley of Eshcol, and searched it out.

25. And they took of the fruit of the land in their hands, and brought *it* down unto us, and brought us word again, and said, *It is* a good land which the Lord our God doth give us.

19. Profecti de Horeb perambulavimus totam solitudinem magnam et terribilem hanc quam vidistis per viam montis Emorrhæi, quemadmodum præceperat Jehova Deus noster nobis, ac pervenimus usque ad Cades Barnea.

20. Et dixi vobis, Pervenistis usque ad montem Emorrhæi quem Jehova Deus noster dat nobis.

21. Vide, dedit Jehova Deus tuus coram te terram, ascende, posside quemadmodum dixit Jehova Deus patrum tuorum tibi, ne timeas, neque consterneris.

22. Accessistis autem ad me omnes vos, et dixistis, Mittamus viros ante nos qui explorent nobis terram, et referant nobis rem, et viam per quam ascendamus, et urbes ad quas veniamus.

23. Quod placuit in oculis meis, et sumpsi ex vobis duodecim viros, virum unum ex quaque tribu.

24. Qui abierunt et ascenderunt in montem, veneruntque usque ad vallem Eschol, et exploraverunt eam.

25. Tuleruntque in manu sua è fructu terræ illius, et attulerunt nobis, retuleruntque nobis rem, ac dixerunt, Bona est terra quam Jehova Deus noster dat nobis.

NUMB. XII. 16. *And afterward the people departed from Hazeroth.* At first sight Moses appears to be at variance with himself: for he here states that he sent the spies at God's command, whereas in Deut. i. 22, he relates that he made this concession at the request of the people;[1] but the

[1] Hengstenberg (Dissertations on the Genuineness of the Pentateuch, vol. ii. p. 344,) discusses this point, in opposition to Vater and De Wette,

two statements are easily reconciled. It is, indeed, unquestionable that God had regard to the infirmity and distrust of the people ; for the spies are not sent to see in what direction the land was to be attacked, with which design two were afterwards sent by Joshua, but God had here no other object than to encourage them, when they else were cowardly and inert, to throw off their inactivity, and eagerly to advance. The necessity of such a remedy was evidently shewn, when they all demanded this of Moses. The second narrative, therefore, is fuller, and in it Moses goes back further than he had done in the first, viz., that it arose from the timidity and pusillanimity of the people that he did not at once hasten whither God invited him ; for, if they had straightway obeyed, they would have won the land of their enemies without any delay ; but they requested that a respite might be given them. It is, then, by no means inconsistent that Moses did, at the request of the people, what God at the same time enjoined, because He saw that they were otherwise hesitating, and but little disposed to advance, and needed this stimulus. For, if the spies had honestly performed their duty, the people would have been led forward as if they had seen the land themselves, which would have been the readiest means for putting an end to all delays.

though he reminds us that " the discrepancy is no new discovery, but has been thoroughly canvassed ; compare Gerhard on Deut., p. 53." " That the contradiction is only apparent (he says) is clear from Numb. xiii. 26 ; for, since those, to whom the answer was brought back, must be identical with the persons who sent out the spies, it appears from this passage that not merely Moses and Aaron, but also the congregation, had a share in giving the commission. The author, therefore, cannot intend to deny this, when, in verse 1 and 2, he refers the matter to God." " The sending out of the spies (he further argues) was a part of God's plan, and hence was expressly commanded by Him, as soon as its indispensable condition, the proposal on the part of the people, had taken place. For one thing, it would insure to the well-disposed a strengthening of their weak faith ; on the other hand, it formed a part of God's design, that the evil-disposed should take occasion by this undertaking to manifest their unbelief, and be ripened by it for judgment. This design we learn from the result, which can never be contrary to the design. If the divine purpose was the essential point, and the proposal of the people the mere *conditio sine quâ non* of its being carried into effect, it will be easily understood how the latter might be passed over in the Book of Numbers, although, as we have already seen, it is pre-supposed. After what has been remarked, Calvin's view of the mutual relation of the two passages will clearly appear to be the correct one."

First, however, the place is described, from whence the spies were sent, viz., at no great distance from mount Sinai, although they had encamped twice, so that it was their third station. It has already been stated in chapter x., that the cloud rested in the wilderness of Paran, which some understand to have been said by anticipation, (*κατὰ πρόληψιν*,) as if Moses had said that, from the time when the people left Mount Sinai, they had not made any permanent halt, until they came to that wilderness, and there pitched their tents. But this opinion is by no means consistent; for it is clear that they stayed some time in Taberah; and many days were spent at the graves of lust, (Kibroth-hattaavah;) for there they were gorged for a month with the flesh of the birds, and then the pestilence attacked them, which cut off many of them, for whose burial it was necessary to provide. Now, their next halt was for more than seven days. It, therefore, appears probable to me that by the word Paran, a different place is not expressed; but that it is merely meant that, though they advanced, they still remained in some part of that wilderness. For, since the wilderness of Paran was in one direction contiguous to Mount Sinai, that name is sometimes given to it; for Moses certainly confounds them elsewhere, as also does the Prophet Habakkuk. (Deut. xxxiii. 3; Hab. iii. 3.)

NUMB. XIII. 2. *Of every tribe of their fathers shall ye send a man.* If all had been taken from one tribe, or from any single portion of the people, their fidelity might have been suspected by the others. God, therefore, would have each tribe assured by its own witness, in order that their report might be more unquestionable. All cause for jealousy was also to be taken away; lest, if any tribe had been passed over, it might have excepted against the messengers, whom it supposed to have been elected in contempt of it. This, then, was the advantage of the equal distribution, lest any sinister suspicion or offence might disturb the unanimity of the whole people. Secondly, it is required that they should be possessed of personal dignity, since God commands that chief men should be chosen, whose testimony would be of greater authority; for it would have been easy to throw discredit upon obscure individuals. Since, however, both precautions were unsuccessful, it appears from hence that there is no counsel so wise and salutary as not to be capable of perversion by the wickedness of mankind. Thus this excellent providence of God rendered the people the more inexcusable. At the same time, God has reminded us once for all by this example that, however those, who seemed to be like pillars, may totter and stumble, or even fall altogether, still our minds must be supported by faith, so as not to give way.

Their names are enumerated, in perpetual remembrance of their ignominy, except in the case of two, Joshua and Caleb; for it was just that their crime should be handed down to all ages, and that the infamy of their perfidiousness should never be blotted out, since they endeavoured, as far as in them lay, to bring to nought the promise and the grace of God.

Moses gave the name of Jehoshua to the son of Nun in the spirit of prophecy, as a presage of the exalted function to which he was destined. Ambition is so rash, that men are often disappointed in the result, when they invent titles of honour of their own accord; but Moses was not induced by the blindness of affection to change the name Oshea into Jehoshua; but God directed his tongue and mind thus to commend, beforehand, him who[1] was to be the future minister of

[1] "Afin que ce nom d'honneur servist à l'authoriser;" in order that this name of honour might serve to give him authority.—*Fr.*

Calvin here alludes to the apparent contradiction arising from the fact that Joshua had already been called by his new name in Exod. xvii. 9; xxiv. 13; xxxiii. 11; and Numb. xi. 28, which, as Hengstenberg remarks, was a topic of discussion as early as the times of Justin Martyr. Hengstenberg reviews the three modes of meeting the difficulty proposed, viz., 1. That he was so called in the earlier passages by *prolepsis*. 2. That Moses now only renewed the name. 3. That a statement is here made of what had taken place a considerable time before. To this view he himself inclines, and says, "That the author here first mentioned that he, whom he had originally called simply Joshua, originally bore the name of Hoshea, was not without good reason. What had been hitherto related of Joshua, belonged to him as a servant of God; the sacred name was, therefore, properly employed. But here Hoshea must stand; for he went to spy out the land, not as a servant of Moses, but as one of 'the heads of the children of Israel,'—one of the plenipotentiaries of the congregation."—Genuineness of Pentateuch, vol. ii. p. 323.

their preservation. Still it cannot be inferred with certainty from this passage at what time the new name was given him; for it is not specified that he was called Jehoshua at the time he was sent out; nay, it is probable that he had been previously thus distinguished, viz., from the period in which he had been associated with Moses as his companion and minister in all important matters.

18. *And see the land what it is.* The counsel of Moses had this object, that the people might be made aware how rich and fertile the land was; for a barren country does not support a large population; and the healthfulness of a locality is inferred from the vigour of its inhabitants. He, therefore, chiefly insists on the goodness of the land and its abundant production of fruits. Still, perhaps, God would intentionally have the Israelites forewarned, that they would have to do with strong and powerful enemies; lest they might be alarmed and discouraged at suddenly beholding them. But the main point was, that the pleasantness and fertility of the land might allure them to take possession of it.

22. *And they ascended by the south, and came unto Hebron.* Their direct course was not, indeed, towards the south, but they proceeded along the southern border, until they came to Rehob and Hamath, after having passed the mountains. Hebron, however, in which Abraham had sojourned, is specified from amongst the other cities; and it is probable that the three sons of the giant, who are here named, were in possession of that city. But some think that Anak is not a proper name, and is used, by *enallage* of the number, for giants. In fact, giants are elsewhere called Anakim. Nor is there any doubt but that these three, who are mentioned, were formidable from their great stature and strength, as we gather from the book of Joshua. It is, then, equivalent to saying that this city was then possessed by warlike men, famous for their prowess. It will, however, appear from the end of the chapter, that Anak was the proper name of a man, whose sons were of excessive height. The antiquity of the city is afterwards signalized by comparison, viz., that it was founded seven years before Zoan, one of the chief cities of

Egypt, and of which mention is often made in Scripture. Heathen writers call it Tanis;[1] and it is situated on one of the seven famous mouths of the Nile, which is called from the city, *Ostium Taniticum.* Now, since the Egyptians gloried in their antiquity above all other nations, it is evident that the land of Canaan was well peopled immediately after the deluge; and this is a sign of its great fertility, for, if the neighbouring countries had been more so, they would not have settled themselves there by preference, when they were at liberty to make their choice. A *prolepsis* is to be noted in the name of the valley of Eshcol: for it was afterwards that it began to be so called by the Israelites in memory of the remarkable cluster of grapes which Moses states to have been brought from hence; and this is immediately after specified.

NUMBERS, CHAPTER XIII.

25. And they returned from searching of the land after forty days.

26. And they went and came to Moses, and to Aaron, and to all the congregation of the children of Israel, unto the wilderness of Paran, to Kadesh; and brought back word unto them, and unto all the congregation, and shewed them the fruit of the land.

27. And they told him, and said, We came unto the land whither thou sentest us, and surely it floweth with milk and honey; and this *is* the fruit of it.

28. Nevertheless the people *be* strong that dwell in the land, and the cities *are* walled, *and* very great: and, moreover, we saw the children of Anak there.

29. The Amalekites dwell in the land of the south; and the Hittites, and the Jebusites, and the Amo-

25. Reversi sunt ab exploranda terra post quadraginta dies.

26. Profecti ergo sunt, et venerunt ad Mosen et Aharon, et ad universum cœtum filiorum Israel, in desertum Paran in Cades: et retulerunt eis rem, atque universo cœtui, ostenderuntque eis fructum terræ.

27. Narraverunt ergo ei: et dixerunt, Pervenimus ad terram ad quam misisti nos; et certe affluit lacte et melle: et ipse est fructus ejus.

28. Nisi quòd fortis est populus qui incolit eam, et urbes munitæ sunt, et magnæ admodum: ac filios Enac vidimus illic.

29. Amalec habitat in terra meridiana: Hitthæus autem, et Jebusæus, et Amorrhæus inhabitant mon-

[1] Thus the word is translated by the LXX. See note on Ps. lxxviii. —*C. Soc. Edit.* Vol. iii. p. 239.

rites, dwell in the mountains; and the Canaanites dwell by the sea, and by the coast of Jordan.

tes: Chananæus verò habitat juxta mare et ad ripam Jordanis.

30. And Caleb stilled the people before Moses, and said, Let us go up at once, and possess it; for we are well able to overcome it.

30. Tacere verò fecit Caleb populum ad Mosen, et dixit, Ascendendo ascendamus et possideamus: nam prævalendo prævalebimus contra eam.

31. But the men that went up with him said, We be not able to go up against the people; for they *are* stronger than we.

31. At viri qui ascenderant cum eo, dixerunt, Non poterimus ascendere contra populum illum, quia fortior est nobis.

32. And they brought up an evil report of the land which they had searched unto the children of Israel, saying, The land, through which we have gone to search it, *is* a land that eateth up the inhabitants thereof; and all the people that we saw in it *are* men of a great stature.

32. Et detraxerunt terræ quam exploraverunt, apud filios Israel, dicendo, Terra per quam transivimus ut exploraremus eam, terra est quæ consumit habitatores suos: et omnis populus quem vidimus in medio ejus, viri proceræ staturæ sunt.

33. And there we saw the giants, the sons of Anak, *which come* of the giants: and we were in our own sight as grasshoppers, and so we were in their sight.

33. Atque illuc vidimus gigantes filios Enac, è gigantibus. Et fuimus sicut locustæ in oculis nostris, sic fuimus in oculis eorum.

25. *And they returned from searching of the land.* The activity and diligence of the twelve men is commended, who in so short a time examined the whole of the land from the desert of Sin to the sea, and along the whole course of the Jordan; and this, too, in the hottest part of the year, when the grapes were beginning to ripen. Thus far, then, they faithfully executed the task intrusted to them. In their report, also, there seems to be nothing unworthy of honest men. They had been commanded by Moses to consider the inhabitants of the land, whether they were strong or weak, and also whether the cities were fortified; and they relate nothing which was not true and fully ascertained by them. In a word, at first sight their relation contains nothing worthy of reprehension. Nevertheless, we may gather from the context that the ten of them, whose desire was to turn away the people, spoke in such discouraging terms of their difficulties, that they produced exactly the contrary effect to what Moses had hoped. No other accusation, however, is as yet alleged against them, than that, by maliciously and deceptively inspiring despondency, they held back the people from entering the land. Although, therefore, they had not

openly lied, they were wanting in sincerity. Perhaps, too, the whole of their address is not recorded; because Moses deemed it sufficient to state their perversity of feeling, in that they added to their praises of the land an exception, which overwhelmed the people's minds with fear. From whence also we gather a useful admonition, that crafty sophists avail nothing with God, when they endeavour to cover their deceit by tortuous prevarications. Wherefore, if we desire to approve our discourse to God, we must take care to lay aside all such unfair evasions, and, rejecting all disguise, to speak simply and from the heart. The ten spies, then, lay a foundation of good faith, in order that they may afterwards be more competent to deceive. The land, they say, is a good one, except that the people are strong; and what is this but that there was little hope that the Israelites would obtain the blessing promised them by God, and that the attempt must by no means be made? With the same view they thunder out[1] the names of several nations, in order to increase the alarm; for, after having reported that they had seen the sons of Anak, they state that their contests would be too arduous with the various peoples, who would advance from all sides to resist them.

30. *And Caleb stilled the people before Moses.* That is, he restrained the murmurs of the people before Moses, against whom they had begun to rise tumultuously. Hence it appears that much was said on both sides which is passed over in silence, for there would have been no need of restraining the violence of the people, unless the contention had waxed warm. His words, however, shew what was the state of the whole case and question, viz., that the ten treacherous spies had dissuaded the people from foolishly advancing to the land, which it was impossible to win; and urged them not to attack rashly very powerful enemies, to whom they would be far from equally matched. But Caleb opposes them with the confidence of victory. We (he says) shall conquer the land, and upon this he grounds his exhortation. Moreover, there is no doubt but that, relying on God's promise, he believed that they would be successful, and thus boldly fore-

[1] "Ils parlent à plene bouche;" they speak with open mouth.—*Fr.*

told it, whilst the others took not at all into consideration that, with the banner of the Lord before them, the people would come into the promised inheritance.

This does not appear to accord with what Moses relates in Deut. i., where he absolves the spies, and casts the whole blame on the people; but the contradiction is easily reconciled, for there he had no other object than to assert the criminality of the Israelites, who, by their contumacy, had for a long time impeded the fulfilment of God's promise. Omitting, therefore, that part of the history which did not affect the matter in hand, he only adverts to that which convicted them of wicked ingratitude, *i.e.*, that the fertility of the land was commended by the spies; and consequently, since the people were abundantly assured of God's liberality, that they sinned grossly by rejecting it. He, therefore, states their crime to have been, that they were rebellious against the mouth or word of Jehovah, viz., because they had refused to follow Him when He invited them.

What Moses here ascribes to Caleb alone, he elsewhere attributes to Joshua also. It is plain, then, that Caleb spoke for both of them, and that Joshua was prudently and modestly silent, lest a tumultuous altercation should arise. It may, however, be probably conjectured that the bravery and firmness of him, who is praised, was the more conspicuous, whilst the honesty of Moses is perceivable, inasmuch as, by his preference of Caleb, he obscures and diminishes the praise due to his own minister.

32. *But the men that went up with him said.* We here see, as in a mirror, how impiety gradually gathers audaciousness in evil. At the outset, the authors of the rebellion were ambiguous in their expressions, and contented themselves with obscure insinuations; they now throw aside all shame, and openly and acrimoniously oppose the address of Caleb, which was certainly nothing less than casting discredit on God's words, and setting at nought His power. God had promised to give the land to the Israelites; they deny that He will do so. He had afforded them many proofs that nothing is difficult to Him: they deny that His aid will suffice against the forces of their enemies. Moreover, they at

length break out into such impudence, that in their falsehood they contradict themselves. They had confessed that the land was rich; they now declare that it consumes or devours its inhabitants, which is entirely the reverse. For this is equivalent to saying, that the wretched men, who cultivated it, wore themselves out with their assiduous labours; or, at any rate, that it was pestilential from the inclemency of its climate; either of which statements was utterly false. The mode in which some understand it, viz., that the giants[1] in their violence committed indiscriminate slaughter, is without foundation; for this evil was by no means to be feared by the people, after the extermination of the inhabitants. I do not doubt, then, but that it means that the cultivation of the land was difficult, and full of much inconvenience.

At the end of the last verse, where it is said, "as grasshoppers," &c., I think the words are inverted, and ought to be thus connected; "As grasshoppers are despised in our eyes, so we were looked down upon by these giants on account of our lowness of stature."

NUMBERS, CHAPTER XIV.

1. And all the congregation lifted up their voice, and cried; and the people wept that night.

2. And all the children of Israel murmured against Moses and against Aaron; and the whole congregation said unto them, Would God that we had died in the land of Egypt! or, would God we had died in this wilderness!

3. And wherefore hath the Lord brought us unto this land, to fall by the sword, that our wives and our children should be a prey? Were it not better for us to return into Egypt?

4. And they said one to another,

1. Tunc sustulit universus cœtus, edideruntque vocem suam, et flevit populus nocte illa.

2. Et murmuraverunt adversus Mosen et adversus Aharon omnes filii Israel: ac dixerunt universa multitudo, Utinam mortui essemus in terra Ægypti: aut in deserto hoc utinam mortui essemus.

3. Et quare Jehova introducit nos in hanc terram, ut cadamus gladio, uxores nostræ et parvuli nostri sint in prædam? Nonne satius esset nobis reverti in Ægyptum?

4. Dixerunt itaque alter ad al-

[1] Corn. à Lapide has the following note on verse 33; "נפלים, *nephilim*, *i.e.*, giants, who are called *nephilim*, that is, *falling*, because they were so tall, that those who saw them fell from terror, or rather *falling*, *i.e.*, making to fall, (the *Kal* being put for the *Hiphil*,) laying prostrate and slaying other men in all directions, for these giants were savage men and truculent tyrants."

Let us make a captain, and let us return into Egypt.

5. Then Moses and Aaron fell on their faces before all the assembly of the congregation of the children of Israel.

6. And Joshua the son of Nun, and Caleb the son of Jephunneh, *which were* of them that searched the land, rent their clothes:

7. And they spake unto all the company of the children of Israel, saying, The land, which we passed through to search it, *is* an exceeding good land.

8. If the Lord delight in us, then he will bring us into this land, and give it us; a land which floweth with milk and honey.

9. Only rebel not ye against the Lord, neither fear ye the people of the land; for they *are* bread for us: their defence is departed from them, and the Lord *is* with us; fear them not.

terum, Constituamus ducem, et revertamur in Ægyptum.

5. Tunc cecidit Moses et Aharon super faciem suam coram universo cœtu congregationis filiorum Israel.

6. Jehosua vero filius Nun, et Caleb filius Jephuneh, de exploratoribus terræ sciderunt vestimenta sua.

7. Ac loquuti sunt ad universam congregationem filiorum Israel, dicendo, Terra per quam transivimus ut exploraremus eam, optima terra est.

8. Si complacitum fuerit Jehovæ in nobis, introducet nos in terram istam, tradetque eam nobis, terram quæ affluit lacte et melle.

9. Tantum ne sitis rebelles Jehovæ, neque timeatis populum terræ hujus: quia *velut* panis noster sunt, recessit præsidium eorum ab ipsis: Jehova autem nobiscum est, ne timeatis eos.

1. *And all the congregation lifted up their voice.* Here we see how easily, by means of a few incentives, sedition is excited in a great multitude; for the people, unless governed by the counsel of others, is like the sea, exposed to many tempests; and the corruption of human nature produces this amongst innumerable other evils, that lies and impostures prevail over truth. There was, indeed, some pretext for the error of the people, in that they saw ten most choice leaders of their tribes dissuading them from entering the land, and only two advising them to proceed. But that credulity, to which they were too much inclined, is without excuse, because it arose from incredulity; for, if the dignity and reputation of ten men availed so much with them, that they were thus easy of belief, ought they not much rather to have given credit to the word of God, who had promised them the land four hundred years before? For when they cried out beneath the oppressive tyranny of the Egyptians, the memory of the promise given to their fathers was not effaced, since the holy Jacob had carefully provided for its transmission. They had recently heard and embraced its confirmation, and in this confidence had come forth from

Egypt. We see, then, that they had already been induced by their own supineness and depravity to recoil from entering the land, because they had thrown aside their confidence in God, so that they might seem to have deliberately laid hold of the opportunity. Still the evil counsellors gave an impulse to them, when they were falling of their accord, and cast them down headlong.

They begin with weeping, which at length bursts out into rage. The cause of their weeping is the fear of death, because they think that they are being carried away to slaughter; and whence does this arise, except because the promised aid of God is of no account with them? Thus it appears how greatly opposed to faith is cowardice, when, on the occurrence of danger, we look only to ourselves. But, whilst the beginning of infidelity is to be withheld by fear from obedience to God, so another worse evil presently follows, when men obstinately resist God, and, because they are unwilling to submit themselves to His word, enter into altercation with Him. This was the case with the Israelites, who, being overwhelmed with grief, at length are stirred up by its impetuosity against Moses and Aaron. And this is wont too often to occur, that impatience bursts forth from the anguish into which our unbelief has brought us. The desire for death, which they conceive, arises from ingratitude and contempt of God's blessing. They wished that they had died either in Egypt or in the wilderness; why, then, had they just before humbly beseeched Moses to propitiate God?

With regard to the words, the old interpreter,[1] taking the particle לו, *lu*, which is optative, for the negative (לא, *lo*,) improperly translates the passage, as if their death in the desert would have been more bitter than in Egypt; whereas they only deplore that they would be exposed to death if they should enter the land of Canaan, as follows in the next verse.

[1] By the old interpreter, *C.* does not here mean, as he generally does, the *V.*, which accords with his own view, "in hâc vastâ solitudine *utinam* pereamus;" on these words Corn. à Lapide says; "Ita hæc legunt et conjungunt, Hebr., Chald., Septuaginta, et Latina Romana. Tollenda ergo est negatio *non*, et distinctio quam habent Biblia Plantiniana."

3. *And wherefore has the Lord brought us into this land?* The pride, and even the madness of their impiety here more fully betrays itself, when they accuse God of deception and cruelty, as if He were betraying them to the Canaanitish nations, and leading them forth to slaughter; for they conclude that they ought not to obey His command, because He would destroy them, and not only so, but that He would at the same time give their wives and children to be a prey. We see how mad is unbelief, when it gives way to itself, since these wretched people do not hesitate to prefer charges against God, and to repay His kindnesses by calling Him their betrayer. But what was the cause of this blasphemous audacity,[1] except that they hear they would have to do with powerful enemies? as if they had not experienced the might of God to be such, that nothing which they might encounter was to be feared whilst He was on their side! At the same time, they also accuse God of weakness, as if He were less powerful than the nations of Canaan. At length their monstrous blindness and senselessness comes to its climax, when they consult as to their return, and, rejecting Moses, set themselves about choosing a leader, who may again deliver them up to Pharaoh. Were they so quickly forgetful how wretched their condition there had been? It was for no fault of theirs, but whilst they were peaceful and harmless guests, that the Egyptians had so cruelly afflicted them, since they were hated by Pharaoh on no other account but because he could not endure their multitude; what, then, was he likely to do, when, for their sakes, he had undergone so many calamities; what humanity, again, was to be expected from that nation which had conspired for their destruction already, when it had suffered no injury from them? Surely there was no house among them which would not long to avenge its first-born! Yet they desire to give themselves up to the will of a most bitter enemy, who, without any cause for ill-will, had proceeded to all sorts of extremities against them. Hence we plainly see that unbelievers are not only blinded by the just vengeance

[1] "D'une audace tant diabolique;" of such diabolical audacity.—*Fr.*

of God, but carried away by a spirit of infatuation, so as to inflict upon themselves the greatest evils.

5. *Then Moses and Aaron fell on their faces.* It is doubtful whether they so humbled themselves towards the people, as to lie prostrate before them, or whether it was in prayer that they fell with their faces on the earth; the latter, however, seems more likely to me, as if, by thus turning themselves to God, they reproved the stupidity of the people. And, in fact, in such a case of obduracy, nothing remained except to call upon God, yet in such sort that the prayer should be made in the sight of all, in order to influence their minds. Otherwise they might have sought some place of retirement; but by this pitiful spectacle they endeavoured to recall the people to their right senses. This, indeed, is beyond dispute, that they sought for nothing on their own account, but were only anxious for the welfare of the people; since, if the people had gone back, they would have been at liberty to sojourn in the land of Canaan, or elsewhere. Yet still they were not merely concerned with regard to the people, but the interruption of God's grace troubled them most, with which the Covenant made with Abraham would also have been buried. In a word, this was justly felt by them to be the same as if they had seen both the glory of God and the salvation of the human race altogether brought to nought. Wherefore they must needs have been more than senseless who were unmoved by this sad sight, especially when Moses, whom God had exalted by so many privileges above all other mortals, was lying prostrate on the earth for their sake.

6. *And Joshua, the son of Nun, and Caleb.* The magnanimity of Joshua is here specified, whereas, before, only Caleb had been praised. But Moses says that they both rent their clothes in token of their excessive sorrow, and even of their abhorrence. For, as is well known, this, amongst the Orientals, was a solemn ceremony in extreme grief, or when they would express their abomination of some crime. Hypocrites have improperly imitated this custom, either when they made a pretence of sorrow, or desired to deceive the simple. But it is plain that Caleb and Joshua were

moved to rend their garments by solemn feelings, nay, by the fervour of their indignation; whilst, at the same time, they seek to reclaim the people from their madness. And, first, they commend the fertility of the land; and then base their hope of obtaining it on the favour or good pleasure of God. Some take the conditional particle אם, *im*, for the causal particle, and translate it, "For *because* God loves us, therefore He will bring us in;" but this I do not approve of, and it is manifestly foreign to the true meaning; for, since the Israelites had in a manner rejected so great a benefit, they were surely unworthy through unbelief of being still pursued by His favour. The condition is, therefore, introduced as if doubtingly, not in order to diminish their hopes, as though it were a mark of uncertainty, but simply that the people should be convinced of their impiety, and repent; as if they had said, If only we afford room for the continuance of God's favour towards us, be ye of good courage. And this they state more clearly soon afterwards, in reproving the stubbornness of the people, where they say, "Only (or but) rebel not ye;" in which words they admonish them that they shut up all the ways whereby God might still pursue the course of His work;[1] and that there is no other obstacle to these wretched people except their own unbelief, which does not permit them to obey God. In this way, then, they assert that God's power is sufficient to perform what He had promised; and then exhort the people to conciliate His favour, from whence they had fallen through their own fault. The particle אך, *ac*, is used emphatically, as though Joshua and Caleb had said that there was no fear of danger, except because the people's minds were set on bringing evil upon themselves. Finally, in their reliance upon God's aid, they exult like conquerors; "They will be bread for us," they say, *i.e.*, we shall devour them without any trouble. And the reason is subjoined, because, if God stands by the Israelites, their enemies will be destitute of all defence. Justly, then, and for the best of reasons they conclude, that although our enemies would otherwise be formidable, they are not to

[1] Addition in *Fr.*, "Quand on ne se soumet point a luy;" when they do not submit themselves to Him.

be feared, if only God, apart from whom there is no strength, be favourable unto us.

The Repetition of the same Narrative.

DEUTERONOMY, CHAPTER I.

26. Notwithstanding ye would not go up, but rebelled against the commandment of the Lord your God:

27. And ye murmured in your tents, and said, Because the Lord hated us, he hath brought us forth out of the land of Egypt, to deliver us into the hand of the Amorites, to destroy us.

28. Whither shall we go up? our brethren have discouraged our heart, saying, The people *is* greater and taller than we; the cities *are* great, and walled up to heaven: and, moreover, we have seen the sons of the Anakims there.

29. Then I said unto you, Dread not, neither be afraid of them.

30. The Lord your God, which goeth before you, he shall fight for you, according to all that he did for you in Egypt before your eyes;

31. And in the wilderness, where thou hast seen how that the Lord thy God bare thee, as a man doth bear his son, in all the way that ye went, until ye came into this place.

32. Yet in this thing ye did not believe the Lord your God,

33. Who went in the way before you, to search you out a place to pitch your tents *in*, in fire by night, to shew you by what way ye should go, and in a cloud by day.

26. Et tamen noluistis ascendere, sed rebellastis verbo Jehovæ Dei vestri.

27. Et murmurastis in tabernaculis vestris dicentes, Propterea quod odio habebat nos Jehova, eduxit nos è terra Ægypti, ut traderet nos in manum Emorrhæi, ut perderet nos.

28. Quo nos ascendimus? fratres nostri dissolverunt cor nostrum, dicendo, Populus iste major et procerior nobis est, urbes magnæ et munitæ usque ad cœlum: et etiam filios gigantum vidimus ibi.

29. Tunc dixi vobis, Ne paveatis neque timeatis ab eis:

30. Jehova Deus vester qui præcedit vos, ipse pugnabit pro vobis, prorsus ut fecit vobiscum in Ægypto in oculis vestris.

31. Et in ipso deserto vidistis quod portaverit Jehova Deus tuus, quemadmodum portare solet homo filium suum, et hoc per totam viam per quam ambulastis, donec veneritis ad locum istum.

32. Atqui ea in re non credidistis Jehovæ Deo vestro,

33. Qui præcedebat vos per viam ad explorandum vobis locum in quo castra figeretis, per ignem in nocte, ut ostenderet vobis viam per quam ambularetis, et per nubem in die.

27. *And ye murmured in your tents.* Elsewhere he says that they also wept; here he only speaks of their murmuring, which better suited his reproof. He then reminds them how malignant had been their ingratitude and perversity in upbraiding God on account of the special blessing which He had conferred upon them, as if He had done them a grievous injury. He could not have afforded them a more manifest

proof of His paternal love towards them than by their deliverance. Most iniquitous, therefore, is their mode of repaying Him, viz., by complaining that they had been cruelly brought forth to die, and by construing into hatred His exceeding great love. It is clear from the next verse that, although Moses does not relate the details in their proper order, there is still no contradiction in his words. A little before, he had seemed to give unqualified praise to the spies, as if they had performed their office honestly and faithfully, but now, from the language of the people, he shews that they were the authors of the revolt, inasmuch as they rendered inert, by the terror they inspired, those whom they ought to have encouraged.

29. *Then I said unto you, Dread not.* He here omits the address of Caleb and Joshua: since he only states briefly the heads of what he had spoken to the people. He merely shews that, when he endeavoured to recall them to their right senses, his efforts and pains were ineffectual. Moreover, he reasons from experience that they might well place their hopes in the assistance of God, because He went before them as a light; and, in proof of this, he reminds them that, after the discomfiture of the Egyptians, He did not fail still to exert His power, so as to protect even to the end those whom He had once delivered. This, then, is his proposition, that although they might be aware of their own weakness, still, through the power of God, they would be conquerors, since He had taken them under His care, and had declared Himself their leader; which he indicates by the expression, "goes before you." And, lest any hesitation should remain, he sets against their present obstacles the miracles of God's power, which they had experienced, not only in the commencement of their redemption, but in the continued progress of their deliverances, when, in their lost and desperate state, He had by ways innumerable restored them from death unto life. Hence he concludes that they ought not to be afraid, not that he would wish them to be altogether free from all fear and care, but so that they might overcome all hinderances, when confidence derived from the ready help of God should prevail in their hearts. He says emphatically

that God had fought "before their eyes," to lead them to fuller conviction by the evidence of their own senses.

31. *And in the wilderness where thou hast seen.* The constant course of God's grace is here commemorated; from whence they might safely infer, that He, who had pursued them with so many benefits, would still be the same in this crowning act. He, therefore, uses the image of *bearing*, because the way would have been by no means passable unless God had borne them, as it were, on His shoulders, just as a father is wont to bear his infant child. Thus, on the one hand, the incredible goodness of God is exalted, who had deigned so far to condescend as to take up the people in His arms; and, on the other hand, the people are reminded of their own infirmity, for, unless upheld by the power of God, they would scarcely have been competent to advance a step. Elsewhere, retaining a portion of this similitude, Moses compares God to an eagle,[1] who bears her young upon her wings, and teaches them to fly. And surely, unless (the Israelites) had been uplifted by supernatural means, they would never have been equal to a hundredth part of the difficulties they encountered.

32. *Yet in this thing ye did not believe the Lord.* He signifies that they had been most prejudiced observers of the works of God, since His power, so often experienced and so thoroughly understood, had not aroused them to confidence in Him. For in the word דבר, *dabar*, which we have translated *thing*, he embraces all the proofs whereby God had testified, that in Him alone there was all that was necessary to insure their complete salvation. And this was, so to speak, real or practical doctrine, when God called upon them to trust Him by stretching forth His hand. Still, He accuses them of unbelief with reference to the promise; for, whilst faith is not only prompt and ready in obedience, but invigorates and quickens the whole man, so the cause of their inertness was that they gave no heed to God who had promised to bestow upon them the land of Canaan, and did not rest upon His covenant. In relation to this also, he

[1] Deut. xxxii. 11. The last sentence of the paragraph in omitted in *Fr.*

says, that God marked out the places and stations where they should pitch their camp, for, unless it had been His design to guide them onwards, this change of places would have been superfluous. It was, therefore, gross supineness not to refer these signs for halting and proceeding to their proper object, since it was equivalent to despising God when He held out His hand to them.

NUMBERS, CHAPTER XIV.

10. But all the congregation bade stone them with stones. And the glory of the Lord appeared in the tabernacle of the congregation before all the children of Israel.	10. Tunc dixit tota multitudo, ut eos lapidibus obruerent: et gloria Jehovæ apparuit in tabernaculo conventionis omnibus filiis Israel.
11. And the Lord said unto Moses, How long will this people provoke me? and how long will it be ere they believe me, for all the signs which I have shewed among them?	11. Tunc dixit Jehova ad Mosen, Usquequò vilipendet me populus iste? et usquequo non credent mihi in cunctis signis quæ feci in medio eorum?
12. I will smite them with the pestilence, and disinherit them, and will make of thee a greater nation and mightier than they.	12. Percutiam eum peste, expellamque eum: te autem faciam in gentem magnam et robustiorem eo.

10. *But all the congregation bade stone them.* When these wicked men began by murmuring against God, and openly casting censure upon Him, no wonder that they should also rage against His servants; for, when we endeavour to subdue pride, it generally begets cruelty; and so also, when iniquity is reproved, it always ends at last in fury. Caleb and Joshua did not constrain them by force of arms, neither did they menace them; but only persuaded them to trust in God's promise, and not to hesitate to advance into the land of Canaan; yet, because in their obstinacy the people had determined not to believe God, they champ the bit, as it were, upon being chastised, and desire to stone their reprovers. How great was the impetuosity of their wrath is manifest from this, that God does not attempt to appease their fury, nor to restrain them by threats, or by His authority, but openly displays His power from heaven, and miraculously protects His servants by the manifestation of His glory, as if He were rescuing them from wild beasts. There is, indeed, no express mention made of the cloud, but we

may infer that the sign to which they were accustomed, was given not merely to terrify them, but also to cast them prostrate, so that they might be deprived of their power to inflict injury, and might desist even against their wills. For the majesty of God, although it truly humbles believers only, yet sometimes subdues the reprobate and the lost, or renders them astounded in all their ferocity.

11. *And the Lord said unto Moses.* God remonstrates with respect to their indomitable obstinacy, because they had just now hesitated not petulantly to despise and reject Him with the most atrocious insults, and notwithstanding all the clearest manifestations of His power. For I know not whether the sense which some give be suitable, when they translate the verb נאץ, *naatz,* "to provoke."[1] Jerome comes nearer to the genuine sense, How long will they detract me? But let us be contented with the genuine intention of God, which He confirms by the succeeding *antithesis,* where He complains that He is disparaged, because they do not take into consideration the many miracles whereby He had abundantly testified His power and loving-kindness; and thus He proves their contempt, because they deliberately refuse credit to the many signs of which the accumulation at least ought to have subdued or corrected their stubbornness.

The denunciation of their final punishment follows, together with a statement of the atrocity of their crime; for the particle "How long" indicates its long continuance, as well as the enduring patience of God. He had, indeed, punished others severely, but only for example's sake, in order that the name of their race should remain undestroyed, whereas he now declares that He will deal with them as with persons in a desperate condition, who cease not to make a mock of His patience. Hence we are taught, that, although God is placable in His nature, still the hope of pardon is deservedly cut off from unbelievers, who are so

[1] *A. V.*, "How long will this people *provoke* me?" *V.* "Usquequo *detrahet* mihi populus iste?" Ainsworth says, "*provoke me,* or *despite, blaspheme, contemptuously provoke me.* So the Apostle expoundeth this word *blaspheme,* in Rom. ii. 24, from Isa. lii. 5; and it implieth also a contempt or despising, Prov. i. 30; xv. 5; Isa. v. 24."

obdurate as that He produces no effect upon them by His hand, or by His countenance, or His word. He then briefly adverts to the use of the signs, viz., that their object was, that the knowledge or experience of them should awaken hopes of success.

If the apparent contradiction offends any one, that God should declare the people to be cast off, when it was already decreed that He would pardon them, a reply may be sought from elsewhere in three words; for God does not here speak of His secret and incomprehensible counsel, but only of the actual circumstances, shewing what the people had deserved, and how horrible was the vengeance which impended,[1] in respect to their wicked and detestable revolt, since it was not His design to keep Moses back from earnest prayer, but to put the sincerity of his piety and the fervency of his zeal to the proof. And, in fact, he does not contravene the prohibition, except upon the previous exhibition of some spark of faith. See Exodus xxxii.

13. And Moses said unto the Lord, Then the Egyptians shall hear *it;* (for thou broughtest up this people in thy might from among them;)	13. Et dixit Moses ad Jehovam, Atqui audient Ægyptii (quia eduxisti in virtute tua populum istum è medio ejus:)
14. And they will tell *it* to the inhabitants of this land: *for* they have heard that thou, Lord, *art* among this people; that thou, Lord, art seen face to face; and *that* thy cloud standeth over them; and *that* thou goest before them, by day-time in a pillar of a cloud, and in a pillar of fire by night.	14. Dicentque habitatori terræ ejus, *qui* audierunt quod tu Jehova sis, in medio hujus populi: quandoquidem oculo ad oculum visus sis tu Jehova: et nubes tua steterit super eos, et in columna nubis præcesseris eos per diem, et in columna ignis per noctem.
15. Now, *if* thou shalt kill *all* this people as one man, then the nations, which have heard the fame of thee, will speak, saying,	15. Si interfeceris populum hunc quasi virum unum, tunc dicent gentes quæ audierint famam tuam.
16. Because the Lord was not able to bring this people into the land which he sware unto them, therefore he hath slain them in the wilderness.	16. Quia absque potentia est Jehova, ut introducat populum istum in terram quam juravit eis, ideo mactavit eos in deserto.
17. And now, I beseech thee, let the power of my Lord be great, according as thou hast spoken, saying,	17. Et nunc magnificetur quæso fortitudo Domini mei, sicut loquutus es, dicens:

[1] "Et quelle punition luy seroit apprestee, si Dieu se vouloit venger d'une revolte si detestable;" and what punishment would be prepared for them, if God chose to take vengeance on so detestable a revolt.—*Fr.*

18. The Lord *is* long-suffering, and of great mercy, forgiving iniquity and transgression, and by no means clearing *the guilty;* visiting the iniquity of the fathers upon the children unto the third and fourth *generation.*

19. Pardon, I beseech thee, the iniquity of this people, according unto the greatness of thy mercy, and as thou hast forgiven this people, from Egypt even until now.

18. Jehova tardus ad iram, et multæ misericordiæ, tollens iniquitatem et peccatum, et innocentem non faciens: visitans iniquitatem patrum in filios super tertiam et quartam generationem.

19. Propitius esto agedum iniquitati populi hujus, secundum magnitudinem clementiæ tuæ, sicut remisisti populo huic ex Ægypto usque nunc.

13. *Then the Egyptians shall hear it.* Moses here, according to his custom, stands "in the breach" of the wall, as it is said in Psalm cvi. 23, to sustain and avert the anger of God, which else would burst forth, since through his intercession it came to pass that the fire was speedily extinguished, and the people were not consumed. In order to support his request, he only objects that God's holy name would be the sport of the wicked, if the people should perish altogether. I have endeavoured to reduce to their proper meaning the words which translators variously render. First, he says, "The Egyptians shall hear, whereas it is a thing sufficiently notorious, and testified by miracles, that this people was rescued from among them by thy might. The same report will also obtain currency among the nations of Canaan, who have already heard that thou art the protector of this people, and have undertaken the charge of governing them. If, therefore, they should altogether perish, all the nations which have heard of thy fame will cast the blame on thee, and will think that thy power is broken down in the midst of its course, so that thou couldst not carry through to the end the work thou hadst undertaken." The substance amounts to this, that because God had manifested by clear and evident signs that He was the deliverer of this people, He would be exposed to the reproach of the wicked, unless He should preserve in safety those whom He had once redeemed. For nothing else would occur to the minds of the heathen nations, except that God was unable to maintain His blessing, however desirous He might be to do so. And assuredly this is no ordinary effect of God's goodness, so to connect the glory of

His name with our salvation, that whatever is adverse to us brings with it reproach upon Him, because the mouth of the wicked will be open to blaspheme. And this will in fact turn to our advantage, if on our part, without dissimulation, and in zealous sincerity, we beseech God to uphold His own glory in saving us; for many boldly plead the name of God in their own behalf, although they are unaffected by any real care or love for it. Moreover, because the more illustrious God's exercise of His power has been, the more insolently are the ungodly disposed to blaspheme, if it has appeared to fail; we must always entreat of Him that He should not desert the work of His hands which He has begun in us. To this effect are the words, "They have heard that thou art seen face to face;" for, if the people's safety were not maintained, the failure would have been imputed to none but God, who had put forth the power of His hand to preserve them. In fine, since their astonishing exodus had been a testimony of God's favour, so, if He had suffered the people to perish in the desert, all would have considered it a sign of His weakness, inasmuch as it was not probable that He should not accomplish what He desired, unless He were unable to do so.

17. *And now, I beseech thee, let the power of my Lord be great.* He derives another ground of confidence from the vision, in which God had more clearly manifested His nature, from whence it appears how much he had profited by it, and what earnest and anxious attention he had paid to it. Hence, however, we derive a general piece of instruction, that there is nothing more efficacious in our prayers than to set His own word before God, and then to found our supplications upon His promises, as if He dictated to us out of His own mouth what we were to ask. Since, then, God had manifested Himself to Moses in that memorable declaration, which we have already considered, he was able to derive from thence a sure directory for prayer; for nothing can be more sure than His own word, on which if our prayers are based, there is no reason to fear that they will be ineffectual, or that their results should disappoint us, since He who has spoken will prove Himself to be true. And, in

fact, this is the reason why He speaks, viz., to afford us the grounds for addressing Him, for else we must needs be dumb.

Since I have expounded the 18th verse elsewhere,[1] let my readers refer to that place.

19. *Pardon, I beeeech thee, the iniquity of this people.* In order to encourage his hope of pardon, he first sets before himself the greatness of God's mercy, and then the past instances by which it had been proved that God was inclined to forgiveness. And, indeed, the mercy of God continually invites us to seek reconciliation whenever we have sinned; and, though iniquities heaped upon iniquities, and the very enormity of our sins, might justly make us afraid, still the abundance of His grace, of which mention is here made, must needs occur to us, so as to swallow up all dread of His wrath. David, also, betaking himself to this refuge, affords us an example how all alarm is to be overcome. (Ps. li. 1.) But, since the bare and abstract recognition of God's goodness is often insufficient for us, Moses applies another stay in the shape of experience: Pardon, (he says,) as thou hast so often done before. For, since the goodness of God is unwearied and inexhaustible, the oftener we have experienced it, the more ought we to be encouraged to implore it; not that we may sink into the licentious indulgence of sin, but lest despair should overwhelm us, when we are lying under the condemnation of God, and our own conscience smites and torments us. In a word, let us regard this as a most effective mode of importunity, when we beseech God by the benefits which we have already experienced, that He will never cease to be gracious.

20. And the Lord said, I have pardoned, according to thy word:

21. But *as* truly *as* I live, all the earth shall be filled with the glory of the Lord.

22. Because all those men which have seen my glory, and my miracles which I did in Egypt, and in the wilderness, have tempted me now these ten times, and have not hearkened to my voice;

20. Tunc dixit Jehova, Peperci secundum sermonem tuum.

21. Veruntamen vivo ego, et replebit gloria mea universam terram.

22. Quoad cunctos homines qui viderunt gloriam meam, et signa mea quæ edidi in Ægypto, et deserto, et tentaverunt me jam decem vicibus, nec paruerunt voci meæ:

[1] See Exod. xxxiv. 6, 7. Vol. iii. pp. 386-388.

23. Surely they shall not see the land which I sware unto their fathers, neither shall any of them that provoked me see it:

24. But my servant Caleb, because he had another spirit with him, and hath followed me fully, him will I bring into the land whereunto he went; and his seed shall possess it.

25. (Now the Amalekites and the Canaanites dwelt in the valley.) To-morrow turn you, and get you into the wilderness, by the way of the Red sea.

23. Si videbunt terram, de qua juravi patribus eorum, omnes, inquam, qui me irritaverunt, non videbunt eam.

24. At servum meum Caleb, eo quòd alius fuit spiritus cum eo, et adimplevit ire post me, ipsum quoque introducam in terram quam ingressus est, et semen ejus hæreditate accipiet eam.

25. Amalec et Chananæus habitat in valle: cras revertimini et proficiscimini in desertum via maris Suph.

20. *And the Lord said, I have pardoned, according to thy word.* God signifies that He pardons for His servant Moses' sake, and makes, as it were, a present to him of those whom He had already devoted to destruction. Hence we gather how much the entreaties of the pious avail with God: as He is said, in Ps. cxlv. 19, to "fulfil the desire of them that fear him." He would, indeed, have done of His own accord what He granted to Moses; but, in order that we may be more earnest in prayer, the use and advantage of prayers is commended, when God declares that He will not only comply with our requests, but even obey them.

But how is it consistent for Him to declare that He had spared those, upon whom He had determined to inflict the most extreme punishment, and whom He deprived of their promised inheritance? I reply that the pardon in question was not granted to the individuals, but to their race and name. For the opinion of some is unnatural, who think that they were released from the penalty of eternal death, and thence that God was propitiated towards them, because He was contented with their temporal punishment. I do not doubt, then, but that Moses was so far heard, as that the seed of Abraham should not be destroyed, and the covenant of God should not fail. For He so dispensed the pardon as to preserve their posterity uninjured, whilst He inflicted on the unbelievers themselves the reward of their rebellion. Thus the conditions of the pardon were of no advantage to the impious rebels, though they opened a way for the faithful fulfilment of His promise.

21. *But as truly as I live, all the earth.* It is, indeed, plain that God here swears by His life and glory: the meaning is only ambiguous in this respect, that some translate it in the past tense, that the earth had been filled with His glory, which had already been displayed in so many miracles. And this seems to accord well with what follows, "Those, who have seen my glory—shall not see the land;" still the future tense suits the context better, viz., that God should call to witness His glory, which He will hereafter assert. Moses feared lest the destruction of the people should be turned into a reproach and contumely against God; God now declares with an oath that He would so vindicate His glory, as that those, who were guilty of so great a crime, should not escape punishment. He proclaims that those should not see the land, who had shut their eyes against the miracles, of which they had been spectators and eye-witnesses, and in their blindness had endeavoured to set them at nought. For, inasmuch as they had not been taught to fear God by so many signs, they were worse than unworthy of beholding the land, the possession of which ought to have been assured to them by those very signs, if God's truth had not been utterly rejected by their ingratitude.

God complains that He had been "tempted" by them "ten times;" because they had not ceased constantly to provoke Him by their frowardness; for it is no fixed or definite number, which is intended, but God would merely indicate that they had done so without measure or end. We have elsewhere[1] shewn what it is to tempt God, viz., to subject His power to the narrow rule of our own senses, and to prescribe to Him the mode in which He is to act, according to our own desires: so as to defer to Him no further than our carnal reason dictates. The source and cause of this tempting of God is subjoined, *i.e.*, when men refuse to listen to His voice; since nothing but obedience, which is the mistress of humility, can restrain our insolence.

24. *But my servant Caleb.* By *synecdoche* Caleb alone is now excepted, although Joshua was a partaker of the same

[1] See *antè*, vol. i. p. 421, on Deut. vi. 16.

grace, as he had been also a sharer in his courageous conduct; but Caleb is especially distinguished, because he had, as it were, uplifted the banner, and had stood forth first to encourage Joshua. The sum of his praise is that he "fulfilled[1] to go after God." The word "will," which some understand, is superfluous, since the expression is complete without any addition. God, therefore, commends Caleb's perseverance in obeying; because he not only promptly exhorted the others, but also proceeded boldly and unhesitatingly, without being deterred by any obstacles. God, however, magnifies his perseverance, because he looked to Him alone in his noble conflict with so great a multitude. For it is an extraordinary case for a person to stand firm, and to hold a straight course in the midst of violent and tempestuous disturbances, when all the world is, as it were, convulsed. Although the word רוח, *ruach*,[2] is sometimes used for the disposition of the mind, yet I have no doubt but that Moses signifies, by *metonymy*, that Caleb was thus influenced by divine inspiration.

25. *Now the Amalekites and the Canaanites.* Some thus resolve these words; "Although the Amalekites dwell in the valley;" and others thus: "Since the Amalekites abide in the valleys to lay ambuscades." Others think that their object is to inspire terror, lest the Israelites should remain too long in the enemy's country, since they would be daily exposed to fresh attacks. I am, however, rather of opinion that they are spoken in reproach. For they had already arrived at the borders of the inhabited land, so that their enemies might be put to the rout at once: whereas God commands them to retire, and thus expels them from the land, which they had actually reached. Still I do not deny that He sets before them the necessity of the case, and thus enforces their obedience; as if He had said, that nothing

[1] *A. V.*, "Followed me fully." "*Hebr.*, he fulfilled after me: so in Deut. i. 36, and Josh. xiv. 8."—Ainsworth. "*Implevit*, subaudi, verbum meum, vel voluntatem meam."—*S. M.*

[2] "This *other spirit* was the spirit of faith, which the Law cannot give, (Gal. iii. 2)—the spirit of adoption of sons, not of bondage to fear again, Rom. viii. 14, 15. By the guidance of this spirit, Caleb constantly followed the Lord, and obtained the promised inheritance."—Ainsworth.

now remained but to retreat, and again to throw themselves into the desert.

26. And the Lord spake unto Moses and unto Aaron, saying,

27. How long *shall I bear with* this evil congregation, which murmur against me? I have heard the murmurings of the children of Israel, which they murmur against me.

28. Say unto them, *As truly as* I live, saith the Lord, as ye have spoken in mine ears, so will I do to you:

29. Your carcases shall fall in this wilderness; and all that were numbered of you, according to your whole number, from twenty years old and upward, which have murmured against me,

30. Doubtless ye shall not come into the land *concerning* which I sware to make you dwell therein, save Caleb the son of Jephunneh, and Joshua the son of Nun.

31. But your little ones, which ye said should be a prey, them will I bring in, and they shall know the land which ye have despised.

32. But *as for* you, your carcases, they shall fall in this wilderness.

33. And your children shall wander in the wilderness forty years, and bear your whoredoms, until your carcases be wasted in the wilderness.

34. After the number of the days in which ye searched the land, *even* forty days, (each day for a year,) shall ye bear your iniquities, *even* forty years; and ye shall know my breach of promise.

35. I the Lord have said, I will surely do it unto all this evil congregation, that are gathered together against me: in this wilderness they shall be consumed, and there they shall die.

36. And the men which Moses sent to search the land, who returned, and made all the congregation to murmur against him, by bringing up a slander upon the land,

26. Loquutus est itaque Jehova ad Mosen et Aharon, dicendo:

27. Usque quo congregationem hanc perversam feram, quæ murmurat adversum me? murmurationes filiorum Israel, quibus ipsi murmurant contra me, audivi.

28. Dic ergo eis, Vivo ego, dicit Jehova, nisi quemadmodum loquuti estis in auribus meis sic fecero vobis.

29. In deserto isto cadent cadavera vestra, et omnes numerati vestri, secundum omnem numerum vestrum, à filio viginti annorum et supra, qui murmurastis contra me.

30. Si vos ingrediemini terram de qua levavi manum meam, ut habitare vos facerem in ea: præter Caleb filium Jephuneh, et Jehosua filium Nun.

31. Ac parvulos vestros, de quibus dixistis, In prædam erunt, ipsos introducam: et cognoscent terram istam quam despexistis.

32. Cadavera autem vestra cadent in deserto hoc.

33. Et filii vestri pastores erunt in deserto hoc quadraginta annis: et portabunt scortationes vestras donec consumantur cadavera vestra in deserto.

34. Secundum numerum dierum quibus explorastis terram quadraginta diebus, unoquoque die pro anno uno, portabitis iniquitates vestras in deserto, et cognoscetis vanitatem meam.

35. Ego Jehova loquutus sum, Si non hoc fecero universæ congregationi huic perversæ, quæ congregata est adversum me, in deserto isto consumentur, ibique morientur.

36. Viri itaque illi quos miserat Moses ad explorandam terram, qui reversi murmurare fecerant adversus eum cunctam congregationem, detrahendo terræ:

37. Even those men that did bring up the evil report upon the land, died by the plague before the Lord.

38. But Joshua the son of Nun, and Caleb the son of Jephunneh, *which were* of the men that went to search the land, lived *still*.

37. Morientur viri illi qui terræ detraxerunt, plaga coram Jehova.

38. Jehosua vero filius Nun, et Caleb filius Jephuneh vivent, ex hominibus illis qui profecti sunt ad explorandam terram.

26. *And the Lord spake unto Moses.*[1] I have translated the *copula* by the word *itaque* (therefore,) to indicate the connexion with what precedes: for Moses does not here recount anything new, but, by way of explanation, repeats a point of great importance, viz., that they, who had refused to enter the land, would be deprived of its possession. He begins with the passionate interrogation:[2] "How long shall this troublesome dregs of a people be borne with, who never cease to murmur against me?" And God says that He "had heard" their turbulent cries; in order that they might more certainly perceive that their pride was intolerable, since God Himself was weary of it, although He is long-suffering and slow to anger. It is in bitter irony that He says He will deal with them in accordance with their own resolution and desire. Nothing, indeed, was further from their intention than to wander in the wilderness, but, since they had held back from entering the land, God says that He will gratify them in a very different sense, viz., that they shall never enjoy the sight of that land, which they had despised. By His oath, He expresses His extreme wrath, as also it is said in Ps. xcv. 11, "Unto whom I sware in my wrath, that they shall not enter into my rest."[3] It was necessary that their stolidity should be thus aroused, lest, when God was so greatly provoked, they should still continue self-satisfied, according to their wont. He aggravates their punishment by another circumstance, *i.e.*, that they were to be deprived of the inheritance which He had sworn to give to Abraham; for the lifting up of the hand[4] (as I have

[1] "The Lord spake *therefore* to Moses," &c.—*Lat.*

[2] "Pathetica interrogatio."—*Lat.* "Or, Dieu use d'un proeme vehement à la façon d'un homme passioné;" now, God uses a vehement exordium, after the fashion of an angry man.—*Fr.*

[3] "Si introibunt in requiem meam."—*Lat.* See *Margin A. V.*, and Heb. iv. 3, 5.

[4] See ver. 30, *Margin A. V. Item*, vol. i. p. 131, on Exod. vi. 8.

said elsewhere) was a form of oath; just as if God were called down from heaven by the outstretched hand to be witness and judge: and, although this does not indeed literally apply to God, still we know that He commonly transfers to Himself the things that belong to men. Moreover, this was a most severe reproof, that they by their wickedness and self-will should nullify a promise, which God had ratified by an oath, in so far, at least, as its fulfilment affected themselves: for He points out immediately afterwards that, although they had rejected the proffered blessing, He would still be true; and would bestow on their little ones that which they had refused for themselves. It is thus that God tempers His judgments against those hypocrites, who falsely profess to honour His name, so as to preserve a seed for the propagation of His Church: nor is He ever so severe towards the reprobate, as to fail in sustaining His mercy towards His elect. Nay, He here declares that He will be gracious towards their children, as a means of inflicting punishment on the fathers. It was an indirect accusation of God, when they lamented over their children, as if they were to be carried away as "a prey;" whereas, God promises that they shall be the possessors of the land, in order to reprove this wicked blasphemy.

33. *And your children shall wander in the wilderness.*[1] He here pronounces that their children shall be in some measure partakers of their punishment, inasmuch as they shall wander in the desert until the time prescribed: for by the word shepherds, He means sojourners,[2] who have no certain or settled residence. To this effect is the similitude in the song of Hezekiah: "My lodging is departed as a shepherd's tent."[3] (Isa. xxxviii. 12.) In short, He declares

[1] *Lat.*, "shall be shepherds." *Margin A. V.*, "or *feed.*"

[2] "Il entend qu'ils seront errans comme estrangers, ayant tousiours un pied levé, et nul arrest;" he means that they shall wander as strangers, having one foot always lifted, and without any stay.—*Fr.*

[3] *A. V.*, "Mine age is departed, &c." A. Barnes's translation pretty nearly agrees with that of *C.*, which he defends in the following note: "The word דורי, which is here used, means properly the revolving period, or circle of human life. The parallelism seems to demand, however, that it should be used in the sense of *dwelling*, or habitation, so as to correspond with the "shepherd's tent." Accordingly, Lowth and Noyes render

that they shall be wandering and unsettled, and lead a life, like shepherds conducting their flocks from place to place.

He calls the wicked rebellions, whereby they had corrupted themselves, metaphorically "whoredoms;" for, from the time that God had espoused them to Himself, their true chastity would have been to embrace His grace in sincere faith, and at the same time to devote themselves to His service; but by rejecting His pure worship, they had broken their sacred marriage-vow like gadding harlots.

This example teaches us how God visits the iniquities of the fathers on their children, and yet chastises no one undeservedly; since the descendants here referred to,[1] although atoning for the fault of others, were still by no means innocent themselves. But in the judgments of God there is always a deep abyss, into which if you fear to be plunged, adore that which it is not lawful to question. Nevertheless, there is no doubt but that thus also God provided for the welfare of those, towards whom He appeared to show some marks of severity. For He waited not only until they had grown up, but also, as was advantageous to themselves, until they had attained the strength of manhood, and until a new generation had sprung up. He assigns a second reason why He postponed the fulfilment of His promise for forty years, viz., that He might repay the ill-spent days by as many years. Having, then, spoken of their children, He again returns to the actual criminals themselves, who were to be consumed in all that long period of time, as if by a lingering disease. The noun תנואת, *tenuoth*, which I have rendered *vanity*,[2] is derived from the verb נוא, *nu*, which signifies to render ineffectual. Translators, however, extract from it various meanings. Some thus construe it: Ye shall

it *habitation*. So also do Gesenius and Rosenmüller. The Arabic word has this signification; and the Hebrew verb דור, also means to *dwell*, to *remain*, as in Chaldee." *C.'s* Latin is here *hospitium*; in his Commentary on Isaiah, *habitatio*.

[1] "Ayant porté la paste au four (comme on dit) pour le peche de leurs pères;" having carried the dough to the oven (as they say) for the sin of their fathers.—*Fr.*

[2] *A. V.*, "My breach of promise. *Margin*, *Or*, altering of my purpose." *Fr.*, "Mensonge."

know whether I am false, or whether my word shall be vain. Others, rendering it *prohibition*, depart more widely from the sense. But, in my judgment, it is an ironical concession, whereby God reproves their detestable pride, which had no other object than to accuse God of falsehood, and to charge Him calumniously with failing to fulfil His words. Unless,[1] perhaps, it should be preferred to take it passively; because the people had endeavoured to annihilate, as it were, God himself. But still I rather adopt this sense, that they should perceive by certain and experimental proof, whether God's promises were frivolous or vain. Moreover, we must bear in mind the admonition of the Prophet, to which I have referred, (Ps. xcv. 11,) and which the Apostle adapts to our present use, (Heb. iv. 6,) viz., that a better rest is now offered to us, from which we are to fear lest our unbelief should withhold us. For it is not sufficient for us that God's hand should once have been extended to us, unless we allow ourselves to be directed by it, until our earthly wanderings are concluded, and it conducts us into our heavenly rest.

36. *And the men, which Moses sent to search the land.* I do not at all approve of the view which some take, that this is recorded by anticipation; for there is no question but that Moses recounts the special punishment which was inflicted by God upon the perfidious spies. He had previously treated of the general punishment of the whole people; when he now relates that the ten men were smitten by the plague, he intimates that God would begin with them, so as to manifest by this conspicuous and notable example how grossly He was offended by their very disgraceful contempt of His grace. Their sudden and unnatural death was, therefore, a kind of presage to all the others of the punishment which awaited them. For, in the first place, the expression, "the plague," is emphatic, as much as to say that they

[1] "Sinon qu'on aimast mieux prendre ce mot en temps passif, Vous cognoistrez mon aneantissement: pource que le peuple s'estoit efforcé d'abolir Dieu;" unless it be preferred to take this word in a passive sense, You shall know my annihilation; because the people had striven to annihilate God.—*Fr.*

should not die in the ordinary course of nature. Again, by "the sight of God,"[1] he means something else than as if he had said, "before God ;" for God was not merely a beholder of their destruction, but in a strange and unusual manner He executed His awful judgment, as if He had publicly ascended the tribunal. And this appeared more clearly by His prolonging the life of Caleb and Joshua, who were the only survivors of that generation until the end of the time prescribed. It is true, indeed, that the verbs[2] are in the past tense ; but, since there is an evident πρόληψις, I have not hesitated to change the tense, which is a sufficiently common idiom of the language ; and thus the connexion of the address is better preserved.

DEUTERONOMY, CHAPTER I.

34. And the Lord heard the voice of your words, and was wroth, and sware, saying,

35. Surely there shall not one of these men of this evil generation see that good land, which I sware to give unto your fathers,

36. Save Caleb the son of Jephunneh, he shall see it ; and to him will I give the land that he hath trodden upon, and to his children, because he hath wholly followed the Lord.

39. Moreover, your little ones, which ye said should be a prey, and your children, which in that day had no knowledge between good and evil, they shall go in thither, and unto them will I give it, and they shall possess it.

40. But *as for* you, turn you, and take your journey into the wilderness, by the way of the Red sea.

34. Audivit autem Jehova vocem verborum vestrorum, iratusque est, ac juravit, dicendo :

35. Non videbit quisquam ex hominibus illis de generatione mala hac terram bonam quam juravi me daturum patribus vestris ;

36. Præter Caleb filium Jephuneh : ipse enim videbit eam, eique dabo terram quam calcavit, et filiis ejus, eo quod adimplevit ire post Jehovam.

39. Etiam parvuli vestri, de quibus dixistis, In prædam erunt, ac filii vestri, qui non norunt hodie bonum nec malum, ipsi intrabunt illuc, illisque dabo eam, et ipsi possidebunt eam.

40. Vos autem conversi proficiscimini in desertum per viam maris Suph.

[1] It will be seen that *C.'s* own translation is, "coram Deo ;" but the *V.* renders the words, "in conspectu Domini."

[2] *A. V.* concludes the denunciation of the Almighty at ver. 35. *C.* continues it to the end of ver. 38 ; and hence arose the necessity for changing the tenses. Vatablus and the Geneva version agree with *C.* ; Dathe with *A. V.*

34. *And the Lord heard the voice of your words.* I have shewn elsewhere what is meant by God's hearing, *i.e.*, that nothing can be concealed from Him, but that He will take account of and judge all our words and deeds. And this is worthy of our observation ; for men would never dare to murmur against Him, unless they promised themselves impunity[1] from His not being present. Secondly, we learn from hence, that God, who is a just Judge, does not proceed hastily and without cause to inflict punishment on men, and that He does not manifest severity without a full examination of the case. He, therefore, means that they deprived themselves of their assured inheritance, when they were close upon receiving it, through their own rebellion and depravity.

39. *Moreover, your little ones.* I have already shewn that God so tempered His judgment that, whilst none of the guilty should escape with impunity, still His faithfulness should remain sure and inviolable, and that the wickedness of men should not make void the covenant which He had made with Abraham. He, therefore, pronounces sentence upon them, that they should never enjoy the inheritance which they had despised : yet declares that He will nevertheless be true in the fulfilment of what He had promised, and will display His mercy towards their children, whom in their despair they had condemned to be a prey to their enemies.

When He limits this grace to their little ones, whose age did not yet allow them to discern between good and evil, He signifies that all who had already arrived at the years of reason, were, from the least to the greatest, accomplices in the crime, since the contagion had spread through the whole body. Surely it was an incredible prodigy, that so great a multitude should be so carried away by diabolical fury, as that nothing should remain unaffected by it, unless perhaps a timely death removed some of the old men rather on account of the vice of others than their own. But, if even

[1] "Sous ombre qu'il ne prend point garde à ce qui ce fait ici bas;" under the pretext that He pays no attention to what is done here below.—*Fr.*

a hundredth part of them had been guiltless of the crime, God would have left some survivors.

"To have no knowledge of good and evil," is equivalent to being unable "to discern between their right hand and their left hand;" by which expression in Jonah, (iv. 11,) God exempts from condemnation those little ones, who have as yet no power of forming a judgment. From hence, however, some have foolishly attempted to prove that infant-children are not defiled by original sin; and that men are involved in no guilt, except such as they have severally contracted by their own voluntary act (*arbitrio*.) For the question here is not as to the nature of the human race; a distinction is simply made between children and those who have consciously and wilfully provoked God's wrath; whereas the corruption, which is the root (of all evils,[1]) although it may not immediately produce its fruit in actual sins, is not[2] therefore non-existent.

NUMBERS, CHAPTER XIV.

39. And Moses told these sayings unto all the children of Israel: and the people mourned greatly.

40. And they rose up early in the morning, and gat them up into the top of the mountain, saying, Lo, we *be here*, and will go up unto the place which the Lord hath promised: for we have sinned.

41. And Moses said, Wherefore now do ye transgress the commandment of the Lord? but it shall not prosper.

42. Go not up, for the Lord *is* not among you; that ye be not smitten before your enemies.

43. For the Amalekites and the Canaanites *are* there before you, and ye shall fall by the sword: because ye are turned away from the Lord, therefore the Lord will not be with you.

39. Loquutus est igitur Moses verba ista omnibus filiis Israel, et luxerunt populus valde.

40. Surrexeruntque mane, et ascenderunt in verticem montis, dicendo: Ecce nos, ut ascendamus ad locum de quo loquutus est Jehova: quia peccavimus.

41. Et dixit Moses, Ut quid transgredimini sermonem Jehovæ? Et (*vel,* quando) hoc non prospere cedet.

42. Ne ascendatis: quia non est Jehova in medio vestri: ne percutiamini coram inimicis vestris.

43. Amalec enim et Chananæus ibi est ante vos, et cadetis gladio. Nam propterea quod aversi estis a sequendo Jehova, neque erit Jehova vobiscum.

[1] Added from *Fr.*

[2] "Ne laisse pas d'estre cachee en nous;" Does not cease to lie hid within us.—*Fr.*

44. But they presumed to go up unto the hill-top: nevertheless, the ark of the covenant of the Lord, and Moses, departed not out of the camp.	44. Sumpserunt tamen animos ut ascenderent in verticem montis. Arca autem fœderis Jehovæ et Moses non recesserunt è medio castrorum.
45. Then the Amalekites came down, and the Canaanites which dwelt in that hill, and smote them, and discomfited them, *even* unto Hormah.	45. Descendit itaque Amalec et Chananæus, qui habitabant in monte illo, percusseruntque eos, et contuderunt usque Horma.

39. *And Moses told all these sayings.* It was, indeed, a just cause for mourning, when they heard that God, whose longsuffering they had so wantonly abused, would hereafter be inexorable. Yet here we have set before our eyes that "sorrow of the world which worketh death," as Paul says, (2 Cor. vii. 10,) when the wicked, as they weep and complain, cease not to murmur against God; nay, when they gnaw the bit with greater obstinacy, and thus, like savage and untameable beasts, rush forward to their destruction in blind desperation. The temporal punishment could not, indeed, be redeemed by any tears; but, if there had been the disposition to repent, their only remedy would have been voluntarily to submit themselves, and calmly to undergo whatever chastisement God might be pleased to inflict. First of all, however, they proudly struggle to shake off the punishment awarded to them, and whilst they pretended penitence, increasingly kick against God. There is no doubt but that it was under the pretence of submission that they prepared themselves on the morrow to advance; but wherefore was this, except that they may overturn God's inviolable decree! Nevertheless, they sought, as if against His will, to make a way for themselves, though He forbade. "Behold us, (they said,) we are ready;" but it was too late; for the opportunity had fled. For, as the Prophet exhorts us to "seek the Lord while he may be found," (Isa. lv. 6,) so also we ought to follow Him when He calls us. But of what avail was this unseasonable alacrity of the people? When God wishes them to retire into the desert, they affect a desire to obey Him by advancing further; and still would have their confession of sin accepted as a sufficient satisfaction.

41. *And Moses said, Wherefore do ye now transgress?* He rejects this feigned penitence, whereby the sinner tries all sorts of shifts,[1] so as not to submit himself to God. "If thou wilt return, O Israel, return unto me," saith the Lord by Jeremiah, (iv. 1.) The first thing, therefore, which we must consider is, what God requires of us; so that it may plainly appear that we truly submit ourselves to His power.

In order to restrain their temerity, Moses reminds them that they will seek in vain for success, when they depart from God's command. And this is a very useful piece of instruction, that His grace will never be wanting to us, if we simply obey His word; but when, in contempt and neglect of His precepts, we are carried away by our own feelings, the event will never be prosperous. If any should object that the wretched people had no other remedy, I have already stated, that they ought to have been contented with this consolation, viz., that banishment from the land of Canaan was not disinheritance from the hope of eternal life. Nay, if they had humbled themselves before God, they might expect that their punishment would have been a profitable help to them. By their misdirected activity they double the evil. After having pointed out their danger, Moses again impresses upon them that God is not with them, because they had deserted Him: and that His blessing was withheld, because they had refused to follow Him at the proper time.

44. *But they presumed to go up unto the hill-top.* It was not, indeed, their intention deliberately to array themselves against God, but rather did they endeavour to appease Him by this means of propitiation. Nor was their self-deceit devoid of a colourable pretext, inasmuch as they were ready cheerfully to welcome death, so as to offer their lives in sacrifice, and thus to compensate for their previous hesitation and inertness. It is thus that the zeal of the wicked is fervent, when it ought to be still; whereas, when God commands, coldness and apathy possess their

[1] "En laquelle les pecheurs tournent à l'entour du pot;" whereby sinners twist round the pot.—*Fr.*

minds, so that they are no more aroused by His voice, than as if they were stones. In a word, when it ought to be quiet, unbelief is always active, prompt, and bold; but when God would have it advance, it is timid, slow, and dead.

In conclusion, Moses adds, that their foolish enterprise was punished; for they were not merely routed and put to flight by their enemies, but utterly destroyed.[1] Hence we gather, that their audacity failed them in the trial, and was deficient in true courage. At the same time he recounts another sign of their senselessness, in that they left behind the ark of God, as well as Moses, and rushed forward, like doomed persons, to be slaughtered. Hence it appears that unbelievers, when carried away by the blind impulse of their zeal, are as much destitute of reason and discretion as if they deliberately conspired for their own destruction.

DEUTERONOMY, CHAPTER I.

41. Then ye answered and said unto me, We have sinned against the Lord, we will go up and fight, according to all that the Lord our God commanded us. And when ye had girded on every man his weapons of war, ye were ready to go up into the hill.

42. And the Lord said unto me, Say unto them, Go not up, neither fight; for I *am* not among you; lest ye be smitten before your enemies.

43. So I spake unto you; and ye would not hear, but rebelled against the commandment of the Lord, and went presumptuously up into the hill.

44. And the Amorites, which dwelt in that mountain, came out against you, and chased you, as bees

41. Et respondistis et dixistis ad me, Peccavimus Jehovæ: nos ascendemus et pugnabimus omnino sicut præcepit nobis Jehova Deus noster. Et accinxistis vos singuli armis suis bellicis, et parastis ascendere in montem.

42. Dixit autem mihi Jehova, Dic eis, Ne ascendatis, neque pugnetis: quia non sum in medio vestri, et ne percutiamini coram inimicis vestris.

43. Loquutus sum hæc apud vos sed non audistis, ac rebelles fuistis ori Jehovæ, et temerè egistis ut ascenderetis in montem.

44. Itaque egressus est Amorrhæus qui habitabat in monte in occursum vestri, et vos persequuti sunt,

[1] "Sed etiam contriti."—*Lat.* "Discomfited them."—*A.V.* The Geneva version renders the word "consumed."—*Hebr.* ויכתום, from כתת, which Taylor renders, "*contundere, conterere.* To beat, to crush, to knock, and mash all to pieces."

do, and destroyed you in Seir, *even* unto Hormah.

45. And ye returned, and wept before the Lord; but the Lord would not hearken to your voice, nor give ear unto you.

46. So ye abode in Kadesh many days, according unto the days that ye abode *there*.

quemadmodum facere solent apes, et contriverunt vos in Seir usque Horma.

45. Et reversi flevistis coram Jehova: sed non exaudivit Jehova vocem vestram, nec auscultavit vobis.

46. Et mansistis in Cades diebus multis, secundum numerum dierum quibus mansistis.

41. *Then ye answered and said unto me.* The repentance was too late, which impelled the Israelites to their unseasonable effort of activity; although, as I have above explained, they did not truly and seriously repent, since, when they ought patiently to have borne the chastening of God, they endeavoured to shake it off, and to drive it far away from them by a new act of disobedience. In a word, they did nothing else but kick against the pricks. But such is the energy of men, when their own fancy leads them, that they will dare anything which God forbids. But herein did their far worse folly betray itself, in that, when they were again withheld, they still refuse to obey. Besides, He does not merely forbid them to fight, but denies them His assistance. What then could be more monstrous than that, in opposition to God's will, and when the hope of His assistance was withdrawn, they should engage in what they had just before obstinately refused to attempt under His auspices, and by His command, and with the sure promise of success? And yet, so does hypocrisy blind men's minds, that they imagined they were correcting and compensating for the evil which they doubled. Moses then relates how they received the reward which they deserved; as much as to say, that, although they might be slow to learn, still they were made acquainted, by the reverse which they experienced, how fatal a thing it is not to obey God: for fools never learn wisdom except beneath the rod.

45. *And ye returned and wept before the Lord.* He here appeals to the testimony of their own conscience; for they never would have been brought to weeping and prayers, except by the force of their own feelings. Since, then, they were abundantly convinced, that a just punishment was inflicted upon their obstinacy, necessity drove them to seek

after God: consequently they had no cause to complain, though God manifested Himself to be implacable.

In the last verse there is an ambiguity in the meaning of these words, " many days, according to the number of the days." Some, rendering the verb in the pluperfect tense, " in which we had remained there,"[1] suppose that they still abode there another forty days. But it is equally probable that an indefinite time is referred to: as if he had said, that the people delayed there a long time, from whence it might be inferred, that they lay like persons stupified, from lack of knowing what to do.

It is Kadesh-barnea to which Moses refers, from whence the spies had been sent forth; and not the Kadesh where Miriam died, and where the people murmured for want of water.

DEUTERONOMY, CHAPTER IX.

22. And at Taberah, and at Massah, and at Kibroth-hattaavah, ye provoked the Lord to wrath.	22. Et in Taberah et in Massah, et in Cibroth Hatthaavah ad iram provocastis Jehovam.
23. Likewise, when the Lord sent you from Kadesh-barnea, saying, Go up and possess the land which I have given you; then ye rebelled against the commandment of the Lord your God, and ye believed him not, nor hearkened to his voice.	23. Et quum misisset vos Jehova de Cades Barnea, dicendo: Ascendite, et possidete terram quam dedi vobis, rebellastis verbo Jehovæ Dei vestri, neque credidistis ei, neque obedivistis voci ejus.
24. Ye have been rebellious against the Lord from the day that I knew you.	24. Rebelles fuistis Jehovæ à die qua cognovi vos.

[1] " Quibus *anteà* manseratis."—Pagninus in Poole. The *V.* has only " Sedistis ergo in Cades-barne multo tempore." On this Corn. à Lapide has the following note: " In Hebrew it is added, *according to the days that ye abode,* which Vatablus thus explains, Ye remained in Kadesh-barnea as many days after the return of the spies, as ye had remained there before their return. Again, the Hebrews themselves, in *Seder Olam,* thus explain it, Ye remained in Kadesh-barnea as many days as ye afterwards remained in all your other stations together, viz., 19 years: for twice 19 make 38, to which if you add the two years that had elapsed before they came to Kadesh-barnea, you will have the forty years of their journeyings in the desert. Nothing like this, however, can be gathered from our version, nor from the Hebrew either; for the expression, ' according to the days that ye abode,' is merely a Hebrew form of repetition, explanatory of what had preceded, and meaning ' for a long time.'—Hence our interpreter has omitted this Hebrew repetition as redundant, and strange to Latin ears."

22. *And at Taberah.* He briefly adverts to several cases whereby he may convince the people of ingratitude and persevering obstinacy, and thus of a corrupt nature: for it is just as if he had said, that they had been rebellious against God not once only, nor in one particular way, but that they had heaped together many offences, so that it was wonderful that God had so often pardoned them. He also recounts the names given to the places as memorials of their sins, in order that they may at length cease to transgress, since, although so often provoked, God had borne with them already too long.

DEUTERONOMY, CHAPTER II.

1. Then we turned, and took our journey into the wilderness, by the way of the Red sea, as the Lord spake unto me; and we compassed mount Seir many days.

1. Postea reversi profecti sumus in desertum per viam maris Suph, quemadmodum loquutus fuerat Jehova ad me, et circumivimus montem Seir diebus multis.

1. *Then we turned and took our journey.* The time in which they struck their camp is not stated in the book of Numbers. This verse, therefore, will aptly connect the history, since otherwise there would be an abruptness in what immediately follows. He then briefly indicates what was the nature of their journeying until the time appointed; viz., that, by wearying themselves in vain in circuitous wanderings, they might, at length, learn to follow God directly, and not to decline from the way which He points out.

LEVITICUS, CHAPTER XXIV.

10. And the son of an Israelitish woman, whose father *was* an Egyptian, went out among the children of Israel; and this son of the Israelitish *woman* and a man of Israel strove together in the camp:

11. And the Israelitish woman's son blasphemed the name *of the Lord*, and cursed. And they brought

10. Egressus est autem filius mulieris Israelitidis, qui erat filius viri Ægyptii, in medio filiorum Israel, et jurgati sunt in castris ipsis filius Israelitidis et vir Israelita.

11. Et transfixit filius mulieris Israelitidis nomen, et maledixit: adduxeruntque eum ad Mosen: nomen

him unto Moses: (and his mother's name *was* Shelomith, the daughter of Dibri, of the tribe of Dan:)

12. And they put him in ward, that the mind of the Lord might be shewed them.

13. And the Lord spake unto Moses, saying,

14. Bring forth him that hath cursed without the camp, and let all that heard *him* lay their hands upon his head, and let all the congregation stone him.

autem matris ejus erat Selomith filia Dibri, de tribu Dan.

12. Et posuerunt eum in custodiam, ut exponeret eis juxta sermonem Jehovæ.

13. Loquutus est autem Jehova ad Mosen, dicendo:

14. Educ blasphemum extra castra, et ponant omnes qui audierunt manus suas super caput ejus, et lapidet eum universus cœtus.

10. *And the son of an Israelitish woman.* In what year, and in what station in the desert this occurred, is uncertain. I have, therefore, thought it advisable to couple together two cases, which are not dissimilar. It is probable that between this instance of punishment, and that which will immediately follow, there was an interval of some time: but the connexion of two similar occurrences seemed best to preserve the order of the history; one of the persons referred to having been stoned for profaning God's sacred name by wicked blasphemy, and the other for despising and violating the Sabbath. It is to be observed that the crime of the former of these gave occasion to the promulgation of a law, which we have expounded elsewhere:[1] in accordance with the common proverb, Good laws spring from bad habits: for, after punishment had been inflicted on this blasphemer, Moses ordained that none should insult the name of God with impunity.

It was providentially ordered by God that the earliest manifestation of this severity should affect the son of an Egyptian: for, inasmuch as God thus harshly avenged the insult of His name upon the offspring of a foreigner and a heathen, far less excusable was impiety in Israelites, whom God had, as it were, taken up from their mothers' womb, and had brought them up in His own bosom. It is true, indeed, that on his mother's side he had sprung from the chosen people, but, being begotten by an Egyptian father, he could not be properly accounted an Israelite. If, then, there had been any room for the exercise of pardon, a

[1] See vol. ii. p. 431, on Lev. xxiv. 15, 16.

specious reason might have been alleged why forgiveness should be more readily extended to a man of an alien and impure origin. The majesty of God's name, however, was ratified by his death. Hence it follows that it is by no means to be permitted that God's name should be exposed with impunity to blasphemies among the sons of the Church.

We may learn from this passage that during their tyrannical oppression many young women married into the Egyptian nation, in order that their affinity might protect their relatives from injuries. It might, however, have been the case that love for his wife attracted the father of this blasphemer into voluntary exile, unless, perhaps, his mother might have been a widow before the departure of the people, so as to be at liberty to take her son with her.

To proceed, he is said to have "gone out," not outside the camp, but in public, so that he might be convicted by witnesses; for he would not have been brought to trial if his crime had been secretly committed within the walls of his own house. This circumstance is also worthy of remark, that, although the blasphemy had escaped him in a quarrel, punishment was still inflicted upon him; and assuredly it is a frivolous subterfuge to require that blasphemies should be pardoned on the ground that they have been uttered in anger; for nothing is more intolerable than that our wrath should vent itself upon God, when we are angry with one of our fellow-creatures. Still it is usual, when a person is accused of blasphemy, to lay the blame on the ebullition of passion, as if God were to endure the penalty whenever we are provoked.

The verb נקב, *nakab,* which some render to *express,* is here rather used for to curse, or to transfix; and the metaphor is an appropriate one, that God's name should be said to be transfixed, when it is insultingly abused.[1]

13. *And the Lord spake unto Moses.* It must be remembered, then, that this punishment was not inflicted upon the blasphemer by man's caprice, or the headstrong zeal of the

[1] See vol. ii. p. 431, and note. "La similitude de transpercer le nom de Dieu convient tres bien; pource que nous disons *deschirer par pieces* ou *despiter.*"—*Fr.*

people, but that Moses was instructed by Divine revelation what sentence was to be pronounced. It has been elsewhere stated[1] why God would have malefactors slain by the hands of the witnesses. Another ceremony is here added, viz., that they should lay their hands upon his head, as if to throw the whole blame upon him.

NUMBERS, CHAPTER XV.

32. And while the children of Israel were in the wilderness, they found a man that gathered sticks upon the Sabbath-day.	32. Quum autem essent filii Israel in deserto, invenerunt virum colligentem ligna die Sabbathi:
33. And they that found him gathering sticks brought him unto Moses and Aaron, and unto all the congregation.	33. Et adduxerunt illum qui invenerunt colligentem ligna, ad Mosen et Aharon, et universam congregationem.
34. And they put him in ward, because it was not declared what should be done to him.	34. Qui posuerunt eum in custodiam: quia nondum patefactum erat quid faciendum esset ei.
35. And the Lord said unto Moses, The man shall be surely put to death: all the congregation shall stone him with stones without the camp.	35. Et dixit Jehova ad Mosen, Moriendo moriatur vir ille: lapidet eum lapidibus universa congregatio extra castra.
36. And all the congregation brought him without the camp, and stoned him with stones, and he died; as the Lord commanded Moses.	36. Eduxerunt ergo eum congregatio extra castra, et lapidaverunt eum lapidibus, et mortuus est, quemadmodum præceperat Jehova Mosi.

32. *And while the children of Israel.* Since we know not in what year, or in what month this happened, it appeared that nothing would be better than to follow the context of Moses. This history shews that the Israelites were not always affected by the same degree of madness, so as to be rebellious against God; since in this instance their moderation is no less manifested than the fervency of their pious zeal. But as one swallow does not make spring, so we shall form an incorrect judgment of men's whole lives from one noble action. The transgressor of the law is brought to Moses and Aaron, whose authority retains the whole people in the path of duty. Their humility is also worthy of praise, in that they quietly wait for the decision of God; and finally,

[1] Vol. ii. p. 83, on Deut. xiii. 9.

must be added, their energy in executing the punishment as soon as God has declared the sentence. You would say that in every point they were rightly conformed to the rules of piety; but, since the most trifling occasion immediately led them astray, their hypocrisy was discovered by this great levity of conduct.

This, however, is the sum of the history, that by the death of one man the obligation of the Sabbath was sanctioned, so that it might henceforth be held in greater reverence. It might indeed be the case that these men, who brought the transgressor of the Sabbath, were careless in other matters, and, as is usual with hypocrites, were excessively rigid in their assertion of the claims of an outward ceremony. From the punishment, however, we may infer that the criminal himself had not erred through inadvertence, but in gross contempt of the Law, so as to think nothing of subverting and corrupting all things sacred. Sometimes, indeed, God has severely avenged inconsideration in the pollution of holy things; but it is probable that He would not have commanded this man to be stoned, unless he had been convicted of wilful crime. Moreover, by this severity God testified how much stress He laid upon the observance of the Sabbath. The reason of this has been elsewhere set forth,[1] viz., that by this mark and symbol He had separated His chosen people from heathen nations. Whence also arose the main reproach against the Jews, when they were called Sabbatarians.[2]

But it must be borne in mind that the worship of God was not to consist in mere idleness and festivity; and therefore that what God enjoined respecting the seventh day had another object: not only that they should then employ themselves in meditating upon His works, but that, renouncing themselves and their own works, they should live unto God.

Furthermore, this case shews us in general that the magis-

[1] Vol. ii. p. 434.

[2] Martial, *lib.* iv., *epigr.* 4, speaks of "jejunia Sabbatariorum," in a connexion which makes it highly probable that it was a kind of nickname for the Jews.

tracy is appointed no less for the maintenance of the First Table, than the Second; so that, if they inflict punishment upon murder, adultery, and theft, they should also vindicate the worship of God: for it is to be observed that the man was not stoned by a mere unreflecting impulse, but by the direct command of God. They knew, indeed, what he had deserved before God's tribunal; but, since no political law had been given on this head, Moses was unwilling to come to any decision except by the authority of God.

NUMBERS, CHAPTER XVI.

1. Now Korah, the son of Izhar, the son of Kohath, the son of Levi: and Dathan and Abiram the sons of Eliab; and On the son of Peleth, sons of Reuben, took *men:*

2. And they rose up before Moses, with certain of the children of Israel, two hundred and fifty princes of the assembly, famous in the congregation, men of renown:

3. And they gathered themselves together against Moses and against Aaron, and said unto them, *Ye take* too much upon you, seeing all the congregation *are* holy, every one of them, and the Lord *is* among them: wherefore then lift ye up yourselves above the congregation of the Lord?

4. And when Moses heard *it,* he fell upon his face:

5. And he spake unto Korah, and unto all his company, saying, Even to-morrow the Lord will shew who *are* his, and *who is* holy; and will cause *him* to come near unto him: even *him* whom he hath chosen will he cause to come near unto him.

6. This do; Take you censers, Korah, and all his company;

7. And put fire therein, and put incense in them before the Lord to-morrow: and it shall be, *that* the man whom the Lord doth choose, he *shall be* holy: *ye take* too much upon you, ye sons of Levi.

8. And Moses said unto Korah, Hear, I pray you, ye sons of Levi;

9. *Seemeth it but* a small thing

1. Tulit autem Corah filius Ishar, filii Cehath, filii Levi, et Dathan et Abiram filii Eliab, et On filius Peleth filii Reuben.

2. Et surrexerunt coram Mose, et viri è filiis Israel ducenti quinquaginta, principes congregationis, vocati ad tempus statutum, viri nominis.

3. Congregatique sunt adversum Mosen et Aharon, ac dixerunt eis, Sat sit vobis: nam tota congregatio, universi ipsi sancti sunt, et in medio eorum est Jehova: quare ergo effertis vos supra congregationem Jehovæ?

4. Quod quum audisset Moses, projecit se in faciem suam.

5. Et loquutus est ad Corah et ad omnem congregationem ejus, dicendo: Manè ostendet Jehova qui sint ejus, et quis sanctus, et ut accedat ad se: et quem elegerit, accedere faciet ad se.

6. Hoc facite, capite vobis acerras, Corah et tota congregatio ejus,

7. Et ponite in illis ignem, imponite quoque in eis incensum coram Jehova cras, et erit, vir quem elegerit Jehova, erit ille sanctus: satis sit vobis filii Levi.

8. Et dixit Moses ad Corah: Audite, quæso, filii Levi.

9. An parum hoc vobis est quod

unto you, that the God of Israel hath separated you from the congregation of Israel, to bring you near to himself, to do the service of the tabernacle of the Lord, and to stand before the congregation to minister unto them?

10. And he hath brought thee near *to him*, and all thy brethren the sons of Levi with thee: and seek ye the priesthood also?

11. For which cause, *both* thou and all thy company *are* gathered together against the Lord: and what *is* Aaron, that ye murmur against him?

separaverit Deus Israelis vos de congregatione Israel, ut accedere faceret vos sibi ut ministretis in ministerio tabernaculi Jehovæ, et ut staretis coram congregatione, ut ministraretis ei.

10. Et accedere fecit te, et omnes fratres tuos, filios Levi tecum: nisi quæratis etiam sacerdotium?

11. Idcirco tu et universa congregatio tua estis qui conveniunt contra Jehovam: at verò Aharon quid est, quod murmurastis adversus eum?

1. *Now Korah, the son of Izhar.* The impious conspiracy is here related of a few men, but these of the highest rank, whose object was to subvert and destroy the divinely-appointed priesthood. They make their attack, indeed, upon Moses, and accuse him of ruling unjustly; for thus it is that turbulent persons are carried away without reason or discrimination; but the only cause why they are set against him is because they suppose him to be the originator of the priesthood, as we easily collect from his reply. For he does not command them to stand forth, in order that they may decide respecting the political government or chieftainship, but that it may be made plain whether God acknowledges them as priests; nor does he reproach the Levites with anything but that, not content with their own lot, they have an unreasonable ambition to obtain the honour of the high-priesthood. It was jealousy, then, that instigated Korah and his companions to set on foot first a quarrel, and then a tumult, respecting the priesthood, because they were indignant that the hope of attaining that honour was taken away from themselves and their posterity for ever. Thus there never was any more deadly or abominable plague in the Church of God, than ambition; inasmuch as it cannot be that those who seek for pre-eminence should range themselves beneath God's yoke. Hence arises the dissolution of legitimate authority, when each one neglects the duties of his position, and aims at his own private advancement.

Now, this conspiracy was the more formidable, because

the sedition did not arise from the dregs of the people, but amongst the princes themselves, who were of high dignity, and held in the greatest estimation. For although there were only four leaders of the faction, there is but little room to doubt but that the purpose of the two hundred and fifty was the same; for they would never have eagerly embarked in a grave and invidious contest for the sake of four men; but the fact was, that an unholy covetousness misled them all, for there was none of them who did not expect some prize as a reward of victory. They not only, then, dissemble their mental disease, but conceal it under an honourable pretext; for they pretend that they are instigated by zeal for the public good, and that their object is the defence of liberty. For, inasmuch as ambition is crafty, it is never destitute of some specious excuse: thus, whilst schismatics are influenced by nothing but pride to disturb the peace of the Church, they always invent plausible motives, whereby they may conciliate in some degree the favour of the ignorant, or even of the unstable and worthless. We must, therefore, cautiously weigh the designs of those who seek to make innovations, and to overthrow a state of things which might be endured; for thorough investigation will make it plain that they aim at something besides what they pretend. By the fact of their so speedily engaging such a multitude of persons in their party, we perceive how disposed man's nature is to the most unpromising and unreasonable revolts in the world. Four worthless men wickedly endeavour to overthrow Moses and Aaron; and straightway two hundred and fifty persons are ready to follow them, not of the populace, but chiefs of the tribes, whose reputation might dazzle the eyes of the simple. Hence we must be the more cautious, lest any bugbears (*larvæ*) should deceive us into making rash innovations.

With respect to the wording of the passage, some refer the verb " he took,"[1] to the other conspirators, as if it were said

[1] *A. V.*, " took *men*." There has been very much discussion among the commentators respecting this word. Holden says, " There is nothing in the Hebrew answering to the word *men*, and the verb is in the singular number; the received version, therefore, can scarcely be correct. The most easy and natural construction of the original is, 'And Korah took

that Korah stirred them up. Others explain it that he instigated himself, and hurried himself onwards by his evil passions. I do not, however, assent to either signification, but take it for "he set to work" (*aggressus est.*) When it is afterwards said that "they rose up before Moses," some understand the words according to their simple meaning, others in a bad sense; and undoubtedly here the expression "before the face of," is equivalent to "against," and thus indicates the wantonness of their aggression. There is more difficulty in the words קרא׳ מועד,[1] *kerei mogned.* All, however, almost with one consent, translate them "great in the congregation;" but since the word קריים, *keriim,* generally signifies persons *called* or *invited,* and מועד, *mogned,* not only an assembly, but also an appointed time, or convention, it seems probable to me that these princes and men of high name are stated to have been present, because they were called according to appointment: as if Moses had said that they were called at a fixed time, or by agreement. For neither do I see any reason why, after the word עדה,[2] *gnedah,* מועד, *mogned,* should be used with the same meaning.

3. *Ye take too much upon you.*[3] Some explain, "Let it suffice," as if they desired to put an end to the tyranny of Moses; but I am rather of opinion that they would thus make a charge of presumptuous and sacrilegious supremacy, as if Moses and Aaron had not only usurped more than their right, but had also robbed God of His supreme authority. They, therefore, reproach the holy men with having impiously subjected to themselves the inheritance of God. Thus we see that God's faithful servants, whatever may be their moderation, are still not exempted from false accusations. Moses was an extraordinary example, not only of integrity, but also of humility and gentleness; yet he is called proud and violent, as if he unworthily oppressed the

(*i. e.*, won over, or drew into a conspiracy with him) both Dathan and Abiram,' &c. This agrees with other parts of Scripture which attribute this rebellion to Korah, chap. xxvii. 3; Jude 11." And this appears to be the general opinion.

[1] *A. V.*, "famous in the congregation." *S. M.* Vocabantur ad concilium.—*W.*

[2] עדה, *A. V.*, "of the assembly."

[3] "Sat sit vobis;" let it be enough for you.—*Lat.*

people of God. Observe further, that God permits His servants to be loaded with such unjust calumnies, in order to teach them that they must expect their reward elsewhere than from the world; and that He may humble them and make trial of their endurance. Let us learn, then, to harden ourselves, so as to be prepared, though we do well, to be evil spoken of. These ungodly and seditious men betray their senselessness as well as their impudence. For by what right do they seek to degrade Moses and Aaron? Because, forsooth, God dwells amongst the people, and all in the congregation are holy! But holiness is neither destructive of subordination, nor does it introduce confusion, nor release believers from the obligation to obey the laws. It is madness in them, then, to infer that those, whom God has sanctified, are not subject to the yoke; yet they maliciously stigmatize as tyranny that care of the people which God has intrusted to His servants, as if they would purposely turn light into darkness.

4. *And when Moses heard it, he fell upon his face.* There is no doubt but that he had recourse to prayer in his perplexity, since he knew that the remedy for so great an evil was only in the hand of God. It is in this respect that the magnanimity of the ungodly differs from the firmness of believers; for it often happens that unbelievers also labour in the defence of a good cause, voluntarily expose themselves to the hatred of many, undergo severe contests, and encounter of their own accord great perils; but with them obstinacy stands in the place of virtue. But those who look to God, since they know that the prosperous or unhappy events of all things are in His power, thus rely upon His providence; and when any adversity occurs, implore His faithfulness and assistance. When, therefore, Moses cast himself upon the earth, this[1] supplication was of more value than all those heroic virtues in which unbelievers have ever seemed to excel.

5. *And he spake unto Korah.* Moses did not inconsiderately choose this mode of divination, but by the dictation of the Spirit maintained the priesthood of his brother by

[1] "Telle humilité à prier;" such humility in prayer.—*Fr.*

this token and testimony; for we know how, in matters of doubt and obscurity, he was accustomed to inquire what God's pleasure was. He did not, therefore, at this time make this proposal hastily and at random, but by the inspiration of the Spirit had recourse to the sure judgment of God. The effect of his prayer was that God suggested an easy and expeditious mode of conquest.

He bids them take their censers, that by their incense-offering it might be manifested whether their oblation was acceptable to God. By deferring it to the morrow he consulted their own safety, if any of them might still be not incurable; for he saw that they were carried away headlong by blind fury, and that they could not be recalled to their senses in a moment. He, therefore, grants them some space of time for repentance, that they might be led to consideration during the night; or perhaps his object was that, the tumult being appeased, he might render them all attentive to the decision of God.

8. *Hear, I pray you, ye sons of Levi.* He addresses the whole body, and yet it is said that his discourse was directed to Korah alone, and this was because he had corrupted others of the Levites, and therefore is first summoned to God's tribunal, so that the whole party might be at the same time included. He was able to expostulate with the Levites at once, because their residence was close to the sanctuary.

He accuses them of ingratitude, because they were not satisfied with the honour with which God had already dignified them, but also sought the high-priesthood. In this they betrayed their despisal of His grace; for, if they had rightly valued the gifts of God, each of them would have quietly contented himself with his lot; especially since, in proportion as a person has been liberally dealt with, his ingratitude is more intolerable, if he aspires to anything higher. We are taught, therefore, that the higher the degree may be to which we have been elevated by God's goodness, the greater is the punishment which our crime deserves, if our ambition still incites us to overleap the bounds of our calling. Nevertheless, such is the perversity of almost all men, that as soon as a person has attained some intermediate position, he uplifts, as it were, the standard of pride[1] and prescribes to himself no limit, until he shall have reached above the clouds. In a word, few are found who do not grow insolent in places of honour. Wherefore we ought to be all the more attentive to this admonition of Moses, that those are most ungrateful to God who despise their lot, which is already honourable, and aim at something higher.

11. *For which cause both thou, and all thy company.* He here lays open their sin, which they had endeavoured to disguise. For they had neither scruple nor shame, as we have seen, in pretending pious zeal. But in one word Moses scatters these mists, telling them that they were instigated by nothing but pride and envy to disturb the condition of the people. We must observe the expression which he uses, that they are in "arms against God;" for, although they might have never confessed to themselves that they had to do with Him, but only that they were contending for the pre-eminence with men; still, because it was their aim to overthrow the order established by God, Moses casts aside all false pretences, and sets before them the simple fact that they are waging war with God, when they are fighting with His servants. If, therefore, we are afraid of contending with Him, let us learn to remain in our right place. For, however they may prevaricate, who disturb the Church through their ambition, in fighting against the servants of God, they attack Himself: and therefore it is needful that He should resist them, to avenge Himself. For war is not waged against God, as the poets feign the giants to have done, when they heaped up mountains, and endeavoured to surmount heaven; but when He is assailed in the person of His servants, and when what He has decreed is in any wise undermined. The vocation of the priests was sacred, so that they who conspired to overthrow it, were the open enemies of God, as much as if they had directed their arms, their strength, and their assaults against Him. We must, therefore, bear in

[1] "Comme si Dieu en l'honorant luy avoit dressé une banniere d'orgueil;" as if God by honouring him had raised for him a banner of pride.—*Fr.*

mind the reason which is subjoined, "And what is Aaron?" for, if Aaron had usurped anything for himself, his temerity and audacity would not have been supported by the countenance of God. Moses, therefore, declares that this is God's cause, because there was nothing human in the ordinance of the priesthood. It was, indeed, an honourable office, so that Aaron justly deserved to be thought something of; but Moses indicates that he had nothing of his own, nor arrogated anything to himself; in a word, that he is nothing in himself, and moreover, that he is not elevated for his own private advantage, and that his dignity is no idle one; but rather a laborious burden placed upon his shoulders for the common welfare of the Church. How utterly ridiculous, then, is the folly of the Pope in comparing all the enemies of his tyranny to Korah, Dathan, and Abiram; for, in order to prove that his cause is connected with that of God, let him shew us the credentials of his calling, and at the same time thoroughly fulfil his office. But what frivolous and vapid trifling it is, when some mimic Aaron sets himself up —produces no divine command or vocation—domineers in obedience to his own lusts, and is rather an actor on the stage than a priest in the temple; that all who reject this spurious dominion should be condemned as schismatics! Wherefore let us hold fast this principle, that war is waged against God when His servants are molested, who are both lawfully called and faithfully exercise their office.

12. And Moses sent to call Dathan and Abiram, the sons of Eliab; which said, We will not come up:

13. *Is it* a small thing that thou hast brought us up out of a land that floweth with milk and honey, to kill us in the wilderness, except thou make thyself altogether a prince over us?

14. Moreover, thou hast not brought us into a land that floweth with milk and honey, or given us inheritance of fields and vineyards: wilt thou put out the eyes of these men? we will not come up.

15. And Moses was very wroth, and said unto the Lord, Respect not thou their offering: I have not

12. Misit etiam Moses ad vocandum Dathan et Abiram filios Eliab: qui responderunt, Non ascendemus.

13. An parum es quod ascendere feceris nos è terra quæ fluit lacte et melle, ut mori nos faceres in deserto, nisi etiam dominando domineris nobis?

14. Atqui certè ad terram quæ fluit lacte et melle non introduxistis nos, neque dedisti nobis hæreditatem agrorum et vinearum: an oculos virorum istorum effodies? Non ascendemus.

15. Iratus est ergo Moses valdè, et dixit ad Jehovam, Ne respicias ad oblationem eorum: ne asellum

taken one ass from them, neither have I hurt one of them.

quidem unum ab eis accepi, neque afflixi quenquam ex ipsis.

12. *And Moses sent to call Dathan and Abiram.* He desired, in this way, if it might be, by his holy admonitions, to withhold them from that destruction, on which they were rushing. Therefore he ceased not to provide for their welfare, though he had thus far experienced that they were altogether in a desperate state. Herein he presented a likeness of the loving-kindness of God, by whose Spirit he was directed; not only because he was unwilling to pass sentence without hearing the cause, but also because he endeavoured to bring them to repentance, that they might not wilfully destroy themselves. Nevertheless it came to pass at this time, as also often afterwards, that not only was the earnestness of the Prophet, with respect to these unbelievers, thrown away, but that it hardened them more and more. For we know what was said by Isaiah; "Make the heart of this people fat, and make their ears heavy, and shut their eyes: lest they see with their eyes, and hear with their ears, and understand with hearts, and convert, and be healed." (Isa. vi. 10.) Thus does it please God to discover the wickedness of the reprobate, in order that they may be rendered the more inexcusable.

13. *Is it a small thing that thou hast brought us.* It is not enough for these wicked men, when they are invited to discussion, contumaciously to repudiate the superiority of Moses, unless they also assail him with counter-accusations. The crime they allege against him must be observed. They reproach him for having led them up out of the land of Egypt: though they cunningly suppress its name, whilst they magniloquently extol its fruitfulness, in order to throw into the shade all that God had promised with respect to the land of Canaan. Nay, they seem to transfer slyly to Egypt the very phrase which Moses had often used, so that thus God's blessing may be, as it were buried. But what gross ingratitude it shewed, to allege as a crime against Moses, God's minister, that deliverance, which was so extraordinary an act of His kindness! In the next place, they reproach him with having brought them into the desert, to

die: and this they enlarge upon in the next verse, and maliciously inquire, Where is the truth of the promises? At length they conclude that Moses is impudent in his deceptions, inasmuch as it plainly appears that the people had been imposed upon by him: as if it were his fault that they had deprived themselves of the possession of the promised land. Moses had exhorted them, by God's command, to enter upon the inheritance promised to them: what dishonesty and petulance, therefore, was it, when they had shut the door against themselves, to complain of Moses, upon whom it had not depended that they were not in the enjoyment of fields and vineyards! In the third place, they taunt Moses with seeking to domineer over a free people. He did indeed preside over them; but how far short of dominion was that moderate control, which was as onerous to Moses, as it was advantageous to the whole people! But this is the condition of God's servants, that their course is through reproaches,[1] though they are conducting themselves aright.

15. *And Moses was very wroth.* Although it might be, that there was something of human passion here, still zeal for God was supreme in his mind, nor did intemperate feelings, if he was at all tempted by them, prevail. Assuredly, it appears probable, from the context, that he was inflamed with holy ardour; since he executes the vengeance of God, as His lawful minister, so that it is plain he neither spoke nor did anything but at the dictation of the Spirit. Nay, we shall soon see that, although he was anxious with regard to the public safety, he required that but a few offenders should be punished, and not that the multitude should perish. Nor does his anger burst forth into revilings: as those, who are carried away by excess, usually assail the enemies by whom they are injured, with their tongue as well as their hands: but he betakes himself to God; nor does he ask more than that they may be brought to shame in their pride. This is, indeed, expounded generally, by many, as if Moses desired that God should have no mercy upon them; but inasmuch as the decision of the quarrel de-

[1] Addition in *Fr.*, "comme dit Sainct Paul."

pended on the approbation or rejection by God of the offering they were about to make, he does not seem to me to pray for more than that God, by refusing their polluted gift, should thus chastise their ambition. At the same time also he shews that his prayer springs from the confidence of a good conscience, when he dares to testify before God that he had injured no man. Now this was the extreme of integrity and disinterestedness, that, when the people owed everything to him, he had not taken even the value of a single ass as the reward of all his labours.

16. And Moses said unto Korah, Be thou and all thy company before the Lord, thou, and they, and Aaron, to-morrow:

17. And take every man his censer, and put incense in them, and bring ye before the Lord every man his censer, two hundred and fifty censers; thou also, and Aaron, each *of you* his censer.

18. And they took every man his censer, and put fire in them, and laid incense thereon, and stood in the door of the tabernacle of the congregation with Moses and Aaron.

19. And Korah gathered all the congregation against them unto the door of the tabernacle of the congregation: and the glory of the Lord appeared unto all the congregation.

20. And the Lord spake unto Moses and unto Aaron, saying,

21. Separate yourselves from among this congregation, that I may consume them in a moment.

22. And they fell upon their faces, and said, O God, the God of the spirits of all flesh, shall one man sin, and wilt thou be wroth with all the congregation?

23. And the Lord spake unto Moses, saying,

24. Speak unto the congregation, saying, Get you up from about the tabernacle of Korah, Dathan, and Abiram.

25. And Moses rose up, and went unto Dathan and Abiram: and the elders of Israel followed him.

16. Postea dixit Moses ad Corah, Tu et universa congregatio tua estote coram Jehova, tu et illi et Aharon cras.

17. Et capite quisque acerram suam, et ponite in illis suffitum, et admovete coram Jehova quisque acerram suam, ducentas quinquaginta acerras, tu quoque et Aharon, quisque acerram suam.

18. Tulerunt igitur quisque acerram suam, et posuerunt in ipsis ignem. posueruntque suffitum, et steterunt ad ostium tabernaculi conventionis, et Moses et Aharon.

19. Congregaverat autem contra ipsos Corah, universam congregationem ad ostium tabernaculi conventionis: et visa est gloria Jehovæ à tota multitudine.

20. Tunc loquutus est Jehova ad Mosen et Aharon, dicendo:

21. Separate vos è medio turbæ ejus, et consumam eos momento.

22. Tunc ceciderunt super facies suas, ac dixerunt, Deus (*vel*, fortis) Deus spirituum in universa carne, num quum vir unus peccaverit, contra totum cœtum excandesces?

23. Loquutus est autem Jehova ad Mosen dicendo:

24. Alloquere congregationem, dicendo, Discedite è circuitu tabernaculi Coræ, Dathan, et Abiram.

25. Surrexit ergo Moses, et venit ad Dathan et Abiram: et sequuti sunt eum seniores Israel.

26. And he spake unto the congregation, saying, Depart, I pray you, from the tents of these wicked men, and touch nothing of theirs, lest ye be consumed in all their sins.

26. Tunc loquutus est ad congregationem, dicens, Recedite nunc à tabernaculis virorum istorum impiorum, neque attingatis quicquam eorum quæ ad illos pertinent, ne fortè pereatis in omnibus peccatis illorum.

27. So they gat up from the tabernacle of Korah, Dathan, and Abiram, on every side: and Dathan and Abiram came out, and stood in the door of their tents, and their wives, and their sons, and their little children.

27. Et recesserunt à tabernaculo Coræ, Dathan et Abiram, è circuitu. Dathan verò et Abiram egressi sunt, ac steterunt ad ostium tabernaculorum suorum, et uxores eorum, et filii eorum, et parvuli eorum.

28. And Moses said, Hereby ye shall know that the Lord hath sent me to do all these works; (for *I have* not *done them* of mine own mind:)

28. Tunc dixit Moses, In hoc scietis quòd Jehova miserit me, ut facerem omnia opera hæc, et quòd non de corde meo:

29. If these men die the common death of all men, or if they be visited after the visitation of all men, *then* the Lord hath not sent me:

29. Si ut moriuntur omnes homines, morientur isti, et visitatione omnium hominum visitabitur super eos, non misit me Jehova:

30. But if the Lord make a new thing, and the earth open her mouth, and swallow them up, with all that *appertain* unto them, and they go down quick into the pit; then ye shall understand that these men have provoked the Lord.

30. Sin autem creationem creaverit Jehova, et aperuit terra os suum, et deglutiverit eos, atque omnia quæ ad illos pertinent, et descenderint viventes in infernum: tum cognoscetis quòd irritaverunt viri isti Jehovam.

31. And it came to pass, as he had made an end of speaking all these words, that the ground clave asunder that *was* under them:

31. Fuit igitur quum consummasset loqui omnia verba ista, rupit sese terra quæ erat sub illis:

32. And the earth opened her mouth, and swallowed them up, and their houses, and all the men that *appertained* unto Korah, and all *their* goods.

32. Aperuitque terra os suum, et deglutivit eos, et domos eorum, atque omnes homines qui erant ipsi Corah, et omnem substantiam:

33. They, and all that *appertained* to them, went down alive into the pit, and the earth closed upon them: and they perished from among the congregation.

33. Descenderuntque ipsi et quotquot ad eos pertinebant viventes, in infernum: ac operuit eos terra, et perierunt è medio congregationis.

34. And all Israel that *were* round about them fled at the cry of them: for they said, Lest the earth swallow us up *also*.

34. Omnis autem Israel qui erant in circuitu eorum, fugerunt ad clamorem eorum: dicebant enim, Ne fortè deglutiat nos terra.

16. *And Moses said unto Korah.* The idea of Moses is not to make an experiment as if in a doubtful matter; but, being assured by the Spirit of prophecy what the event would be, he summons Korah before the tribunal of God,

that he may receive the sentence of condemnation which he deserves. Nor does he inveigle him so as to destroy him unawares, but rather still endeavours to cure his madness, if it were possible to do so. For the sacred incense-offering was calculated to inspire him with alarm, lest, by rashly attempting more than was lawful, he should effect his own destruction, especially after so memorable an example had been made in the case of Nadab and Abihu. Moses, however, in reliance on God's command, does not hesitate to engage in an open contest, in order that the judgment of God might be the more conspicuous.

18. *And they took every man his censer.* It is manifest how greatly they were blinded by pride, since, although admonished both by the confidence of Moses and also by the previous examples, they still obstinately go forward. Surely if any spark of the fear of God had remained in them, their censers would straightway have fallen from their hands; but Korah seems to have sought, as it were, deliberately how he might cast aside all fear, and totally bereave himself of his senses. For in the next verse, Moses narrates how ostentatiously he hardened himself in his rebellion, before he should offer the incense; for he gathered the people together to his party, in order that the magnificence of his array might overwhelm the grace of God, which opposed him. Herein also his senselessness is clearly seen, when he seeks to fortify himself against God by the favour of the mob, as if he had desired to extinguish the light of the sun by interposing a little smoke. Now, let us learn so to condemn his folly, as that nothing similar may happen in ourselves; for all ambitious persons are affected by the same disease. They collect their forces by endeavouring to ingratiate themselves with men; and, if the world approves of them, they are inebriated with such fatal confidence, as to spit at the very clouds. But we shall soon see how God, by a single breath, dissipates all their ungodly conspiracies.

On the other side, the levity of the people is set before our eyes. For some time they had been all accustomed to the duly-appointed priesthood, which they knew to be instituted by God; yet only a single night is required to make them revolt to Korah. And, in fact, as we are by nature slow to act aright, so also we are carried away to evil in a moment, as soon as some villain lifts up his finger.

21. *Separate yourselves from among this congregation.* Again does God declare that He will bear the people's great impiety no longer, but will destroy them all to a man. Just, therefore, as He had commanded Lot to depart from Sodom, nay, had drawn him out by the hand of the angel, when He desired to destroy that city, so He now commands Moses and Aaron to give Him room to exercise His wrath. In this He declares His extraordinary favour towards them; as if He were not free to execute vengeance, until they had gone out of the way, lest the destruction should reach themselves. In speaking thus, however, He does not absolutely affirm what He had determined in His secret counsel, but only pronounces what the authors of this wickedness had deserved. It is, therefore, just as if He were ascending His judgment-seat. Thus Moses by his intercession by no means changed His eternal decree; but, by appeasing Him, delivered the people from the punishment they had merited. In the same sense God is said to be influenced by our prayers; not that after the manner of men He assumes new feelings, but, in order to shew the more than paternal love with which He honours us, He, as it were, indulges us, when He listens to our desires. Hence we gather that even by this express denunciation Moses was not prohibited from praying; because his faith in the adoption of the people was not destroyed. For we have already said that this principle, that the covenant which God had made with Abraham could not be made void, was so thoroughly engraven upon his mind, that it surmounted whatever obstacles might present themselves. Resting, therefore, on the gratuitous promise, which depended not on men, his prayer was the offspring of faith. For the saints do not always reason accurately and subtilely as to the form of their prayers; but, after they have once embraced that which suffices to awaken in them confidence in prayer, viz., God's word, their whole attention is so directed to it, that they pass over the things which seem apparently to contradict it.

Nor can we doubt but that it was God's design, when He delivered his terrible sentence as to the destruction of the people, to quicken the earnestness of Moses in prayer, since necessity more and more inflames the zeal of the pious. In short, Moses was always consistent in his care for the well-being of the people.

22. *O God, the God of the spirits of all flesh.* The old interpreter renders the first אל, *el*, as an adjective, in which some others have followed him;[1] but, in my opinion, the name of God is rather repeated by way of adding force to the sentence. It does not, however, so clearly appear to me why all render the word *flesh* in the genitive case. But, since I do not think that the ל, *lamed*, is superfluous here, but that it is used for ב, *beth*, as often elsewhere, I have accurately expressed the sense by my translation, "*in* all flesh."[2] There is no question but that Moses applies this epithet to God in connexion with the present matter; as if he desired to induce God to preserve His own work, just as a potter spares the vessels formed by himself. To the same effect is the prayer of Isaiah: "But now, O Lord, thou art our father; we are the clay, and thou our potter; and we all are the work of thy hand. Be not wroth very sore," (Isa. lxiv. 8, 9:) for hence he alleges a reason why God should relent, and be inclined to mercy. There is this difference, that Isaiah refers to that special grace wherewith God had embraced His people, whereas Moses carries his address further, viz., to the general grace of creation. It is of little importance whether we choose to expound this[3] with

[1] In the clause under consideration, אל, *El*, is immediately followed by אלהי, *Elohey*, the form given to Elohim, when it is to be used in connexion with the next word. The different roots of El and Elohim seem to indicate that El has an especial reference to the power of the Deity, and Elohim to His authority as a judge. There being no practicable equivalent distinction in Latin or English, and the word *Almighty* being appropriated to rendering שדי, *Shaddai*, *C.* and our *A. V.* do but repeat the word God, whilst the *V.* and *S. M.* have *fortissime Deus;* but *C.* saw in *S. M.'s* notes, *Aut sic, O Deus, Deus.*—*W.*

[2] *C.'s* supposition, that the preposition ל prefixed to *all*, is equivalent to ב, or *in*, would not facilitate the version. Noldius, giving instances where the ל prefixed has the effect of a genitive, cites this passage amongst others.—*W.*

[3] "Le mot de chair;" the word *flesh*.—*Fr.*

reference to all animals, or only to the human race, since Moses merely prays that, since God is the Creator and Maker of the world, He should not destroy the men whom He has formed, but rather have pity upon them, as being His work. In passing, however, we may infer from this passage,[1] that all (men) have their separate souls, for God is not said to have inspired all flesh with life, but to have created their spirits. Hence the monstrous delusion of the Manicheans is refuted, that our souls are so infused by the transmission of the Spirit of God, as that there should still be only one spirit.[2] But if it be preferred to include the animals, we must mark the grades of distinction between the spirit of man and the spirit of a dog or an ass. It is, however, more fitting to restrict it to men.

24. *Speak unto the congregation, saying.* It is evident, from this answer, that Moses was heard as regarded the general preservation of the people, on condition, however, that they should give proof of their repentance, by deserting the authors of the wicked rebellion; for, when God commands them to retire from amongst them, He indirectly implies, that, if they remain mixed up with them, they shall share in the same destruction. Yet it is probable that the

[1] Addition in *Fr.*, "Moyennant qu'il soit prins des hommes, comme c'est le plus vray-semblable;" supposing it be taken as having reference to men, as is the more probable conjecture.

[2] "Lesquels pensent que les ames procedent de la substance de Dieu;" who think that our souls proceed from the substance of God.—*Fr.*

This doctrine of the Manicheans is often referred to in the writings of Augustine. The Benedictine Editors, in their index to his works, point out by citations the following particulars: "Manichæorum error circà animam. Docent animam nostram hoc esse quod Deus est; esse partem, seu particulam Dei; animas non solum hominum, sed etiam pecorum, de Dei esse substantiâ, et partes Dei asserunt."

The word which I have translated *transmission*, is in the Latin *ex traduce*, a well-known metaphor in theological controversy, derived from the practice of *inarching*, or grafting *by approach*, when two neighbouring branches are tied together so as to cohere and form one, whilst the parent stocks, to which they belong, continue still to possess a separate and individual vitality. Thus Prudentius, Apoth. 919-921.

Vitandus tamen error erit, ne *traduce* carnis
Transfundi in sobolem credatur fons animarum,
Sanguinis exemplo, &c.

C. makes frequent allusions to this heretical doctrine as having been resuscitated by Servetus, amongst his other pantheistic notions. See Instit. Book i. ch. xv. § 5. *C. Soc. Edit.*, vol. i. p. 223; and also on Ps. civ. 30. *C. Soc. Edit.*, vol. iv. p. 168.

elders who "followed" Moses, held to his side, and continued firm in the performance of their duty. And, indeed, it is not at all consistent that Caleb and Joshua, and such like, were ever drawn away into so great a sin. We must not, therefore, take what is said of the whole congregation without exception. When Moses, in his delivery of God's command, does not address Korah, Dathan, and Abiram by their names, but calls them "these wicked men," it is not the reviling of anger, but an urgent mode of exhortation; for, had he not thus vehemently marked his detestation of them, there was danger lest his words should have been but coldly received by many, and lest they should have been of little avail. To the same effect also is what he immediately adds: "Lest ye be consumed in all their sins;" as if he had said, Lest the contagion of so many and such great crimes should infect yourselves. Since they obeyed Moses, it is plain that many of the multitude had been carried away before by folly and levity, for deliberate iniquity would not have been so quickly or so easily corrected. But on the other hand, the marvellous stolidity of Dathan and Abiram is described, in that they came forth unawed, with their wives and children. Still it is not to be doubted but that they were terrified, after they saw themselves to be stripped of all aid and favour; but although the withdrawal of the people disturbed them, they nevertheless stood like maniacs; nor did fear subdue them or prevent them from proceeding in their fatal audacity to their doom. Thus[1] do the wicked often stand astounded, yet in their fear they by no means think of appeasing God.

28. *And Moses said, Hereby ye shall know.* Moses now begins more clearly to show wherefore he has brought the rebels to this open contest, viz., that God may sanction before the whole people, by a terrible exertion of His power, the system established by Himself. For it was no ordinary effort of confidence to concede the victory to His enemies, unless the earth should swallow them up alive. But, inasmuch as this was to be a most conspicuous judgment of God, he arouses their attention by the striking words he uses. If they should be cut off by a sudden death, he would have

[1] This final sentence omitted in *Fr.*

justly boasted that his cause was approved by God; but not content with this, he desires to be accounted a mere impostor, if they should die the common death of men. In order to express the strangeness of the miracle, whereby men's senses should be ravished, he employs the word *create*[1] emphatically; as much as to say, that the mode of their death would be no less unusual than as if God should add something to His creation, and change the face of the world. Thus David, when he prays that his enemies should go down alive into hell (*infernos*) or the grave, seems to allude to this history, (Ps. lv. 23;) for although that descent be understood to mean sudden death overtaking the wicked in a moment in the midst of their happiness and security, still, he at the same time indicates by it this horrible retribution, which had occurred in times past, inasmuch as memorable punishments pass into proverbial instances of God's wrath.

34. *And all Israel that were round about them.* We must suppose that the people were standing around, expecting at a distance the event that was to take place; for they had previously retired from the tents, in token of their separation (from this wicked company.)[2] That they should now fly in confusion, lest the same destruction should overwhelm themselves, is a sign of their bad conscience, which is always troubled in itself, and agitates the wicked with sore inquietude. It is needful, indeed, that even the pious should be alarmed by God's judgments, in order that their consternation or dread should instruct them[3] in his holy fear, and therefore they never reflect without dread on the punishments which God has inflicted upon the crimes of men. But, since hypocrites carry in their hearts a hot iron, as it were, they fall down like dead men, as if the lightning fell from God upon their own heads. Thus we shall presently see that this blind fear profited them but little.

35. And there came out a fire from the Lord, and consumed the two hundred and fifty men that offered incense.	35. Porro ignis egressus est à Jehova, et consumpsit ducentos illos, et quinquaginta viros offerentes suffitum.
36. And the Lord spake unto Moses, saying,	36. Tunc loquutus est Jehova ad Mosen, dicendo:

[1] *A. V.*, "Make a new thing;" margin, "Create a creature."
[2] Added from *Fr.*
[3] "A s'humilier devant luy;" to humble themselves before Him.—*Fr.*

37. Speak unto Eleazar the son of Aaron the priest, that he take up the censers out of the burning, and scatter thou the fire yonder; for they are hallowed.

38. The censers of these sinners against their own souls, let them make them broad plates *for* a covering of the altar; for they offered them before the Lord, therefore they are hallowed: and they shall be a sign unto the children of Israel.

39. And Eleazar the priest took the brazen censers, wherewith they that were burnt had offered, and they were made broad *plates for* a covering of the altar;

40. *To be* a memorial unto the children of Israel that no stranger, which *is* not of the seed of Aaron, come near to offer incense before the Lord, that he be not as Korah, and as his company; as the Lord said to him by the hand of Moses.

37. Dic ad Eleazar filium Aharon sacerdotis, ut tollat acerras è medio incendii, et ignem dispergat longius, quia sanctificatæ sunt.

38. Quod ad acerras istorum qui scelerati fuerunt in animas suas, ut faciant ex illis extensiones laminarum, opertorium altaris: quia obtulerunt in ipsis coram Jehova, et sanctificatæ sunt: et erunt in signum filiis Israel.

39. Tulit itaque Eleazar sacerdos acerras æreas quibus obtulerant combusti, et extenderunt eas operimentum altaris.

40. Memoriale filiis Israel, ut non accedat quisquam alienus qui non sit è semine Aharon, ut offerat suffitum coram Jehova, ne sit sicut Corah et cœtus ejus: quemadmodum ei præceperat Jehova per manum Mosis.

35. *And there came out a fire from the Lord.* The diversity of the punishments had the effect of awakening more astonishment in the people, than as if all had been destroyed in the same manner, although God's anger raged more fiercely against the original authors of the evil, so as to make it manifest that each received a recompense according to the measure of his iniquity. He says that a fire went forth from Jehovah, because it was not kindled naturally, nor accidentally, but was accompanied by conspicuous marks, which showed that it was sent by Him. Yet I do not reject the opinions of others, viz., that God thundered from heaven, since thus His power would have been more manifestly exerted.

37. *Speak unto Eleazar the son of Aaron.* Since there is no manifestation of God's wrath so conspicuous as not to be forgotten too often by man's stupidity, God was willing to anticipate this evil, and set up a monument for posterity, lest the recollection of this memorable judgment should ever be obscured. He commands, therefore, that a covering for the altar should be made of the censers, in order that none should rashly intrude himself to make the sacred offerings. When He calls them "hallowed," some understand that it

was sinful to transfer them to profane purposes, because they had once been devoted to the service of God. I am, however, rather of opinion that they were set apart (*sacratas*) as things accursed (*anathemata.*) Thus the fire which had been upon them is scattered afar, in order that the altar should be cleansed from its pollution. Although, however, there was the same pollution in the censers, yet God would have them preserved as accursed, so that all posterity might understand that none but the priests were to be admitted to the sacrifices. Nor is it superfluous for Him to speak of the rebels as having acted criminally "against their own souls;" but it was in order that the memory of their punishment might be in a manner engraved upon those brazen enclosures, in order to awaken continued dread.

40. *To be a memorial unto the children of Israel.* This passage again confirms what I have just said, that God's judgments, which ought to remain in full remembrance in every age, straightway escape, and are blotted out from men's minds, unless they are provided with certain aids to meditate upon them. This, however, does not happen so much from ignorance as neglect. Wherefore we ought to be the more attentive to the aids to memory, which may retain us in the path of duty.

41. But on the morrow all the congregation of the children of Israel murmured against Moses and against Aaron, saying, Ye have killed the people of the Lord.

42. And it came to pass, when the congregation was gathered against Moses and against Aaron, that they looked toward the tabernacle of the congregation; and, behold, the cloud covered it, and the glory of the Lord appeared.

43. And Moses and Aaron came before the tabernacle of the congregation.

44. And the Lord spake unto Moses, saying,

45. Get you up from among this congregation, that I may consume them as in a moment. And they fell upon their faces.

46. And Moses said unto Aaron, Take a censer, and put fire therein

41. Et murmuraverunt universus cœtus filiorum Israel postridie contra Mosen et Aharon, dicendo, Vos interfecistis populum Jehovæ.

42. Fuit autem quum se congregaret universus cœtus contra Mosen et Aharon, verterunt faciem ad tabernaculum conventionis, et ecce operuit illud nubes et conspecta est gloria Jehovæ.

43. Venit ergo Moses et Aharon coram tabernaculo conventionis.

44. Et loquutus est Jehova ad Mosen, dicendo:

45. Recedite è medio congregationis hujus, et consumam eos momento. Tunc projecerunt se super faciem suam.

46. Dixitque Moses ad Aharon, Cape acerram, et pone in ea ignem

from off the altar, and put on incense, and go quickly unto the congregation, and make an atonement for them: for there is wrath gone out from the Lord; the plague is begun.

ex altari, et injice suffitum et perge citò ad congregationem, et expia eos: egressus est enim furor à facie Jehovæ, cœpitque percussio.

47. And Aaron took as Moses commanded, and ran into the midst of the congregation; and, behold, the plague was begun among the people: and he put on incense, and made an atonement for the people.

47. Tulit ergo Aharon quemadmodum dixerat Moses, et cucurrit in medium congregationis: et ecce incœperat percussio in populo, posuitque suffitum et expiavit populum.

48. And he stood between the dead and the living; and the plague was stayed.

48. Et quum staret inter mortuos et viventes, cessavit percussio.

49. Now they that died in the plague were fourteen thousand and seven hundred, besides them that died about the matter of Korah.

49. Fuerunt autem qui mortui sunt plaga illa, quatuordecim millia et septingenti, præter mortuos super negotio Corah.

50. And Aaron returned unto Moses unto the door of the tabernacle of the congregation: and the plague was stayed.

50. Postea reversus est Aharon ad Mosen ad ostium tabernaculi conventionis, quum percussio esset cohibita.

41. *But on the morrow all the congregation.* There is something more than monstrous in this madness of theirs. The conflagration was yet smoking, wherein God had appeared as the awful avenger of pride: the chasm in which the leaders of the rebellion had been swallowed up, must still have been almost before their eyes. God had commanded the plates to be molten, which might record that severe judgment through many succeeding ages. All had confessed by their alarm and hasty flight that there was danger lest they should themselves also be exposed to similar punishments. Yet, on the next day, as if they desired deliberately to provoke God, who was still, as it were, armed, they accuse God's holy servants of having been the authors of the destruction, though they had never lifted a finger against their enemies. Was it in the power of Moses to command the earth to open? Could he draw down the fire from heaven at his will? Since, then, both the chasm and the fire were manifest tokens of God's wonderful power, why do not these madmen reflect that they are engaging in fatal warfare against Him? For to what purpose was this extraordinary mode of punishment, except that in their terror they might learn to humble themselves beneath God's hand? Yet hence did they only derive greater wildness in their audacity, as if they desired to perish voluntarily with

these sinners, whose punishment they had just been shuddering at. In two ways they betray their senselessness; first, by substituting Moses and Aaron as guilty of the murder, in place of God; and, secondly, by sanctifying these putrid corpses, as if in despite of God. They accuse Moses and Aaron of the slaughter, of which God had plainly shewn Himself to be the author, as they themselves had been compelled to feel. But such is the blindness of the reprobate with respect to God's works, that His glory rather stupifies them than excites their admiration. The foulest ingratitude was also added; for they do not consider that only a very few hours had elapsed since they had been preserved by the intercession of Moses from impending destruction. Thus, in their desire to avenge the death of a few, they call those the killers of the people of the Lord, to whom they ought to have been grateful for the safety of all. Again, what arrogance it is to count among the people of God, as if against His will, those reprobates, when He had not only cut them off from His Church, but had also exterminated them from the world, and from the human race! But thus do the wicked wax wanton against God under the very cover of His gifts, and especially they do not hesitate to mock Him with empty titles and outward signs, as the masks of their iniquity.

42. *And it came to pass when the congregation.* From the fact that Moses and Aaron were protected by the covering of the cloud, we gather how uncontrollable was the rage of the people. For, although the glory of God only stood over the tabernacle, so that Moses and Aaron were still exposed to stoning, and any other acts of violence, yet it so dazzled the eyes of these wicked men, that they could not touch the holy persons. Nor can we doubt but that they betook themselves to the sanctuary, because, in the extremity of their danger, the only hope that remained to them was in the help of God. When, therefore, they had fled to this sacred asylum, God received them under the shadow of His wings. Thus did He testify, that the prayers and hopes of His people are never in vain, but that He succours them whenever they call upon Him. For although, now-a-days, He does not appear in a visible abode, still He is nigh unto

all those who cast their cares upon Him. It might, indeed, have been the case that the sign of God's glory was seen by none but Moses and Aaron, in order that they might be fully assured that God was near to help them; but, since the expression is indefinite, it is probable that God threatened also the frantic multitude, lest they should proceed to any further acts of violence, although the light was presented in vain to them in their blindness.

45. *Get you up from among this congregation.* I have expounded the meaning of this expression a little above, namely, that as God regards His people with constant and peculiar love, so He defers His vengeance against the wicked, until these people are set apart, and placed in safety. For He declares that, as soon as Moses and Aaron have secured themselves, all the rest shall perish in a moment. But incredible was the kindness of both of them, thus humbly to intercede for so ungrateful a people, who deserved to die a hundred times over; for, forgetful of their own lives, which they saw to be imperilled, they were ready to make atonement for the guilt, so as to rescue from death those abandoned wretches who were plotting their destruction. I do not, however, understand this, "Get you up," merely with reference to place, for they were already separated, having taken refuge in the tabernacle; but it is just as if God had commanded them to sever themselves from the people, and, quitting them altogether, and casting away all care for the public welfare, to provide for their own private safety.

46. *And Moses said unto Aaron.* The expiation of so great a sin did not indeed depend on the incense-offering, nor are we to imagine that God is appeased by the savour of frankincense; but thus was a symbol set before this gross-hearted people, whereby they might be alike aroused to repentance and faith; for however insensible they might be in their rebellion, yet the dignity of the priesthood was so conspicuous in the censer, that they ought to have been awakened by it to reverence. For who would not view his impiety with horror, when he is made conscious of having despised and violated that sanctity wherein the Divine power displays itself for life or death? The sight of the censer might have justly availed to subdue their hardness of heart,

so that at last they might begin to condemn and detest their unrighteous act. The second warning which it gave them was no less profitable, *i.e.*, that they might perceive that God was only propitiated towards them by virtue of a mediator; but, in so far as the actual state of things allowed, the visible type directed them to the absent Saviour. Since, however, men corrupt and obscure the truth by their fond inventions, His majesty is asserted by the Divine institution of sacrifice. Whilst Aaron, the typical priest, stands forth, until the true, and only, and perpetual Mediator shall be revealed.

The verb כפר, *caphar*, properly signifies, as I have said elsewhere, to reconcile God to men through the medium of an expiation (*piaculum;*) but, since here it refers to the people, the sense of Moses is rightly expressed by a single word, as one may say, to purge, or lustrate from pollution.

48. *And he stood between the living and the dead.* If you understand that the living were everywhere mingled with the dead, you may conjecture that God's wrath did not so fall upon one part of the camp, as to destroy all that came in its way without exception, as had been the case in the other revolt, but that He selected those who had sinned most grievously. But it is probable that Aaron proceeded so far as to leave behind those who still remained uninjured, and, in the very place where the destruction had occurred, encountered the wrath of God, and arrested its course. Hence it was that both the fervour of his zeal might be the better perceived, and his office of appeasing God was more fully confirmed by its actual success. For what more evident miracle could be required, than when the slaughter, which had both begun to rage suddenly, and then to proceed in a course no less rapid than continuous, was stopped by the arrival of Aaron, exactly as if a hedge had been set up against it? The efficacy of the priesthood in propitiating God, is therefore both clearly and briefly set before us; and hence we are taught, that though we are so close to the reprobate when they perish, as that their destruction should reach to ourselves, still that we shall be safe from all evil, if only Christ intercede for us.

49. *Now they that died in the plague.* Already three hundred, or thereabouts, had been destroyed on account of the conspiracy made with Korah; now a much larger num-

ber was added. And this, forsooth, is what the wicked reap from their obstinacy, that God being more and more provoked redoubles His punishments; even as He threatens that, unless those whom He chastises shall repent, He will deal "seven times more" severely with them. (Lev. xxvi. 18.) Wherefore let us learn, when we are warned by His rebukes, to humble ourselves betimes beneath His mighty hand, since nothing is worse than to kick against the pricks; and let us always bear in mind what the psalm says, "Be ye not as the horse or as the mule, whose mouth must be held with bit and bridle; . . . (because) many sorrows shall be to the wicked." (Ps. xxxii. 9, 10.) They rebelliously exclaimed that the people of the Lord were slain, when three hundred had perished; they now experience how much better it would have been to be dumb before God, and to give glory to His holy severity, than, instead of three hundred, to devote to destruction nearly fifty times as many. Let us, then, remember the admonition of Paul: "Let us beware lest we murmur, lest perchance the destroyer should destroy us,"[1] (1 Cor. x. 10;) for nothing is less tolerable in us than that we should frowardly presume to speak evil of God, when Scripture so often exhorts us to be silent in His presence.

NUMBERS, CHAPTER XVII.

1. And the Lord spake unto Moses, saying,	1. Et loquutus est Jehova ad Mosen, dicendo,
2. Speak unto the children of Israel, and take of every one of them a rod, according to the house of *their* fathers, of all their princes, according to the house of their fathers, twelve rods: write thou every man's name upon his rod.	2. Alloquere filios Israel, et cape ab eis singulas virgas per domos patrum, à cunctis scilicet principibus eorum, juxta domos patrum suorum, duodecim virgas: et uniuscujusque nomen scribes super virgam ejus.
3. And thou shalt write Aaron's name upon the rod of Levi: for one rod *shall be* for the head of the house of their fathers.	3. Nomen autem Aharon scribes super virgam Levi: quia virga una erit capiti domus patrum suorum.
4. And thou shalt lay them up in the tabernacle of the congregation before the testimony, where I will meet with you.	4. Reponesque illas in tabernaculo conventionis coram testimonio ubi conveniam vobiscum.
5. And it shall come to pass, *that*	5. Et erit, vir ille quem elegero,

[1] It will be seen that he gives the substance, and not the actual words, of St. Paul's exhortation.

the man's rod, whom I shall choose, shall blossom; and I will make to cease from me the murmurings of the children of Israel, whereby they murmur against you.

6. And Moses spake unto the children of Israel, and every one of their princes gave him a rod apiece, for each prince one, according to their fathers' houses, *even* twelve rods; and the rod of Aaron *was* among their rods.

7. And Moses laid up the rods before the Lord in the tabernacle of witness.

8. And it came to pass, that on the morrow Moses went into the tabernacle of witness; and, behold, the rod of Aaron, for the house of Levi, was budded, and brought forth buds, and bloomed blossoms, and yielded almonds.

9. And Moses brought out all the rods from before the Lord unto all the children of Israel: and they looked, and took every man his rod.

10. And the Lord said unto Moses, Bring Aaron's rod again before the testimony, to be kept for a token against the rebels; and thou shalt quite take away their murmurings from me, that they die not.

11. And Moses did *so:* as the Lord commanded him, so did he.

12. And the children of Israel spake unto Moses, saying, Behold, we die, we perish, we all perish.

13. Whosoever cometh any thing near unto the tabernacle of the Lord shall die: shall we be consumed with dying?

illius virga florebit; et *ita* quiescere faciam à me murmurationes filiorum Israel quibus murmurant adversum vos.

6. Loquutus est ergo Moses ad filios Israel, et dederunt illi omnes principes eorum virgam; singuli principes virgam per domos patrum suorum, duodecim scilicet virgas; virga autem Aharon erat in medio virgarum eorum.

7. Et posuit Moses virgas coram Jehova in tabernaculo testimonii.

8. Et fuit, postridie venit Moses ad tabernaculum testimonii, et ecce germinaverat virga Aharon è domo Levi, ac produxerat germinationem, protuleratque flores, ad maturitatemque perduxerat amygdala.

9. Et protulit Moses omnes virgas illas à facie Jehovæ ad omnes filios Israel: qui viderunt, et acceperunt singuli virgam suam.

10. Dixit autem Jehova ad Mosen, Refer virgam Aharon coram testimonio in custodiam, in signum filiis rebellibus; et cessare facies murmurationes eorum apud me, ut non moriantur.

11. Et fecit Moses quemadmodum præceperat Jehova, sic fecit.

12. Et dixerunt filii Israel ad Mosen, dicendo, Ecce mortui sumus, periimus, omnes nos periimus.

13. Quicunque accesserit, qui accesserit, *inquam*, ad tabernaculum Jehovæ, morietur; nunquid consumendi sumus moriendo?

1. *And the Lord spake unto Moses.* Howsoever stubborn the Israelites might be, yet their hardness of heart being now subdued, and their pride broken down, they ought to have acknowledged the authority of the priesthood, and to have perpetually held it in pious reverence. But it is plain from the confirmation of it, which is now added, that they were not yet thoroughly overcome. For God never appoints anything in vain; the remedy, therefore, was necessary, that He now applied to that disease of obstinacy which He perceived still to maintain its secret hold upon their hearts.

Herein we also behold His inestimable goodness, when He not only had regard to the relief of their infirmity, but even struggled with their depravity and perverseness, in order to restore them to their senses. In the same way also He now deals with us, for He not only strengthens the weakness of our faith by many aids, but He puts constraint upon our light and inconstant minds, and retains us in the path of duty though we strive against Him. He likewise anticipates our wilfulness, so as to keep us from growing presumptuous, or rouses us up when we are disposed to be slothful. In fact, it is our business so to apply to our use whatever helps to faith and piety He sets before us, as to be assured that they are so many pieces of evidence to convict us of unbelief. Although, therefore, the majesty of the priesthood had been already sufficiently, and more than sufficiently established, still God saw that in the extreme perversity of the people there would be no end to their murmurs and rebellions, unless a final ratification were added, and that, too, in a season of repose, inasmuch as, whilst the sedition was in progress, they were not so disposed and ready to learn. By this confirmation, then, He set aside whatever doubts could at any time arise, when Aaron's rod, severed as it was from the tree, was the only one of the twelve which blossomed. For it was no natural circumstance that a branch which derived no sap from the root, and which at that season of the year would have been dry upon the tree, should produce flowers and fruit, when it was cast before the Ark of the Covenant, whilst the others, although altogether similar, remained dry and dead.

2. *Speak unto the children of Israel.* They are mistaken who suppose that to the twelve rods there was another added for the tribe of Levi;[1] for, since there was no question here as to the possession of the land, there was no occasion at all for the division of the tribe of Joseph into two parts. We know, too, that it was endowed with a double portion, because the Levites had no inheritance; and in this case the circumstances were different, because all the other tribes were contending for the priesthood with the tribe of Levi

[1] So, amongst others, Corn. à Lapide. C.'s view is that of the Jewish Commentators.

alone. Hence it was, then, that rods were given to each of them, in accordance with the origin of their race. But, when Aaron's rod is said to have been "in the midst of them,"[1] it is in the usual phrase of the Hebrew language, because it was mixed with them as one of their number. And this is expressly stated, to shew us that all ground for cavilling might be taken from the ungodly, since all the rods were cast promiscuously into the same bundle, so that none should be distinguished above the others, and thus nothing could be ascribed to the collusion of men. If any should object that by these means the rivalry was not extinguished which the other Levites had with the house of Aaron, since his own name alone was inscribed upon the rod, so that there would be no comparison between the families; I reply, that since the power of God manifested itself distinctly in the name of Aaron, the rejection of the others was sufficiently shewn forth by his election; for, if this honour had been common to the others, God would have defrauded them by giving distinction to him alone. Besides, no other plan could have been adopted for putting an end to this quarrel; for if there had been several rods for one tribe, the whole people would have complained of the inequality. It was necessary, then, that all should be brought to the contest on equal terms, so that the difference between them might be seen to depend upon God's good pleasure. But if the name of Levi had been inscribed, all its families would have claimed the right of succession, as if common to them all. There was, therefore, no other course open but that God should prefer to the whole people one individual chosen from amongst the members of his own kindred and tribe.

4. *And thou shalt lay them up in the tabernacle.* The place itself had not a little to do with the effectual decision of the matter; because it was clearly manifested that God was the author of the miracle, and consequently that the priesthood proceeded from Him. For we have elsewhere said that the whole government of the Church so entirely depends upon His decree, that men are not permitted to interfere with it. Wherefore He set the ark of the covenant in opposition to the voices of the whole people, in order to testify

[1] *A. V.*, "Among them," verse 6.

that no further dispute was to be raised respecting the priest, whom He had appointed by His own declaration and authority. At the same time, it had the effect of consoling the people, and silencing their complaints that the rods of all the tribes were brought in common into the sanctuary before God; for, although a peculiar dignity was accorded to that of Aaron alone, still the people ceased not to be a priestly kingdom. Hence it follows, that the honourable privilege conferred on one family contributed to the public welfare of all; so far was it from being the case that their inferiority ought to have caused them pain or envy.

5. *And it shall come to pass, that the man's rod.* Aaron, indeed, had been previously chosen; but the expression here refers to his manifestation;[1] because God is said again to choose those, whom He has chosen by His secret counsel, when He brings them forth into the sight of men with their peculiar marks of distinction; and this not once only, but as often as He confirms their election by new indications. And this seems to be spoken of by way of concession, as if God would pass over all His former decrees, and invite the people afresh to take cognizance of the matter. With this view He states that He will put an end to all the malevolent and noisy detractions of the people, so that Aaron may henceforth exercise his office without controversy; for, although not even thus was their perverseness altogether cured, still their insolence was restrained.

8. *And it came to pass, that on the morrow.* It is not without cause that the time is notified, for by no skill could it be brought about that a rod should blossom in the lapse of a single night. Again, all suspicion of fraud was removed by the fact that Moses departed when he had placed the rods in the sanctuary, and, returning on the next day, brought out the bundle of rods before them all. But in this respect was the power of God principally shewn forth, that in so short a space of time not only flowers, but fruits also, were formed upon a dry bough, which could not have occurred but by the reversal of the order of nature. And further, the time of year is to be taken into account, which was by no means in accordance with such maturity, Now, by

[1] *Fr.*, "A la seconde declaration."

this miracle the dignity of the typical priesthood was undoubtedly ratified to the ancient people under the Law; but, in so much as the truth itself is more excellent than its figure or image, the intention of God unquestionably was to assert the priesthood of His only-begotten Son rather than that of Aaron. Hence the profit to be derived from this miracle most especially pertains to us,[1] in order that we may embrace the Priest presented to us by God with the veneration He deserves. I pass by the frivolous allegories[2] in which others take delight. And in fact it ought to be abundantly sufficient for us, that the power of God which might direct the people to the Mediator, appeared of old under a visible symbol; but when the Son of God came, whatever He then represented to their sight was spiritually revealed in Him: for not only was He a sprout (*surculus*) from the stem of Jesse, as He is called by Isaiah (xi. 1); and a stone hewn without the art or labour of man, under which form He was shewn to Daniel (ii. 34); but by His resurrection He was separated from the whole human race. For this, too, we must diligently observe, that it is not enough that He should obtain with us the prerogative and title of Priest, unless He is so only and indivisibly. Hence it is plain that His honour is in the Papacy torn in pieces by foul and intolerable sacrilege, when they invent innumerable mediators.

10. *And the Lord said unto Moses.* What God had prescribed concerning the censers, He now commands as to the rod, *i.e.*, that it should be preserved as a monument for future ages; because men are forgetful and slow to consider His works, and not only so, but because they bury their memory as if of deliberate malice. He bids, therefore, and not without reproach, that this sign should be laid up in safety, saying, that this is done on account of their perverseness. At the same time, however, He commends His paternal love

[1] "Nous appartient plus qu'aux Juifs;" pertains to us more than to the Jews.—*Fr.*

Corn. á Lapide reports many of these,—

"*Symbolicè et tropologicè*, (he says,) this rod signifies what sort of person a pontifex and pastor ought to be, viz., watchful, active, laborious, and austere, such as were St. Nicholas of Myra, St. Andrew the Carmelite, Pius II., and Cardinal Julian Cesarinus.

"*Allegoricè*, it is Christ; or the Virgin Mary, whose flower is Christ.

"*Anagogicè*, it is a symbol of the resurrection."

and pity, in that, whilst He chastises their pride, He provides for their welfare. For, as they were given to rebellion, they would still have provoked His wrath by new murmurings. He says, then, that He anticipates them, and restrains their impetuous fury, lest they should die. Thus in humbling us, He not only punishes our transgressions, but He has regard to what is profitable for us, and proves that He cares for us.

12. *And the children of Israel spake unto Moses.* It was indeed somewhat better to be alarmed by admiration of God's power than as if they had despised it in brutal stupidity; but there is a medium between torpor or obstinacy, and consternation. It is true that believers tremble at the judgments of God, and, in proportion as each of us has advanced in piety, so we are the more affected by a sense of His anger. But this fear humbles believers in such a manner that they nevertheless seek after God; whilst the reprobate so tremble as fretfully to desire to drive God far away from them. Hence it arose that the Israelites, stunned as it were by God's severity, which they deemed excessive, deplored their wretched lot; for, inasmuch as they had no sense of God's goodness, the chastisement to them was like a gibbet rather than a medicine. They exclaim, therefore, that they are destroyed, because God so severely avenges His polluted worship; as if all such instances of rigour were not profitable for the purpose of rendering them more heedful and cautious. No doubt this servile fear sometimes prepares men for repentance; but nothing is more perilous than to rest in it, because it first engenders bitterness and indignation, and at length drives them to despair. Howsoever formidable, then, may be God's severity, let us learn at the same time to apprehend His mercy, so that we may be prepared to endure willingly with meek and quiet minds the punishments which we have deserved. In short, this passage shews how little progress the Israelites had made, since the rods of God so greatly exasperated them, that they cut themselves off from all hope of salvation. For this is the meaning of the words, "Shall we be consumed with dying?" as if it were not the case that God, on the contrary, was preserving them from death, when in His paternal solicitude He warned them of their danger.

NUMBERS, CHAPTER XX.

1. Then came the children of Israel, *even* the whole congregation, into the desert of Zin, in the first month: and the people abode in Kadesh; and Miriam died there, and was buried there.

1. Pervenerunt autem filii Israel universa congregatio, in desertum Sin, mense primo, et mansit populus in Cades: ubi mortua est Maria, et sepulta illic fuit:

2. And there was no water for the congregation: and they gathered themselves together against Moses and against Aaron.

2. Quumque non esset aqua congregationi, convenerunt adversus Mosen et Aharon.

3. And the people chode with Moses, and spake, saying, Would God that we had died when our brethren died before the Lord!

3. Et jurgatus est populus cum Mose, ac dixerunt in hunc modum, Et utinam obiissemus quando obierunt fratres nostri coram Jehova.

4. And why have ye brought up the congregation of the Lord into this wilderness, that we and our cattle should die there?

4. Et quare venire fecistis congregationem Jehovæ in desertum istud: ut moriamur hic nos et jumenta nostra.

5. And wherefore have ye made us to come up out of Egypt, to bring us in unto this evil place? it *is* no place of seed, or of figs, or of vines, or of pomegranates; neither *is* there any water to drink.

5. Et quare ascendere fecistis nos ex Ægypto, ut venire faceretis nos ad locum malum istum, non locum sementis, ficuum, et vinearum, et malogranatorum, et in quo aqua nulla est ad bibendum?

6. And Moses and Aaron went from the presence of the assembly unto the door of the tabernacle of the congregation, and they fell upon their faces: and the glory of the Lord appeared unto them.

6. Abierunt ergo Moses et Aharon à conspectu congregationis ad ostium tabernaculi conventionis, et projecerunt se super faciem suam: apparuitque gloria Jehovæ super eos.

7. And the Lord spake unto Moses, saying,

7. Et loquutus est Jehova ad Mosen, dicendo:

8. Take the rod, and gather thou the assembly together, thou and Aaron thy brother, and speak ye unto the rock before their eyes; and it shall give forth his water, and thou shalt bring forth to them water out of the rock: so thou shalt give the congregation and their beasts drink.

8. Accipe virgam, et congrega cœtum tu et Aharon frater tuus, et loquimini petræ in oculis eorum, et dabit aquam suam, educesque illis aquam è petra, et potum dabis cœtui ac jumentis eorum.

9. And Moses took the rod from before the Lord, as he commanded him.

9. Tulit ergo Moses virgam à conspectu Jehovæ, quemadmodum præceperat ei:

10. And Moses and Aaron gathered the congregation together before the rock, and he said unto them, Hear now, ye rebels; must we fetch you water out of this rock?

10. Et congregaverunt Moses et Aharon congregationem ante petram, dixitque illis, Audite nunc ô rebelles, Nunquid de petra hac educemus vobis aquam?

11. And Moses lifted up his hand, and with his rod he smote the rock twice; and the water came out

11. Et elevavit Moses manum suam, percussitque petram virga sua duabus vicibus: tunc egressæ sunt

abundantly, and the congregation drank, and their beasts *also*.

12. And the Lord spake unto Moses and Aaron, Because ye believed me not, to sanctify me in the eyes of the children of Israel, therefore ye shall not bring this congregation into the land which I have given them.

13. This *is* the water of Meribah; because the children of Israel strove with the Lord, and he was sanctified in them.

aquæ multæ, et bibit congregatio ac jumenta eorum.

12. Et dixit Jehova ad Mosen et Aharon, Propterea quòd non credidistis mihi, ut sanctificaretis me in oculis filiorum Israel, idcirco non introducetis congregationem istam in terram quam dedi illis.

13. Istæ sunt aquæ jurgii, pro quibus jurgati sunt filii Israel cum Jehova, et sanctificavit se in illis.

1. *Then came the children of Israel.* In the twenty-third chapter of this book many intermediate stations are mentioned, which are not here referred to: perhaps because, from the time that God compelled them to draw back, they had made no advance for thirty whole years, but had wandered about by circuitous paths. In connecting the history, therefore, in this place he relates that they passed from the desert of Paran to the desert of Sin; because they then began to direct their journey straight towards the land of Canaan, and to advance more closely to it, so as at length to conclude their wanderings. When he tells us that Miriam died here, we may infer from hence that her life was greatly prolonged. It is probable that she was a girl of ten or twelve years of age, when Moses was born, since she was able to provide adroitly for his safety, (Exod. ii. 4;) for although her name is not actually given, yet it may be reasonably supposed that she was the person who fetched her mother to nurse the child that had been exposed. She reached the age, then, of about 130 years,[1] an unusual length of life, and especially for a woman.

2. *And there was no water for the congregation.* We have already seen a similar, though not the same, history. For, when the people had hardly come out of Egypt, they began to rebel in Rephidim on account of the scarcity of water; and now, after thirty-eight years, or thereabouts, a new sedition arose in Kadesh, because there, too, they wanted water. Their first murmuring, indeed, sufficiently shewed how great was their depravity and contumacy; for, when

[1] "Ainsi elle a passe six vingts ans;" thus she was more than six-score years of age.—*Fr.*

God gave them their food from heaven every day, why did they not supplicate Him for water, so that their sustenance might be complete? Yet, not less with foul ingratitude than with impious refractoriness, they assail God with reproaches, and complain that they are deceived and betrayed. But this second rebellion is far worse; for, when they had experienced that it was in God's power to extract plenty of water from the barren rock, why do they not now implore His aid? why does not that marvellous interference in their behalf recur to their minds? Yet, in their madness, they clamour that they have been more cruelly dealt with than as if they had been swallowed up by the earth, or consumed by fire from heaven, as if there were no remedy for their thirst. Assuredly this was incredible stupidity, designedly, as it were, to shut the gate of God's grace, and to cast themselves into despair. It is true that they rebel against Moses and Aaron; but they direct their complaints like darts against God Himself. They deem it a very great injustice that they had been brought into the desert, as if they had not in their own impious obstinacy themselves preferred the desert to the land of Canaan, and were deserving, therefore, of pining, in want of all things, to death itself. Perversely, then, do they throw the blame, which belongs to themselves alone, upon the ministers of their salvation. With truth, indeed, do they call the place evil and barren; but God would not have wished to keep them imprisoned there, unless they had voluntarily refused the land flowing with milk and honey, after it had been set before their eyes, and an easy entrance to it had been accorded to them under the guidance and authority of God. Thus the Prophet, in Psalm cv., in recounting the history of their redemption, before he descends to the punishments inflicted upon their sins, relates that they were brought forth by God "with joy" and "with gladness."[1] But, further, taking occasion from the inconvenience they experienced from thirst, they maliciously heap together other complaints. There was no lack of food to satisfy their hunger, and such as was pleasant to the taste; yet they complain exactly as

[1] These expressions occur, Ps. cv. 43. It is in Ps. cvi. that the Psalmist proceeds to narrate the history of their rebellions and punishments.

if hunger oppressed them as well as thirst. God daily rained for them food from heaven, which it was mere sport for them to gather; but the ground of their murmuring is that they had not to fatigue themselves with ploughing and sowing. Behold to what senselessness men are driven by preposterous lust, and by contempt of God's present blessings! The climax of their madness, however, is that they lament their fate in not having been swallowed up with Korah and his companions, or consumed by fire from heaven. They had been overwhelmed with great fear at that melancholy spectacle; and justly so, for God had exhibited a prodigy, terrible throughout all ages. Now they quarrel with Him because His lightnings did not smite them also. Nor do they only lament that they were not destroyed by that particular kind of death, but they wilfully provoke God's vengeance upon their heads, which ought to have terrified them more than a hundred deaths: for it is emphatically added, that those, with whom they desired to be associated, had "died *before the Lord.*" They acknowledge, therefore, that the destruction, which they imprecate upon themselves, had come to pass not by chance, but by the manifest judgment of God, as if they were angry with God for having spared themselves. Most truly do they call them their *brethren,* to whom they were only too like; yet is it in brutal arrogance that they desire to be accounted God's Church; for, whilst they professedly connect themselves with the adverse faction, they arrogate falsely this title to themselves.

6. *And Moses and Aaron went from the presence.* It is probable that they fled in fear, inasmuch as the tabernacle was a kind of refuge for them from the violence of the people. Still, we may conjecture from other passages that they had consideration not only for themselves, but for the wretched people, howsoever unworthy of it they might be. So also, when they throw themselves upon their faces, I understand that they did so, not so much (to pray) that God would protect them from the wrath of their enemies, but also that He would calm these madmen by some appropriate remedy. Still their agitation appears to have been such as to deprive them of their ordinary self-restraint. Neither, indeed, does God try their faith and patience, as He

often did on other occasions; perhaps because He saw that they were too much overwhelmed to be able to persevere inflexibly in pious zeal, patience, and care for the public good. Consequently the appearance to them of God's glory was a support for their weakness, as in a case of extremity.

This example shews us how earnestly God should be entreated constantly to support us with new supplies of His grace, since otherwise the boldest of us all would fail at every moment. The invincible resolution of Moses had so often overcome every obstacle, that there seemed to be no fear of his being in danger of falling; yet the conqueror in so many struggles at length stumbles in a single act. Hence we should more carefully bear in mind the exhortation of Paul: Because "it is God which worketh in us both to will and to do of his good pleasure," we should "work out our own salvation with fear and trembling." (Phil. ii. 12, 13.)

8. *Take the rod.* It is unquestionable that the faith of Moses had now begun to waver; but we gather from his prompt obedience that it had not altogether failed; for he wastes no time in discussion, but comes straight to the rock in order that he may perform God's command. His faith, then, was only so smothered, that its hidden vigour at once directed him to his duty. Thus is it that the saints sometimes, whilst they totter like children, still advance toward their mark.

By the sight of "the rod," God would recall both to Moses and the people so many miracles, which were well fitted to awaken confidence for the future; just as if He were uplifting the standard of His power. The command to speak to the rock is not unattended with a severe reproach, as if He had said, that in the lifeless elements there was more reason and intelligence than in men themselves. And assuredly it was a thing much to be ashamed of, that the rock, as if it could hear and was endued with sense, should obey God's voice, whilst the people, to whom the Law had been given, remained in deafness and stupidity.

10. *And Moses and Aaron gathered the congregation together.* There is no doubt but that Moses was perplexed between hope and doubt, so that, although he committed the event to God, he was still to a certain extent oppressed

with anxiety; for he would never have been so ready and prompt in obeying, and especially in such an unusually arduous matter, if he had been without faith. Aaron and himself had recently hidden themselves in alarm; it was, therefore, a task of no slight difficulty straightway to call the people, from whom they had fled, and voluntarily to encounter their madness. Thus far, then, we see nothing but a readiness to obey, conjoined with magnanimity, which is deserving of no common praise; but inasmuch as the unbelief of Moses is condemned by the heavenly Judge, in whose hands is the sovereign power, and at whose word we all stand or fall, we must acquiesce in His sentence. We scarcely perceive anything reprehensible in this matter, yet, since God declares that the fall of Moses displeased Him, we must abide by His decision rather than our own. And hence, too, let us learn that our works, on the surface of which nothing but virtue is apparent, are often abounding in secret defects, which escape the eyes of men, but are manifest to God alone.

If it be asked in what respect Moses transgressed, the origin of his transgression was unbelief; for it is not allowable, when this species of sin is expressly referred to in the answer of God, to imagine that it was anything else. But it is doubtful in what point he was incredulous; unless it be that in asking whether he could fetch water out of the rock, he seems to reject as if it were impossible and absurd what God had promised to do. And, in fact, he was so entirely taken up by considerations of their contumacy, that he did not acknowledge the grace of God. He inquires whether he shall fetch water out of the rock? whereas he ought to have recollected that this had already been permitted to him by God. It became him, then, confidently to assert that God had again promised the same thing, rather than to speak with hesitation.

Others think that he sinned, because he was not contented with a single blow, but smote the rock twice. And this perhaps did arise from distrust. But the origin of the fault was that he did not simply embrace God's promise, and strenuously discharge the duty assigned to him as an evidence of his faith. Although, therefore, his smiting the rock twice might have been a token of his want of confidence, still it was only an aggravation of the evil, and not its origin or cause. Thus, then, we must always come back to this, that Moses did not give God the glory, because he rather considered what the people had deserved, than estimated the power of God according to His word. And this, too, his previous reprimand denotes, when, in accusing the Israelites of rebellion, he shews, indeed, that he was inflamed with holy zeal; yet, at the same time, he does not bestir himself with suitable confidence in order to their conviction; nay, in a manner he confesses that the power of God fails beneath their wickedness. Thus it is said in Ps. cvi. 32, 33, "That it went ill with Moses for their sakes, because they provoked his spirit, so that he spoke with his mouth:"[1] for the Prophet does not there excuse Moses; but shews that in consequence of the wickedness of the people, he was carried away by inconsiderate fervour, so as to deny that what God had promised should take place. Hence let us learn that, when we are angered by the sins of others, we should beware lest a temptation of an opposite kind should take possession of our minds.

12. *And the Lord spake unto Moses and Aaron.* God here both sets forth their crime, and pronounces its punishment. Now, whilst unbelief is in itself a gross and detestable evil, God aggravates its guilt by declaring its consequence, viz., that He was defrauded of His glory, when Moses and Aaron, who ought to have been the proclaimers of the miracle, lay as it were confounded with shame. For, whereas their confidence, by exciting attention, would have sanctified God's name, so by their mistrust it came to pass that all were led to think that there was nothing to be hoped from His assistance.

When Moses not only ingenuously confesses his guilt, but also relates how he was condemned by God, and, in order that his disgrace may be more complete, introduces Him speaking as from His judgment-seat, this does not a little tend to establish the truth of his doctrine. For what human

[1] *A. V.*, "He spake unadvisedly."

being, unless he had renounced all carnal affections, would voluntarily endure to declare himself guilty before all the world? His angelic virtues were sufficient to exempt him from all suspicion. Having erred in one particular only, he proclaims the disgrace which he might have concealed, and does not hesitate to disparage himself, in order to magnify the goodness of God. And surely it is obvious from this passage that, whenever God had before pardoned the people at the request of Moses, the pardon was no less gratuitous than as if he had not interceded for them. For the intercession of Moses ceases on this occasion, yet God does not fail to deal kindly with them in their unworthiness, according to His wont.

13. *This is the water of Meribah.*[1] This name was given to the place in order that the ingratitude of their fathers might be detestable to their descendants, and hence the mercy of God more illustrious. Thus the Prophet, referring to it, says: "That the generation to come might know them,—that they might not forget the works of God,—and might not be as their fathers, a stubborn and rebellious generation; a generation that set not their heart aright, and whose spirit was not stedfast with God." (Ps. lxxviii. 6, 7, 8.) And elsewhere both the name of Meribah and that of Massah are employed, in order that the Israelites might learn not to imitate their fathers, (Ps. xcv. 8;[2]) although Moses here uses the plural number, whereas he has the singular in Exodus xvii.

The expression at the end of the verse, that God "was sanctified" among the children of Israel, is not used in approval, but rather in reproof, of their conduct. Israel is called elsewhere God's "holiness,"[3] (Ps. cxiv. 2,) because God magnificently displayed His glory in their deliverance; but He is here said to have sanctified Himself in a different

[1] *Lat.*, "These are the waters of strife." See margin *A. V.*

[2] In *C.'s* translation of this verse he retains the proper names Meribah and Massah, which in *A. V.* are rendered, "in the *provocation*, and in the day of *temptation*." See *C. Soc. Edit.*, vol. iv. p. 40; and Mr. Anderson's note.

[3] *A. V.*, "Judah was his sanctuary." *V.* "Facta est Judæa sanctificatio ejus." See *C. Soc. Edit.* of Psalms, vol. iv. pp. 336, 337.

sense, because, by the overthrow of their iniquity and frowardness, He rescued His holy name from contempt. In fine, it was a proof of His inestimable mercy, that the water, which might have justly been destructive to them, was not only given to be the sustenance of their bodies, but also was converted into an aid for their salvation; for which reason Paul says that this was "spiritual drink." (1 Cor. x. 4.)

A Repetition of the same History.

DEUTERONOMY, CHAPTER I.

37. Also the Lord was angry with me for your sakes, saying, Thou also shalt not go in thither.	37. Etiam contra me iratus est Jehova propter vos, dicendo: Etiam tu non ingredieris illuc.
38. *But* Joshua the son of Nun, which standeth before thee, he shall go in thither: encourage him; for he shall cause Israel to inherit it.	38. Jehosua filius Nun, qui stat coram te, ipse ingredietur illuc: ipsum robora, quandoquidem illam in hæreditatem distribuet Israeli.

37. *Also the Lord was angry with me.* It is in no cowardly spirit that he transfers to them the guilt of unfaithfulness, which he had confessed for himself; but, since he had only fallen in consequence of being overwhelmed by their obstinate wickedness, he justly reproaches them with the fact that God was wroth with him on account of their sin. If under this pretext he had attempted to extenuate his guilt before God, or to substitute their criminality for his own, he would have done nothing else than double the evil: but, in reproving the people, he rightly and appropriately complained that the cause of his sin had arisen from them. As if he had said that they were so perverse that even he had been corrupted by them, and drawn into association with their guilt and its punishment. He here, however, adds respecting Joshua what he had before passed over in silence. His appointment as successor to Moses served to encourage the people; for it was a notable ground for hope that they should hear a provision already made, that after the death of Moses they should not be destitute of a leader, who would rule them under the auspices of God.

Why God preferred this man to all others, especially when

Caleb is more highly praised elsewhere, is only known to Himself. We know that He chooses according to His own will those whom He destines to any charge, so that the dignity of men may depend upon His gratuitous favour. "To stand before" a person is equivalent to being at hand to do his bidding; and it seems that this was stated to be the condition of Joshua, in order that the punishment might be more manifest; inasmuch as, by an entire inversion, a successor is given to Moses, who had been his servant.

NUMBERS, CHAPTER XX.

14. And Moses sent messengers from Kadesh unto the king of Edom, Thus saith thy brother Israel, Thou knowest all the travel that hath befallen us;

15. How our fathers went down into Egypt, and we have dwelt in Egypt a long time; and the Egyptians vexed us and our fathers:

16. And when we cried unto the Lord, he heard our voice, and sent an angel, and hath brought us forth out of Egypt; and, behold, we *are* in Kadesh, a city in the uttermost of thy border.

17. Let us pass, I pray thee, through thy country: we will not pass through the fields, or through the vineyards, neither will we drink *of* the water of the wells: we will go by the king's *high*-way, we will not turn to the right hand nor to the left, until we have passed thy borders.

18. And Edom said unto him, Thou shalt not pass by me, lest I come out against thee with the sword.

19. And the children of Israel said unto him, We will go by the high-way; and if I and my cattle drink of thy water, then I will pay for it: I will only (without *doing* any thing *else*) go through on my feet.

20. And he said, Thou shalt not

14. Misit autem Moses nuntium è Cades ad regem Edom, Sic dicit frater tuus Israel, Tu nosti omnem laborem qui apprehendit nos.

15. Quia descenderunt patres nostri in Ægyptum, et mansimus in Ægypto diebus multis, afflixeruntque nos Ægyptii, et patres nostros.

16. Et clamavimus ad Jehovam, qui exaudivit vocem nostram, et misit angelum qui nos eduxit ex Ægypto. Et ecce, sumus in Cades, urbe in extremitate termini tui.

17. Transeamus, agedum, per terram tuam, non transibimus per agros aut per vineas, neque bibemus aquam putei, via regia gradiemur: neque declinabimus ad dexteram aut ad sinistram, donec transierimus terminum tuum.

18. Cui respondit Edom, Non transibis per me, ne fortè cum gladio egrediar in occursum tui.

19. Et dixerunt ei filii Israel, Per viam ascendemus: quòd si aquas tuas biberimus ego et animalia mea, dabo pretium illarum. Tantummodo sine negotio transeam pedibus meis.

20. Verùm dixit, Non transibis.

go through. And Edom came out against him with much people, and with a strong hand.

Et egressus est in occursum ejus cum populo multo, et manu forti.

21. Thus Edom refused to give Israel passage through his border: wherefore Israel turned away from him.

21. Renuit igitur Edom permittere Israeli, ut transiret per terminum suum: tunc Israel declinavit ab eo.

22. And the children of Israel, *even* the whole congregation, journeyed from Kadesh, and came unto mount Hor.

22. Et profecti sunt è Cades, veneruntque filii Israel, tota congregatio ad montem Hor.

A Repetition of the same History.

DEUT. II. 2. And the Lord spake unto me, saying,

3. Ye have compassed this mountain long enough: turn you northward.

4. And command thou the people, saying, Ye *are* to pass through the coast of your brethren the children of Esau, which dwell in Seir, and they shall be afraid of you: take ye good heed unto yourselves therefore.

5. Meddle not with them; for I will not give you of their land, no, not so much as a foot-breadth; because I have given mount Seir unto Esau *for* a possession.

6. Ye shall buy meat of them for money, that ye may eat; and ye shall also buy water of them for money, that ye may drink.

7. For the Lord thy God hath blessed thee in all the works of thy hand: he knoweth thy walking through this great wilderness: these forty years the Lord thy God *hath been* with thee; thou hast lacked nothing.

8. And when we passed by from our brethren the children of Esau, which dwelt in Seir, through the way of the plain from Elath, and from Ezion-gaber, we turned and passed by the way of the wilderness of Moab.

2. Postea loquutus est ad me Jehova, dicendo:

3. Sufficit vobis circuisse montem istum: convertite vos ad aquilonem.

4. Populo autem præcipe dicendo, Vos nunc transituri estis per terminum fratrum vestrorum filiorum Esau qui habitabant in Seir: timebunt autem à vobis, cavete diligenter:

5. Ne irritetis eos, non enim daturus sum vobis de terra eorum usque ad calcationem plantæ pedis: quia in hæreditatem ipsi Esau dedi montem Seir.

6. Cibum emetis ab eis argento, et comedetis: et etiam aquam emetis ab eis argento, et bibetis.

7. Siquidem Jehova Deus tuus benedixit tibi in omni opere manus tuæ, et novit quòd ambules per desertum magnum istud: jam quadraginta annis Jehova Deus tuus fuit tecum, neque indiguisti aliquo.

8. Et transivimus à fratribus nostris filiis Esau, qui habitabant in Seir, per viam solitudinis ab Elath et ab Esion-gaber: conversi autem transivimus ad viam deserti Moab.

NUMB. XX. 14. *And Moses sent messengers from Kadesh.* His first narrative does not explain the cause of the embassy, but from the account in Deuteronomy it is plain that peace[1]

[1] "Sauf conduit, et amitié;" safe conduct and friendship.—*Fr.*

was sought for from the Edomites as brethren by the command of God. God, therefore, prescribes the conditions of peace and war; lest the Israelites should rashly attack any, who were not to be reckoned enemies, although they might act towards them with little humanity. Undoubtedly this would seem hard to His people that they were to leave a country, which was close to them, untouched, and to seek a more distant place of abode. But God restrains their impatience for a twofold reason; first, because it was unjust and by no means humane to assail their kindred; and both these nations were descended from Isaac, and their original ancestors were twin brothers. Circumcision, too, was common to them both, a mark of their being of the same origin, and a bond of fraternal connexion. But the other reason ought to have had more weight in restraining them, because it was unlawful to cast the children of Esau out of the possession, which they had obtained by a similar right as that whereby the land of Canaan had been promised to the posterity of Jacob. If, therefore, they desired to enjoy their own inheritance, the decree was not to be violated which God had pronounced by the mouth of Isaac, (Gen. xxvii. 39;) especially since Esau the founder of the race (of the Edomites) had fixed his home in Mount Seir by the secret inspiration of God, and to that place had his posterity been confined. God, therefore, now admonishes them that it would have been an act of sacrilegious audacity, if the Israelites should attempt to overthrow the prophecy of Isaac, by which Esau had been declared the possessor of a rich and fertile soil.

Deut. ii. 4.—*And they shall be afraid of you.* This temptation was the more provoking, when they heard not only that the embassy would be vain, but that although Edom should receive them with injustice and hostility, they were still to abstain from violence and arms. For there might be some reason in this, that when they presented their request in a friendly manner, they would have a legitimate cause of war, if Edom should reject their demands. But this further condition might appear altogether intolerable that they were to do nothing against those who refused to let them pass quietly through their land. Hence, however, it more fully appears how the Israelites were gradually, and by various kinds of chastisement, subdued to obedience, whereas they would otherwise have fiercely and petulantly exclaimed that they had been dealt with unkindly by God; since thus their condition would be worse than the universal law of nations allowed. In this matter, then, their wanderings, for eight and thirty years, had much efficacy in bringing them back to the right way.

NUMB. XX. 14.—*Thou knowest all the travel that hath befallen us.* This preface was well calculated to conciliate favour, when the sons of Jacob, descended from the same blood, familiarly approached the Edomites: for their connexion ought to have rendered them hospitable. But there are two principal points whereby Moses endeavoured to influence the mind of the king of Edom, so that he should grant them a passage through his dominions. The first is derived from the ordinary feelings of humanity; for nature dictates that aid should be extended to the wretched, who are unjustly oppressed. In this view, he says, that the afflictions which they had endured were notorious; viz., that as sojourners in Egypt they had been tyrannically harassed and oppressed. In saying that "the Egyptians vexed us and our fathers," although they were not, at that time, endowed with capacity for estimating the injuries inflicted upon them,[1] yet it is not without reason that they complain that these injuries had been inflicted on themselves, which affected their whole body and name, especially since the final act of cruelty directly concerned them, when Pharaoh commanded all the male infants to be destroyed. The second argument is more effective: since nothing can be less in accordance with propriety than to deny our assistance to those whose welfare God recommends to us by His own example. In order, then, that they may obtain help from their brethren, they make mention of the grace of God, which at that time

[1] "Ils prennent sur eux les injures qui avoyent este faites devant qu'ils les peussents sentir, n'estans point encore nez, ou estans petits enfans;" they take upon themselves the injuries which had been done before they could feel them, not being yet born, or being but little children.—*Fr.*

might have been everywhere celebrated. When, therefore, this message is given to their ambassadors, We cried unto the Lord, who hath heard us, their design was to exhort the Edomites to be imitators of God, who had been merciful in delivering His people. If any should object that the cry of the people had not been praiseworthy, as not having arisen from a true and sincere faith, nor from a serious feeling of the heart, the reply is easy, that the Israelites were not here boasting of any merit of their own, as if they had prayed duly and perfectly, but that they were simply professing their innocence, since they could not have had recourse to God, unless they had been unjustly oppressed. The fact, then, that God had heard them, had the effect of commending their cause. They prove, however, from the result, that God was their deliverer: because their exodus had been incredible; although this point is but lightly touched upon.

Their notion is a poor one, who understand Moses by "the angel:" since by this name they unquestionably magnify the miracles which God had wrought.[1] Now, although the angels encamp around the servants of God—and it is certain that many angels had been the ministers of the people's safety—still they especially designate, as the angel, Him who had been often before called Jehovah, and in whom the majesty of God perfectly shone forth. Paul, however, teaches that he was Christ. (1 Cor. x. 4.)

19. *And the children of Israel said unto him.* It is doubtful whether or not the ambassadors were sent a second time, in order to remove all unjust suspicions, and to appease the ferocity (of the Edomites.) It is probable, however, that we have the relation of what was done in one and the same expedition. The sum is, that the Israelites tried every means, in order that a free and unmolested passage might be accorded them by the Edomites: whence their repulse might appear the more harsh and intolerable. But God, by this test, would prove the obedience of His people.

[1] *C.* found in *S.M.* that Rabbi Salomon interpreted the ambiguous word מלאך, *messenger*, here, instead of *angel;* and said that the messenger was Moses.—*W.*

As regards the Edomites, although by rashly taking up arms they would have drawn upon themselves just destruction, still God spared them for a time; not by freely pardoning them, but by deferring their punishment, as He is wont to do, until its due season.

DEUT. II. 7.—*For the Lord thy God hath blessed thee.* This reason is added, lest the people should be grieved at spending their money, of which they had not much, in buying meat and drink. There are, however, two clauses; first, that they were so enriched by God's bounty, that they were fully supplied with the means of buying food; and, secondly, that they must not doubt but that He would relieve their necessity, if it were required, since He had thus far provided for them, and had not suffered them to want anything. He, therefore, encourages them to hope, in consideration of their past experience; because God would take care of them, as He had before been accustomed to do.

The question, however, arises, how God could say, that He had blessed the work of their hands, when they had had no commerce with other nations, so as to make the smallest gains whatever. But I thus understand it, viz., that although they were gratuitously sustained in the wilderness, and had not expended a single penny in buying even shoe-latchets, still their cattle had increased, and, besides, they had made some profits by their daily labour; not by receiving, indeed, daily wages, but by providing for themselves furniture and other necessaries.

NUMBERS, CHAPTER XX.

23. And the Lord spake unto Moses and Aaron in mount Hor, by the coast of the land of Edom, saying,

24. Aaron shall be gathered unto his people; for he shall not enter into the land which I have given unto the children of Israel, because ye rebelled against my word at the water of Meribah.

25. Take Aaron and Eleazar his

23. Dixit autem Jehova ad Mosen et Aharon in monte Hor, in finibus terræ Edom, dicendo:

24. Congregabitur Aharon ad populos suos. Non enim ingredietur terram quam dedi filiis Israel: eo quod rebelles fueritis ori meo in aquis jurgii.

25. Accipe Aharon et Eleazar

son, and bring them up unto mount Hor;

26. And strip Aaron of his garments, and put them upon Eleazar his son: and Aaron shall be gathered *unto his people*, and shall die there.

27. And Moses did as the Lord commanded: and they went up into mount Hor, in the sight of all the congregation.

28. And Moses stripped Aaron of his garments, and put them upon Eleazar his son; and Aaron died there in the top of the mount: and Moses and Eleazar came down from the mount.

29. And when all the congregation saw that Aaron was dead, they mourned for Aaron thirty days, *even* all the house of Israel.

filium ejus, et ascendere fac eos in Hor montem.

26. Tunc exues Aharon vestibus suis, quibus indues Eleazar filium ejus: quia Aharon colligetur, et morietur ibi.

27. Fecitque Moses quemadmodum præceperat Jehova. Et ascenderunt in Hor montem in oculis totius congregationis.

28. Et exuit Moses Aharon vestibus suis, et induit illis Eleazar filium ejus, mortuusque est Aharon ibi in vertice montis. Tunc descendit Moses et Eleazar de monte.

29. Videns autem tota congregatio quòd obiisset Aharon, fleverunt eum triginta diebus tota domus Israel.

A Repetition of the same History.

NUMB. XXXIII. 38. And Aaron the priest went up into mount Hor, at the commandment of the Lord, and died there, in the fortieth year after the children of Israel were come out of the land of Egypt, in the first *day* of the fifth month.

39. And Aaron *was* an hundred and twenty and three years old when he died in mount Hor.

38. Ascendit autem Aharon sacerdos in Hor montem secundùm sermonem Jehovæ: et mortuus est ibi anno quadragesimo ex quo egressi sunt filii Israel è terra Ægypti, mense quinto, primo die mensis.

39. Erat Aharon natus centum ac viginti tres annos quando mortuus est in Hor monte.

NUMB. XX. 23.—*And the Lord spake unto Moses.* First of all, in the death of Aaron, we must consider the execution of the sentence, whereby he had been condemned; for God wished to shew that He had not threatened either him or Moses in vain, with what then occurred, as children are wont to be threatened. If Aaron had died without any such prediction, since he might have seemed from his extreme age to have but discharged the debt of nature, as it is called, the people might have been so overcome by their grief, as to have no inclination to proceed. But now, when, in the death of one man, the condemnation of their public and common guilt is clearly manifested, such great severity on God's part against the high-priest, who had before propitiated God towards them all by his intercession, must have been a very sharp spur to them all. For it must needs have suggested itself to them, that God was no longer to be trifled with, before whom not even this sacred dignity could escape punishment. This was the reason why Aaron was called forth to die in the sight of all, that the survivors might learn to live to God, inasmuch as He instructed them to obey by this notable example. For the rebuke is added not so much for the sake of Moses and Aaron, viz., that they should not enter the land, because they had been rebellious against God's word, as that the people might perceive that they deserved to perish ten times over; since, by their contumacy, they had exasperated the holy men, so that in the excess of their zeal they had almost fallen away from the faith.

25. *Take Aaron and Eleazar his son.* Aaron's successor was to be designated whilst he was himself still living; first of all, that the perpetuity of the priesthood might be secured; and, secondly, lest the people, with their usual temerity, should take upon themselves the election in a matter depending on the will of God alone. For, unless Eleazar had been appointed priest whilst his father was yet alive, the office itself might fall into disesteem, since the high dignity of any individual is often odious. Lest, therefore, their perverse envy might impel them to repudiate the priesthood, God anticipates them, and provides that religion, which ought to be perpetual, should not perish together with the men. Again, we know how great was the audacity of this people in innovation; lest, then, they should, at their own caprice, take to themselves a priest from another tribe, it was well that he of whom God approved, should be firmly established, so as to be received without controversy as the true and lawful one. In this matter an external symbol was made use of, in that Eleazar was invested with the sacred garments; nor does this refer to the shirt, or the slippers, but to the sacerdotal ornaments. The effect, therefore, of this ceremony was as if Aaron should resign the office, which he had discharged till that day, to his son. Moreover, it is worthy of observation that Aaron not only

voluntarily cedes his dignity, but his life also. By this proof his faith was confirmed, for had he not been persuaded that an inheritance was laid up for him in heaven, he would not have so calmly migrated from the world. Since, however, he composes himself to die, just as if he were but lying down on his bed, it is altogether beyond a doubt that his mind was lifted up to the hope of a blessed resurrection, from whence arises a cheerful readiness to die. And it is probable that his faith was elevated and strengthened when he saw that the testimony of God's grace, on which the safety of the people depended, was made to rest upon the person of his son. For it was exactly as if the image of the Mediator were set visibly before his eyes. This consolation, then, being of no ordinary character, rendered him superior to the terrors of death. Meanwhile, Eleazar succeeded, in the presence of the people, so that his authority might not hereafter be exposed to their murmurs.

29. *And when all the congregation saw.* This has been an error common to almost all nations and ages, but which reigned peculiarly amongst the people of Israel—to pay due honour to God's holy servants, rather after their deaths than in their lives. They had frequently wished to stone Aaron; they had raised great tumults, in order to cast him down from the dignity in which God had placed him; now, forgetting their malignity and envy, they lament for him when dead.

The question, however, occurs, whether the mourning for a month, which is here recorded, was praiseworthy or not? But it could not be otherwise than improper, inasmuch as it was a means of aggravating their grief; for men are naturally only too much inclined to excessive grief, even although they do not indulge it; and besides, the hope of a better life avails to mitigate sorrow. Hence we infer, that those are endued with scarcely any taste of eternal salvation, who give way to immoderate grief. But, since believers have another cause for mourning, *i. e.*, to exercise themselves both in the fear of God, and in the hope and desire of the future resurrection, this solemn mourning has not been unreasonably received as a general custom. Since death is a mirror of God's curse upon the whole human race, it is profitable for us, whenever any of our belongings dies, to mourn our common lot, so as to humble ourselves beneath God's hand. Besides, if mourning is directed to its proper end, it in a manner unites the living with the dead; so that in death itself the communion of the new and immortal life shines forth. And further, the weakness of the ancient people had need of being propped and supported by such aids as this; for, amidst their dark shadows, it would not have been easy to rise above the world, unless they had been taught that the dead still belonged to them, and that there remained some bond of connexion between them. But if the utility (of this custom) be corrupted by its abuse, it is not just that what is right in itself should be blamed for the fault of men.

NUMB. XXXIII. 39. *And Aaron was an hundred and twenty and three years old.* It is not without reason that the great age of Aaron is expressly stated, inasmuch as his life had been prolonged to an unusual period, for the good of the people. At the age of an hundred he had already exceeded the ordinary extent of life; whereas, by God's extraordinary blessing, he survived until the people were about to pass into the promised land. Hence their ingratitude was the more base in not acknowledging this paternal care of God, since it was for their advantage that He preserved so long the minister of His grace.

DEUTERONOMY, CHAPTER X.

6. And the children of Israel took their journey from Beeroth of the children of Jaakan to Mosera: there Aaron died, and there he was buried; and Eleazar his son ministered in the priest's office in his stead.

7. From thence they journeyed unto Gudgodah; and from Gudgodah to Jotbath, a land of rivers of waters.

6. Filii autem Israel profecti sunt de Beeroth filiorum Jaacan in Moserah: illic mortuus est Aharon, et illic sepultus est, functusque est sacerdotio Eleazar filius ejus pro eo.

7. Inde profecti sunt in Gudgodah, et de Gudgodah in Jobath terram torrentium aquarum.

6. *And the children of Israel.* Since it is not the design of Moses to specify the stations here, as he does in Numbers

xxxiii., but only to mark the place in which Aaron died, I have therefore thought fit to connect what we read here with the preceding narrative. In the death of Aaron, they might recognise the punishment of their own rebellion. But that Eleazar should be substituted in his place, was a sign of the paternal grace of God, who did not suffer them to be deprived of this blessing. This succession, too, was to be a perpetual rule for the future, so that the sacerdotal dignity, according to God's prescription, should remain in that family.

He here specifies the names of certain places, which he omits in the passage above cited; for he there states that the Israelites went straight from Kadesh-barnea to Mount Hor; and then makes them pass on to Zalmonah and Punon, perhaps because the places had different names, or because they did not pitch their camp in Gudgodah, or Jotbath; although the advantages of the spot might have invited them to stop in a well-watered valley, for it is called "the land of torrents," through which an abundance of water flowed.

I do not advert to what every reader will readily observe for himself, that in the discourse of Moses the order of the history is inverted; for he says that the Levites were separated from the rest of the people, after the death of Aaron.

NUMBERS, CHAPTER XXI.

1. And when king Arad the Canaanite, which dwelt in the south, heard tell that Israel came by the way of the spies, then he fought against Israel, and took *some* of them prisoners.

2. And Israel vowed a vow unto the Lord, and said, If thou wilt indeed deliver this people into my hand, then I will utterly destroy their cities.

3. And the Lord hearkened to the voice of Israel, and delivered up the Canaanites; and they utterly destroyed them and their cities: and he called the name of the place Hormah.

1. Quum audisset Chananæus rex Arad habitans in meridie quod veniret Israel per viam exploratorum, pugnavit cum Israele, et abduxit ab eo prædam (*vel*, captivitatem.)

2. Vovit ergo Israel votum Jehovæ, et dixit, Si tradendo tradideris populum istum in manum meam, delebo urbes eorum.

3. Et exaudivit Jehova vocem Israelis, et dedit Chananæum, et delevit eos ac urbes eorum: vocavitque nomen loci illius Horma.

A Repetition of the same History.

NUMB. XXXIII. 40. And king Arad the Canaanite, which dwelt in the south in the land of Canaan, heard of the coming of the children of Israel.

40. Audivit autem Chananæus rex Arad (is verò habitabat in meridie in terra Chanaan) quum ingrederentur filii Israel.

NUMB. XXI. 1. *And when king Arad the Canaanite.* It is not altogether agreed among commentators who this king Arad was. Some think that he was an Amalekite, but this error is refuted by the fact that the Amalekites had already attempted in vain to interrupt the journey of the people. Nor is it credible that after so great a slaughter, they would have endeavoured to do so again, especially since their territories remained untouched. Besides, it would have been absurd to call the Amalekites Canaanites, since they derived their origin not from Canaan but from Esau, and thus were connected with the Israelites by a common descent from Shem. We shall, however, rightly understand this as referring to the Amorites, who were certainly reckoned among the Canaanites, as being of the same race; as Moses tells us in his first book, (Gen. x. 16, and xv. 21;) nay, he elsewhere designates all the people of Canaan by the name of Amorites. Moreover, in the thirty-fourth chapter of this book, we shall see that their boundaries reached to mount Hor and Kadesh-barnea. Since, then, the Amorites were in this neighbourhood towards the south, the name will suit them very well. That king Arad, however, alone made war upon them, arose from the paternal providence of God, who wished to accustom His people to the conquest of their enemies by degrees. If all these nations had united their forces, and made a combined attack upon an unwarlike people, it would have succumbed in astonishment and fear. But it was easier for them to defend themselves against a single nation. And yet, in the first combat, God permitted the Israelites to be routed, so that the victorious Canaanite took some booty, or led away some captives. And this also was useful to the Israelites, in order that, mistrusting their own strength, they might humbly betake themselves to the succour of God; for it behoved them to learn that, unless they were aided from on high, they would be altogether insufficient, when they had to resist many powerful nations, since they had not been able to withstand even a single people.

With respect to "the way of the spies," some understand that, as the people had been taught by Joshua and Caleb, they followed the footsteps of those who had been sent to explore the land; but, inasmuch as it appears that the course was a different one, I know not whether this opinion is very tenable. Thus, some take the word דרך, *derek*, to mean "after the manner of,"[1] which appears to be harsh and constrained. Thus, then, I explain it, Since they had to advance through unknown regions, spies were sent on, according to custom, to direct the whole march; and hence king Arad knew that his territory was to be invaded, before the army had proceeded so far.

2. *And Israel vowed a vow unto the Lord.* This was a manifestation of piety, when they had sustained a loss, not to cast away hope, nor to murmur against God; but to encourage themselves by entreating His aid. To this state of submissiveness they had been subdued by the chastisements of God, although the continuance of their obedience, as we shall presently see, was not of long duration. Any one at first sight would say that there was something absurd in this vow; but we gather from the result, that it was lawful and approved by God; for the sign of His approbation was that He hearkened to the vows and cry of the people. I admit, indeed, that God sometimes answers defective prayers, but there is no doubt whatever but that Moses here commends their piety in the vow. We must consider, then, how it was lawful for them to offer the destruction of cities and the wasting of lands to God as a sacrifice of sweet savour; and the reply to this question will be easy, if we bear in mind that the vow did not originate in inconsiderate zeal, but rather in the command of God. It seems cruel to destroy an entire nation; but God had not only decreed its destruction, but had appointed the Israelites to execute His sentence. Hence the vow, of which we are now treating, was not idly spoken, being founded on

[1] It is again *S. M.* who has mentioned this opinion.—*W.*

God's word, which is the first rule for vowing rightly. It was, indeed, allowable for them to spare the cities, in order to possess them themselves; but it was also allowable to devote them as an offering (*in anathema*) of first-fruits to God, as we are elsewhere told of the city of Jericho. This at any rate we must conclude, that although God had not openly and expressly commanded the cities to be utterly destroyed, still this vow was dictated by the Holy Spirit, lest the people should yield to sloth, and set themselves down in a single corner, but that, having desolated and wasted this region, they might encourage themselves the more to further progress. The verb חרם, *charam*, which Moses employs, signifies, indeed, *to destroy*, and from it is derived the word חרמה, *chormah*, or *Hormah*, which implies a species of anathema, as if they devoted the land to the curse of God. Moses, however, adds, that the people performed the vow, under the obligation of which they had laid themselves; and praiseworthy indeed was their magnanimity, in refusing to avail themselves of a comfortable home by destroying the cities, which they had acquired by the right of war.

We know not whether the cities were destroyed immediately after the victory over their enemies; indeed, I rather conjecture that there was some interval of time, because the people did not straightway enter the boundaries of the promised land. And this more clearly appears from chapter xxxiii., where, after this battle was fought, certain stations are enumerated, which are in another direction. It is probable, therefore, that they fought outside the boundaries of the Canaanites, and that, when the people came here soon afterwards, the land was finally put to the sword.

NUMB. xxxiii. 40.—*And king Arad the Canaanite.* Although Moses gives no account of a battle, yet he briefly revives the recollection of the previous history; as much as to say, that in this part of their journey the Israelites at length met with their enemy, since they then began to fight with one of the nations of Canaan. In a word, the meaning is, that this was the beginning of their warfare, when the land which God had promised them as an inheritance was about to be occupied.

NUMBERS, CHAPTER XXI.

4. And they journeyed from mount Hor by the way of the Red sea, to compass the land of Edom: and the soul of the people was much discouraged because of the way.

5. And the people spake against God, and against Moses, Wherefore have ye brought us up out of Egypt to die in the wilderness? for *there is* no bread, neither *is there any* water; and our soul loatheth this light bread.

6. And the Lord sent fiery serpents among the people, and they bit the people; and much people of Israel died.

7. Therefore the people came to Moses, and said, We have sinned; for we have spoken against the Lord, and against thee: pray unto the Lord, that he take away the serpents from us. And Moses prayed for the people.

8. And the Lord said unto Moses, Make thee a fiery serpent, and set it upon a pole: and it shall come to pass, that every one that is bitten, when he looketh upon it, shall live.

9. And Moses made a serpent of brass, and put it upon a pole; and it came to pass, that if a serpent had bitten any man, when he beheld the serpent of brass, he lived.

4. Et profecti sunt de Hor monte per viam maris Suph, ut circuirent terram Edom: et angustiis affecta est anima populi in via.

5. Itaque loquutus est populus contra Deum et Mosen, Ut quid ascendere nos fecistis ex Ægypto, ut moreremur in deserto? Non est enim panis neque aqua. Et tædet animam nostram super pane levi (*aut*, vili.)

6. Misit igitur Jehova in populum serpentes urentes, qui momorderunt populum: ita ut moreretur populus multus ex Israele.

7. Tunc venit populus ad Mosen, et dixerunt, Peccavimus, quia loquuti sumus contra Jehovam et contra te: ora Jehovam ut auferat à nobis serpentes istos. Et oravit Moses pro populo.

8. Et dixit Jehova ad Mosen, Fac tibi urentem, et pone eum super vexillum: et erit, quicunque morsus fuerit, et aspexerit illum, tunc vivet.

9. Fecit ergo Moses serpentem æneum, quem posuit supra vexillum: et fuit, quando momorderat serpens quenquam, aspiciebat ad serpentem æneum, et vivebat.

4. *And they journeyed from mount Hor.* This also is narrated in their praise, that they bore the weariness of a long and circuitous march, when they were already worn down by their wanderings for forty years. Moses, therefore, tells us that, since God had forbidden them to pass the borders of Edom, they went by another way; but immediately afterwards he adds, that they basely rebelled, without being provoked to do so by any new cause. They had before been rebellious under the pressure of hunger or thirst, or some other inconvenience; but now, when there

were no grounds for doing so, they malignantly exasperate themselves against God. Some understand that they were afflicted in mind because of the way,[1] so that the ב, *beth*, indicates the cause of their grief and trouble. It might, indeed, be the case that their passage through the mountains was steep and difficult; but a pleasant region was almost in sight, gently to attract them onward. Again, they falsely complain of want of water, in which respect God had already applied a remedy. Nothing, then, could be more unfair than odiously to recall to memory a past evil, in which they had experienced the special aid of God. But their depravity is more thoroughly laid open in their loathing of the manna, as a food affording but little nutriment, or contemptible.

The verb[2] קצר, *katzar*, is used first, which signifies to *constrain;* thus some explain it, that they were rendered anxious by distress. But since the same word is used for to *shorten*, others translate it that their minds were broken down with weariness, so as to faint by the way. In any case, a voluntary bitterness is indicated, whereby they were possessed, so that their alacrity in advancing altogether failed them. The verb[3] קצה, *katzah*, which Jerome renders *sickens*, is not used simply for disgust, but signifies that weariness which excruciates or agonizes the mind.

They call the manna "light" food; as much as to say that it inflates rather than satisfies or nourishes; or, as I deem more probable, the word קלקל, *kelokel*, is used metaphorically for vile, or contemptible, and valueless.

[1] *Heb.*, בדרך. *Lat.*, in viâ. *A. V.*, "because of the way." "*In* often noteth the cause of a thing; as, 'the Lord's soul was grieved in (*that is*, for, *or* because of) the misery of Israel,' Judg. x. 16; or, according to the like phrase in Zech. xi. 8, their soul 'loatheth the way,' both for the longsomeness of it, and for the many wants and troubles they found therein."—Ainsworth *in loco.*

[2] *A. V.*, "discouraged;" *margin*, "*or*, grieved; *Heb.* shortened." קצר, To shorten, to cut short, to cut off, and hence to reap. *S. M.* says, "Their spirit was shortened, *i.e.*, became impatient; being a species of antithesis to longanimity, or long forbearing."—*W.*

[3] *A. V.*, "loatheth." קצה is likewise *to cut off*, but is said by the lexicographers to borrow a meaning in this instance from קוץ, to *loathe*, and *be weary of*. It would be simpler to say that קצה is the præt. 3d. pers. of קוץ, and that a feminine verb is required by the subs. נפשנו.—*W.*

5. *And the people spake against God and against Moses.* Either because they murmured against God in the person of Moses, or else because their impiety broke forth to such a furious extent, that they openly blasphemed against God; and this latter opinion is most in accordance with the words, because by their use of the plural number they accuse two parties together.[1] But, inasmuch as Moses had nothing separate from God, no one could enter into a contest with him without warring also against God Himself. Here, however, as I have said, their insolence proceeded still further, so as not only to rail against the minister, but to vomit forth also their wicked blasphemy against God Himself, as if He had injured them most grossly by their deliverance.

6. *And the Lord sent fiery serpents.* Their ingratitude was justly and profitably chastised by this punishment; for they were practically taught that it was only through God's paternal care that they had been previously free from innumerable evils, and that He was possessed of manifold forms of punishment, whereby to take vengeance on the wicked.

Although deserts are full of many poisonous animals, still it is probable that these serpents suddenly arose, and were created for this special purpose; as if God, in His determination to correct the people's pride, should call into being new enemies to trouble them. For they were made to feel how great their folly was to rebel against God, when they were not able to cope with the serpents. This, then, was an admirable plan for humbling them, contemptuously to bring these serpents into the field against them, and thus to convince them of their weakness. Consequently, they both confess their guilt and acknowledge that there was no other remedy for them except to obtain pardon from God. These two things, as we are aware, are necessary in order to appease God, first, that the sinner should be dissatisfied with himself and self-condemned; and, secondly, that he should seek to be reconciled to God. The people seem faithfully to fulfil both of these conditions, when they of

[1] Addition in *Fr.*, "sinon qu'ils s'addressent aussi à Aaron;" unless they also address Aaron.

their own accord acknowledge their guilt, and humbly have recourse to God's mercy. It is through the influence of terror that they implore the prayers of Moses, since they count themselves unworthy of favour, unless an advocate (*patronus*) should intercede for them. This would, indeed, be erroneous, that those who are conscience-struck should invite an intercessor to stand between them and God, unless they, too, should unite their own prayers with his; for nothing is more contrary to faith than such a state of alarm as prevents us from calling upon God. Still the kindness of Moses, and his accustomed gentleness is perceived by this, that he is so readily disposed to listen to these wicked ones; and God also, on His part, shews that the prayer of a righteous man is not unavailing, when He heals the wound He had inflicted.[1]

8. *Make thee a fiery serpent.* Nothing would, at first sight, appear more unreasonable than that a brazen serpent should be made, the sight of which should extirpate the deadly poison; but this apparent absurdity was far better suited to render the grace of God conspicuous than as if there had been anything natural in the remedy. If the serpents had been immediately removed, they would have deemed it to be an accidental occurrence, and that the evil had vanished by natural means. If, in the aid afforded, anything had been applied, bearing an affinity to fit and appropriate remedies, then also the power and goodness of God would have been thrown into the shade. In order, therefore, that they might perceive themselves to be rescued from death by the mere grace of God alone, a mode of preservation was chosen so discordant with human reason, as to be almost a subject for laughter. At the same time it had the effect of trying the obedience of the people, to prescribe a mode of seeking preservation, which brought all their senses into subjection and captivity. It was a foolish thing to turn the eyes to a serpent of brass, to prevent the ill effects of a poisonous bite; for what, according to man's judgment, could a lifeless statue, lifted up on high, profit? But it is the peculiar virtue of faith, that we should willingly be fools,

[1] Addition in *Fr.*, "si tost;" so speedily.

in order that we may learn to be wise only from the mouth of God. This afterwards more clearly appeared in the substance of this type: for, when Christ compares Himself to this serpent which Moses lifted up in the wilderness, (John iii. 14,) it was not a mere common similitude which He employs, but He teaches us, that what had been shewn forth in this dark shadow, was completed in Himself. And, surely, unless the brazen serpent had been a symbol of spiritual grace, it would not have been laid up like a precious treasure, and diligently preserved for many ages in God's sanctuary. The analogy, also, is very perfect; since Christ, in order to rescue us from death, put on our flesh, not, indeed, subject to sin, but representing "the likeness of sinful flesh," as Paul says. (Rom. viii. 3.) Hence follows, what I have above adverted to, that since "the world by wisdom knew not God," He was manifested in the foolishness of the cross. (1 Cor. i. 21.) If, then, we desire to obtain salvation, let us not be ashamed to seek it from the curse of Christ, which was typified in the image of the serpent.

Its lifting up is poorly and incorrectly, in my opinion, explained by some, as foreshadowing the crucifixion,[1] whereas it ought rather to be referred to the preaching of the Gospel: for Moses was commanded to set up the serpent on high, that it might be conspicuous on every side. And the word נס, *nes*, is used both for a standard, and the mast of a ship, or any other high pole: which is in accordance with the prophecy of Isaiah, where he says that Christ should be "for an ensign" to all nations, (Isa. xi. 10:) which we know to have been the case, by the spreading of the doctrine of the Gospel through the whole world, with which the look of faith corresponds. For, just as no healing was conveyed from the serpent to any who did not turn their eyes towards

[1] *C.* here is opposed to the great body of the commentators, although he has with him "some of reverent account in the Church," as Attersoll calls them. Perhaps it may be admissible to include, with Lampe, both views: "*Exaltatio* serpentis hujus in *pertica* primo quidem designat exaltationem in cruce, ita tamen ut pertica simul possit emblema gerere præconii Evangelici, per quod Christus crucifixus mundo innotuit."—In Johan. iii. 14.

it, when set up on high, so the look of faith only causes the death of Christ to bring salvation to us. Although, therefore, God would give relief to their actual distress, it is still unquestionable that He even then admonished all believers that the venomous bites of the devil could only be cured by their directing their minds and senses by faith on Christ.

The brazen serpent is, furthermore, a proof to us how inclined to superstition the human race is, since posterity worshipped it as an idol, until it was reduced to powder by the holy king Hezekiah. (1 Kings xviii. 4.)

10. And the children of Israel set forward, and pitched in Oboth.

11. And they journeyed from Oboth, and pitched at Ije-abarim, in the wilderness which is before Moab, toward the sun-rising.

12. From thence they removed, and pitched in the valley of Zared.

13. From thence they removed, and pitched on the other side of Arnon, which *is* in the wilderness that cometh out of the coasts of the Amorites: for Arnon *is* the border of Moab, between Moab and the Amorites.

14. Wherefore it is said in the book of the wars of the Lord, What he did in the Red sea, and in the brooks of Arnon.

15. And at the stream of the brooks that goeth down to the dwelling of Ar, and lieth upon the border of Moab,

16. And from thence *they went* to Beer: that *is* the well whereof the Lord spake unto Moses, Gather the people together, and I will give them water.

11. Then Israel sang this song, Spring up, O well; sing ye unto it:

18. The princes digged the well, the nobles of the people digged it, by *the direction of* the lawgiver, with their staves. And from the wilderness *they went* to Mattanah;

19. And from Mattanah to Nahaliel; and from Nahaliel to Bamoth;

20. And from Bamoth *in* the valley, that *is* in the country of

10. Et profecti sunt filii Israel, et castrametati sunt in Oboth.

11. Profecti verò ex Oboth castrametati sunt in Ije-abarim in deserto, quod erat in conspectu Moab ab ortu solis.

12. Inde profecti castrametati sunt in valle Zered.

13. Profecti deinde illinc castrametati sunt citra Arnon, quæ est in deserto, et portenditur à termino Emorrhæi. Arnon enim est terminus Moab inter Moab et Emorrhæum.

14. Idcirco dicetur in narratione præliorum Jehovæ, Vaheb in Suphah, et torrentes ad Arnon.

15. Et decursum torrentium, qui pergit ut quiescat in Ar, et recumbit in termino Moab.

16. Illinc in Beer. Is est puteus de quo dixerat Jehova ad Mosen, Congrega populum, et dabo illis aquam.

17. Tunc cecinit Israel carmen hoc, Ascende Beer, canite ei.

18. Puteus quem foderunt principes, foderunt eum principes populi cum legislatore baculis suis. Et è deserto in Mathanah.

19. Et è Mathanah in Nahaliel: et de Nahaliel in Bamoth.

20. Et de Bamoth Hagaie, quæ est in regione Moab, in vertice collis,

Moab, to the top of Pisgah, which looketh toward Jeshimon.	et respicit contra faciem deserti, (*vel*, Gessimon.)

10. *And the children of Israel set forth.* Moses does not here enumerate all the stations, which will be mentioned hereafter, when he recapitulates them all separately and in order: for, in hastening to record certain memorable circumstances, he passes over those of minor importance, which, however, he does not omit elsewhere; since the account of their circuitous course, when they were turning away from the Edomites, was of some moment. For it was, as we have observed, no ordinary proof of obedience, when God had forbidden them to attack the Edomites, that they should undertake a difficult and rugged march. Still in this place Moses deemed it sufficient to mark the principal places in which they stopped. Meanwhile, what I have stated appears to be the case, that he hastens onwards to relate circumstances of much importance, for, when they came to Arnon, he highly magnifies the power of God, with which He succoured His people.

13. *From thence they removed, and pitched.* I will presently add, what Moses relates in Deuteronomy respecting the Moabites and Ammonites. Since here he only briefly touches upon the main facts, he only specifies that the people came to the borders of their enemies, where it was necessary to give battle, because there was no means of entering the land of Canaan, except by force of arms. Here, then, was the end of their journeying, for, when the Amorites were conquered, they began to inhabit their cities. He, therefore, immediately adds, that this place would be memorable in all ages, because in it God again exerted His power, by putting to flight their enemies. Still translators appear to me to be mistaken as to the meaning of the words. Almost all of them render the word ספר, *sepher*, "the book;" and afterwards eagerly discuss what book it is, without coming to any satisfactory conclusion. I rather understand it to mean "narration;" as if Moses had said, that when the wars of Jehovah shall be recounted, the memory of this place would be celebrated; as David, when he is recounting, and magnifying God's mercies,

expressly mentions that king Sihon and Og were conquered.

There is also another ambiguity in the following words: for some suppose *Vaheb* to be the proper name of a city, and *Suphah* a noun common, which they translate "in a whirlwind;"[1] but, since the shore of the Red Sea was not habitable, I do not see how mention could be suitably made of any city situated there. But if they think it was a city near Arnon, it is surprising that it should never be spoken of elsewhere, and yet here referred to, as if it were well known. I therefore rather incline to their opinion, who explain it as a verb, and suppose that ו (*vau*) is used for י (*yod*,) so that the sense should be; As God had begun to fight gloriously for the Israelites at the Red Sea, so also He continued the same grace at Arnon. I admit, that if the points be scrupulously insisted upon, this meaning would not be altogether accordant with grammar; but I prefer eliciting a probable meaning at the cost of a single point, than to go out of the way in search of poor conjectures, as they do who imagine *Vaheb* to be the proper name of a place. Appropriately, indeed, does Moses compare Arnon with the Red Sea, in order to shew that God's grace, at its end, is thoroughly in accordance with its commencement. He had mightily fought against the Egyptians, and had destroyed the army of Pharaoh in the Red Sea, but small would have been the fruit of this deliverance, unless, with equal efficacy, He had succoured His people when they had to contend with the Canaanitish nations: for the question

[1] את־והב בסופה *eth-vaheb b'suphah.* None of the most ancient translations can be said to be in unison with the present reading of the Hebrew in this clause. The *LXX.* appear to have read זהב, and render it τὴν Ζωὸβ ἐφλόγισε. The Chaldee Paraphrast, Onkelos, has על ימא דסוף, "By the sea of Suph," *i.e.*, the Red Sea. The Syriac has, "A flame with a whirlwind," translating סופה, instead of treating it as a proper name, and having apparently read some form of להב instead of את־והב. The *V.* has, "Sicut fecit in mari rubro;" our *A.V.* "What he did in the Red Sea," but in the Margin, "Vaheb in Suphah." The translation of *S. M.* agrees with that in the text of *A.V.;* but in his notes he says, "Kimchi interprets והב to be the name of a place, but R. Salomon treats it as equivalent to יהב, *he gave*, and expounds the clause thus, As God gave many signs by the Red Sea, so was He wonderful in his works by the brook Arnon.—*W.*

here is not as to God's blessings in general, but only as to the victories, wherein it was manifested that the Israelites did not fight without the approval and guidance of God. Moses, therefore, does not recount the miracles performed in the desert: but only says, that in the history of the wars of God the name of Arnon would be equally renowned with that of the Red Sea. Still, in the word Arnon it must be observed that there is a *synecdoche;* for Moses comprehends in it all the subsequent battles. Since, therefore, from the time that the people arrived at Arnon, where their enemies came forth to meet them, God again lifted up His standard, and gloriously honoured His people by continued victories—hence the special celebrity of the place arose. There is a poetical repetition in the verse, where, for the torrents, the stream of the torrents[1] is spoken of, which descends to Ar, and reposes in the border of Moab.

16. *And from thence* they went *to Beer.* Some think that a circumstance is here narrated, which had never been mentioned before, since a song is recorded, which we do not find elsewhere. But since Moses repeats the same words which he had used before, and speaks as of a very notorious matter, that he was there commanded to assemble the people, to partake of the water which God had given, it appears probable to me that the name was given to the place, whereby both God's goodness and the people's ingratitude might be testified to posterity. I do not, however, contend that this is the same place, from whence we previously read that water was extracted: for it was not there only that the people was satisfied by drinking it, but it flowed forth beside them wherever they went. In which sense Paul writes that "the Rock followed them," (1 Cor. x. 4;) not that the rock was torn from its roots, but because God miraculously drew on the water which flowed from it, so that it should accompany them, and thus continually supply them with drink. And this we gather also from the next verse, where Moses says, that the people "sang this song, Ascend, Beer."[2] For when they saw that, contrary to nature, the

[1] *A.V.* "the brooks"—"the stream of the brooks."
[2] See *Margin A.V.* The original word for a well is באר, *Beer.—W.*

water rose into higher levels from the source which was recently called into existence, so as to supply them with drink in dry places, they began to pay more attention to the miracle, and to celebrate the grace of God. Still it might be the case that the water did not flow down like a river, but bubbled up from the open veins of the earth, whenever it was required. At any rate, by its ascent he indicates an extraordinary effect produced by God. When it is said, that "the princes digged the well," there is, in my opinion, an implied contrast between a few persons, and those but little fitted for manual labours, and a great body of engineers. Whenever armies have need of water, the soldiers dig wells with much labour; here quite another mode of proceeding is expressed, viz., that the leaders of the people, together with Moses, dug the well, not by artificial or mechanical means, but by the simple touch of a staff. Moses, indeed, speaks of "staves," in the plural number, because mention of the princes is made; but I have no doubt but that the rod of Moses is contrasted with all other implements, in order to exalt the power and grace of God. I think, too, that the name of Beer was given to the place, where that water forsook the Israelites; since they had come to well-watered regions, which would supply water in abundance without miraculous interference. Let us, however, learn from this canticle, that, although the people had at first impiously rebelled against God, still, by long experience of the blessing, they were at length induced to gratitude, so as to burst forth into praise of God. Hence we gather, that they were not obstinate in their senselessness.

DEUTERONOMY, CHAPTER II.

9. And the Lord said unto me, Distress not the Moabites, neither contend with them in battle: for I will not give thee of their land *for* a possession; because I have given Ar unto the children of Lot *for* a possession.

10. The Emims dwelt therein in

9. Et dixit mihi Jehova, Ne oppugnes Moab, neque lacessas eum bello, quia non dabo tibi è terra ejus possessionem; filiis enim Lot dedi Ar in hæreditatem.

10. Emim antea habitabant in

times past, a people great, and many, and tall, as the Anakims;

11. Which also were accounted giants, as the Anakims; but the Moabites call them Emims.

12. The Horims also dwelt in Seir beforetime; but the children of Esau succeeded them, when they had destroyed them from before them, and dwelt in their stead, as Israel did unto the land of his possession, which the Lord gave unto them.

13. Now rise up, *said I,* and get you over the brook Zered: and we went over the brook Zered.

14. And the space in which we came from Kadesh-barnea, until we were come over the brook Zered, *was* thirty and eight years; until all the generation of the men of war were wasted out from among the host, as the Lord sware unto them.

15. For indeed the hand of the Lord was against them, to destroy them from among the host, until they were consumed.

16. So it came to pass, when all the men of war were consumed and dead from among the people,

17. That the Lord spake unto me, saying,

18. Thou art to pass over through Ar, the coast of Moab, this day:

19. And *when* thou comest nigh over against the children of Ammon, distress them not, nor meddle with them: for I will not give thee of the land of the children of Ammon *any* possession, because I have given it unto the children of Lot *for* a possession.

20. (That also was accounted a land of giants: giants dwelt therein in old time; and the Ammonites call them Zamzummims;

21. A people great, and many, and tall, as the Anakims; but the Lord destroyed them before them, and they succeeded them, and dwelt in their stead:

22. As he did to the children of Esau which dwelt in Seir, when he destroyed the Horims from before them; and they succeeded them, and

ea, populus magnus et multus, et excelsus, sicut Anacim.

11. Gigantes reputabantur etiam ipsi sicut Anacim; et Moabitæ vocarunt eos Emim.

12. In Seir autem habitaverunt Horim antea, quos filii Esau expulerunt, et perdiderunt à facie sua, habitaveruntque loco ipsorum, quemadmodum Israel in terra possessionis suæ quam dedit illis Jehova.

13. Nunc surgite et transite torrentem Zered: et transivimus torrentem Zered.

14. Dies autem quibus ambulavimus de Cades-barnea, donec transiremus torrentem Zered, fuerunt triginta-octo anni, donec consumeretur tota generatio virorum bellatorum de medio castrorum, quemadmodum juraverat Jehova illis.

15. Præterea manus Jehovæ fuit in eos, ut perderet eos è medio castrorum, donec consumeret eos.

16. Et fuit, postquam consumpti fuerunt omnes viri bellatores, ut morerentur è medio populi.

17. Tunc loquutus est Jehova ad me, dicendo:

18. Tu transiturus es hodie terminum Moab, nempe Ar.

19. Et accedes ad viciniam filiorum Ammon, ne obsideas eos, neque irrites eos, quia non daturus sum tibi de terra filiorum Ammon possessionem aliquam: nam filiis Lot dedi illam in possessionem.

20. Terra gigantum reputata fuit etiam ipsa: gigantes habitaverunt in ea olim, quos Ammonitæ vocabant Zamzumim.

21. Populus magnus et multus et excelsus sicut Anacim: et perdidit eos Jehova à facie eorum, possederuntque eos, et habitaverunt loco ipsorum.

22. Quemadmodum fecit filiis Esau, habitantibus in Seir, propter quos disperdidit Horæos à facie eorum, et possederunt eos, habitave-

dwelt in their stead, even unto this day:	runtque loco ipsorum usque in hanc diem.
23. And the Avims which dwelt in Hazerim, *even* unto Azzah, the Caphtorims, which came forth out of Caphtor, destroyed them, and dwelt in their stead.)	23. Et Avæos qui habitabant in Haserim usque Azzah, Caphthorim qui egressi sunt de Caphthor, perdiderunt eos, et habitaverunt loco ipsorum.

9. *And the Lord said unto me, Distress not the Moabites.* He had previously forbidden them to enter the land of Edom, unless consent were obtained. A similar prohibition is now added with respect to the Moabites, because God had allotted to them the territory which they inhabited. As I have said, this was painful and burdensome, that they should cherish kindness and fraternal good-will towards those who treated them with hostility; but God desired in this respect also to prove the obedience of His people. He did not, then, take into consideration what this nation had deserved; but, inasmuch as they were the descendants of Lot, and consequently of the race of Abraham, He desired to treat them with special favour. For the division of the whole world appertains to Him, so as to distribute to its various peoples whatever part He chooses, and to fix the bounds wherein they should confine themselves. If any object that the people of Canaan had also their limits assigned to them, and ought not, therefore, to have been expelled from the lands in which their forefathers had for many ages inhabited, the reply is easy, viz., that God is always free to take away what He has given, and to readjust the boundaries imposed by His will, when the sins of men deserve that this should be done. When, therefore, He declares that He had given their land to the Moabites, it is not according to the ordinary force of the expression, but by a fixed decree that their habitation should remain sure and undisturbed.

10. *The Emims dwelt therein in times past.* This is a confirmation of the foregoing declaration, which is, however, inserted by way of parenthesis by Moses himself; for the ninth verse, which I have just expounded, is followed regularly by the thirteenth, "Now rise up," &c. For, after God had turned away the people from the borders of Moab, He shews them in what direction they must pass over; but

Moses, interrupting the address of God, explains how the Moabites had obtained that territory, though they were strangers, and had no land of their own on which they might set their foot. For Lot was no less an alien than Abraham; Moses, therefore, states how by special privilege the posterity of Lot became masters of that land which giants had previously possessed. For it was not by human means that, having driven out the giants, who were formidable to all men, they had obtained the peaceful occupation, and even the dominion of that land, which might have seemed to be invincible, from the valour and strength of its inhabitants. He says, therefore, that the giants dwelt there, as also in Mount Seir; and that both were overcome and destroyed, not so much by the hand and arms of men as by the power of God, so that their land might be cleared for possession as well for the children of Esau as for those of Lot. Now, since God elsewhere declares that He had given Mount Seir to Esau as an inheritance, according as He had promised to his father Isaac, it follows that the Moabites had obtained their land also by the same Divine authority. The comparison which is made between Edom and the Israelites does not hold good in all respects; for, although Esau was sustained by this consolation, that his inheritance should be of "the fatness of the earth," (Gen. xxvii. 39,) it might still be the case that with regard to himself and his posterity, their possession should not be legitimate; whereas God so promised the land of Canaan to the race of Abraham, that the Israelites received the dominion over it, as if from His own hand, as it is said in Psalm cxxxvi. 21. In this respect, too, there was a difference, because the land of Canaan was chosen as that in which God should gather His Church, in which He should be purely worshipped, and which should be an earnest to the faithful of the heavenly and eternal rest. But, as elsewhere, the distinction between the sons of Esau and Jacob is marked, so now Moses[1] magnifies God's special blessing towards them both.

[1] "Moyse dit ici qu'ils ont eu cela de commun, que Dieu les a voulu loger;" Moses says here that they had this in common, that God had chosen to give them their dwelling-places.—*Fr.*

13. *Now rise up.* He now proceeds with what he had begun in verse 9, viz., that God had commanded them to pass by the land of Seir, and to advance to the brook Zered; as much as to say, that after they had been subdued by their misfortunes, they were prohibited from further progress, until God should open the way before them, and thus they should follow Him as their leader, and not make a passage for themselves at their own discretion.

He afterwards specifies the period of delay which they had been compelled by God to pass in the desert, after they had once reached the borders of the promised land. He says, then, that after thirty-eight years they had at length returned to the land from whence they had been obliged to retire; and briefly reminds them how long the course of their deliverance had been interrupted through their own fault, since they had gone forth to enjoy the promised land. He calls those "warlike men," or, in the Hebrew, "men of war," whose age entitled them to bear arms, *i.e.*, who had exceeded their twentieth year.

When mention is elsewhere made of forty years, the two years are then included which were spent both in Mount Sinai and in other places; and with good reason, because, during that time also, their sins prevented them from passing to the enjoyment of their inheritance immediately after the promulgation of the law.

19. *And when thou comest nigh over against the children of Ammon.* God now makes provision as to the Ammonites, since their condition was the same as that of the Moabites, inasmuch as they were descended from the two daughters of Lot. It might, indeed, seem wonderful that, since the memory of their origin was detestable, these two nations should have been so dear to God. Ammon and Moab had been born of an incestuous connexion. It was, therefore, more reasonable that this tragical circumstance should have been buried by their destruction, than that they should have been distinguished by God's favour from the common lot of other nations, as if their nobility rendered them superior to others. But let us learn from hence, that since God's judgments, like a deep abyss, are beyond our apprehension,

they should be regarded with reverence. Lot's distinguished piety is expressly declared. The disgraceful crime, which he committed when drunk, it pleased God so to mark with perpetual infamy, as still to impress upon it some signs of His mercy, although this was done especially for the sake of Abraham himself. It is unquestionable, however, that God recommends the posterity of Lot to the Israelites on this ground, that they may more willingly exercise kindness towards them, and abstain from all injury, when they had to do with two nations whom they see to be cared for by God Himself, for the sake of their common relationship to Abraham.

Furthermore, by the same argument whereby he had before proved that both Edomites and Moabites, relying on God's help, had occupied the lands over which they had dominion, he now establishes that the land which the Ammonites possessed had been granted them by God, viz., because in their conquest and overthrow of the giants they had surpassed the limits of human bravery, and thus God had given a proof of His special and unusual favour towards them. For neither by the ordinary course of nature could two men increase to so great a multitude.

Now, although the Hebrews call the Cappadocians *Caphthorim*,[1] we do not know whether the giants, whose country was taken possession of by the Ammonites, sprung from them. But, if this be admitted, they had a long journey, attended by many dangers, after they left their country; and again, since they must have passed through rich and fertile regions, it is strange that they should have penetrated to those mountains. It might, however, be the case, that, making forays as robbers, they nowhere found a quiet resting-place until a less cultivated region presented itself.

[1] Bochart remarks that all ancient writers are unanimous in supposing Caphthor to be Cappadocia, and the Caphthorim Cappadocians; but he assigns to them that part of Cappadocia only which bordered on Colchis. *Phaleg.* Book iv. chap. xxxii.—See *C.* on Jer. xlvii. 4, *C. Soc. Edit.*, vol. iv. p. 614.

NUMBERS, CHAPTER XXI.

21. And Israel sent messengers unto Sihon king of the Amorites, saying,

22. Let me pass through thy land: we will not turn into the fields, or into the vineyards; we will not drink *of* the waters of the well; *but* we will go along by the king's *high*-way, until we be past thy borders.

23. And Sihon would not suffer Israel to pass through his border; but Sihon gathered all his people together, and went out against Israel into the wilderness: and he came to Jahaz, and fought against Israel.

24. And Israel smote him with the edge of the sword, and possessed his land from Arnon unto Jabbok, even unto the children of Ammon: for the border of the children of Ammon *was* strong.

25. And Israel took all these cities: and Israel dwelt in all the cities of the Amorites, in Heshbon, and in all the villages thereof.

26. For Heshbon *was* the city of Sihon the king of the Amorites, who had fought against the former king of Moab, and taken all his land out of his hand, even unto Arnon.

27. Wherefore they that speak in proverbs say, Come into Heshbon, let the city of Sihon be built and prepared;

28. For there is a fire gone out of Heshbon, a flame from the city of Sihon: it hath consumed Ar of Moab, *and* the lords of the high places of Arnon.

29. Woe to thee, Moab! thou art undone, O people of Chemosh! he hath given his sons that escaped, and his daughters, into captivity, unto Sihon king of the Amorites.

30. We have shot at them: Heshbon is perished even unto Dibon, and we have laid them waste even unto Nophah, which *reacheth* unto Medeba.

31. Thus Israel dwelt in the land of the Amorites.

21. Misit Israel legatos ad Sihon regem Æmorrhæorum, dicendo:

22. Transeam per terram tuam: non declinabimus per agros, neque per vineam: non bibemus aquas puteorum, via regia pergemus, donec transierimus terminum tuum.

23. At non permisit Sihon Israeli ut transiret per terminum suum. Itaque congregavit Sihon universum populum suum, et egressus est obviam Israeli in desertum, venitque in Jahaz et pugnavit cum Israele.

24. Et percussit eum Israel in ore gladii, et hæreditate accepit terram ejus ab Arnon usque ad Jabbok usque ad filios Ammon: quia munitus erat terminus filiorum Ammon.

25. Et accepit Israel omnes istas urbes, et habitavit Israel in omnibus urbibus Æmorrhæi, in Hesbon, et in omnibus oppidis ejus.

26. Hesbon erat urbs Sihon regis Æmorrhæi. Nam ipse pugnaverat contra regem Moab primùm, et acceperat omnem terram ejus è manu usque ad Arnon.

27. Idcirco dicunt parabolicè loquentes, Venite in Hesbon, ædificetur et instauretur urbs ipsi Sihon:

28. Quia ignis egressus est de Hesbon, et flamma ex urbe Sihon consumpsit Ar Moab et dominos excelsorum Arnon.

29. Væ tibi Moab, periisti popule Chemos, dedit filios suos in fugam, et filias suas in captivitatem regis Æmorrhæi Sihon.

30. Et lucerna eorum periit ab Hesbon usque ad Dibon, et delevimus usque ad Nophah, quæ est ad Medebah.

31. Habitavit itaque Israel in terra Æmorrhæi.

32. And Moses sent to spy out Jaazer, and they took the villages thereof, and drove out the Amorites that *were* there.

32. Misit deinde Moses ad explorandum Jaazer, et ceperunt oppida ejus, et expulit Æmorrhæum qui erat ibi.

A Repetition of the same History.

DEUT. II. 24. Rise ye up, take your journey, and pass over the river Arnon: behold, I have given into thine hand Sihon the Amorite, king of Heshbon, and his land; begin to possess *it*, and contend with him in battle.

25. This day will I begin to put the dread of thee, and the fear of thee, upon the nations *that are* under the whole heaven, who shall hear report of thee, and shall tremble, and be in anguish because of thee.

26. And I sent messengers out of the wilderness of Kedemoth unto Sihon king of Heshbon, with words of peace, saying,

27. Let me pass through thy land: I will go along by the high-way, I will neither turn unto the right hand nor to the left.

28. Thou shalt sell me meat for money, that I may eat; and give me water for money, that I may drink: only I will pass through on my feet,

29. (As the children of Esau which dwell in Seir, and the Moabites which dwell in Ar, did unto me,) until I shall pass over Jordan, into the land which the Lord our God giveth us.

30. But Sihon king of Heshbon would not let us pass by him: for the Lord thy God hardened his spirit, and made his heart obstinate, that he might deliver him into thy hand, as *appeareth* this day.

31. And the Lord said unto me, Behold, I have begun to give Sihon and his land before thee: begin to possess, that thou mayest inherit his land.

32. Then Sihon came out against us, he and all his people, to fight at Jahaz.

24. Surgite, proficiscimini, et transite torrentem Arnon. Vide, dedi in manum tuam Sihon regem Hesbon, Æmorrhæum et terram ejus, incipe possidere, et dimica prælio cum eo.

25. Hodie incipiam dare pavorem tui et formidinem tui super faciem populorum qui sunt sub toto cœlo, qui audierunt famam tuam, et pavebunt, timebuntque a facie tua.

26. Et misi nuntios è deserto Cedemoth ad Sihon regem Hesbon verbis pacificis, dicendo:

27. Transeam per terram tuam, per viam ambulabo, non declinabo ad dexteram nec ad sinistram.

28. Cibum argento vendes mihi ut comedam: aquam argento dabis mihi ut bibam, tantum transibo pedibus meis:

29. Quemadmodum fecerunt mihi filii Esau qui habitant in Seir, et Moabitæ qui habitant in Ar: donec transiero Jordanem ad terram quam Jehova Deus noster dat nobis.

30. Et noluit Sihon rex Hesbon ut transiremus per sua. Induraverat enim Jehova Deus tuus spiritum ejus: et obfirmaverat cor ejus, ut daret eum in manu tua, ut hodie est.

31. Dixit autem Jehova ad me, Vide, jam cœpi dare coram te Sihon, et terram ejus, incipe possidere, ut possideas terram ejus.

32. Egressus est autem Sihon in occursum nostrum ipse et universus populus ejus ad prælium in Jahaz.

33. And the Lord our God delivered him before us; and we smote him, and his sons, and all his people.	33. Et tradidit illum Jehova Deus noster coram nobis, percussimusque eum et filios ejus, et totum populum ejus.
34. And we took all his cities at that time, and utterly destroyed the men, and the women, and the little ones, of every city; we left none to remain:	34. Cepimus quoque omnes urbes ejus eo tempore, et destruximus omnes urbes, viros et mulieres, et parvulos: non reliquimus superstitem.
35. Only the cattle we took for a prey unto ourselves, and the spoil of the cities which we took.	35. Veruntamen jumenta prædati sumus nobis, et spolia urbium quas cepimus.
36. From Aroer, which *is* by the brink of the river of Arnon, and *from* the city that *is* by the river, even unto Gilead, there was not one city too strong for us: the Lord our God delivered all unto us.	36. Ab Aroer quæ est juxta ripam torrentis Arnon, et urbe quæ est in valle, usque ad Gillad, non fuit urbs quæ effugerit à nobis, omnes tradidit Jehova Deus noster coram nobis.
37. Only unto the land of the children of Ammon thou camest not, *nor* unto any place of the river Jabbok, nor unto the cities in the mountains, nor unto whatsoever the Lord our God forbade us.	37. Tantummodo ad terram filiorum Ammon non accessisti, omnem locum torrentis Jabboc, et urbes montanas, atque omnia de quibus præcepit Jehova Deus noster.

NUMB. XXI. 21. *And Israel sent messengers.* The second narration, which I have subjoined from Deuteronomy, is the fuller; nevertheless, a question arises from it, for what reason this embassy was sent to king Sihon, whose kingdom was already devoted to the Israelites: for it seems to be altogether inconsistent to offer conditions of peace when war is decreed. God commands His people to take up arms: He declares that they shall be victorious, so as to occupy the land of Sihon by right of war; what, then, can be more absurd than to request of him that they might pass through his land in peace? If this attempt were made by Moses without the command of God, such an excess of kindness was not devoid of guilt, inasmuch as it was an act of much temerity to promise what God had appointed otherwise. But, if we should say that the messengers went with the authority, and at the command of God, under what pretext shall the deceptiveness of the act be excused? for it is very improper to flatter with soothing words and promises those whom you have destined to destruction. The conclusion I come to is, that although the event was not unknown to God, still the embassy was sent, nevertheless, by His command

and decree, in order to lay open the obstinate ferocity of the nation. But, since the secret judgments of God far surmount our senses, let us learn to reverence their height; and let this sober view restrain our boldness like a rein, viz., that although the reason for the works of God be unknown to us, still it always exists with Him. God knew that the messengers would speak to the deaf, and yet it is not in vain that He bids them go; for, since the kingdom of Sihon was not properly included in the promised land, it was not lawful for the children of Israel to make war upon it until they had been provoked by an unjust refusal. Thus, then, I connect the history. Before they had been assured at God's command of the event, and the victory, they sent the messengers, who demanded that a pacific passage should be accorded to them; and that then the permission to have recourse to arms was granted. If any prefer to think that, before Moses attempted to preserve peace, he had been made acquainted with all that would occur, I will not contend the point; but I deem it more probable that he had expectations of the peace which he sought, because the judgment of God had not yet been declared. If, therefore, Sihon had allowed himself to be propitiated, Moses would never have dared to deal with him as an enemy; but he rather simply and honestly promised peace, which he intended to preserve; God, however, had otherwise appointed, as the event presently shewed. Still He was not inconsistent with Himself, or variable, in sending the messengers to an irreclaimable and obstinately perverse man; for thus was all excuse taken away when he had voluntarily provoked to war a people who were ready and willing to maintain peace and equity. But rather may we see in this history, as in a glass, that, whilst God earnestly invites the reprobate to repentance and the hope of salvation, He has no other object than that they may be rendered inexcusable by the detection of their impiety. Hence is their ignorance refuted, who gather from this that it is free for all promiscuously to embrace God's grace, because its promulgation (*doctrina*) is common, and directed to all without exception; as if God was not aware of what Sihon would answer when He would have him attracted to equity by friendly and peaceful words; or as if, on his free will, the purpose of God was suspended as to the war, which was soon after carried forward by His decree.

But inasmuch as what is here briefly recorded, would be obscure in itself, we must explain it by the other narrative, where it is thus written,—

DEUT. II. 24. *Rise ye up, take your journey.* I have lately said that the order is here inverted, for what soon after follows, "And I sent messengers out of the wilderness," &c., ver. 26, Moses, in my opinion, has inserted by way of parenthesis: it will, therefore, be suitably rendered in the pluperfect tense, "But I had sent," &c. Thus there will be no ambiguity in the sense that, when the messengers had returned without effecting their purpose, God sustained the weariness of the people by this consolation, as though He had said, Sihon has not, with impunity, repudiated the peace offered to him, since it will now be permitted you to assail him in lawful war. And assuredly this signal for the expedition to advance depends on the declaration which is subjoined in ver. 30, as we may readily gather from the context; for Moses there repeats what we here read respecting their passage in somewhat different words; and again does God testify that He has given Sihon into the hands of the people, and exhorts Moses to go down boldly to the battle. Moreover, the cause is there specified why (Sihon) had been so arrogant and contemptuous in his rejection of the embassy, viz., because God had "hardened his spirit, and made his heart obstinate." From whence again it appears how poor is the sophistry of those who imagine that God idly regards from heaven what men are about to do.[1] They dare not, indeed, despoil Him of foreknowledge; but what can be more absurd than that He foreknows nothing except what men please? But Scripture, as we see, has not placed God in a watch-tower, from which He may behold at a distance what things are about to be; but teaches that He is the director (*moderatorem*) of all things; and that He subjects to His will, not only the events of things, but the designs

[1] Addition in *Fr.*, "sans disposer de leur volonte;" without disposing their will.

and affections of men also. As, therefore, we have before seen how the heart of Pharaoh was hardened, so now Moses ascribes to God the obstinacy of king Sihon. How base a subterfuge is the exception which some make as to His *permission*, sufficiently appears from the end which Moses points out.[1] For why did God harden the heart of Sihon? that "He might deliver him into the hand" of His people to be slain; because He willed that he should perish, and had destined his land for the Israelites. If God only permitted Sihon to grow hardened, His decree was either nought, or mutable, and evanescent, since it depended on the changeable will of man. Putting aside, then, all childish trifling, we must conclude that God by His secret inspiration moves, forms, governs, and draws men's hearts, so that even by the wicked He executes whatever He has decreed. At the same time it is to be observed that the wicked are not impelled to hardness of heart by extrinsic force, but that they voluntarily harden themselves; so that in this same hardness of heart God may be seen to be a just judge, however incomprehensible His counsel may be, and however the impiety of men may betray itself, who are their own instigators, and the authors of their own sin. Emphatically does Moses inculcate the same thing twice over, viz., that the spirit of Sihon was hardened by God, and his heart made obstinate, in order that God's paternal favour towards His chosen people might be more conspicuous; because from the obstinacy of the blinded king He afforded them a just cause for war, and an opportunity for victory.

NUMB. XXI. 25.—*And Israel took all these cities.* As if speaking of something present, he uses the demonstrative pronoun, and says, "these cities," just as if he were pointing them out to the eyes of his readers. The word which we have rendered "towns" (*oppida*,)[2] others translate "country-

[1] "Or il appert par la fin que Moyse specifie combien ceste tergiversation est frivole, de dire que Dieu permet sans rien ordonner;" now, it appears by the end which Moses specifies, how frivolous is that subterfuge, to say that God permits without ordaining anything.—*Fr.*

[2] Par ce mot, que nous avons translaté *villages*, il nous faut aussi entendre les bourgades, et metairies;" by this word, which we have translated *villages*, we must also understand the hamlets and farm-houses.—*Fr.* See marg. *A. V.*

houses" (*villas,*) or "hamlets" (*viculos.*) In the Hebrew, Moses calls by the name of "daughters" all the villages and lesser towns, whose mother-city (*metropolis*) was Heshbon. By these words, however, Moses indicates that, by the right of war, all these places had fallen into the hands of the Israelites, as the lot of their inheritance; for, as I have lately said, God had not yet openly declared that they should be masters of this part of the country. They would consequently have over-passed their boundaries, unless these had been added to the land of Canaan. This is the reason why God openly declares that they possessed them by His authority. But when he says that the cities were destroyed, and all their inhabitants exterminated, so that neither women nor children were spared, let us understand that they dealt not thus cruelly of their own impulse, or in heedless violence, but that whatsoever was on the other side of Jordan was devoted to destruction by God, that they might always have their minds fixed on the promised land, and might never give way to listlessness, which would have been the case if an easy occupation of it had invited them to repose. Although, therefore, God delivered over the land to them hereafter, and suffered them to enrich themselves with its booty and spoils, yet He would not have it retained as a place of residence, and therefore commanded them to destroy its cities and villages, in order that they might seek their rest elsewhere. In fine, since they were abundantly disposed to be slothful, it was expedient that all snares should be removed, and that by the very desolation they might be urged forward whither God called them.

26. *For Heshbon was the city of Sihon.* It is not without cause that Moses relates how the country near Heshbon had passed into the hands of the Amorites, because a long time afterwards this was sought for as a pretext for war by the Ammonites, when they saw that the people were brought into a low estate. In the time of Jephthah, therefore, having collected a great army, an irruption was made by them; and they made this their excuse, that they took up arms to recover what was their own, from Arnon as far as Jabbok, and as far as Jordan. Consequently, God would have it

testified in the sacred records, as Jephthah then replied to the Ammonites, that this part of the land was taken from king Sihon, when the children of Israel were marching peacefully through the borders of the Ammonites. Designedly, then, did Moses, in order to sanction the right of the people, insert in these authentic registers, as it were, what had formerly occurred, namely, that the Amorites had had the dominion over that part of the country, without interference from the Ammonites; nor was there any question that the Amorites had secure and peaceful possession of it. Hence it follows that it passed to the Israelites, so that there were no grounds why, three hundred years afterwards, the Ammonites should reclaim what had so long been lost and abandoned by them. And, in order that posterity might know that there was then no obscurity about the matter, he records an ancient canticle, from which it appears that the Ammonites were so completely overcome, that their enemies triumphed magnificently over them, and cut off all hope of their restoration. Here, however, the question arises, why the king of Ammon, rather than the king of Moab, set on foot that war; for we clearly gather from the song, that the land was taken from the Moabites. But for men who are bent on rapine and robbery, it is sufficient to allege any trivial pretext, and often to glory in the rights of others. There doubtless remained a report that the Amorites had been driven out of their territories,[1] which they had obtained by force of arms. The Ammonites pass over in silence what had been forgotten in the lapse of many ages, and set up this false title, that, although the Israelites had conquered the Amorites, still their victory conferred upon them no right to occupy what the Amorites unjustly and forcibly held. With this object Moses inserted the account he here gives.

27. *Wherefore, they that speak in proverbs.* That is, an old saying, or proverbial sentence remains, and is well known. The song, however, appears to have been composed in the character of those who, when prepared to engage in war, mutually exhorted each other, "Come into Heshbon," *i. e.*, run to the standard of king Sihon; hasten to his home,

[1] "Par les enfans d'Israel;" by the children of Israel.—*Fr.*

and his chief place of abode, in order that we may thence go forth to battle. These expressions, "build and prepare," I interpret as being used for enlarge, adorn, and enrich; for it is probable that this city was not overthrown, but they foretell that the city would be renovated, when a larger dominion had been gained. And this is more fully confirmed by what immediately follows, when it is said that "a fire had gone forth from Heshbon," which consumed Ar of Moab, and all its neighbourhood. As to the "lords of the high places of Arnon," some understand the priests who presided in the temples; others extend them to all the inhabitants in general; but, in my opinion, it will not be unsuitable to refer them to the idols themselves, since it appears from the next verse that the conquerors were so insolently elated, as not only to despise the men themselves, but their gods also; for when they say, "Thou art undone, O people of Chemosh," there is no doubt but that they mockingly reproach them with the fact that they had been badly defended by the gods whom they worshipped.[1] And, in point of fact, ungodly men, when in prosperity, uplift their horns to heaven, as if they would assail the divinity which was opposed to them. They, therefore, deride Chemosh, because he made "his sons" or worshippers to be fugitives or captives.

In the word *lantern*[2] he makes use of a common metaphor. Some follow the Chaldee interpreter, and render it *kingdom;* but it has a wider signification; for it includes all the component parts of a happy and prosperous state.[3] The meaning, therefore, is, that their glory and all their wealth

[1] "Par Chamos, qu'ils adoroyent comme leur patron;" by Chemosh, whom they worshipped as their patron.—*Fr.*

[2] ונירם, *vaniram: A. V.*, "we have shot at them." Our translators have regarded ניר, the central syllable of this composite word, as the first future plural of ירה, *be shot* or *cast;* and *S. M.* has noticed this explanation as more probably right than the one which he has adopted in his text, and which supposes ניר to be a substantive, namely, a *lantern*. The Chaldee Paraphrast and the *V.* have regarded this substantive as a metaphor for the ruling power. If it had been a substantive, its place, in ordinary construction, should have been after the verb אבד, *perished*, whereas it precedes that verb, which has Heshbon following it, in the proper position for its nominative.—*W.*

[3] "Elle comprend les biens, l'honneur, le repos, et la reputation;" it comprehends goods, honour, repose, and reputation.—*Fr.*

was annihilated. The cities of Dibon and Medeba are situated on the extreme borders, near the river Arnon, so that by these he designates all the intermediate plain.

NUMBERS, CHAPTER XXI.

33. And they turned, and went up by the way of Bashan: and Og the king of Bashan went out against them, he, and all his people, to the battle at Edrei.

34. And the Lord said unto Moses, Fear him not: for I have delivered him into thy hand, and all his people, and his land; and thou shalt do to him as thou didst unto Sihon king of the Amorites, which dwelt at Heshbon.

35. So they smote him and his sons, and all his people, until there was none left him alive: and they possessed his land.

33. Conversi autem ascenderunt per viam Basan, et egressus est Og rex Basan in occursum ipsis, ipse et universus populus ejus ad prælium in Edrei.

34. Tunc dixit Jehova ad Mosen, Ne timeas eum: quia in manu tua dedi eum et universum populum ejus, ac terram ejus: faciesque ei quemadmodum fecisti Sihon regi Æmorrhæorum qui habitabat in Hesbon.

35. Et percusserunt eum et filios ejus, universumque populum ejus: ut non remanserit ei superstes: et possederunt terram ejus.

DEUT. III. 1. Then we turned, and went up the way to Bashan: and Og the king of Bashan came out against us, he and all his people, to battle at Edrei.

2. And the Lord said unto me, Fear him not: for I will deliver him, and all his people, and his land, into thy hand; and thou shalt do unto him as thou didst unto Sihon king of the Amorites, which dwelt at Heshbon.

3. So the Lord our God delivered into our hands Og also, the king of Bashan, and all his people: and we smote him, until none was left to him remaining.

4. And we took all his cities at that time; there was not a city which we took not from them, threescore cities, all the region of Argob, the kingdom of Og in Bashan.

5. All these cities *were* fenced with high walls, gates, and bars; besides unwalled towns a great many.

6. And we utterly destroyed them, as we did unto Sihon king of Hesh-

1. Conversi autem ascendimus per viam Basan et egressus est Og rex Basan nobis in occursum, ipse et universus populus ejus ad prælium in Edrei.

2. Et dixit Jehova ad me, Ne timeas illum, nam in manu tua dedi eum, et universum populum ejus, ac terram ejus: faciesque ei quemadmodum fecisti Sihon regi Æmorrhæorum qui habitabat in Hesbon.

3. Tradidit itaque Jehova Deus noster etiam Og regem Basan, et universum populum ejus: percussimus eum, ut non reliquerimus ei superstitem.

4. Cepimus quoque omnes urbes ejus eo tempore: non fuit urbs ulla quam non ceperimus ab eis, nempe sexaginta urbes, omnem regionem Argob regni Og, in Basan.

5. Omnes autem istæ urbes erant munitæ muris altis, portis et vectibus: præter urbes non muratas multas valdè.

6. Quas vastavimus, quemadmodum fecimus Sihon regi Hesbon,

bon, utterly destroying the men, women, and children, of every city.

7. But all the cattle, and the spoil of the cities, we took for a prey to ourselves.

8. And we took at that time, out of the hand of the two kings of the Amorites, the land that *was* on this side Jordan, from the river of Arnon unto mount Hermon;

9. (*Which* Hermon the Sidonians call Sirion, and the Amorites call it Shenir;)

10. All the cities of the plain, and all Gilead, and all Bashan, unto Salchah, and Edrei, cities of the kingdom of Og in Bashan:

11. For only Og king of Bashan remained of the remnant of giants; behold, his bedstead *was* a bedstead of iron: *is* it not in Rabbath of the children of Ammon? nine cubits *was* the length thereof, and four cubits the breadth of it, after the cubit of a man.

vastando omnem urbem, viros, mulieres, et parvulos.

7. Omnia autem jumenta et spolia urbium prædati sumus nobis.

8. Tulimus itaque eo tempore terram è manu duorum regum Emorrhæorum, quæ erat trans Jordanem, à torrente Arnon usque ad montem Hermon.

(9. Sidonii vocant Hermon, Sirion, et Emorrhæi vocant eum Senir.)

10. Omnes urbes planitiei, et totum Gilad, et omnem Basan usque ad Salchah, et Edrei, urbes regni Og in Basan.

11. Solus quippe Og rex Basan remanserat ex reliquis gigantibus: ecce lectus ejus, lectus ferreus, nonne est in Rabbath filiorum Ammon? novem cubitorum longitudo ejus, et quatuor cubitorum latitudo ejus ad cubitum hominis.

NUMB. XXI. 33. *And they turned and went up.* Here there is another victory of the people described, wherein they again experienced the continued favour of God, in order that they may be aroused to greater alacrity, and courageously prepare themselves for farther progress; for they might confidently expect that, with God for their leader, all things would succeed prosperously with them. The region of Bashan, as Scripture informs us in many places, was fertile, and famous for its rich pastures; but Moses here also testifies to its great extent. It was, then, no ordinary proof of God's favour and aid, that they should take it in a moment, as it were. It is not, therefore, without cause, that, in the Psalm, God's power and goodness is magnified in reference to these victories; because He "slew mighty kings, Sihon king of the Amorites, and Og king of Bashan, and gave their land for a heritage, a heritage unto his people." (Ps. cxxxv. 10-12.) For, although the Israelites were superior in numbers, yet there is no doubt but that, when this king dared to go forth to battle, he trusted in his forces, and deemed himself equal to resistance. Hence did God's grace shine forth the more conspicuously; and, indeed, in order that he may extol its greatness the more, Moses afterwards also relates that sixty cities were taken.[1]

34. *And the Lord said unto Moses.* God first of all exhorts His people to confidence. He then commands that the men as well as the cities and villages should be destroyed, so that nothing should be preserved except the booty. He indeed addresses Moses only, but his injunctions are directed to all, because Moses, who was already sufficiently energetic, had not so much need of being spurred on as the others. God, however, had regard to the future also, lest the recollection of the blessing should be lost through the ingratitude of the people. In promising them victory, therefore, He desired to have the praise of it bestowed upon Himself.

I have already shewn why He commanded the cities to be overthrown, and all the houses utterly destroyed, namely, lest convenient habitations should tempt the people to torpor, when they were required to hasten onwards to the promised rest; for those who had been ready in the wilderness to retire, and to go back into Egypt, would have eagerly taken possession of this fertile land, and reposed themselves as in a delightful nest. By its desolation, therefore, they were compelled to abandon it. Its possession, indeed, was afterwards granted to the tribes of Reuben, and Gad, and half of Manasseh; but on condition that they should leave their herds there, and accompany their brethren through the whole expedition, not deserting them till the Canaanitish nations were destroyed.

DEUT. III. 4. *And we took all the cities.* He here more fully relates what he had briefly touched upon in Numbers. He says that sixty *well-fortified cities* were taken, besides the villages. Hence we infer both the extent of the country, and also the special power of God in the aid He afforded them, in that they took, in so short a time, so many cities well closed in, and begirt with high walls; as if they were merely travelling through a peaceful land in security, and with nothing to do.

After the eighth verse, he repeats connectedly what he had separately related respecting the two kingdoms; and in order that the places might be more certainly identified, he mentions two other names for mount Hermon, stating that it was called

[1] Addition in *Fr*, "sans les bourgades;" not reckoning the villages.

Sirion by the Sidonians, and Shenir by the Amorites. Finally, he adds that Og, king of Bashan, was a giant, and the only survivor of that race. As a memorial of his lofty stature, he alleges his iron bedstead, the length of which was as much as nine cubits, according to the common measure of that period. By this circumstance he again magnifies the marvellous help of God, in that he was overcome by the children of Israel, who might, by his stature, have singly terrified a whole army.

The enormous stature of the giants is apparent from this passage. Herodotus records,[1] that the body of Orestes, disinterred by command of the oracle, was seven cubits in length. Pliny,[2] although he does not cite his authority, subscribes to this testimony. Gellius[3] thinks that this was fabulous, as also what Homer[4] writes with respect to the diminution of men's height in process of time; but his erroneous view is confuted by almost universal consent. What Pliny[5] himself relates is indeed incredible, that in Crete a body was discovered, by an opening of the earth, forty-six cubits long, which some thought to be the body of Orion, and others of Etion. But if we believe that there were giants, (which is not only affirmed by the sacred Scriptures, but also recorded by almost all ancient writers,) we need not be surprised if they were more than eight cubits in height. Although, however, the race of giants began to disappear in the time of Moses, still, in after ages, there existed persons who approached to this ancient stature,[6] as in the time of Augustus and Claudius there was one man about ten feet in height, and another nine feet nine inches. Moses, therefore, intimates nothing more than that this monstrous race of men gradually died out, so that the enormous height of Og, king of Bashan, was an unusual sight.

[1] Herod. Clio, § 68. [2] Pliny, vii. 16. [3] Gellius, lib. iii. x.
[4] Homer, *Il.* lib. xii. 381-3, 446-9; lib. xx. 286, 7. [5] Pliny, lib. vii. 16.
[6] *Fr.* "Comme sous l'empire d'Auguste il y avoit un homme haut de dix pieds, et sous l'empire de Claude un un peu moindre;" as under the empire of Augustus there was a man ten feet high, and, under that of Claudius, one somewhat shorter. Pliny, *loc. cit.*, records the exhibition at Rome, by the Emperor Claudius, of an Arab named Gabbara, whose height was nine feet nine inches; and adds, that in the reign of Augustus, there lived *two* persons, Posio and Secundilla, who were half a foot higher than Gabbara, and who, on account of their wonderful size, were buried in the cemetery of the Sallustian gardens.

NUMBERS, CHAPTER XXII.

1. And the children of Israel set forward, and pitched in the plains of Moab, on this side Jordan *by* Jericho.

2. And Balak the son of Zippor saw all that Israel had done to the Amorites.

3. And Moab was sore afraid of the people, because they *were* many; and Moab was distressed because of the children of Israel.

4. And Moab said unto the elders of Midian, Now shall this company lick up all *that are* round about us, as the ox licketh up the grass of the field. And Balak the son of Zippor *was* king of the Moabites at that time.

5. He sent messengers therefore unto Baalam the son of Beor, to Pethor, which *is* by the river of the land of the children of his people, to call him, saying, Behold, there is a people come out from Egypt: behold, they cover the face of the earth, and they abide over against me.

6. Come now, therefore, I pray thee, curse me this people; for they *are* too mighty for me: peradventure I shall prevail, *that* we may smite them, and *that* I may drive them out of the land: for I wot that he whom thou blessest *is* blessed, and he whom thou cursest is cursed.

7. And the elders of Moab and the elders of Midian departed with the rewards of divination in their hand; and they came unto Baalam, and spake unto him the words of Balak.

8. And he said unto them, Lodge here this night, and I will bring you word again, as the Lord shall speak unto me. And the princes of Moab abode with Balaam.

9. And God came unto Balaam, and said, What men *are* these with thee?

10. And Balaam said unto God, Balak the son of Zippor, king of Moab, hath sent unto me, *saying*,

1. Inde profecti sunt filii Israel, et castrametati sunt in campestribus Moab trans Jordanem Jericho.

2. Quum autem vidisset Balac filius Sippor quæcunque fecerat Israel Emorrhæo:

3. Timuit Moab propter populum valdè, quòd multus esset: et anxius fuit Moab propter filios Israel.

4. Dixit igitur Moab ad seniores Madian, Nunc lambet congregatio hæc omnes circuitus nostros, quemadmodum lambit bos gramen agri. Porro Balac filius Sippor erat rex Moab tempore illo.

5. Misit igitur legatos ad Balaam filium Beor in Pethor, quæ erat juxta flumen terræ filiorum populi sui, ut vocaret eum, dicendo, En populus egressus est ex Ægypto, ecce, operuit superficiem terræ, et habitat contra me.

6. Nunc ergo veni, obsecro, maledic mihi populum hunc, quia fortior me est: fortè potero, et percutiam eum, expellamque è terra. Novi enim quòd cui benedixeris benedictus erit, et cui maledixeris maledictus erit.

7. Profecti ergo sunt seniores Madian, et divinationes in manu eorum: et pervenerunt ad Balaam, et retulerunt ei verba Balac.

8. Ille verò dixit eis, Pernoctate hic nocte ista, et reddam vobis responsum, quemadmodum loquetur Jehova ad me. Manseruntque principes Moab cum Balaam.

9. Et venit Deus ad Balaam, ac dixit, Qui sunt viri isti qui sunt apud te?

10. Respondit Balaam Deo, Balac filius Sippor rex Moab misit ad me:

11. Behold, *there is* a people come out of Egypt, which covereth the face of the earth: come now, curse me them; peradventure I shall be able to overcome them, and drive them out.

12. And God said unto Baalam, Thou shalt not go with them; thou shalt not curse the people: for they *are* blessed.

13. And Balaam rose up in the morning, and said unto the princes of Balak, Get you into your land: for the Lord refuseth to give me leave to go with you.

14. And the princes of Moab rose up, and they went unto Balak, and said, Balaam refuseth to come with us.

11. En populus iste qui egressus est ex Ægypto operuit superficiem terræ: nunc ergo veni, maledic mihi illi: fortè potero pugnare cum eo, et expellere eum.

12. Et dixit Deus ad Balaam, Ne eas cum illis, neque maledicas populo qui benedictus est.

13. Surrexit itaque Balaam manè, et dixit ad principes Balac, Revertimini ad terram vestram: quia renuit Jehova concedere mihi, ut eam vobiscum.

14. Et surrexerunt principes Moab, et pervenerunt ad Balac, ac dixerunt, Renuit Balaam venire nobiscum.

1. *And the children of Israel set forward.* This narrative contains many circumstances worthy of record: First, it shews that there is no stone which Satan does not turn for the destruction of the Church, and that, after he has assailed her in vain by force of arms, he attacks her by snares and secret artifices, whilst the ungodly also work under his impulse, as far as they are able, to overthrow her by deceit, and to make the promises of God, and His unchangeable decree for the preservation of the Church which He has chosen, of none effect. But God shews, on the other hand, that He so watches over His own, as to turn to their salvation whatever plots their enemies may devise for their destruction. He likewise represents as in a mirror how foolish and vain are their attempts who endeavour to undermine the grace of God; and especially He demonstrates that God's truth will always be so completely victorious as to receive the testimony even of its professed enemies; just as Balaam was made to proclaim it. These and other observations, however, will be better made in their several places.

We have already seen that there was no reason why Balak should devise any evil against God's people, since he had no inconvenience to fear from them. Their faith had been voluntarily pledged; security had been promised him, and a treaty proposed. When, therefore, he and all the Moabites prepare themselves, and arouse their neighbours for resistance, they were ungrateful to God as well as men. In his very alarm we see the truth of what Scripture declares, viz., that the reprobate are always agitated by groundless terrors; and this is the just reward of those who seek not peace with God, that they should be constantly harassed by wretched disquietude. By special privilege God had exempted the Moabites from being at all interfered with; but they invent for themselves causes of anxiety, because they see that God's people had overcome great and powerful kings. For as the brightness of the sun is painful and injurious to those who have weak eyes, so the blessings which God bestows upon the Church, in token of His paternal favour, torment the reprobate and stir them up to envy. If the Moabites had prudently considered their own advantage, they might have easily so arranged with their old connections as to provide for their own tranquillity; but now, by provoking their ill-will, they make the worst bargain possible for themselves. Nor is it the unwise alarm of Balak only which is described, but that of the whole nation of Moab. At first, indeed, the king's name is introduced alone, but immediately afterwards Moses includes them all without exception. Hence it is plain that this error was universal, by the contagion of which they presently corrupt others also. For they invite the Midianites to associate themselves with them in the work of repulsing the Israelites. The pretext alleged is, that as oxen consume the grass of the field, so there was imminent danger lest, if the people of Israel were not resisted, they should as it were lick up and devour all the nations; whereas they had experienced quite the reverse, for the people had turned aside of their own accord into circuitous paths, in order to avoid doing them injury. This forbearance would have delivered them from all anxiety, unless their own malignity had taught them to entertain foul suspicions; for why had not the Israelites made a direct aggression upon their territories, except because they were desirous to leave them safe and intact? Otherwise they would have boldly made a way for themselves by force of arms.

5. *He sent messengers therefore unto Balaam.* This pas-

sage shews us, like many others, that the errors wherein Satan entangles unbelievers are derived from good principles. The modesty of king Balak appears to be worthy of praise, in that, conscious of his own weakness, and placing no confidence in human aid, he sets about imploring the help of God. For this is our only safe refuge, although earthly aids may fail us, still to maintain our courage, and to rely upon God, who is all-sufficient in Himself, and independent of external means. Thus far, then, Balak acts rightly, for he seeks nothing more than to conciliate God's favour, nor places his confidence of victory in anything but God's good-will; but, when he seeks for God amiss by circuitous ways, he departs far from Him. And this is a common error with all hypocrites and unbelievers, that, whilst they aspire after God, they wander into indirect paths of their own. Balak desires Divine deliverance from his danger; but the means are of his own device, when he would purchase incantations from a mercenary prophet; thus it is, that he binds down God, and subjects Him to his own inventions. He knows, he says, that the power of blessing and cursing appertained to Balaam; but whence arose this persuasion, unless,[1] by catching at the mere empty name of Prophet, he separates God from Himself? He ought first to have inquired what the will of God was, and to have addressed prayer in earnest faith to Him, in order to propitiate Him; whereas, omitting the main thing, he is satisfied with a mere venal blessing. We gather, therefore, from his anxiety to obtain peace and pardon from God, that there was some seed of religion implanted in his mind. The reverence which he pays to the Prophet is also a sign of his piety. But that he desires to win over God by his own vain inventions is a proof of foolish superstition; and that he seeks to lay Him under obligation to himself, of impious pride.[2]

I know not how it came into the mind of the Chaldee

[1] "Si ce n'est qu'en prenant à la volee le titre vain de Prophete sans son effet, il separe Dieu de soy-mesme, ou le veust couper par pieces?" unless it be that, laying hold at random of the empty title of Prophet without its essence, he separates God from himself, and would cut him in pieces?—*Fr.*

[2] "D'un orgueil diabolique;" of diabolical arrogance.—*Fr.*

interpreter to suppose that Pethor was on the banks of the Euphrates; nor is it probable that (Balaam) was fetched from so great a distance. Neither would his celebrity have extended from so distant a place to these nations. I am persuaded that it is the proper name of a place, because the termination of the word *Petorah* does not admit of its being an epithet, such as "the soothsayer," as Jerome has rendered it. Although, however, the country is not specified, it is probably gathered from the context that Balaam was a Midianite; and for this reason I conceive the Midianites were sought in alliance, in order that they might gain over their fellow-countrymen.

It is a poor exposition of what follows in verse 7, that they had "the divinations in their hand,"[1] to refer it to the art of divination, or even that they were accompanied by those who were skilful in the same science. It is more simple to interpret it of their commission, as though Moses said that the messengers were instructed as to what they sought of Balaam, viz., that he should curse the people of Israel, for there is no absurdity in supposing that Moses again repeats what he had related in the preceding verse. Still, I am not indisposed to accept the view which others take, viz., that they took with them the reward or price of divination, for there have been in all ages hireling prophets who made a sale of their revelations; and since even amongst the Israelites many impostors thus set themselves up for hire, this abuse had much vogue (among them.) Hence it was that Saul and his servant hesitated to go to Samuel, because they had not any gift at hand to offer him, until the servant replied that he had the fourth part of a shekel of silver, as if Samuel set up his prophecies for sale, as was commonly the case. (1 Sam. ix. 7, 8.) Ezekiel, indeed, charges the false prophets with this, that they sold themselves for a trifling bribe.

[1] *A. V.*, "The rewards of divination;" Ainsworth says, "So Targum Jonathan expoundeth it, *The fruits of divination sealed in their hand;* and thus *Besorah*, i.e., *good tidings*, is used for *the reward of good tidings*, in 2 Sam. iv. 10." "Non raro Hebræi rem ponunt pro pretio rei; ut Exod. xxi. 10, *humiliatio*, i.e., pretium pudicitiæ."—Bonfrerius in Poole.

8. *And he said unto them, Lodge here this night.* Inasmuch as he waits for a revelation from the true God, it is probable that he was not a magician or sorcerer, whose only power to divine arose from superstition or evil arts. We shall, indeed, see hereafter, that he was accustomed to use many impostures and deceptions; but it will be plain, from the evidence of facts, that he was furnished with the gift of prophecy. Not that he is to be reckoned among the true prophets whom God set over His Church, because neither was the perpetual office of prophesying conferred upon him, nor was it conjoined with that of teaching. For those servants of His, to whom God intrusted the office of prophesying, He so directed by His Spirit, that they never spoke except out of His mouth. And although they did not foresee all that was to happen, but only according to the measure of their revelation, still He concealed nothing from them which it was profitable for them to know. Hence the expression of Amos, "Surely the Lord God will do nothing, but he revealeth his secret unto his servants the prophets." (Amos iii. 7.) In a word, they were the organs of the Holy Spirit for all necessary predictions; and the credit due to their prophecies was of an equable and constant character, so that they never spoke absurdly or in vain. Besides, they were endowed with the power of adapting their prophecies to a just object and use. Thus, after the Law was promulgated, they were its interpreters. In prosperity they bore witness to the grace of God; in adversity, to His judgments. In fine, their business was to ratify God's covenant, whereby He reconciles men to Himself through Christ. Far different was the case with Balaam, and such like, who were only endued with a particular gift,[1] so that they truly foretold some things, and were mistaken in others; and, indeed, they only uttered bare revelations without any admixture of doctrine. God willed, indeed, that such should exist even among heathen nations, so that some sparks of light should shine amidst their darkness, and thus the excuse of ignorance should be taken away. Indeed, all those who have dared to delude the world by their impostures have usurped

[1] "Pour predire ceci ou cela;" to predict this or that.—*Fr.*

the name of prophet; and although the word *divination* is honourable and sacred, it has been improperly applied to the art of deception, and the liberty to lie, as it is the custom of the devil to profane God's name by its impious abuse. Still, there were some among the Gentiles who occasionally predicted future events by divine inspiration; and this was especially the case before the Law was given, inasmuch as God had not then distinguished His elect people from others by this mark. At this time, it is true, the promise had been given, "The Lord thy God will raise up unto thee prophets,"[1] &c., (Deut. xviii. 15.); but it was not yet generally known, and therefore God was unwilling that the nations should be deprived of their soothsayers, who still were very different from those true prophets, whose call was clear and legitimate.

I have said thus much briefly with reference to Balaam, whom God addresses in a vision by night, or dream, no less familiarly than any of His own servants; but only on a particular point. By the inquiry, "What men are these with thee?" He indirectly reproves his improper desires. At first sight he pretends a holy anxiety to obey, when he dares to attempt nothing without God's permission, and refuses to stir a foot, until he shall have received His answer. Yet secret covetousness influences him to obtain from God, by bargaining as it were, what he still feels not to be right. God glances at this astuteness, when He inquires respecting the men; as much as to say, that there was no reason why he should detain them a moment, since their demand should have been peremptorily refused. And, assuredly, if he had been free, he would have hastened at once to obey the wishes of king Balak, even contrary to the will of God. He now requests that permission should be given him; as if he desired to have the reins, which withheld him from his evil purposes, slackened, when he would have willingly shaken them off altogether, if he were not well aware that he could do nothing further than God would permit. Nor, indeed, does he regard what is lawful and right; but only seeks that his mouth may be opened to curse with impunity.

12. *Thou shalt not go with them.* If there were any room

[1] *A. V.*, "A Prophet." See *C.'s* Comment. *in loco*, vol. i. p. 433.

for doubt, God peremptorily removes it, and confirms the prohibition; because it was unlawful to curse, those whom He had blessed. For nothing more is permitted to prophets than that they should be the witnesses, or ambassadors (*internuntii,*) or heralds of the grace which God freely deigns to bestow at His own pleasure upon whom He will. Moreover, God is said to *bless* those whom He has embraced with His favour, and to whom He experimentally declares Himself to be propitious, when He displays His liberality towards them. Of this *blessing* He willed that the prophets should be His ministers in such a manner that the power should still remain altogether in His own hands. If, therefore, they usurp to themselves the prerogative of blessing without His commission, their act is not merely frivolous and inefficacious, but even blasphemous. Justly, then, does Ezekiel convict of falsehood and deception those false prophets, who, by their flatteries, encourage the souls which were doomed to die; whilst they slay by their terrors and threats those to whom God had promised life. (Ezek. xiii. 2 and 22.) Hence we gather, how vain it is for hypocrites, as they are wont to do, to purchase pardon from men in order to propitiate God; and also that we need not be afraid of those degenerate ministers,[1] who desire to domineer tyrannically in virtue of their office, although they launch their fulminations against the innocent.

It is plain, however, that Balaam's obedience to God's command does not proceed from the heart. His words, indeed, might deceive the simple, from their appearance of humility; "I will not go, because God forbids it;" but there is no doubt but that, led as he was to gratify them by ambition and by avarice, he indicates that he would be disposed to undertake the journey, unless he were forbidden by God. If his heart had been sincere, the honest reply he should have given was obvious, viz., that it was vain to send either for himself or any one else, in order that Balak might resist the inviolable decree of God. If he had thus heartily and unequivocally given glory to God, another embassy would not have been sent to him; but by his faltering ex-

[1] "Les ministres masqués;" the masked ministers.—*Fr.*

cuse he appeared to inflame the desire of the foolish king, in order to sell his curse at a higher price; for we know that this is the usual way with impostors, that they obtain higher pay for themselves in proportion to the difficulty of the matter. Still, however, if we compare the mercenary prophets of the Pope with Balaam, his servile and enforced submission will deserve no little praise by the side of their detestable and indomitable folly, who, in despite of God, hesitate not to burst forth in impious curses. The truth, which they oppugn, is conspicuous: that terrible judgment, which (God) denounces by the mouth of Isaiah, rings in their ears, " Woe unto them that put darkness for light, and light for darkness," (Isa. v. 20;) nevertheless they proceed, and in their brutal madness vomit forth their blasphemies not only to the destruction of the Church, but, if it were possible, to the extinction of all religion.

15. And Balak sent yet again princes, more, and more honourable than they.

16. And they came to Balaam, and said to him, Thus saith Balak the son of Zippor, Let nothing, I pray thee, hinder thee from coming unto me;

17. For I will promote thee unto very great honour, and I will do whatsoever thou sayest unto me: come therefore, I pray thee, curse me this people.

18. And Balaam answered and said unto the servants of Balak, If Balak would give me his house full of silver and gold, I cannot go beyond the word of the Lord my God, to do less or more.

19. Now therefore, I pray you, tarry ye also here this night, that I may know what the Lord will say unto me more.

20. And God came unto Balaam at night, and said unto him, If the men come to call thee, rise up, *and* go with them; but yet the word which I shall say unto thee, that shalt thou do.

21. And Balaam rose up in the

15. Rursus ergo misit Balac principes plures, et nobiliores istis.

16. Qui venientes ad Balaam dixerunt ei, Sic dixit Balac filius Sippor, Noli quæso prohibere teipsum ne venias ad me:

17. Nam honorando honorabo te valdè, et quicquid dixeris mihi, faciam: veni igitur obsecro, et maledic mihi populo huic.

18. Respondens autem Balaam dixit servis Balac, Etiamsi daturus sit mihi Balac plenam domum suam argento et auro, non possim transgredi sermonem Jehovæ Dei mei, ut faciam aliquid, sive parvum, sive magnum.

19. Nunc ergo manete, obsecro, hic vos quoque hac nocte, ut sciam quid addet Jehova loqui mihi.

20. Tunc venit Deus ad Balaam nocte, et dixit ei, Si vocandum te venerint viri isti, surge, vade cum eis: veruntamen quod dixero tibi, illud facies.

21. Surrexit itaque Balaam manè,

morning, and saddled his ass, and went with the princes of Moab.

et stravit asinam suam, et perrexit cum principibus Moab.

22. And God's anger was kindled because he went: and the angel of the Lord stood in the way for an adversary against him. (Now he was riding upon his ass, and his two servants *were* with him.)

22. Iratus verò est furor Dei quòd ipse iret cum illis: stetitque angelus Jehovæ in ipsa via, in adversarium illi: ipse autem equitabat super asinam suam, et duo pueri ejus erant cum eo.

23. And the ass saw the angel of the Lord standing in the way, and his sword drawn in his hand: and the ass turned aside out of the way, and went into the field; and Balaam smote the ass, to turn her into the way.

23. At videns asina angelum Jehovæ stantem in via, et gladium ejus evaginatum in manu ejus, declinavit illa è via, et ivit in agrum: itaque percussit Balaam asinam ut declinare faceret eam in viam.

24. But the angel of the Lord stood in a path of the vineyards, a wall *being* on this side, and a wall on that side.

24. Stetitque postea angelus Jehovæ in semita vinearum: maceria una erat hinc, et maceria altera inde.

25. And when the ass saw the angel of the Lord, she thrust herself unto the wall, and crushed Balaam's foot against the wall; and he smote her again.

25. Videns verò secundò asina angelum Jehovæ, coarctavit sese parieti, coarctavit quoque pedem Balaam ad parietem: propterea addidit percutere eam.

26. And the angel of the Lord went further, and stood in a narrow place, where *was* no way to turn either to the right hand or to the left.

26. Addidit præterea angelus Jehovæ transire, et stetit in loco angusto ubi nulla erat via ad declinandum sive ad dextram sive ad sinistram.

27. And when the ass saw the angel of the Lord, she fell down under Balaam: and Balaam's anger was kindled, and he smote the ass with a staff.

27. Quum autem vidisset asina angelum Jehovæ, succubuit sub Balaam, unde iratus furor Balaam percussit asinam baculo.

28. And the Lord opened the mouth of the ass; and she said unto Balaam, What have I done unto thee, that thou hast smitten me these three times?

28. Et aperuit Jehova os asinæ, dixitque illa ad Balaam, Quid feci tibi, quòd percussisti me jam tribus vicibus:

29. And Balaam said unto the ass, Because thou hast mocked me: I would there were a sword in mine hand, for now would I kill thee.

29. Tunc dixit Balaam ad asinam, Quia illusisti mihi, utinam esset gladius in manu mea, certe nunc occiderem te.

30. And the ass said unto Balaam, *Am* not I thine ass, upon which thou hast ridden ever since *I was* thine unto this day? was I ever wont to do so unto thee? And he said, Nay.

30. Dixit autem asina ad Balaam, Nonne sum asina tua? super me equitasti ex quo esse cœpisti usque ad diem hanc, nunquid solita sum facere tibi sic? Qui respondit, Nequaquam.

31. Then the Lord opened the eyes of Balaam, and he saw the angel of the Lord standing in the way, and his sword drawn in his hand: and he bowed down his head, and fell flat on his face.

31. Et detexit Jehova oculos Balaam, viditque angelum Jehovæ stantem in via, et gladium ejus evaginatum in manu ejus: tum demisso capite adoravit pronus in faciem suam.

32. And the angel of the Lord said unto him, Wherefore hast thou smitten thine ass these three times? Behold, I went out to withstand thee, because *thy* way is perverse before me:

32. Et alloquutus est eum angelus Jehovæ, Quare percussisti asinam tuam jam tribus vicibus? en ego egressus sum in adversarium tibi, quia declinavit à via coram me.

33. And the ass saw me, and turned from me these three times: unless she had turned from me, surely now also I had slain thee, and saved her alive.

33. Et vidit me asina, declinavitque ante me jam tribus vicibus: quòd si non declinasset à facie mea, jam nunc etiam te occidissem, et ipsam vivam reservassem.

34. And Balaam said unto the angel of the Lord, I have sinned; for I knew not that thou stoodest in the way against me: now therefore, if it displease thee, I will get me back again.

34. Dixit igitur Balaam ad angelum Jehovæ, Peccavi: non enim sciebam quòd tu stares in occursum mei in via: nunc autem si malum est in oculis tuis, revertar mihi.

35. And the angel of the Lord said unto Balaam, Go with the men: but only the word that I shall speak unto thee, that thou shalt speak. So Balaam went with the princes of Balak.

35. Angelus verò Jehovæ dixit ad Balaam, Vade cum istis viris: veruntamen verbum quod loquar ad te illud loqueris. Abiit igitur Balaam cum principibus Balac:

36. And when Balak heard that Balaam was come, he went out to meet him unto a city of Moab, which *is* in the border of Arnon, which *is* in the utmost coast.

36. Audiens verò Balac quòd adveniret Balaam, egressus est in occursum ejus in civitatem quandam Moab, quæ erat juxta terminum Arnon, quæ est in extremo finium.

37. And Balak said unto Balaam, Did I not earnestly send unto thee to call thee? wherefore camest thou not unto me? am I not able indeed to promote thee to honour?

37. Et dixit Balac ad Balaam, Annon mittendo misi ad te ad accersendum te? an verè non possum honorare te?

38. And Balaam said unto Balak, Lo, I am come unto thee: have I now any power at all to say any thing? the word that God putteth in my mouth, that shall I speak.

38. Respondit autem Balaam ad Balac, Ecce veni ad te: nunc autem nunquid omnino potero loqui quicquam? Verbum quod posuerit Deus in ore meo, illud loquar.

39. And Balaam went with Balak, and they came unto Kirjath-huzoth.

39. Et perrexit Balaam cum Balac, et pervenerunt in civitatem Husoth:

40. And Balak offered oxen and sheep, and sent to Balaam, and to the princes that *were* with him.

40. Et mactavit Balac boves, et oves: misitque ad Balaam et ad principes qui cum ipso erant.

41. And it came to pass on the morrow, that Balak took Balaam, and brought him up into the high places of Baal, that thence he might see the utmost *part* of the people.

41. Postera autem die accepit Balac ipsum Balaam, et ascendere fecit eum in excelsa Baal, et vidit illinc extremum populi.

15. *And Balak sent yet again princes.* Here we see that, however humbly ungodly men implore God's grace, still they do not lay aside their pride; as if their grandeur could avail to dazzle the eyes of God. In order, therefore, to make

Him comply with their wishes, they think it enough to display their magnificent ceremonies; and, indeed, whatever modesty superstition may pretend, it always swells with secret confidence. Thus Balak, in order to obtain favour, makes a show of his dignity and power, and deems that Balaam will be thus at his service. Although, however, the impostor shews much more spirit in this his second reply than before, still his hypocrisy is soon discovered, and he betrays the duplicity of his mind. It is, indeed, a noble speech, and indicative of much magnanimity, "If Balak would give me his house full of silver and gold, I will not disobey the command of God:" but why does he not instantly banish from him altogether these unholy traffickers, who are instigating him to transgression? We see, then, that he speaks rather in a spirit of boasting, than to ascribe to God the glory due to Him; for his desire was to acquire for himself the title and credit of a holy Prophet by this parade of obedience. In the meantime, when he begs that a season of delay should be granted him for the purpose of inquiring what God's pleasure was, he is convicted of impious rebellion. He does not dare openly, and in flagrant contempt of God, to put himself forward for the purpose of cursing God's people: and so far well: but why does he not acquiesce in the Divine decision? why, when he has been assured whether a matter was lawful or not, does he still doubtingly inquire? For thus does he deliberate, and question whether that which God has once prescribed ought to be certain and unchangeable; nay, he endeavours to force God to alter His determination. From the time that he had heard, "Thou shalt not go," upon what pretence was it permissible to continue the controversy? This, then, is the object of Balaam's endeavour, that God, by withdrawing the decision which He had pronounced, should deny Himself; and this was an act of most blasphemous impiety. Still many such persons will be found now-a-days, who, though fully assured of the will of God, cease not nevertheless to countermine it, so that they may at length attain the end, towards which they are hurried by their lawless cupidity. At the outset, it is anything but their desire to know what is right; or, when they know it, to follow it: but ambition instigates some, lust inflames others, and others are urged forward by avarice: in a word, evil affections preside over every deliberation. Straightway God interposes some obstacle, and compels them, whether they will or no, to understand what they ought to do. They proceed, however, notwithstanding; and, inasmuch as the way is closed, they endeavour by subterfuges, by crooked paths or evasions, to elude the sure word of God; and, although they appear to do this modestly, because they hesitate until permission shall have been obtained from God, yet herein does their impudence betray itself, that they do not cease to importune God and His prophets, until they have extorted what they have already heard to be unlawful. It is plain, therefore, that all those are disciples of Balaam, who try the indulgence of God, that He may at length permit them to attempt what He has once refused.

20. *And God came to Balaam at night.* Although God is far from being deceitful, still hypocrites with their quibbles deserve that He should delude their craft. If we more closely consider the desire of Balaam, it was that God should belie Himself. For, if he was persuaded that He was truthful, what else was there to be hoped except that He should ratify His reply ten times over? Nevertheless, he wickedly lies to God, when he asks for a permission to go, which would convict God Himself of capriciousness and inconstancy. God, therefore, ironically permits what He had before forbidden. If any should deem it to be absurd that God, who is truth itself, should speak deceptively, the answer is easily found, viz., that God was guilty of no falsehood, but that He loosed the reins to a man obstinate in his own perverseness, just as a person might emancipate a wayward and grossly immoral son, because he will not suffer himself to be ruled. For, had not his ungodly covetousness blinded Balaam, the meaning of this ironical permission was not difficult to be understood. Hence, then, let hypocrites learn, that they profit nothing by their vain pretences, although God may indulge them for a time, since He at length taketh the wily in their own craftiness; wherefore,

nothing is better than, in pure and simple teachableness, to inquire what He would have us do, that we may instantly succumb, nor try to alter a word or a syllable as soon as He shall have deigned to open His holy mouth to instruct us. For to call in question what has been decided by Him, what is it but to compel Him by our importunity to bend Himself to our wishes?

22. *And God's anger was kindled because he went.* How is it consistent that God should be angry when Balaam had attempted nothing, thus far, contrary to His command? But we must bear in mind, what I have lately hinted, that God apparently permits much which He does not approve. He allowed the people in the wilderness to eat flesh: He permitted men to give a writing of divorce to their wives, and even to marry several at once; still it was not right for them to eat the flesh, nor were divorce and polygamy free from culpability. At any rate, Balaam sinned by pertinaciously urging what was sinful, and thus deserved the punishment of death, though God was pleased to mitigate it. On this point it behoves us also to be soberly wise, lest, when God's secret judgments differ from our moral sense, we should cry out against Him. That prophet, who, having faithfully delivered his message, tasted bread on his way back, and this at the instigation of another prophet, so that he only fell through carelessness and want of reflection, He punished with death, (1 Kings xiii.;) in this case, the punishment which He inflicts upon an impostor and cheat, who[1] prostitutes his tongue for hire, is no harsher than to terrify him by threats. Here the temerity of the flesh would willingly lay hold of the occasion to find fault with God; but the fact was, that the punishment which awaited Balaam, and from which he did not finally escape, was delayed for a certain period in order to display more brightly the glory of God. Wherefore, if a doubt ever pervades our minds, when the reason for any of God's works is not apparent, let us learn at once to repress it.

The external manifestation of God's anger is afterwards

[1] "Qui vouloit vendre la grace du sainct Esprit;" who would sell the grace of the Holy Spirit.—*Fr.*

described; *i.e.*, that the Angel meets him with a drawn sword; wherein we may observe that, to the great disgrace of the Prophet, the glory of the Angel was first revealed to the ass. For, although the Angel had assumed a body, by the sight of which a brute-animal might be affected, how did it come to pass that the ass was terrified at this alarming sight, whilst the eyes of the Prophet were closed against it, unless because God wished to brand the stupidity of this faithless man with a mark of ignominy? He had previously boasted of his extraordinary visions; a vision now escapes him which was manifest to the eyes of a beast. Whence did such blindness as this arise, except from avarice, by which he was so stupified as to prefer filthy lucre to the holy calling of God? In a word, in him was fulfilled, what Scripture so often denounces against the reprobate, that he was struck by a spirit of dizziness and folly so as to be unable to perceive anything. I have already said, that although angels are naturally invisible, yet that they assume bodies whenever God so pleases, and act in the character of human beings. Who supplied the Angel with a sword? Even He, who created all things out of nothing. If any curious person should go further, and inquire of what material the sword was made? it will be easy to reprove his folly by another question, viz., Whether it is easier for mortal man or for God to apply iron and steel to their various purposes? And it might be the case that a bright light shone from the sword, as when the Cherubim were placed with swords to shut the entrance of Paradise against Adam. In a word, God clothed His Angel in such a form as might strike with terror both the brute-animal and the false prophet. But He began with the ass, in order to put the stolidity of the wicked man more completely to shame.

Moses proceeds to relate how the ass, first of all, was turned aside out of the way, and then, when she was met in a narrow place, how she tremblingly started back so as to crush her master's foot against the wall, and at length how she fell down under him. Surely this miserable impostor ought to have been awakened, if he had not been fascinated by the devil. But Moses carefully details all these circumstances, in order to show that he was not only deprived of common sense, but so utterly astounded, as to pay no attention to a most illustrious miracle.

28. *And the Lord opened the mouth of the ass.* Sceptical persons criticize this passage, and ridicule it, as if Moses related an incredible fable. And, indeed, their scoff appears to be plausible, when they object that there is a great difference between the bray of an ass and an articulate voice; but, however they may now indulge in such wanton observations, they will at length be made to feel how seriously and reverently we ought to speak of the marvellous works of God, by their jokes and trifling about which they seek to appear facetious. Now, since their chattering is unworthy of a lengthened refutation, let us be satisfied by the contempt into which it is thrown by a single expression of Moses, when he says that God "opened the mouth of the ass." For whence would men possess the faculty of speech, unless God had opened their mouth at the first creation of the world? Whence comes it that magpies and parrots imitate the human voice, unless it were the will of God to manifest in them a specimen of a certain extraordinary power? Who is there, then, who shall now impose a law upon the Maker of the world, to prevent Him from adapting the mouth of a beast to the utterance of words? Unless perhaps they would suppose Him to be bound irrevocably, because He has once appointed a certain order in nature, to abstain from displaying His power by miracles. If the ass had been changed into a man, we should have been bound to reverence this proof of God's incomprehensible power;[1] now, when we are told that merely a few words were drawn from it without intelligence or judgment, as if a sound of any kind were diffused through the air, shall the miracle be regarded as a fable? Moreover, if unclean spirits utter words in spectral illusions, why shall God be unable to endow mute tongues with the faculty of speech? Let us, then, learn to reverence with becoming humility the sentence which God executed on the false prophet. He might

[1] Addition in *Fr.*, "Plutost que d'en faire nos farceries;" rather than to make our mock at it.

have chastised him directly by the words of the Angel; but, because the reproof would not have been sufficiently severe if unattended by gross ignominy, He ordained that a beast should instruct him. The voice of the Angel was, indeed, added afterwards; but, since he had been so unteachable, he is treated according to his desert, when, after having made some proficiency in the school of the ass, he begins to listen to God. And, further, the ass convicts him of being dull, and deluded in mind in this respect, that he was not aroused by this unusual circumstance. For she says that she had never before been refractory. If, therefore, there had been any spark of apprehension in the wretched man, he ought to have reflected as to what was the meaning of this novel proceeding and sudden change. Thus was he awakened from his lethargy, in order that he might listen more attentively to what the Angel afterwards spoke.

31. *Then the Lord opened the eyes of Balaam.* This passage teaches us, that whatever be the acuteness of our senses, it is not only implanted in us by God, but also either sustained or extinguished by His secret inspiration. Balaam's eyes are opened; consequently there was a veil before them previously, which prevented him from seeing what was manifest. Thus God at His pleasure makes dull the senses of those who seem to themselves to be very acute; since perception is His special gift.

By this example we are shewn as in a mirror how hypocrites fear God, viz., when they are influenced by His presence; for as soon as they can withdraw themselves, they revel like fugitive slaves. Balaam saw the angel threatening him with a drawn sword, and he hung down his head, and adored; that is to say, because the vengeance of God was impending. But this fear by no means induced him to true correction of himself. He confesses, indeed, that he had sinned, and puts forth some fruit of repentance in that he is ready to return home; but he betrays a servile and compulsory fear, which only trembles at the thought of punishment. "I knew not (he says) that thou stoodest in the way." Unless, therefore, the Angel had been armed for his punishment, he was proceeding in security, as if impunity were conceded to him. Another expression also discovers his craft and perfidiousness. He is ready to return, if his proceeding should *displease* God; as if he had not known before that it was by no means pleasing to God. This, then, is a ridiculous condition, as if he were in doubt on a point which was abundantly clear. If he really feared God, and in pure sincerity of heart, he ought at once to have renounced an expedition which was wicked in itself, and improperly undertaken. For what avail was it to say, "I have sinned," if he thinks that he can prosecute the journey he had begun in opposition to God? Let us, therefore, learn, when God's will is positively known, to have recourse to no crooked subterfuges, whereby we may delay to perform it.

When the Angel says: Unless the ass had turned aside, that he should have slain Balaam without injuring her, he intimates not only that, in accordance with God's justice and loving-kindness, he would have spared the harmless animal, but that by the very sagacity of the beast,—as though she had deprecated God's anger,—the life of her master, who was else unworthy of mercy, had been redeemed.

35. *And the angel of the Lord said unto Balaam.* Again this wicked man is ironically permitted to do what could not be carried out without sin. But, as I have said before, he was so conscious of his ungodly covetousness, that he knowingly and wilfully deceived himself, instead of being deceived. At the same time, we must observe that, as Paul calls God's wisdom "manifold," (Eph. iii. 10,) so His will is declared in various ways, as if He were inconsistent with Himself, though it always actually remains the same. Certain it is, that it was a mere pretence of Balaam, that he went at the command or permission of God. Nevertheless, this answer was given him, "Go," &c. God, indeed, cast derision on the pertinacious folly of this wicked man, and did not approve as proper that which, as far as words went, He permitted; meanwhile, these two things are consistent with each other, that God did not approve what He condemned, and yet chose that it should be done. For, even when He executes His purpose by means of wicked men, He does not

prescribe to them that they are to act thus. He willed to require punishment of Solomon by the hands of Jeroboam, and that the impiety of the house of Ahab should have vengeance inflicted upon it by Jehu; and still it was not right of Jeroboam to upset what God had declared, *i.e.*, that the posterity of David should continue upon the throne; and Jehu also, although he had been anointed by the Prophet, still was guilty of a criminal act in seizing the kingdom: inasmuch as nothing but ambition impelled him to it. As far as relates to the history before us, it was His will to prove by the mouth of Balaam how effectual and unchangeable was His determination as to the adoption of the people, whereby His truth and faithfulness might be more conspicuously shewn forth. Nevertheless, Balaam sinned, in that he was attracted, like a hound, by the scent of gain, to sell his curses for money.

36. *And when Balak heard that Balaam was come.* This passage admirably represents to us the spirit of all those who are devoted to their various superstitions without a sincere fear of God. They are cringing to their false prophets; they meanly flatter them, and hardly stop short of worshipping them, so that nothing more obsequious can be imagined; yet they inwardly cherish pride, which breaks out when they by no means expect it. The king goes forth to meet the prophet, and to pay due honours to himself and his office. It is a great condescension; for it is equivalent to laying his crown and sceptre at his feet: but his dissimulation soon discovers itself, when, expostulating with Balaam, he boasts of his power and riches, wherewith he was able to reward him. Now this is precisely as if he should make the prophetical office subservient to money, and claim the dominion over its revelations by means of his wealth. However great, then, may be the servility with which superstitious persons flatter their idols and priests, still they never lay aside their proud spirits. Such zeal we may see in the Papists, who are as prodigal as possible of the reverence which they parade towards their prelates and monks; but on this condition, that they will be, on their part, complacent to their lusts. If, therefore, a priest (*sacrificus*) will not gratify his

worshippers, they inveigh against him with as much bitterness as if he were any swine-herd.

The answer of Balaam at first sight breathes nothing but piety: "I have come, (he says,) but I must needs speak as God shall command." Whereby he signifies, that, as far as civility required, and inasmuch as depended upon himself, he would have complied with the wishes of the king; but that, in regard to his office as a prophet, he was not at liberty to do this, inasmuch as he would disregard the favour of all mankind, in order that he might obey the commands of God alone.

39. *And Balaam went with Balak.* Moses proceeds to relate how honourably and sumptuously Balaam was received. And first, he records that he was taken to the city of Huzoth;[1] which some would understand as a proper name, others as a noun appellative. In whichever way you take it, it denotes the extent of the city, which was divided into various streets. Secondly, Moses tells us that an abundance of animals were slain in preparation for the feast, and that guests were invited to banquet with Balaam himself.[2] The object of all this is, that Balaam was enticed by blandishments, in order that he might be ashamed to refuse anything to so munificent a king, by whom he had been treated not merely in a friendly, but in a liberal manner; just as if Balaam stood in the place of God, or as if the grace of God Himself were marketable. At length Moses adds that Balaam was brought up into the high places of Baal, that from this elevation he might more conveniently see the camp of the people. Moses, however, says that he only saw the extreme part of the camp; because the whole country was mountainous, and the view was obstructed by distance; still, in my opinion, the sanctity of the spot was the reason why it was chosen by Balak. He, therefore, brought Balaam to a temple, as it were, in order the more to conciliate God's favour. Hence, too, it is apparent that this impostor had no fixed or solid views with regard to the service of God, but

[1] *A. V.*, "Kirjath-huzoth." *Margin*, "a city of streets."

[2] "Et que Balaam a este accompagné de gens honorables;" and that Balaam was accompanied by persons of honour. —*Fr.*

that he worshipped idols promiscuously amongst the heathen, either because he was involved in the same superstitions, or because he made no difficulty in complying with any customs or rites, in order to curry favour. For there have always been[1] trimmers in the world, who for flattery's sake have corrupted religion by various devices, and have mingled heaven with earth.

NUMBERS, CHAPTER XXIII.

1. And Balaam said unto Balak, Build me here seven altars, and prepare me here seven oxen and seven rams.

2. And Balak did as Balaam had spoken: and Balak and Balaam offered on *every* altar a bullock and a ram.

3. And Balaam said unto Balak, Stand by thy burnt-offering, and I will go; peradventure the Lord will come to meet me; and whatsoever he sheweth me I will tell thee. And he went to an high place.

4. And God met Balaam: and he said unto him, I have prepared seven altars, and I have offered upon *every* altar a bullock and a ram.

5. And the Lord put a word in Balaam's mouth, and said, Return unto Balak, and thus thou shalt speak.

6. And he returned unto him, and, lo, he stood by his burnt-sacrifice, he and all the princes of Moab.

7. And he took up his parable, and said, Balak the king of Moab hath brought me from Aram, out of the mountains of the east, *saying*, Come, curse me Jacob; and come, defy Israel.

8. How shall I curse, whom God hath not cursed? or how shall I defy, *whom* the Lord hath not defied?

9. For from the top of the rocks I see him, and from the hills I be-

1. Et dixit Balaam ad Balac, Ædifica mihi hic septem altaria, appara quoque mihi hic septem juvencos, et septem arietes.

2. Fecitque Balac quemadmodum dixerat Balaam, et obtulit Balac et Balaam juvencum et arietem in altari.

3. Tunc dixit Balaam ipsi Balac, Consiste juxta holocaustum tuum, et ibo si fortè occurrat Jehova obviam mihi, et quicquid ostenderit mihi narrabo tibi. Abiit itaque in excelsum.

4. Et occurrit Deus ipsi Balaam, dixitque illi, Septem altaria disposui, et obtuli juvencum in quolibet altari.

5. Posuit autem Jehova verbum in ore Balaam, dixitque illi, Revertere ad Balac, et sic loqueris.

6. Et reversus est ad eum, et ecce, stabat juxta holocaustum suum, ipse et omnes principes Moab.

7. Assumpsitque parabolam suam, ac dixit, De Aram adduxit me Balac rex Moab, de montibus Orientis, dicendo, Veni, maledic mihi Jacob, et veni, detestare Israelem.

8. Cur maledicam, et non maledixit Deus? et cur detestabor eum quem non detestatus est Jehova?

9. Siquidem de vertice petrarum videbo eum, et de collibus intuebor

[1] *Lat.*, "medii homines." *Fr.*, "des nageurs entre deux eaux;" swimmers between two waters.

hold him: lo, the people shall dwell alone, and shall not be reckoned among the nations.	illum: ecce, populus confidenter habitabit, et inter gentes non reputabitur.
10. Who can count the dust of Jacob, and the number of the fourth *part* of Israel? Let me die the death of the righteous, and let my last end be like his!	10. Quis numerabit pulverem in Jacob, ac numerabit quartam partem Israelis? Moriatur anima mea morte rectorum, et sit novissimum meum sicut ipsius.
11. And Balak said unto Balaam, What hast thou done unto me? I took thee to curse mine enemies, and, behold, thou hast blessed *them* altogether.	11. Tunc dixit Balac ad Balaam, Quid fecisti mihi; ut malediceres inimicis meis, sumpsi te, et ecce, benedixisti benedicendo.
12. And he answered and said, Must I not take heed to speak that which the Lord hath put in my mouth?	12. Qui respondens dixit, Nonne quod posuerit Jehova in ore meo, id observabo ad loquendum?

1. *Build me here seven altars.* We more positively conclude from hence that this degenerate prophet had been by no means wont to prophesy in accordance with pure revelations from God, but that the art of divination, in which he boasted, had some affinity to magical exorcisms, and was infected with many errors and deceptions. Still this did not prevent him from being sometimes a true prophet by the inspiration of God's Spirit; because, as has been already said, whilst the world was plunged in darkness, it was God's will that some little sparks of light should still shine, in order to render even the most ignorant inexcusable. Since, therefore, Balaam was only endowed with a special gift, he borrowed devices in various directions, which savoured of nothing but the illusions of the devil, and were utterly foreign to the true and legitimate method of consulting (God.) Hence came the seven victims and the seven altars; for, although God, by consecrating the seventh day unto Himself, as also in the seven lamps, and other things, indicated that there was something of perfection in that number; nevertheless, afterwards, many strange superstitions were invented, and under this pretence Satan cunningly deluded wretched men, by persuading them that secret virtues were contained in this number seven. This frivolous subtlety prevailed also among profane writers, so that they sought the confirmation of the error throughout all nature. Thus they allege the seven planets, as many Pleiades, the *Septem-*

triones,[1] and as many circles or zones; and again, that infants do not come into the world alive till the seventh month. Many such things they heap together in order to prove that some hidden mystery is implied in the number seven. This contagion reached the Christians also: for on this point the ancients[2] sometimes philosophize too refinedly, and have in general preferred to corrupt (Scripture) rather than not to restrict the gifts of the Spirit to this number, and to establish the sevenfold grace of the Holy Ghost. It is plain that Balaam was infected by this fanciful notion, when he endeavours to draw down God by seven altars, and twice seven sacrifices. Let us, however, learn from Balak's prompt compliance, that the superstitious neither spare expense, nor refuse anything which is demanded by the masters of their errors. Wherefore we must beware lest we be rashly credulous; whilst at the same time we take care lest, when it is clear what we ought to do, we should be withheld by discreditable supineness, when unbelievers hasten so eagerly and speedily to their own destruction.

3. *And Balaam said unto Balak.* In this respect, also, he imitates the true servants of God: for he seeks retirement, because God has almost always appeared unto His servants when they have been separated from the company of men. You would say that he was another Moses, when he exhorts the king to persevering prayer, and, in order that he may be more earnest in supplication, bids him remain perfectly still by the altars. Meanwhile he withdraws himself from the crowd, and the eyes of the witnesses, so that he may be more ready to receive the revelation. Since, however, there was no sincerity in him, we may probably conclude, that in vain ostentation he imitated the servants of God, that, like one of God's councillors, he might bring forth the secrets

[1] "The seven stars, or Charles's wain."—Ainsworth. "Sed ego quidem cum L. Aelio, et M. Varrone sentio, qui *triones* rustico certo vocabulo boves appellatos scribunt, quasi quosdam *terriones*, hoc est, arandæ colendæque terræ idoneos. Itaque hoc sidus, quod a figurâ posituràque ipsâ, quia simile plaustro videtur, antiqui Græcorum, αμαξαν, dixerunt, nostri quoque veteres a bubus junctis *septemtriones* appellarunt; id est, a septem stellis, ex quibus quasi juncti *triones* figurantur."—A. Gell. ii. 21.

[2] "Les anciens docteurs."—*Fr.*

from the shrines of heaven. I know not why some render the word שְׁפִי, *shephi, alone,* others, *sad* :[1] it is more suitable to take it for *a high place ;* which other similar passages confirm. The impostor, therefore, retired into a higher place, or summit, in order that he might come forth from thence more surely established as a prophet by his familiar intercourse with God.

4. *And God met Balaam.* It is wonderful that God should have determined to have anything in common with the pollutions of Balaam ; since there is no communion between light and darkness, and He detests all association with demons ; but, however hateful to God the impiety of Balaam was, this did not prevent Him from making use of him in this particular act. This *meeting* him, then, was by no means a proof of His favour, as if he approved of the seven altars, and sanctioned these superstitions ; but as He well knows how to apply corrupt instruments to His use, so by the mouth of this false prophet, He promulgated the covenant, which He had made with Abraham, to foreign and heathen nations.

In truth, he boasts of his seven altars, as if he had duly propitiated God. Thus do hypocrites arrogantly trust that they deserve well of God, when they do but provoke His anger. God, however, passes over this corrupt worship, and proceeds with what He had determined ; for He sends Balaam to be a proclaimer and witness of the sureness of His grace towards His chosen people. He supplies, indeed, His servants with what they speak, and controls their tongues ; for neither would they be sufficient to think anything, unless the ability were bestowed by Him ; and no one can say that Jesus is the Lord, but by the Holy Ghost. Still the holy Prophets were in suchwise organs of the Spirit, that they gave forth from the heart the treasures which God had deposited with them. In this view, Jeremiah says that

[1] *A.V.* " an high place." *Margin,* " he went solitary." " Onkelos explains the word שפי as יחידי, *alone ;* but Kimchi interprets it as גבוה, *a high place.* Rabbi Jehuda expounds is it as נשבר, *affected with grief,* &c."—*S.M.* There is a curious error in the *Fr.*, evidently arising from its dictation to an amanuensis, " le mot que j'ay translaté *Amen,*" *i.e.*, " *à mont,*" as it stands in the *Fr.* Text.

he "did eat the words of God," (Jer. xv. 16;) and Ezekiel, that he ate the roll on which his prophecies were written. (Ezek. iii. 1.) For we must not conceive an inspiration (ἐνθουσιασμὸς) such as that by which the heathens supposed their diviners to be carried away, so that the heavenly *afflatus* transported them, or threw them into ecstasies; but rather did that take place in them, which David declares of himself: "I believed, therefore have I spoken," (Ps. cxvi. 10:) and God illuminated their senses before He guided their tongues. The case of Balaam was different, whose mind was alienated while he delivered the words which were put into his mouth.[1]

7. *And he took up his parable and said.* The word משל, *mashal,* signifies all weighty and notable sayings, especially when expressed in exalted language. The meaning, therefore, is, that Balaam began to speak eloquently, and in no ordinary strain. Nor can it be doubted but that he aroused Balak's attention by this grandeur of language through God's secret influence; that the wretched man might acknowledge that Balaam now spoke in no mortal fashion, but that there was something of divine inspiration in his words, so that his mind might be the more deeply affected by the revelation. The sum of what he said was to this effect, that there was not merely perversity and folly in Balak's design to curse the people, but that whatever he attempted would be vain and useless, since he was fighting against God. At the same time, he renounces for himself that power, which Balak was persuaded that he eminently possessed: for Moses has already recorded the words of Balak before spoken, "I know that he whom thou cursest is cursed," as if the power of God were transferred to him, so that he might exercise it according to his will. But what was this, but to depose God from His supremacy? Consequently this abominable imagination is refuted by the mouth of Balaam, when he attributes the right of blessing to God alone. "How (he says) should I curse except according to God's command?" not that God always restrains the wicked from declaring what

[1] Addition in *Fr.;* "comme une pie en cage, ainsi qu'on dit;" like pie in a cage, as they say.

is opposed to His truth: for we know that they often prate at random, vomit forth their blasphemies by the mouthful, obscure the light by their falsehoods, and endeavour, as far as in them lies, to overthrow the faithfulness of God. But inasmuch as Balaam was compelled to play a different part, viz., to proclaim the revelation suggested to him by God, he confesses that his tongue was tied, so that he could not utter a single syllable against God's command.

Since mention is made of Syria, some have supposed that Balaam was fetched from Mesopotamia; and some colour was given to this mistake, because the art of divination had its rise amongst the Chaldeans. But, as has been said before, it is not credible that the fame of the man should have extended so far; and again, in the short time during which the people remained there, how could an embassy have been twice sent to a distant country? for they would have occupied at least six months. Besides, we shall soon see that he was slain among the Midianites. But it is very probable that the country was included under the name of Aram or Syria, which even profane authors describe as contiguous to Arabia, towards the Red Sea. Now, since, in reference to the land of Moab, Midian was to the eastward, and, moreover, was high and mountainous, it is rightly added that he was called "from the mountains of the east;" and thus does he designate a place well known to the Moabites, on account of its neighbourhood to them.

9. *For from the top of the rocks I see him.* Unless I am mistaken, the meaning is that, although he only beheld the people from afar, so that he could not accurately perceive their power from so high and distant a spot, still they portended to him something great and formidable. A closer view generally intimidates men; besides, a body of twenty thousand men then dazzles our sight, as if the number were five times as great: whilst the real extent of a thing is also more accurately ascertained. But Balaam declares, in the spirit of prophecy, that he sees far more in the people of God than their distance from him would allow; for, posted as he was on a high eminence, he would have only beheld them as dwarfs with the ordinary vision of men. He says, that

"the people shall dwell alone," as being by no means in want of external support: for לבדד, *lebadad*, is equivalent to *solitarily* or *separately*. It is said of the people, therefore, that they shall dwell in such a manner as to be content with their own condition, neither desiring the wealth or power of others, nor seeking their aid. The fact that the people had recourse at one time to the Egyptians, at another to the Assyrians, and entangled themselves in improper alliances, is not repugnant to this prophecy, in which the question is not as to the virtue of the people, but only as to the blessing of God, which is again celebrated in the same words in Deut. xxxiii. 28.

What follows, that "they shall not be reckoned among the nations," must not be understood in depreciation of them, as if it were said that they should be of no credit or position; but the elect people is exalted above all others in dignity and excellence, as though he had said that there should be no nation under heaven equal to or comparable with them. And, although there were other kingdoms more illustrious for the flourishing condition of their people, and superior both in the number of their inhabitants, and in all kinds of prosperity, still this people never forfeited their pre-eminence, since they were distinguished, not so much by wealth and external endowments, as by the adoption of God. Thus, Mount Sion is called noble above all other mountains, because God had there chosen to make His abode. Others explain it that the people should be alone, so as not to be brought into comparison with the Gentiles, inasmuch as its religion should be separate from the whole world, and unmingled with heathen corruptions. The exposition which I have given is, however, more simple.

10. *Who can count the dust of Jacob?* Hence it is plain that what Balaam was to say was suggested to him by God, since he quotes the words of God's solemn promise, wherein the seed of Abraham is compared to the dust of the earth. Still, we must bear in mind what I have just adverted to, that, although that multitude was reduced to a small number by the sin of the people, nevertheless this was not declared in vain, inasmuch as that little body at length expanded

itself so as to fill the whole world. Speaking by *hyperbole*, then, he says that their offspring would be infinite, since the fourth part will be almost innumerable. His aspiration at the conclusion is more emphatic than a simple affirmation. "I would (he says) that I might share with them their last end!"[1] For, in the first place, every one longs for what is most for his good; and again, Balaam confesses himself unworthy to be reckoned among the elect people of God. Hence it might be easily inferred how foolishly Balak trusted to his curse. Further, in these words he refers to everlasting felicity; as much as to say that (Israel) would be blessed in death as in life. At the same time he is a witness to our future immortality; not that he had reflected in himself wherefore the death of the righteous would be desirable, but God extorted this confession from an unholy man, so that, either unwillingly or thoughtlessly, he exclaimed that God so persevered in the extension of His paternal favour towards His people, that He did not cease to be gracious to them even in their death. Hence it follows, that the grace of God extends beyond the bounds of this perishing life. Wherefore this declaration contains a remarkable testimony to our future immortality. For although Balaam, perhaps, did not thoroughly consider what he desired, still, there is no doubt but that he truly professed that he wished it for himself. Nevertheless, as hypocrites are wont to do, he did but conceive an evanescent wish, for it was in no real seriousness that he sought what he was convinced was best.[2]

The Israelites are called *righteous* (*recti*,) as also in other places, not on account of their own righteousness, but in

[1] Corn. à Lapide has a curious note on "the death of the righteous," contrasting the happy deaths of some, whom he deemed righteous, with those of others, whom he counted enemies of the Church. Amongst the latter he refers to Calvin himself. "Calvin, excruciated, according to Beza, by divers diseases, was in addition preyed upon by lice, as Jerome Bolsec, a physician of Lyons, and formerly his disciple, reports in his Life, ch. xxii. Hence observe, that those who persecute the Church, were, by God's just judgment, eaten by worms. Such was the case with Huneric, Herod, Antiochus, the emperors Maximinianus and Arnulphus, and Calvin."

[2] "Qu'il desireroit d'estre en pareille condition avecques le peuple d'Israel;" that he desired to be in a like condition with the people of Israel.—*Fr.*

accordance with God's good pleasure, who had deigned to separate them from the unclean nations.

11. *And Balak said unto Balaam.* The proud man again reproaches the false prophet, as if he had fairly purchased of him the right of prophecy.[1] Behold how the reprobate seek God by crooked paths, and desire to have nothing to do with Him, unless He yields to their improper wishes—in a word, unless they render Him submissive to them. Balaam, therefore, is compelled to repress this stupid arrogance, by pleading God's command, and declaring that nothing more was allowed him than to announce what God prescribed. But we must remember that this was only spoken in reference to a particular act, when, as far as his words went, he acted the part of a true prophet, although his feelings were altogether on the other side.

13. And Balak said unto him, Come, I pray thee, with me unto another place, from whence thou mayest see them: thou shalt see but the utmost part of them, and shalt not see them all; and curse me them from thence.

14. And he brought him into the field of Zophim, to the top of Pisgah, and built seven altars, and offered a bullock and a ram on *every* altar.

15. And he said unto Balak, Stand here by thy burnt-offering, while I meet *the Lord* yonder.

16. And the Lord met Balaam, and put a word in his mouth, and said, Go again unto Balak, and say thus.

17. And when he came to him, behold, he stood by his burnt-offering, and the princes of Moab with him. And Balak said unto him, What hath the Lord spoken?

18. And he took up his parable, and said, Rise up, Balak, and hear; hearken unto me, thou son of Zippor.

19. God *is* not a man, that he should lie; neither the son of man,

13. Tunc dixit ad eum Balac: Veni obsecro mecum ad alterum locum, unde videas illum (tantummodo extremum ejus vidisti, et totum ipsum non vidisti) et ei maledic mihi inde.

14. Et tulit eum in locum sublimem, in verticem Pisgah: ædificavitque septem altaria et obtulit juvencum et arietem in altari.

15. Dixit autem ad Balac, Consiste hic juxta holocaustum tuum, et ego occurram illic.

16. Occurrit verò Jehova ipsi Balaam, et posuit verbum in ore ejus, dixitque, Revertere ad Balac, et sic loqueris.

17. Venit itaque ad eum, et ecce, ille stabat juxta holocaustum suum, et principes Moab cum illo: cui dixit Balac, Quid loquutus est Jehova?

18. Tunc assumpsit parabolam suam, et dixit, Surge Balac, et audi, ausculta verba mea, fili Sippor.

19. Non est homo Deus, ut mentiatur, et filius hominis, ut pœniteat

[1] L'authorité de le faire parler comme il veudroit;" the authority to make him speak whatever he chose.—*Fr.*

that he should repent: hath he said, and shall he not do *it?* or hath he spoken, and shall he not make it good?

20. Behold, I have received *commandment* to bless: and he hath blessed; and I cannot reverse it.

21. He hath not beheld iniquity in Jacob, neither hath he seen perverseness in Israel: the Lord his God *is* with him, and the shout of a king *is* among them.

22. God brought them out of Egypt: he hath as it were the strength of an unicorn.

23. Surely *there is* no enchantment against Jacob, neither *is there* any divination against Israel: according to this time it shall be said of Jacob and of Israel, What hath God wrought!

24. Behold, the people shall rise up as a great lion, and lift up himself as a young lion: he shall not lie down until he eat *of* the prey, and drink the blood of the slain.

eum: ipse dixit, et non faciet? loquutus est, et non præstabit illud?

20. Ecce ut benedicerem accepi: et benedixit *benedictione,* et non revocabo eam.

21. Non aspexit iniquitatem in Jacob, nec vidit violentiam in Israel. Jehova Deus ejus est cum eo, et clangor regis in eo.

22. Deus eduxit eos ex Ægypto: sicut robur unicornis est ei.

23. Non est augurium in Jacob, nec est divinatio in Israel: secundum hoc tempus dicetur de Jacob, et Israele, Quid operatus est Deus?

24. En populus tanquam leo surget, et tanquam leunculus elevabitur: non accubabit donec comederit prædam, et sanguinem occisorum biberit.

13. *And Balak said unto him.* Balak did, as almost all superstitious persons usually do; for, because with them nothing is certain or established, they are carried about from one speculation to another, and try now this and now that expedient. But especially do they imagine that there is some magical power in the sight, as if the eyes contributed partly to the efficacy of their incantations. It appears from profane writers that this was formerly a commonly received opinion, that the gaze of the enchanter had much effect upon his art. Balak, therefore, removes his sorcerer to another place, that there he might the better exercise his divinations. There is some ambiguity in the words. Some render them thus, "Come to another place, that thou mayest see from thence,[1] mayest see a part, and not the whole," as if Balak feared that the multitude itself frightened Balaam, or

[1] So *A. V.*, after the *LXX.* and *V.* Marckius comes to the conclusion that there is no sufficient reason for *C.'s* proposed alteration of the Hebrew tense, in the latter clauses of the verse; for he thinks that Balaam's expression in verse 9, "For from the top of the rocks I see him, and from the hills I behold him," is rather to be understood of a more complete, than of an obscurer view.

diminished the power of his incantations. Their opinion, however, is the more probable, who take the verb *see,* where it is used the second time, in the perfect tense, so that the sense is, "Come to a place where thou mayest behold them; for as yet thou hast not seen the whole, but only a part;" for we know how common a thing with the Hebrews is such an employment of one tense for another. With respect to the place to which Balaam was taken, it little matters whether we believe שדה צפים, *sedeh tzophim,* and פסגה, *pis'gah,* to be nouns proper or appellative, since it is sufficiently clear that, if they were given to the place, it was on account of its position; for it is very likely that there was a level place upon the hill, which might justly be called "The hill of the spies."

17. *And when he came to him.* Balak inquires what God had answered, although he had rejected the previous revelation. Thus do hypocrites profess anxious solicitude in inquiring the will of God, whilst the knowledge of it is intolerable to them. Therefore their extreme earnestness in inquiry is nothing but mere dissimulation. Besides, Balak hunts, as it were, for the answer of God by a distant divination, whereas a testimony to God's will was all the time engraven upon his heart. But this is the just punishment of perverse curiosity, when the wicked endeavour to impose a law upon God, that He may submit to their wishes. Balak omits nothing in regard to outward ceremonies; he humbly attends upon the altars for the purpose of propitiating God; but in the meantime he would have Him obedient to himself, and cannot endure to listen to Him, unless He speaks to him in flattering and deceptive terms.

18. *And he took up his parable and said.* We have already explained the meaning of this expression, namely, to make use of glowing and elevated language, in order the more to awaken the attention of the hearer. The same also is the object of the preface, "Rise up, Balak, and hear; hearken unto me, thou son of Zippor;" for such repetitions are mostly emphatic, and indicate something uncommon.

When he declares that "God cannot lie, because he is not like men," it is a severe kind of censure, as much as to say,

"Would you make God a liar?" for it became requisite that the frantic eagerness of Balak should be repressed, and prevented from proceeding any further. Hence, however, a lesson of supreme utility may be extracted, namely, that men are altogether wrong when they form their estimate of God from their own disposition and habits. Still, almost all men labour under this mistake. For how comes it that we are so prone to waver, except because we weigh God's promises in our own scale? In order, therefore, that we may learn to lift up our minds above the world, whenever the faithfulness and certainty of God's word are in question, it is well for us to reflect how great the distance is between ourselves and God. Men are wont to lie, because they are fickle and changeable in their plans, or because sometimes they are unable to accomplish what they have promised; but change of purpose arises either from levity or bad faith, or because we repent of what we have spoken foolishly and inconsiderately. But to God nothing of this sort occurs; for He is neither deceived, nor does He deceitfully promise anything, nor, as James says, is there with Him any "shadow of turning." (James i. 7.) We now understand to what this dissimilitude between God and men refers, namely, that we should not travesty God according to our own notions, but, in our consideration of His nature, should remember that He is liable to no changes, since He is far above all heavens. As to the meaning of the repentance of God, of which mention is often made, let my readers seek it elsewhere in its proper place. We must, however, at the same time, observe the application of the lesson; for the words "God is true," would have no efficacy in themselves, unless they are applied to their appropriate use, *i.e.*, that we should with unhesitating faith acquiesce in His promises, and seriously tremble at His threats. For with the same object it is said that the word of God is pure and perfect, and is compared with gold refined seven times in the fire; and this also is the tendency of the conclusion, which is presently added: "Shall He not fulfil what He has spoken?" Balak desired to have the people cursed, whom God had adopted: Balaam declares that this is impossible, because God is unchangeable in that which He has decreed. In a word, he teaches us the same truth as Paul does, that the election of his people is "without repentance," because it is founded on the gratuitous liberality of God. (Rom. xi. 29.) If, then, this saying was extorted from the hireling false prophet, how inexcusable will be our stupidity, if our minds vary and waver in embracing God's word, as if He Himself were variable.

20. *Behold I have received* commandment *to bless.* He signifies that a command to bless had been given him, and a positive law laid down for him. For, as has been said, he was not free and independent in this matter; but God had bound him to exercise the prophetic office, even against his own will. Hence he declares that it is not in his power to alter the revelation, of which he is the minister and witness. But there is a remarkable expression introduced in the midst of his declaration, viz., that God himself had blessed; whereby he intimates that the lot of men, whether adverse or prosperous, depends on the authority of God alone; and that no other commission is given to the prophets, except to promulgate what God has appointed; as if he had said, It belongs to God alone to decree what the condition of men is to be; He has chosen me to proclaim His blessing; it is not in my power either to reverse or withdraw it. Now, since Balaam here sustains the character of a true Prophet, we may gather from his words that no other power of binding or loosing is given to the ministers of the Word, except that they should faithfully bring forward what they may have received from God.

21. *He hath not beheld iniquity in Jacob.* Some understand by און, *aven,* עמל, *gnamal,* idols,[1] which bring nothing but deadly labour and trouble to their worshippers; as if it were said that Israel was pure and untainted by such offences, in that they duly served the one true God. But how will it be correct to say that God saw not idolatry in the people, when they had so openly fallen into it? For, although the golden calf was only made on one occasion, still their manifold and almost constant rebellions were such

[1] So the *V.*, "Non est idolum in Jacob, nec videtur simulachrum in Israel."

as to forbid these wicked and perverse men from being thus absolved. Since, however, these two words in connexion signify all sorts of iniquities, which tend to men's hurt, or to the infliction of harm and loss, a more proper meaning will be, that such iniquity is not seen in Jacob as to include him with the nations that are given to violence and crime. Nevertheless, even if we take it thus, the former question still arises; for we know that the Israelites were scarcely better than the worst of mankind. Some reply feebly, that it was not seen, because God did not impute it; but, in my opinion, nothing else is meant by these words but that the people were pleasing to God, because He had sanctified them. If any object, that they were not therefore any the more just or innocent, the answer is easy—that it is not here declared what they were, but only God's grace is magnified, who deigned to exalt them as a holy nation. In this way Jerusalem was the holy city and the royal abode of God, though it was a den of thieves. On this ground Paul says that the children of Abraham were "holy branches," (Rom. xi. 16,) because they sprang from a holy root. In the same sense they are everywhere called God's children, however degenerate they might be. God, therefore, is said to have seen no iniquity in them, with reference to His adoption; not that they were worthy of such exalted praise, as if a distinction were drawn between them and the other nations —not on account of their deserts, but from the mere good pleasure of God. Thus Paul elsewhere, after he has compared them with the Gentiles, and has shewn that they are their superiors in no respect, at length adds, "What advantage then hath the Jew? or what profit is there of circumcision? Much (he says) every way;" and adduces a mark of distinction which does not proceed from themselves.[1] (Rom. iii. 1.) In a word, because it had pleased God to choose that people, He rather manifested His love towards Himself and His own grace, than towards their life and conduct.

Others take this passage otherwise, viz., that God did not behold iniquity, nor see perverseness in Jacob, because He

[1] *i.e.*, "That unto them were committed the oracles of God."

was not willing that he should be unrighteously grieved or afflicted; as if it were said, If any one should wish unjustly to injure this people, God will permit no violence or injustice to be done to them, but will rather defend them as their shield. But if this sense be preferred, I should rather be disposed to take the verb indefinitely, as if it were said, Perverseness shall not be seen in Jacob; for when the Hebrews use the verb without a nominative, they extend the matter in question into a general proposition, and then the verb in the active voice may be suitably resolved into the passive. And thus the context will run better, since it is added immediately afterwards, "The Lord his God is with him," whereby the reason seems to be given why perverseness (*molestia*) should not be seen *against* Jacob, viz., because God would be at hand to render him aid. For we know that His infinite power suffices to defend the safety of His Church, so that not even the gates of hell should prevail against it.

What follows directly afterwards, "The shout or the rejoicing of a king is among them," I understand to be that God will always give them cause for triumph; for the word which the old interpreter elsewhere renders rejoicing (*jubilationem,*) seems here to be used for songs of rejoicing; but, since it also signifies the sound of a trumpet, it will not be inappropriate to take it as that the people shall be terrible to their enemies, because they shall boldly rush forward, or go down to the battle, as if God sounded the trumpet.

22. *God brought them out of Egypt.* He assigns a reason for their constant success, *i.e.*, because God has once redeemed this people, He will not forsake the work which He has begun. The argument is drawn from the continued course of God's blessings; for, since they flow from an inexhaustible fountain, their progress is incessant. This, however, specially refers to the state of the Church, for He will never cease to be gracious to His children, until He has led them to the very end of their course. Rightly, therefore, does Balaam conclude that, because God has once redeemed His people, He will be the perpetual guardian of their welfare. He afterwards teaches that the power where-

with God defends His people shall be invincible, for this is the meaning of the similitude of the unicorn.

23. *Surely there is no enchantment.* This passage is commonly expounded as an encomium on the people, because they are not given to enchantments and magical superstitions, as God also had strictly enjoined upon them in His law that they should not pollute themselves by such defilements. Others thus explain it, The Israelites shall not want enchanters, because by the Urim and Thummim, or by the Prophets, God would reveal to them whatever should be profitable for them. Their opinion is more correct who thus interpret it, No enchantment and no divination avails against the Israelites. Let us now proceed to explain this more clearly. Balaam, in my judgment, confesses that there is no room for His enchantments, or that his customary arts fail him now, because their efficacy and power cannot affect the Israelites. And this confession harmonizes with the words of Pharaoh's magicians, when they said, "This is the finger of God," (Exod. viii. 19;) after they had pertinaciously contended, until God compelled them to yield. Thus now Balaam declares that the elect people were defended from on high, so that his divinations were ineffectual, and his enchantments vain.

The other clause of the verse appears to me to be simply to this effect, that God would henceforth perform mighty works for the defence of His people which should be related with admiration. The translation which some give is constrained and far-fetched, "As at this time it shall be said, What has God wrought in Israel?" for Balaam rather would say, that great should be the progress of God's grace, the beginnings only of which then appeared; and in short, he declares that henceforth memorable should be the performances of God in behalf of His people, which should supply abundant subjects for history.

24. *Behold, the people shall rise up as a great lion.* This comparison is not in every respect accurate; for it does not signify that the Israelites should be cruel or rapacious, but merely bold and strong, and prompt in their resistance if any should provoke them. In the next chapter, it will

occur again with a slight change in the words. What Balaam here predicates generally of the whole people, is applied in the blessings of Jacob to the tribe of Judah alone, (Gen. xlix. 9,) because it especially excelled in bravery. The sum is, that however the people of Israel might be attacked on every side, it should be endued with invincible fortitude, to overcome all assaults, or to repel them vigorously. Let us, finally, remember that this courage, wherewith Israel was to defend itself against all its enemies, was counted amongst the gifts of God; as if Balaam had said that they should be preserved by the help of God.

25. And Balak said unto Balaam, Neither curse them at all, nor bless them at all.

26. But Balaam answered and said unto Balak, Told not I thee, saying, All that the Lord speaketh, that I must do?

27. And Balak said unto Balaam, Come, I pray thee, I will bring thee unto another place; peradventure it will please God that thou mayest curse me them from thence.

28. And Balak brought Balaam unto the top of Peor, that looketh toward Jeshimon.

29. And Balaam said unto Balak, Build me here seven altars, and prepare me here seven bullocks and seven rams.

30. And Balak did as Balaam had said, and offered a bullock and a ram on *every* altar.

25. Dixit autem Balac ad Balaam Neque maledicas ei, neque benedicas.

26. Cui respondit Balaam, dicens: Annon dixi tibi, Quicquid dixerit Jehova id faciam?

27. Tunc dixit Balac ad Balaam, Veni agedum, ducam te ad locum alium, si fortè inde placebit Deo ut maledicas ei mihi.

28. Sumpsit ergo Balac ipsum Balaam in verticem Peor qui respicit versus desertum (*vel,* Jesimon.)

29. Dixit autem Balaam ad Balac, Ædifica mihi hic septem altaria, et appara mihi hic septem juvencos, et septem arietes.

30. Fecit itaque Balac quemadmodum dixerat Balaam, et obtulit juvencum et arietem in *unoquoque* altari.

25. *And Balak said unto Balaam.* Here we may behold as in a mirror how wretchedly unbelievers are driven to and fro, so as to alternate between vain hopes and fears, though by their changes of purpose they are still brought back to the same errors, as if their blind passion led them through a labyrinth. When Balak sees that he is deceived in his opinion, he seeks at least that the hireling prophet should neither profit nor injure. This, however, is exactly as if he would have God to lie idle; but presently he recovers his spirits, and endeavours to repurchase the curse, which

in his penitence he had abandoned. For this cause he drags Balaam to another place, although he had already discovered that this was in vain. But thus pertinaciously do unbelievers prosecute their wicked efforts: whilst, at the same time, the disquietude which agitates them with doubts is the just reward of their temerity.

26. *But Balaam answered and said.* The mercenary prophet here confesses that he has no more power of himself to be silent than to speak. Nor is there any doubt but that he would excuse himself with servility to the proud king, to whom he would willingly have sold himself; as if, in his desire to avert the odium and blame from himself, he would state that he was carried away against his will by the Divine *afflatus.* At the same time he throws back the blame on Balak himself, who, though warned in time, had still foolishly sent to fetch him. The rest I have already expounded.

NUMBERS, CHAPTER XXIV.

1. And when Balaam saw that it pleased the Lord to bless Israel, he went not, as at other times, to seek for enchantments, but he set his face toward the wilderness.

2. And Balaam lifted up his eyes, and he saw Israel abiding *in his tents* according to their tribes; and the Spirit of God came upon him.

3. And he took up his parable, and said, Balaam the son of Beor hath said, and the man whose eyes are open hath said:

4. He hath said, which heard the words of God, which saw the vision of the Almighty, falling *into a trance,* but having his eyes open:

5. How goodly are thy tents, O Jacob! *and* thy tabernacles, O Israel!

6. As the valleys are they spread forth, as gardens by the river's side, as the trees of lign-aloes, which the Lord hath planted, *and* as cedar-trees beside the waters.

1. Quum autem videret Balaam quod placeret Jehovæ, ut benediceret Israeli, non abiit sicut semel et iterum in occursum auguriorum: sed posuit versus desertum faciem suam.

2. Ac quum elevasset oculos suos, vidit Israelem dispositum per tribus suas: fuitque super eum Spiritus Dei.

3. Tunc assumpsit parabolam suam, et ait, Dicit Balaam filius Beor, dicit vir reconditus oculo.

4. Dicit qui audivit eloquia Dei, qui visionem Omnipotentis vidit, qui cadit et aperiuntur oculi ejus.

5. Quam pulchra tabernacula tua Jacob, habitacula tua Israel!

6. Sicut valles diffusæ, sicut horti juxta flumen, sicut arbores aloes, quas plantavit Jehova, sicut cedri juxta aquas.

7. He shall pour the water out of his buckets, and his seed *shall be* in many waters; and his king shall be higher than Agag, and his kingdom shall be exalted.

8. God brought him forth out of Egypt: he hath as it were the strength of an unicorn: he shall eat up the nations his enemies, and shall break their bones, and pierce *them* through with his arrows.

9. He couched, he lay down as a lion, and as a great lion: who shall stir him up? Blessed *is* he that blesseth thee, and cursed *is* he that curseth thee.

7. Defluet aqua è situla ejus, et semen ejus in aquis multis, et elevabitur rex ejus super Agag, et extolletur regnum ejus.

8. Deus eduxit eum ex Ægypto: sicut vires unicornis ei. Consumet gentes hostes suos, et ossa eorum conteret, et sagittis suis confodiet (*vel*, sagittas suas tinget sanguine.)

9. Incurvabit se ut accubet tanquam leo minor, et tanquam leo major: quis excitabit eum? Quisquis benedixerit tibi, erit benedictus: et quisquis maledixerit tibi, erit maledictus.

1. *And when Balaam saw that it pleased the Lord.* It is evident that Balaam, in order to gratify the wicked king for the sake of the reward, endeavoured by various shifts and expedients to obtain an answer in accordance with his wishes. Thus do the wicked seek to propitiate God by delusive means, just as we soothe children by coaxing. And God for some time allowed him[1] to gloat upon his fallacious oracle. He now, however, lays closer constraint upon him, and, breaking off all delay, dictates an answer, which He compels him to deliver. For his obedience is not here praised as if, when he understood the will of God, he yielded voluntarily and abandoned his monstrous cupidity; but, because now there was no more room for subterfuge, he dared not stir his foot, as if God had put forth His hand to retain him in his place.

When it is said that "the Spirit of God was upon him,"[2] after he turned his eyes "toward the wilderness" and beheld the camp of Israel, how they were marshalled "according to their tribes," we must understand it thus: not that he was influenced by a sincere feeling of good-will, so that the sight itself suggested grounds for blessing; but that he was induced by the inspiration of the same Spirit, who afterwards put forth His influence in the prophecy itself. It is

[1] "Inhiare fallaci oraculo."—*Lat.* "Q'uil fust comme à la chasse, pour obtenir quelque fausse revelation;" to be, as it were, in chase of some false revelation.—*Fr.*

[2] *A. V.*, "came upon him."

said, then, that the Spirit of God was upon him, not as if it had begun to inspire him at that particular moment when he cast his eyes upon the camp of Israel; but because it prompted him to look in that direction, in order that the impulse of prophecy might be stronger in him, as respecting a thing actually before his eyes. But after the Spirit had thus affected his senses, or at any rate had prepared them to be fit instruments for the execution of his office, it then also directed his tongue to prophesy; but in an extraordinary manner, so that a divine majesty shone forth in the sudden change, as if he were transformed into a new man. In a word, "the Spirit of God was upon him," shewing by manifest token that He was the author of his address, and that he did not speak of his own natural intelligence. To the same intent it is said that "he took up his parable," because[1] the character of his address was marked with unusual grandeur and magnificent brilliancy.

3. *And the man whose eyes are open*[2] *hath said.* This preface has no other object than to prove that he is a true prophet of God, and that he has received the blessing, which he pronounces, from divine revelation; and indeed his boast was true as regarded this special act, though it might be the case that pride and ambition impelled him thus to vaunt. It is, however, probable that he prefaced his prophecy in this way by the inspiration of the Spirit, in order to demand more credit for what he said. From a consideration of this purpose we may the better gather the meaning of his words. Balaam dignifies himself with titles, by which he may claim for himself the prophetic office; whatever, therefore, he predicates of himself, we may know to be the attributes of true prophets, whose marks and distinctions he borrows. To this end he says that he is "hidden in his eye," by which he means that he does not see in the ordinary manner, but that he is endued with the power of

[1] "Sa façon de parler a eu une gravité authentique, pour toucher plus au vif ceux qui l'orroyent;" his manner of speaking possessed a genuine grandeur, in order to touch more closely to the quick those that might hear it.—*Fr.*

[2] "Reconditus oculo;" covered in the eye.—*Lat.* "Qui a l'œil couvert;" who has the eye covered.—*Fr.*

secret vision. Interpreters agree that שתם, *shethum,* is equivalent to סתם, *sethum,* which is *closed* or *hidden.* Thus some render it in the pluperfect tense: The man who had his eyes closed; and this they refer to the blindness of Balaam, since his ass saw more clearly than himself. Others, who perceive this gloss to be too poor, expound it by *antiphrasis,* Whose eye was open; but, since this interpretation, too, is unnatural, I have no doubt but that he says his eyes were hidden, because in their secret vision they have more than human power.[1] For David makes use of the word to signify mysteries, when he says: "Thou hast manifested to me the hidden things[2] of wisdom." (Ps. li. 6.) Unless, perhaps, we may prefer that he was called the man with hidden eyes, as despising all human things, and as one with whom there is no respect of persons; the former interpretation, however, is the more suitable. And assuredly, when he adds immediately afterwards, the hearer of "the words of God, which saw the vision of the Almighty," it must be taken expositively. To the same effect is what is added in conclusion: "He who falls,[3] and his eyes are opened;" for the exposition which some give, that his mind was awake whilst he was asleep as regarded his body, is far-fetched; and there is a tameness in the opinion of those who refer it to the previous history, where it is recorded that, after Balaam had fallen under the ass, his eyes were opened to

[1] This word has occasioned much discussion among the commentators. *A. V.* subjoins in the margin: "*Heb.* who had his eyes shut, *but now* opened." Ainsworth says: "*Shethum,* the original word, is of contrary significance to *Sethum,* that is, *closed* or *shut up;* however, some take it to be of the same meaning, which may then be explained thus, *The man* who had his *eye shut,* but now open. And *eye* is put for *eyes,* understanding the eyes of his mind opened by the spirit of prophecy; though some of the Hebrews (as Jarchi here observeth) have from hence conjectured that Balaam was blind of one eye!" Dathe, in accordance with the most ancient interpreters, (*LXX.* Onkelos, and the Syriac,) agrees with the text of *A. V.*

[2] *A. V.* "And in the hidden *part* thou shalt make me to know wisdom." *C.'s* exposition *in loco* appears rather to agree with *A. V.* than with his citation in this place. "Some interpret בסתום, *besathum,* as if he here declared that God had discovered secret mysteries to him, or things hidden from the human understanding. He seems rather to mean that wisdom had been discovered to his mind in a secret and intimate manner." See Cal. Soc. edit. of Psalms, vol. ii. pp. 292, 293, and note.

[3] *A. V.,* "falling *into a trance,* but having his eyes open."

see the angel (chap. xxii. 31.) Comparing himself, therefore, to the prophets, he says that he fell down in order to receive his visions; for we often read that the prophets were prostrated, or lost their strength, and lay almost lifeless, when God revealed Himself to them; for thus did it please God to cast down His servants as to the flesh, in order to lift them up above the world, and to empty them of their own strength, in order to replenish them with heavenly virtue.

5. *How goodly are thy tents, O Jacob!* The internal condition of prosperity enjoyed by the people is described by various similitudes akin to each other, and expressive of the same thing. He compares them to valleys and well-watered gardens, and then to trees which were rendered succulent by abundance of moisture, and finally to fields whose seeds imbibe fatness from the waters. The word we translate "*valleys* spread forth," some prefer to render "streams;" and the Hebrew word signifies both; but the course of the metaphors requires that valleys should be rather understood. For the same reason I have given the translation "aloe-trees;" for, although the word אהלים, *ohelim*, often means "tabernacles," I have no doubt but that it here refers to trees, so as to correspond with what follows as to the cedars. They are called trees "which the Lord hath planted," as surpassing the ordinary growth of nature in their peculiar excellency, and exhibiting something more noble than the effect of human labour and skill.

In the concluding similitude the interpreters have erred, in my opinion. Some translate it, "His seed (*is*) many waters;" others, "on many waters;" but[1] the literal translation which I have given runs far better, viz., that he is like a rich and fertile field, whose seed is steeped in much water.

Thus far Balaam has been speaking of God's blessing,

[1] Ainsworth says: "This *seed* may be understood, as before, of children; and *many waters*, of many peoples, as in Rev. xvii. 15; Isa. lvii. 19; Ps. cxliv. 7. Or *seed* may mean *corn* sown in watery, moist, and fruitful places, to bring forth much increase; as Isa. xxxii. 20." *C.'s* own translation is, after all, equivocal; however, his opinion may incline to the literal meaning of the word *seed*.

which shall enrich the people with an abundance of all good things.

7. *And his king shall be higher than Agag.* He now begins to enlarge on their outward prosperity, viz., that the people of Israel shall be powerful and flourishing, and endowed with a warlike spirit to resist the assaults of their enemies; for it would not be sufficient that they should abound with all blessings, unless the ability to defend them should also be superadded. It is by no means a probable conjecture that he speaks of Saul who made prisoner of their king, Agag, in the battle with the Amalekites; but their opinion is the more correct one, who suppose that this was a name common to all the kings of that nation. It was, therefore, God's intention to declare the superiority of His chosen people to the Amalekites; nor need we be surprised that they should be thus brought into especial antagonism with them, not only because they were the constant enemies of Israel, but because their power was then excessively great, as we shall very soon see: "Amalek was the first of nations," &c. (verse 20.)

Although for a long time afterwards, there was no king in Israel, still there is no absurdity in the fact that the commonwealth should be designated by the name of "king," and "kingdom;" especially since God had postponed the full accomplishment of His grace until the time of the establishment of the kingdom. Hence, in this prophecy, Balaam, however little he might have been aware of it, embraced the time of David; and consequently he predicted things which were only accomplished in Christ, on whom the adoption was founded.

What follows has been already expounded, viz., that God, in delivering His people, had made it plain that He would have them remain in safety and perpetuity; and that He was able to bring this to pass.

9. *Blessed is he that blesseth thee.* This mode of expression signifies that the Israelites were elected by God, on these terms, that He would account as conferred upon Himself whatever injury or benefit they might receive. Nor is there anything new in this, that God should declare

that He would be an enemy to the enemies of His Church; and, on the other hand, a friend to her friends, which is a token of the high favour with which He regards her. Hence, however, we are taught, that whatever good offices are performed towards the Church, are conferred upon God Himself, who will recompense them faithfully: and, at the same time, that believers cannot be injured, without His avenging them: even as He says; "He that toucheth you toucheth the apple of *my* eye." (Zech. ii. 8.) If any should object that Balaam himself went unrewarded, although he blessed the people, the reply is an easy one, that he was unworthy of any praise, who was by no means disposed in the people's favour of his own accord, and out of pure and generous feeling; but who was forcibly drawn in a direction whither he was unwilling to go. Meanwhile, this point remains unshaken, that whosoever have contributed their labours for the Church's welfare, and have been her faithful helpers, shall be sure partakers of the blessing which is here promised.

10. And Balak's anger was kindled against Balaam, and he smote his hands together: and Balak said unto Balaam, I called thee to curse mine enemies, and, behold, thou hast altogether blessed *them* these three times.

11. Therefore now flee thou to thy place: I thought to promote thee unto great honour; but, lo, the Lord hath kept thee back from honour.

12. And Balaam said unto Balak, Spake I not also to thy messengers, which thou sentest unto me, saying,

13. If Balak would give me his house full of silver and gold, I cannot go beyond the commandment of the Lord, to do *either* good or bad of mine own mind; *but* what the Lord saith, that will I speak?

14. And now, behold, I go unto my people: come *therefore, and* I will advertise thee what this people shall do to thy people in the latter days.

15. And he took up his parable, and said, Balaam the son of Beor

10. Et excanduit furor Balac contra Balaam, et percussit manus suas, ac dixit ipsi Balaam, Ut malediceres inimicis meis vocavi te, et ecce, benedixisti benedicendo jam tribus vicibus.

11. Nunc ergo fuge in locum tuum: dixeram, Honorando honorabo te, et ecce, privavit te Jehova gloria.

12. Cui respondit Balaam, Annon etiam nuntiis tuis quos miseras ad me loquutus sum, dicendo:

13. Si dederit mihi Balac plenam domum suam argento et auro, non potero transgredi sermonem Jehovæ, ut faciat bonum sive malum è corde meo: quod loquetur Jehova, illud loquar?

14. Nunc itaque ecce, ego discedo ad populum meum: age, consulam tibi quid facturus sit populus iste populo tuo in novissimis diebus.

15. Tunc assumpsit parabolam suam, et dixit, Dixit Balaam filius

hath said, and the man whose eyes are open hath said;

16. He hath said, which heard the words of God, and knew the knowledge of the most High, *which* saw the vision of the Almighty, falling *into a trance*, but having his eyes open.

Beor, dixit, inquam, vir apertum habens oculum.

16. Dixit audiens eloquia Dei, et sciens scientiam Excelsi, videns visionem Omnipotentis: cadens, et discoopertum habens oculum.

10. *And Balak's anger was kindled against Balaam.* Inasmuch as the obstinacy of the wicked is not overcome, so that they should submit themselves to God, when He would bring their lusts under the yoke, it must needs be that, when they are still further pressed, they are carried away into passion. Thus now, Balak, after murmurings and expostulations, bursts forth into impetuous wrath, and rejects, and drives away with reproaches from his presence Balaam, whom he had hitherto been endeavouring to cajole. For, when he smites his hands together, it is because he can no longer restrain himself. He is especially indignant, because Balaam had not hesitated freely and openly to bear witness to the blessing of the children of Israel, against whom he was so full of hatred. For nothing is more galling to kings than when they see private individuals regarding their presence at least without alarm. Since he determines to give no reward to the untoward and ill-starred prophet, he throws the blame upon God, lest he should himself incur discredit from this, as if he were illiberal. And, indeed, what he says is true, that God had kept back Balaam from honour; yet impiously, and, as it were, reproachfully, does he lay the blame upon God, and, in fact, accuses Him of being the cause of the non-fulfilment of his promise.

12. *And Balaam said unto Balak.* Balaam speaks the truth, indeed, yet in a bad spirit, as we have seen: for he excuses himself with servility[1] to Balak, that it did not depend on himself that he did not comply with his wishes, but that God had stood in the way. For he grieves at the loss of his reward; and however grandly he may declaim on the supremacy of God, he still signifies that he has rather acted upon compulsion than willingly executed what was enjoined

[1] "Il fait le chien couchant."—*Fr.*

upon him. By "the word (*sermonem*) of Jehovah,"[1] he means not only His decree, but what had been dictated to him, and which he would have still greatly desired to alter; but he indicates that he was bound by the power of the Spirit to declare, even against his own will, whatever revelation he received. Thus the word "do" refers to his tongue, or his charge as a prophet; since he had not been hired by Balak to perform any manual act, but only to injure the people by his words. The word "heart"[2] is contrasted with the revelation of the Spirit; for impostors are said to speak out of their own heart, when they falsely make use of God's name to cover their own inventions. He, therefore, declares that he was not at liberty to speak "of his own heart," because he was the minister of the Spirit.

14. *And now, behold, I go unto my people.* Since the counsel which he gave is not here expressly mentioned,[3] it is the opinion of some that his address is unfinished, and they suppose that he referred to the cunning advice so destructive to the people, which will be presently related; *i.e.*, that the Moabitish women should prostitute themselves. Others rather imagine that Balaam counselled Balak to rest quiet, since the prosperity of the Israelites would do no harm to the Moabites in his lifetime. I, however, take it simply for to teach, or to admonish what would be for his advantage. Thus he commends his prophecy, in order that Balak may willingly submit to it. Still, when he speaks of the "latter days," he signifies that there was no cause for Balak himself to fear or be anxious; since the punishment of his nation would be deferred for a long time. In the meantime we see what Balak had gained by his trouble; for, whereas he had hitherto only heard.the people of Israel blessed, he is not compelled to listen to what is more painful still, viz., the ruin of his own nation. This is the reward of those who strive against God.

15. *Balaam the son of Beor hath said.* Inasmuch as he

[1] "The commandment of the Lord."—*A. V.*
[2] "Of mine own mind."—*A. V.*
[3] *C.* translates איעצך, which *A. V.* renders, "I will advertise thee," *consulam tibi*, I will counsel thee: so also Ainsworth.

was preparing to treat of most important matters, it is not without reason that he renews his preface, in order to obtain more authority for his prophecy: and although it was not without ambition that he proclaimed these magnificent titles, still we cannot doubt but that God would ratify by them what he had determined to deliver through the mouth of the prophet. It was requisite that this worthless man, whose doctrine would otherwise have been contemptible, should be marked out by Divine indications; and thus it was that he assumed a character that he did not possess, and attributed to himself what only belongs to true prophets. I have before explained how the open and the closed eye are spoken of in the same sense, though for different reasons: for he calls the eye "hidden," as perceiving the secret things of darkness, which are incomprehensible to the human sense; but he claims for himself "open eyes," in that he beholds, by prophetic vision, what he is about to say, as if he would deny that he was going to speak of things which were obscure, and scarcely intelligible to himself.

17. I shall see him, but not now; I shall behold him, but not nigh: there shall come a Star out of Jacob, and a Sceptre shall rise out of Israel, and shall smite the corners of Moab, and destroy all the children of Sheth.

18. And Edom shall be a possession, Seir also shall be a possession for his enemies: and Israel shall do valiantly.

19. Out of Jacob shall come he that shall have dominion, and shall destroy him that remaineth of the city.

20. And when he looked on Amalek, he took up his parable, and said, Amalek *was* the first of the nations; but his latter end *shall be* that he perish for ever.

21. And he looked on the Kenites, and took up his parable, and said, Strong is thy dwelling-place, and thou puttest thy nest in a rock:

22. Nevertheless the Kenite shall be wasted, until Asshur shall carry thee away captive.

23. And he took up his parable,

17. Video eum: sed non modo: intueor illum: sed non propè: procedet stella ex Jacob, et surget sceptrum ex Israele: et confodiet principes (*vel*, angulos) Moab, et destruet omnes filios Seth.

18. Et erit Edom possessa et possidebitur Seir ab inimicis Seir, et Israel faciet virtutem.

19. Et dominabitur ex Jacob, et perdet reliquias ex civitate.

20. Et quum vidisset Amalec, assumpsit parabolam suam, et dixit, Principium gentium Amalec, ideo novissimum ejus usque ad perditionem.

21. Viso etiam Cenæo, assumpsit parabolam suam, et dixit, Robustum habitaculum tuum, et ponis in petra nidum tuum.

22. Certe expelletur Cain, usquequo Assur captivum te ducet.

23. Assumpsit item parabolam,

and said, Alas! who shall live when God doeth this?	et dixit, Væ quis vivet quum statuerit istud?
24. And ships *shall come* from the coast of Chittim, and shall afflict Asshur, and shall afflict Eber, and he also shall perish for ever.	24. Et naves è littore Chitthim quæ affligant Assur, affligent Heber, sed hoc quoque usque ad perditionem.
25. And Balaam rose up, and went and returned to his place; and Balak also went his way.	25. Surrexit itaque Balaam, et abiit, reversusque est in locum suum: atque etiam Balac abiit in viam suam.

17. *I shall see him, but not now.*[1] Though the verbs are in the future tense, they are used for the present; and again, the pronoun *him* designates some one who has not yet been mentioned; and this is a tolerably common usage with the Hebrews, especially when referring to Jerusalem, or God, or some very distinguished man. The relative is, therefore, here put *κατ' ἐξοχὴν* for the antecedent: and although there can be no doubt but that he alluded to the people of Israel, it is still a question whether he designates the head or the whole body; on which point I do not make much contention, since it is substantially the same thing.

The reason why Balaam postpones his prophecies to a distant period, is in order to afford consolation to Balak, for, as much as he possibly can, he seeks to avoid his ill-will, and therefore assures him that, although he denounces evil, it was not to be feared at an early period, since he treats of things which were as yet far off.

The second clause must be unquestionably restricted to the head of the people, called metaphorically "a Star," and then expressly referred to without a figure; for this repetition is common with the Hebrews, by which they particularize the same thing twice over. Assuredly he means nothing else by "the Sceptre," except what he had indicated by the "Star;" and thus he connects the prosperity of the people with the kingdom. Hence we gather that its state was not perfect until it began to be governed by the hand of a king. For, inasmuch as the adoption of the family of Abraham was founded on Christ, only sparks of God's blessing shone forth until its completed brightness was manifested in Christ. It must be observed, therefore, that when Balaam begins to prophesy of God's grace towards the people of Israel, he

[1] "I see him," &c.—*Lat.*

directs us at once to the sceptre, as if it were the true and certain mirror of God's favour. And, in fact, God never manifested Himself as the Father of His people except by Christ. I admit, indeed, that some beginnings existed in the person of David, but they were very far from exhibiting the fulness of the reality: for the glory of his kingdom was not lasting, nay, its chief dignity was speedily impaired by the rebellion of the ten tribes, and was finally altogether extinguished; and when David's power was at its height, his dominion never extended beyond the neighbouring nations. The coming forth of the Star and the Sceptre, therefore, of which Balaam speaks explicitly, refers to Christ; and what we read in the Psalm corresponds with this prophecy; "The Lord shall send the sceptre[1] of thy strength out of Sion." (Ps. cx. 2.) Hence it follows that the blessing, of which Balaam speaks, descends even to us; for, if the prosperity of the ancient people, their rest, their well-ordered government, their dignity, safety, and glory, proceeded from the sceptre as its unmixed source, there is no doubt but that Christ by His coming accomplished all these things more fully for us.

The destruction of the nation of Moab is added as an adjunct of the kingdom. And first, indeed, Balaam declares that "its princes shall be transfixed." If any prefer to read its "corners,"[2] the expression is metaphorical, implying that the Sceptre will break through its munitions, or destroy what may seem to be strongest. I do not doubt but that the same thing is confirmed in what is said of "the children of Sheth;" for those who take it generally for the whole human race,[3] violently wrest the text by their gloss. Balaam is speaking of the neighbouring nations; and, when in the next verse he goes on to specify Edom, he adds Mount Seir

[1] *A. V.*, "The rod."

[2] Dr. Boothroyd has a curious conjecture on this passage. He says, "Most of the ancients, after *LXX.*, give to פאתי the signification of chiefs, princes, or the like. They are supposed to have read פחתי. But I am persuaded that פאתי is the genuine reading, and to be taken here in the same sense as in Jer. xlviii. 45, where a very similar passage occurs: and in both places, it is my belief, the word signifies *whiskers*."

[3] "*The children of Seth*, *i.e.*, all men; so the Chaldee."—Corn. à Lapide *in loco*.

by way of explanation. Since the form of the two sentences is identical, it is probable that none others than the Moabites are meant by the children of Sheth. Still the question arises why Balaam attributes to a single nation what was common to all, for all who were of the descendants of Sheth equally derived their origin from Noah. Some think that they boasted of this descent in order to conceal their shame, for we know that the founder of this nation sprang from an incestuous connexion. But another more satisfactory reason occurs to me, viz., that they boasted, like the Amalekites, of the extreme antiquity of their race ; since, therefore, they desired to be reckoned amongst the most ancient nations, it will not be improbable that by this ironical appellation their vain-glory was reproved. It may, however, have been the case that some one amongst the descendants of Moab was distinguished by this name. Still, as I have lately said, the Moabites as well as the Edomites were subdued by David, for David thus justly celebrates his triumphs over them, " Moab is my wash-pot ; over Edom will I cast out my shoe," (Ps. lx. 8 ;) but then was merely typified, what Christ at length fulfilled, in that He reduced under His sway all adverse and hostile nations. Therefore it is said, he " shall destroy him that remaineth of the cities," *i.e.*, all enemies whom He shall find to be incorrigible.

20. *And when he looked on Amalek.* This people had already been destined to destruction by a Divine decree ; but what God had before declared, is here again ratified by Moses. Although the vengeance, which God was about to take, lay dormant for many ages, it was at length experimentally proved that God had not threatened in vain. But, whilst it is true that they were destroyed by Saul, still we learn from the history that some still survived, and again inhabited their land. In order, therefore, to arrive at the entire accomplishment of this prophecy, we must come to Christ, whose kingdom is the eternal destruction of all the wicked. Poor and unsatisfactory is the view of some commentators,[1] who think that Amalek is called " the first of

[1] " So all the paraphrasts," says Drusius, in Poole's Syn. See margin *A. V.*, and the gloss in the Geneva Bible.

the nations," because they first took up arms against Israel, and encountered them in order to prevent their advance. Rather is the pride of Amalek indirectly rebuked, because they claimed superiority for themselves over other nations, and this on the score of their antiquity, as if they had been created together with the sun and moon. There is then a pointed comparison between this noble origin, and the slaughter which awaited them at their end.

21. *And he looked on the Kenites.* I have not yet referred to the sense in which Balaam is said to have *seen* the Kenites, as well as the other nations; and now, also, I should refrain from doing so, if some did not attribute it to prophetical vision, in which opinion I cannot agree: for Moses relates as a matter of history that Balaam turned his face in the directions in which they respectively lived: and, although he did not actually see the people themselves, the sight of the place in which they dwelt was sufficient for the purpose of prophecy.

By the Kenites I understand the Midianites, who were contiguous to the Amalekites; for it is altogether unreasonable to refer the name to the descendants of Jethro. Forty years had not yet elapsed since Jethro had left his son with Moses; and his was only one small family in the wilderness of Midian, whereas mention is here made of a people already celebrated. Balaam, therefore, designates by *synecdoche* the Midianites, and devotes them also to the punishment they well deserved. Of this Gideon was in some measure the minister and executioner, when he routed their immense army with three hundred men; and his victory is celebrated in Ps. lxxxiii. 11, and Isa. ix. 4. It is probable that their power was broken at that time.

22. *Until Asshur shall carry thee away captive.* It is a harsh and unnatural construction to apply this to the Kenites; and the majority, indeed, consent that it should be referred to the Israelites; yet they differ as to the meaning of it, for some take it affirmatively, that the Kenites should be wasted, until the Assyrians should conquer the Israelites and carry them away captive; some, however,

take it interrogatively,[1] as if it were an abrupt exclamation, How long shall Asshur hold thee captive? Thus they conceive the prolonged exile of the people is indicated. Undoubtedly it was the purpose of the Spirit to shew, by way of correction, that their prosperity, which had been previously mentioned, should be mixed with heavy afflictions: for slavery is a bitter thing, and exile even worse. Hence we gather that, though the Church is blessed by God, it is still in such a way as that it shall not cease to be exposed to various calamities. The interrogation, therefore, will be most appropriate.

24. *And ships shall come from the coast of Chittim.* It is unquestionable that the word Chittim is sometimes used for the Greeks. Some, indeed, imagine that the Macedonians alone are strictly called by this name; it is, however, plain that it is applied generally to the whole of Greece. But since the countries beyond the sea were not so well known to the Jews as to allow of their distinguishing them, Scripture sometimes transfers this same name to Italy. Without doubt in Daniel, (xi. 30,) "the ships of Chittim" must be taken for those of Italy or Rome;[2] because the angel there predicts that the ships of Chittim would come, which should overcome, and render frustrate the efforts of Antiochus; which was plainly brought to pass by the mission of Popilius. With regard to the present passage, first of all the Greeks under Alexander afflicted both Judea and Assyria; and then another affliction followed at the hands of the Romans. Since, however, Balaam has begun to prophesy of the kingdom of Christ, it is probable that the Romans are included together with the Greeks. But from hence we more clearly perceive, what I have lately adverted to, that the children of God are not so exempted from common evils as not to be often involved in them promiscuously with un-

[1] It will be seen that the *A. V.* renders the clause interrogatively in the margin, though with a slight difference from the sense of *C.*

[2] See *C.* on Daniel, (*C. Soc. Edit.*,) vol. ii. pp. 316, 317, 318. "Writers on the geography of the Bible entertain remarkably different ideas as to the country or countries intended by this denomination. The most probable opinion seems to us to be that which considers that the Hebrews used it to express, in a general sense, all the coasts and islands of the Mediterranean Sea, so far as known to them."—Illustr. Com. *in loco.*

believers, as if their conditions were precisely identical. Although the Hebrews are placed on a par with the Assyrians as their companions in misfortune, still a consolation is added, *i.e.*, that the Assyrians also shall perish like Chittim, when they have persecuted the Church.

What Moses adds in conclusion, viz., that Balaam returned to his people, and Balak also went to his place, tends to the commendation of God's grace, since He dissipates the evil counsels of the wicked like clouds, and overthrows their machinations; even as Moses commemorates elsewhere this peculiar blessing of God.[1] Micah, too, celebrates this amongst other Divine mercies: " O my people, (he says,) remember now what Balak king of Moab consulted, and what Balaam the son of Beor answered him," &c. (Micah vi. 5.) The sum is, that the enemies of the chosen people departed in dishonour without accomplishing their purpose, since God put them to confusion.

NUMBERS, CHAPTER XXV.

1. And Israel abode in Shittim, and the people began to commit whoredom with the daughters of Moab.	1. Postquam autem mansit Israel in Sittim, cœpit populus scortari cum filiabus Moab.
2. And they called the people unto the sacrifices of their gods: and the people did eat, and bowed down to their gods.	2. Et vocaverunt populum ad sacrificia deorum suorum, comeditque populus, et adoraverunt deos earum.
3. And Israel joined himself unto Baal-peor: and the anger of the Lord was kindled against Israel.	3. Et adjunxit sese Israel ipsi Baal-peor, accensusque est furor Jehovæ contra Israelem.
4. And the Lord said unto Moses, Take all the heads of the people, and hang them up before the Lord against the sun, that the fierce anger of the Lord may be turned away from Israel.	4. Et dixit Jehova ad Mosen, Assume omnes principes populi, tunc suspende eos Jehovæ, coram sole: et avertetur ira excandescentiæ Jehovæ ab Israele.
5. And Moses said unto the judges of Israel, Slay ye every one his men that were joined unto Baal-peor.	5. Dixit ergo Moses ad judices Israel, Occidite quisque viros suos qui adjunxerunt se ipsi Baal-peor.
6. And, behold, one of the children of Israel came, and brought	6. Et ecce, quidam de filiis Israel venit, et adduxit fratribus suis Ma-

[1] This deliverance is commemorated by Moses again in Deut. xxiii. 4, 5, 6; but the *Fr.* reads Joshua for Moses, and refers to Josh. xxiv. 9.

unto his brethren a Midianitish woman, in the sight of Moses, and in the sight of all the congregation of the children of Israel, who *were* weeping *before* the door of the tabernacle of the congregation.	dianitidem in oculis Mosis atque in oculis totius congregationis filiorum Israel: ipsi autem flebant ad ostium tabernaculi conventionis.
7. And when Phinehas, the son of Eleazar, the son of Aaron the priest, saw *it*, he rose up from among the congregation, and took a javelin in his hand;	7. Quod quum vidisset Phinees filius Eleazar filii Aharon sacerdotis, surrexit de medio congregationis, et accepit lanceam in manu sua.
8. And he went after the man of Israel into the tent, and thrust both of them through, the man of Israel, and the woman through her belly. So the plague was stayed from the children of Israel.	8. Ingressusque est post virum Israel in tabernaculum, et transfixit ambos ipsos, virum Israel et mulierem illam in ventre ejus: et repressa fuit plaga à filiis Israel.
9. And those that died in the plague were twenty and four thousand.	9. Et mortui sunt plaga illa quatuor et viginti millia.

1. *And Israel abode in Shittim.* From this narrative we learn assuredly that the people were no more able to bear prosperity than adversity. Heretofore, either worn out by fatigue, or rendered impatient by abstinence and famine, they had often rebelled against God; now, when they have entered a habitable land, and are resting in the midst of fruitful fields, they are incited by their more comfortable dwelling-places, and more pleasant mode of life, to lasciviousness, and the indulgence of filthy lusts. Moses relates how, when they had given way to their lust, they fell at the same time into whoredom and idolatry. We shall presently see that this arose from the counsel of Balaam, that the Moabites should prostitute their women to the Israelites, in order to entice them by their blandishments to unholy worship. Balaam had learnt by experience that God's favour was an invincible safeguard to protect the people from all injury. He, therefore, invents a plan whereby they may destroy themselves, by not only depriving themselves of God's protection, but also by provoking His wrath against them. By this fan, then, Balaam stirred up the fire, which impelled these poor wretches, inflamed by blind lechery, to another crime, by which they might arouse against themselves the enmity of God. Consequently Paul, referring to this history, informs us that the punishment, which will be mentioned

immediately, was inflicted upon them for fornication. (1 Cor. x. 8.) For, although it was God's design to avenge the violation of His worship, still it is fitting to examine into the origin and source of the evil. Just as, if a drunken man has killed a person, the murder will be imputed to his drunkenness, so Paul, seeing the Israelites impelled by fornication to idolatry, sets before us the punishment as a warning to deter us from fornication, which was the primary cause of their chastisement, and the means of their corruption. Since, then, the fall from one sin to another is so easy, let us hence learn to be more watchful, lest Satan should entangle us in his snares. Let us also observe that he creeps upon us by degrees in order to entrap us. The Moabitish damsels did not straightway solicit the Israelites to worship their idols, but first invite them to their banquets, and thus tempt them to idolatry; for, if mention had been made at first of idol-worship, perhaps they might have shuddered at the atrocity of the crime, to which they allowed themselves to be beguiled by degrees. Now, to be present at a feast, which was celebrated in honour of false gods, was a kind of indirect renunciation of the true God; and when they had been attracted thus far, they threw aside all shame, and abandoned themselves to that extreme act whereby they transfer the honour due only to the one true God, to false and imaginary deities.

3. *And Israel joined himself to Baal-peor.* Moses amplifies their crime by this expression, that they bound themselves to the idol in an impious alliance; and thus he alludes to that holy union whereby God had connected Himself with the people, and accuses them of broken faith and wicked rebellion. Nevertheless, it is probable that the people were not impelled by superstition, but enticed by the wiles of the women to offer worship to idols which they despised. Yet we are told how God declared that they were "joined" to the idol, which they merely pretended to worship, in order to comply with the ungodly wishes of the women. Hence, therefore, this general instruction may be gathered, that when we turn aside from pure religion, we in a manner connect ourselves with idols, so as to coa-

lesce in one body with them, and conspire to renounce the true God.

Baal was then the general name of almost all idols; but an epithet is added to the idol of the Moabites, taken from Mount Peor; nor does it appear that we need go in quest of any other etymology, since the name of this mountain has recently been mentioned. It was on the same principle as in Popery, when they name their Marys after particular places,[1] where the most famous statues are worshipped.

4. *And the Lord said unto Moses.* We have often seen before how God executed His judgments by His own hand, as if He put it forth from heaven; He now imposes this office on Moses, although it is evident from the context that he was not appointed to execute it alone, but that the other judges were associated with him; for it immediately follows that Moses intrusted the same charge to them, and thus, what was obscure, on account of the brevity with which it is recorded, is more clearly expressed. At any rate, it was a notable judgment of God Himself, though He employed men as its ministers. Nor does Paul in vain exhort[2] us by this example to beware of fornication.

The mode of the punishment, however, was diverse, for the lower orders were slain (by pestilence,) but the leaders were hanged upon the gallows, that the sight might awaken more terror; for by "the heads of the people" he means those of the highest repute, whose ignominy must have been most notable, because the eyes of all men are generally upon the great and noble. Hence, also, they deservedly incur the heavier punishment, because obscure persons do less harm by their example, nor are their acts so generally the objects of imitation. Let, therefore, those who are held in esteem beware lest they provoke others to sin by their evil deeds, for, in proportion to each man's pre-eminence, the less excuse he deserves. Others interpret it differently, as if Moses were commanded to fetch the princes to give their sentence against the criminals; thus by the pronoun "them," they under-

[1] "Comme qui diroit nostre Dame de Laurette, ou de Boulogne, ou de Cleri;" as one might say, our Lady of Loretto, or Bologna, or Cleri.—*Fr.*

[2] "Les Corinthiens."—*Fr.*

stood whosoever should be convicted; but it is hardly probable that so great a multitude were hanged, and therefore I do not doubt but that reference is made to their peculiar punishment.

6. *And, behold, one of the children of Israel came.* Moses here relates a case which was foul and detestable beyond others. There is no doubt but that many, in the midst of such gross licentiousness as had now for some time generally prevailed, had filled the camp with various scandalous offences; but there was something peculiarly enormous in the atrocity of this act, in that this impious despiser of God wantonly insulted both God and men amidst the tears and lamentations of all, as if he were triumphing over all shame and modesty. The multitude were weeping before the tabernacle, that is to say, all the pious who trembled at the thought of approaching calamity, since they were fully persuaded that this licentiousness, accompanied by idolatry and sacrilege, would not be unpunished; meanwhile, this abandoned man rushes forward, and, in mockery of their tears, leads his harlot in procession as it were. No wonder, therefore, that God should have exercised such severity, when things had come to this extremity. But it must be observed that the order of the history is inverted, since it is not credible that, after the Judges had begun to perform their office, such an iniquity should be committed. But this narrative is thus inserted, in order that it may be more apparent how necessary it was to proceed speedily to severe chastisement, since otherwise it would have been impossible to apply a remedy in time to so desperate an evil.

7. *And when Phinehas, the son of Eleazar.* The courage of Phinehas is celebrated, who, whilst the rest were hesitating, inflamed with holy zeal, hastens forward to inflict punishment. The backwardness of others is therefore condemned by implication, though their tears were praiseworthy; but, since they were almost stupified by grief, their virtue was not clear from all defect. And certainly, whilst the yet unbridled licentiousness of the people was foaming like a tempestuous sea, we cannot wonder that the minds of the good were altogether or partially disabled. Hence

was the zeal of Phinehas the more distinguished, when he did not hesitate to provoke so many worthless and wicked persons infuriated by their lechery. If any object that he transgressed the limits of his calling, when he laid hold of the sword with which God had not armed him, to inflict capital punishment, the reply is obvious, that our calling is not always confined to its ordinary office, inasmuch as God sometimes requires new and unusual acts of His servants. As a priest, it was not the office of Phinehas to punish crime, but he was called by the special inspiration of God, so that, in his private capacity, he had the Holy Spirit as his guide. These circumstances, indeed, ought not to be regarded as an example, so that a general rule may be laid down from them; though, at the same time, God preserves His free right to appoint His servants by privilege to act in His behalf as He shall see fit. God's judgment of this case may be certainly inferred from its approval, so that we may correctly argue that Phinehas was under His own guidance, since He immediately afterwards declared that He was pleased with the act, as is also stated in Psalm cvi. 30, 31.

Now, if any private person should in his preposterous zeal take upon himself to punish a similar crime, in vain will he boast that he is an imitator of Phinehas, unless he shall be thoroughly assured of the command of God. Let the answer of Christ, therefore, always be borne in mind by us, whereby he restrained His disciples, when they desired, like Elijah, to pray that those who had not received them should be destroyed by fire from heaven, "Ye know not what manner of spirit ye are of." (Luke ix. 54, 55.) In order, therefore, that our zeal may be approved by God, it must be tempered by spiritual prudence, and directed by His authority; in a word, the Holy Spirit must go before and dictate what is right.

9. *And those that died in the plague.* Paul, when he says that only twenty-three thousand died, appears to differ from Moses; but we know that the exact account of numbers is not always observed, and it is probable that *about* twenty-four thousand were slain. Paul, therefore, subtracted one

thousand, and was content with the lesser number;[1] from which, however, we may perceive how severe and terrible was the punishment, teaching us to beware of provoking God by fornication. For, as it is a monstrous thing that so great a multitude should have been infected by this foul and shameful sin, so God's fearful judgment against adulterers and fornicators is set before us. We have already seen that, although they were guilty of a wicked rebellion, still the punishment is justly ascribed to their lust, which impelled them to idolatry.

10. And the Lord spake unto Moses, saying,

11. Phinehas, the son of Eleazar, the son of Aaron the priest, hath turned my wrath away from the children of Israel, while he was zealous for my sake among them, that I consumed not the children of Israel in my jealousy.

12. Wherefore say, Behold, I give unto him my covenant of peace:

13. And he shall have it, and his seed after him, *even* the covenant of an everlasting priesthood; because he was zealous for his God, and made an atonement for the children of Israel.

14. Now the name of the Israelite that was slain, *even* that was slain with the Midianitish woman, *was* Zimri, the son of Salu, a prince of a chief house among the Simeonites.

15. And the name of the Midianitish woman that was slain *was* Cozbi, the daughter of Zur: he *was* head over a people, *and* of a chief house in Midian.

10. Tunc loquutus est Jehova ad Mosen, dicendo:

11. Phinees filius Eleazar filii Aharon sacerdotis avertit excandescentiam meam à filiis Israel, quum zelatus est ipse zelum meum in medio eorum, et non consumpsi filios Israel in zelo meo.

12. Idcirco dic, Ecce, ego do ei pactum meum, pacis.

13. Et erit ei et semini ejus post eum, pactum sacerdotii perpetui, eo quod zelatus est pro Deo suo, et expiavit filios Israel.

14. Porro nomen viri Israel percussi, qui percussus est cum Madianitide, erat Zimri filius Salu, princeps familiæ tribus Simeon.

15. Nomen vero mulieris occisæ Madianitidis Chozbi filia Sur, principis populorum; princeps domus paternæ in Madian erat.

[1] *C.* in his Commentary on 1 Cor. x. 8, enlarges somewhat more on this point: "There perished in one day twenty-three thousand, or, as Moses says, twenty-four thousand. Though they differ as to number, it is easy to reconcile them, as it is no unusual thing, when it is not intended to number exactly and minutely each head, to put down a number that comes near it, as among the Romans there were those that received the name of *centumviri*, (the *hundred*,) while in reality there were two above the hundred. As there were, therefore, about twenty-four thousand that were overthrown by the Lord's hand—that is, above twenty-three thousand, Moses has set down the number *above* the mark, and Paul the number *below* it, and in this way there is in reality no difference."—Cal. Soc. Edit., vol. i. p. 324.

16. And the Lord spake unto Moses, saying,

17. Vex the Midianites, and smite them:

18. For they vex you with their wiles, wherewith they have beguiled you in the matter of Peor, and in the matter of Cozbi, the daughter of a prince of Midian, their sister, which was slain in the day of the plague for Peor's sake.

16. Loquutus est autem Jehova ad Mosen, dicendo:

17. Angustiis affice Madianitas, et percutias eos:

18. Quia ipsi afflixerunt vos fraudibus suis, quibus fraudulenter egerunt contra vos in negotio Peor, et in negotio Chozbi filiæ principis Madian sororis suæ, quæ percussa est in die plagæ propter Peor.

10. *And the Lord spake unto Moses.* In these words God makes it appear that He was the author of the death (of Zimri and Cozbi;[1]) not only because He was thus propitiated towards the people, but because He calls the zeal of Phinehas His own.[2] It will, however, accord equally well whether we take it actively or passively, viz., either that Phinehas was inflamed with zeal to vindicate God's glory, or that he took upon him the zeal of God Himself. Whichever be preferred, God refers to Himself what was done by Phinehas. When He declares that He was appeased by the punishment inflicted, let us not imagine that there was a meritorious satisfaction, whereby the Papists feign that their punishments are redeemed before God. For although the just chastisements of sin are sacrifices of sweet savour, they are by no means expiations to reconcile God. Besides, there is no question here of compensation, but what is meant is, that it was a means of appeasing God, when the ungodliness of the people which had, as it were, fanned up His wrath into a flame, was repressed by this severe correction. Thus, in Ps. cvi., the atonement is ascribed not to the act of Phinehas, but only to his prayer,[3] because, in right of his priesthood, he had humbly interceded for the people. At the same time, the statement of Paul is true, that those are not judged

[1] Added from *Fr.*

[2] *Margin, A.V.*, "*Heb.*, with my zeal."

[3] Ps. cvi. 30. *A.V.*, "Then stood up Phinehas, and *executed judgment;*" in the English Prayer-book, the Chaldee, Syriac, and other versions, "and *prayed;*" with this, however, *C.*, in his Commentary, does not agree: "Some render the word פלל, *pillel, to pray,* (he says;) but the other rendering, to *execute justice,* is more in accordance with the context."—Cal. Soc. Edit., vol. iv. p. 230.

by God who voluntarily judge themselves, (1 Cor. xi. 31,) since, by their penitence, they in a manner prevent His judgment.

A perpetual priesthood is promised to Phinehas as his reward. If any object, that he thus obtained nothing new, since, in accordance with the rule of the law, he was the undoubted successor of his father, I reply, that it is not uncommon that what God had already freely promised, He declares that he will give by way of reward. Thus, what had been promised to Abraham before the birth of Isaac, is again repeated after he was prepared to sacrifice him, (Gen. xxii. 16:) "Because thou hast done this thing, and hast not withheld thy son," therefore, "in blessing I will bless thee, and in thy seed shall all the nations of the earth be blessed." Besides, the privilege of a single individual is not simply in question here, but it refers to a perpetual succession, as if God had promised that his posterity should never fail. And assuredly, the change which took place at the commencement of Solomon's reign, is not repugnant to this promise, for it may be probably inferred that Zadoc, no less than Abiathar, was of the race of Phinehas. This covenant is called a "covenant of peace," because it was to be surely established; consequently, it may be properly rendered, "My covenant in peace." At any rate, it indicates prosperity, as if He had said that Phinehas, together with his posterity, should prosperously execute the sacerdotal office.

14. *Now the name of the Israelite.* Even as the memory of the just is blessed, so also it was equitable that the author of this foul sin should be condemned to perpetual infamy. It appears, however, from the fact of a part of the disgrace being thrown upon the whole tribe, how greatly displeasing to God was this gross enormity. For although the tribe of Simeon is not here actually involved in the charge of participating in the sin, yet are they all branded with the common mark of ignominy for their humiliation, in order that each one of them may learn severely to correct whomsoever amongst his relatives he may see offending, and by no means to encourage their vices, if he desires to do credit to

the founder of his race.[1] It is recorded that both Zimri and the Midianitish woman were of noble and principal families, not only that we may be taught that God's judgment is no respecter of persons (*ἀπροσωπόληπτον*,) in that it does not spare rank, but also that the higher a person may be in position, the greater is the disgrace he is exposed to if he conduct himself dishonourably, since their very dignity renders men's actions more conspicuous.

Because the paternal house of the harlot is said to have been in Midian, some conjecture that she was born in the land of Moab, or, at any rate, brought up there among her maternal relatives; but, as the matter is unimportant, I leave it undecided.

17. *Vex the Midianites, and smite them.* Inasmuch as God constantly forbids His people to take vengeance, it is surprising that the people of Israel should now be instigated to do so; as if they were not already more than enough disposed to it. We must bear in mind, however, that since God, who is the just avenger of all wickedness, often makes use of men's instrumentality, and constitutes them the lawful ministers for the exercise of His vengeance, it must not be altogether condemned without exception, but only such vengeance as men themselves are impelled to by carnal passions. If any one is injured, straightway he is carried away to the desire of vengeance by the stimulus of his own private injury; and this is manifestly wrong: but if a person is led to inflict punishment by a just and well-regulated zeal towards God, it is not his own cause, but that of God which he undertakes. God did not, therefore, desire to give reins to His people's anger, so as to repay the Midianites as they had deserved in the violence of its impulse; but He armed them with His own sword for their punishment; as if He had declared that there was a just cause for their war, and that they need not fear the charge of cruelty, if they exterminated such obnoxious enemies. For, although Balaam alone had imagined this snare, still the guilt is laid upon the whole people. In the meantime, the punishment

[1] "Car c'est le vray moyen d'honorer sa famille et son sang;" for this is the true way to honour one's family and blood.—*Fr.*

of the Moabites is delayed, although they had apparently inflicted the grosser injury. Because no good reason here appears why God should mercifully bear with the one nation, whilst He hastens speedily to the punishment of the others, let us learn to regard His judgments with reverence, and not to presume to discuss them further than is lawful. Let it be sufficient for us to know that war was justly declared against the Midianites, because it was not their fault that Israel was not ruined by their iniquitous impiety.[1]

The Repetition of the same History.

DEUTERONOMY, CHAPTER IV.

3. Your eyes have seen what the Lord did because of Baal-peor: for all the men that followed Baal-peor, the Lord thy God hath destroyed them from among you.

4. But ye that did cleave unto the Lord your God *are* alive every one of you this day.

3. Oculi vestri viderunt quæ fecit Jehova propter Baal-Peor, omnem enim hominem qui perrexerat post Baal-Peor perdidit Jehova Deus tuus è medio tui.

4. Vos autem qui adhæsistis Jehovæ Deo vestro vivitis universi hodie.

3. *Your eyes have seen what the Lord did.* This enlargement more clearly shews that so conspicuous was the example given in the punishment, that it could not be hidden from even the most ignorant; for Moses does not here address those of refined judgment, but the common people generally, who had only been spectators. Assuredly, if God's vengeance had been less manifest, he would not have so confidently appealed to them as witnesses; hence was their stolidity the less excusable, if they were blind to so plain and notorious a fact.

His praise of their constancy I refer to the present case alone; for it is abundantly clear that they did not persevere in cleaving to God. The meaning is, that there was a manifest discrimination in this Divine chastisement, so that the death of the ungodly multitude should preserve the pure worship of God among the survivors.

[1] "Par l'impieté à laquelle ils l'induisoyent;" by the impiety to which they induced them.—*Fr.*

NUMBERS, CHAPTER XXVI.

1. And it came to pass after the plague, that the Lord spake unto Moses, and unto Eleazar the son of Aaron the priest, saying,

2. Take the sum of all the congregation of the children of Israel, from twenty years old and upward, throughout their fathers' house, all that are able to go to war in Israel.

3. And Moses and Eleazar the priest spake with them in the plains of Moab, by Jordan, *near* Jericho, saying,

4. *Take the sum of the people,* from twenty years old and upward; as the Lord commanded Moses and the children of Israel, which went forth out of the land of Egypt.

5. Reuben, the eldest son of Israel: the children of Reuben; Hanoch, *of whom cometh* the family of the Hanochites: of Pallu, the family of the Palluites:

6. Of Hezron, the family of the Hezronites: of Carmi, the family of the Carmites.

7. These *are* the families of the Reubenites, and they that were numbered of them were forty and three thousand and seven hundred and thirty.

8. And the sons of Pallu; Eliab.

9. And the sons of Eliab; Nemuel, and Dathan, and Abiram. This *is that* Dathan and Abiram *which were* famous in the congregation, who strove against Moses and against Aaron in the company of Korah, when they strove against the Lord:

10. And the earth opened her mouth, and swallowed them up together with Korah, when that company died, what time the fire devoured two hundred and fifty men: and they became a sign.

11. Notwithstanding the children of Korah died not.

12. The sons of Simeon, after their families: of Nemuel, the family of the Nemuelites; of Jamin, the

1. Et fuit, post plagam loquutus est Jehova ad Mosen et Eleazar filium Aharon sacerdotis, dicendo:

2. Tollite summam universæ congregationis filiorum Israel, à filio viginti annorum et supra, per domum patrum suorum, omnium egredientium ad bellum in Israele.

3. Itaque loquutus est Moses et Eleazar sacerdos cum illis in campestribus Moab, juxta Jordanem Jericho, dicendo:

4. Numerate universam congregationem filiorum Israel, à filio viginti annorum et suprà: quemadmodum præceperat Jehova Mosi et filiis Israel qui egressi erant è terra Ægypti.

5. Ruben fuit primogenitus Israelis, filii Ruben fuerunt aliquot: de Henoc fuit familia Henochitarum: de Phallu, familia Phalluitarum:

6. De Hesron, familia Hesronitarum: de Charmi, familia Charmitarum.

7. Istæ sunt familiæ Rubenitarum: et fuerunt numerati eorum tria et quadraginta millia septingenti et triginta.

8. Et ex filiis Phallu, Eliab.

9. Filii autem Eliab, Nebuel, Dathan et Abiron: isti sunt Dathan et Abiron majores synagogæ qui rixati sunt contra Mosen et Aharon in congregatione Core, quum rixarentur ipsi contra Jehovam.

10. Et aperuit terra os suum, et deglutivit eos et Core, quando mortua est congregatio, dum consumpsit ignis ducentos quinquaginta viros: qui fuerunt in signum.

11. Filii verò Core non sunt mortui.

12. Filii Simeon per familias suas: de Nemuel, familia Nemuelitarum: de Jamin, familia Jamini-

family of the Jaminites: of Jachin, the family of the Jachinites:

13. Of Zerah, the family of the Zarhites: of Shaul, the family of the Shaulites.

14. These *are* the families of the Simeonites, twenty and two thousand and two hundred.

15. The children of Gad, after their families: of Zephon, the family of the Zephonites: of Haggi, the family of the Haggites: of Shuni, the family of the Shunites:

16. Of Ozni, the family of the Oznites: of Eri, the family of the Erites:

17. Of Arod, the family of the Arodites: of Areli, the family of the Arelites.

18. These *are* the families of the children of Gad, according to those that were numbered of them, forty thousand and five hundred.

19. The sons of Judah *were* Er and Onan: and Er and Onan died in the land of Canaan.

20. And the sons of Judah, after their families, were: of Shelah, the family of the Shelanites: of Pharez, the family of the Pharzites: of Zerah, the family of the Zarhites:

21. And the sons of Pharez were: of Hezron, the family of the Hezronites: of Hamul, the family of the Hamulites.

22. These *are* the families of Judah, according to those that were numbered of them, threescore and sixteen thousand and five hundred.

23. *Of* the sons of Issachar, after their families: *of* Tola, the family of the Tolaites: of Pua, the family of the Punites:

24. Of Jashub, the family of the Jashubites: of Shimron, the family of the Shimronites.

25. These *are* the families of Issachar, according to those that were numbered of them, threescore and four thousand and three hundred.

26. *Of* the sons of Zebulun, after their families: of Sered, the family of the Sardites: of Elon, the family of the Elonites: of Jahleel, the family of the Jahleelites.

tarum: de Jachin, familia Jachinitarum:

13. De Zare, familia Zareitarum: de Saul, familia Saulitarum.

14. Istæ sunt familiæ Simeonitarum: duo et viginti millia et ducenti.

15. Filii Gad per familias suas: de Sephon, familia Sephonitarum: de Haggi, familia Haggitarum: de Suni, familia Sunitarum:

16. De Ozni, familia Oznitarum: de Eri, familia Eritarum:

17. De Arod, familia Aroditarum: de Areli, familia Arelitarum.

18. Istæ sunt familiæ filiorum Gad juxta numeratos suos quadraginta millia et quingenti.

19. Filii Jehudah, Er et Onam: et mortuus est Er et Onam in terra Chanaan.

20. Fuerunt inquam filii Jehudah per familias suas: de Selah, familia Selanitarum: de Phares, familia Pharesitarum: de Zare, familia Zareitarum:

21. Fuerunt autem filii Phares, de Hesron, familia Hesronitarum: de Hamul, familia Hamulitarum.

22. Istæ sunt familiæ Jehudah per numeratos suos, sex et septuaginta millia et quingenti.

23. Filii Issachar per familias suas, de Thola, familia Tholaitarum, de Phua, familia Phuitarum:

24. De Jasub, familia Jasubitarum: de Simron, familia Simronitarum.

25. Istæ sunt familiæ Issachar juxta numeratos suos, quatuor et sexaginta millia ac trecenti.

26. Filii Zabulon per familias suas: de Sered, familia Sereditarum: de Elon, familia Elonitarum: de Jahleel, familia Jahleelitarum.

27. These *are* the families of the Zebulunites, according to those that were numbered of them, threescore thousand and five hundred.

27. Istæ sunt familiæ Zabulonitarum juxta numeratos suos, sexaginta millia et quingenti.

28. The sons of Joseph, after their families, *were* Manasseh and Ephraim.

28. Filii Joseph per familias suas, Manasse et Ephraim.

29. Of the sons of Manasseh: of Machir, the family of the Machirites: and Machir begat Gilead: of Gilead *come* the family of the Gileadites.

29. Filii Manasse, de Machir, familia Machiritarum: et Machir genuit Galaad: de Galaad, familia Galaaditarum.

30. These are the sons of Gilead: *of* Jeezer, the family of the Jeezerites: of Helek, the family of the Helekites:

30. Isti sunt filii Galaad: de Jezer, familia Jezeritarum: de Helec, familia Helecitarum:

31. And *of* Asriel, the family of the Asrielites: and *of* Shechem, the family of the Shechemites:

31. Et de Asriel, familia Asraelitarum: de Sechem, familia Sechemitarum:

32. And *of* Shemida, the family of the Shemidaites: and *of* Hepher, the family of the Hepherites.

32. Et de Semida, familia Semidatarum: et de Hepher, familia Hepheritarum:

33. And Zelophehad the son of Hepher had no sons, but daughters: and the names of the daughters of Zelophehad *were* Mahlah, and Noah, Hoglah, Milcah, and Tirzah.

33. Et Salphaad filio Hepher non fuerunt filii, sed filiæ: quarum hæc nomina Malhad et Noah, Hoglah et Milchah, et Thirsah.

34. These *are* the families of Manasseh, and those that were numbered of them, fifty and two thousand and seven hundred.

34. Istæ sunt familiæ Manasse: numerati autem eorum, duo et quinquaginta millia et septingenti.

35. These *are* the sons of Ephraim, after their families: of Shuthelah, the family of the Shuthalhites: of Becher, the family of the Bachrites: of Tahan, the family of the Tahanites.

35. Isti sunt filii Ephraim per familias suas: de Suthelah, familia Suthelitarum: de Becher, familia Bechritarum: de Thaban, familia Thabanitarum.

36. And these *are* the sons of Shuthelah: of Eran, the family of the Eranites.

36. Et isti sunt filii Suthelah: de Eran, familia Eranitarum.

37. These *are* the families of the sons of Ephraim, according to those that were numbered of them, thirty and two thousand and five hundred. These *are* the sons of Joseph, after their families.

37. Istæ sunt familiæ filiorum Ephraim juxta numeratos suos, triginta duo millia et quingenti: isti sunt filii Joseph per familias suas.

38. The sons of Benjamin after their families: of Bela, the family of the Belaites: of Ashbel, the family of the Ashbelites: of Ahiram, the family of the Ahiramites:

38. Filii Benjamin per familias suas: de Bela, familia Belitarum: de Asbel, familia Asbelitarum: de Ahiram, familia Ahiramitarum.

39. Of Shupham, the family of the Shuphamites: of Hupham, the family of the Huphamites.

39. De Sephupham, familia Suphamitarum: de Hupham, familia Huphamitarum.

40. And the sons of Bela were Ard and Naaman: *of Ard*, the family of the Ardites: *and* of Naaman, the family of the Naamites.

40. Fuerunt autem filii Bela, Arde et Nahaman: de Arde, familia Arditarum: de Naaman, familia Naamanitarum.

41. These *are* the sons of Benjamin, after their families: and they that were numbered of them *were* forty and five thousand and six hundred.

41. Isti sunt filii Benjamin juxta familias suas, et numeratos suos, quadraginta quinque millia et sexcenti.

42. These *are* the sons of Dan, after their families: of Shuham, the families of the Shuhamites. These *are* the families of Dan, after their families.

42. Isti sunt filii Dan per familias suas: de Suham, familia Suhamitarum: istæ sunt familiæ Dan per familias suas.

43. All the families of the Shuhamites, according to those that were numbered of them, *were* threescore and four thousand and four hundred.

43. Omnes familiæ Suhamitarum juxta numeratos suos, sexaginta quatuor millia et quadringenti:

44. *Of* the children of Asher, after their families: of Jimna, the family of the Jimnites: of Jesui, the family of the Jesuites: of Beriah, the family of the Beriites.

44. Filii Asser per familias suas: de Imnah, familia Imnahitarum: de Isui, familia Isuitarum: de Beriah, familia Beriitarum.

45. Of the sons of Beriah: of Heber, the family of the Heberites: of Malchiel, the family of the Malchielites.

45. De filiis Beriah, de Heber, familia Hebritarum: de Malchiel, familia Malchielitarum.

46. And the name of the daughter of Asher *was* Sarah.

46. Nomen autem, filiæ Aser erat Sarah.

47. These *are* the families of the sons of Asher, according to those that were numbered of them, *who were* fifty and three thousand and four hundred.

47. Illæ sunt familiæ filiorum Aser juxta numeratos suos, quinquaginta tria millia et quadringenti.

48. *Of* the sons of Naphtali, after their families: of Jahzeel, the family of the Jahzeelites: of Guni, the family of the Gunites:

48. Filii Nephthali per familias suas: de Jesiel, familia Jesielitarum: de Guni, familia Gunitarum:

49. Of Jezer, the family of the Jezerites: of Shillem, the family of the Shillemites.

49. De Jeser, familia Jesrilitarum: de Sillen, familia Sillenitarum.

50. These *are* the families of Naphtali, according to their families: and they that were numbered of them *were* forty and five thousand and four hundred.

50. Istæ sunt familiæ Nephthali per familias suas: numerati autem eorum, quadraginta quinque millia et quadringenti.

51. These *were* the numbered of the children of Israel, six hundred thousand, and a thousand seven hundred and thirty.

51. Isti sunt numerati filiorum Israel, sexcenta millia, et mille septingenti ac triginta.

52. And the Lord spake unto Moses, saying,

52. Loquutus est autem Jehova ad Mosen, dicendo:

53. Unto these the land shall be divided for an inheritance, according to the number of names.

54. To many thou shalt give the more inheritance, and to few thou shalt give the less inheritance: to every one shall his inheritance be given according to those that were numbered of him.

55. Notwithstanding the land shall be divided by lot: according to the names of the tribes of their fathers they shall inherit.

56. According to the lot shall the possession thereof be divided between many and few.

57. And these *are* they that were numbered of the Levites, after their families: of Gershon, the family of the Gershonites: of Kohath, the family of the Kohathites: of Merari, the family of the Merarites.

58. These *are* the families of the Levites: the family of the Libnites, the family of the Hebronites, the family of the Mahlites, the family of the Mushites, the family of the Korathites. And Kohath begat Amram.

59. And the name of Amram's wife *was* Jochebed, the daughter of Levi, whom *her mother* bare to Levi in Egypt: and she bare unto Amram Aaron and Moses, and Miriam their sister.

60. And unto Aaron was born Nadab and Abihu, Eleazar and Ithamar.

61. And Nadab and Abihu died, when they offered strange fire before the Lord.

62. And those that were numbered of them were twenty and three thousand, all males, from a month old and upward: for they were not numbered among the children of Israel, because there was no inheritance given them among the children of Israel.

63. These *are* they that were numbered by Moses and Eleazar the priest, who numbered the children of Israel in the plains of Moab, by Jordan, *near* Jericho.

53. Istis dividetur terra illa in possessionem secundum numerum nominum.

54. Numerosiori dabis possessionem majorem: et pauciori diminues possessionem suam: unicuique secundum numeratos suos dabitur hæreditas sua.

55. Veruntamen sorte dividetur terra, per nomina tribuum patrum suorum hæreditatem accipient.

56. Secundum sortes dividetur hæreditas ejus inter multum et paucum.

57. Isti autem sunt numerati Levitarum per familias suas, de Gerson, familia Gersonitarum: de Cehath, familia Cehathitarum: de Merari, familia Meraritarum.

58. Istæ sunt familiæ Levitarum, familia Libnitarum, familia Hebronitarum, familia Mathlitarum, familia Musitarum, familia Corhitarum. Cehath autem genuit Amram.

59. Nomen verò uxoris Amram Jochebed filia Levi, quam peperit ipsi Levi in Ægypto, et quæ peperit ipsi Amram, Aharon et Mosen, et Mariam sororem eorum.

60. Natique sunt ipsi Aharon, Nadab et Abihu, et Eleazar et Ithamar.

61. Porro mortui sunt Nadab et Abihu dum offerrent ignem alienum coram Jehova.

62. Et fuerunt numerati eorum, viginti tria millia: omnes mares à filio mensis et suprà: non enim numerati fuerant inter filios Israel, quòd data non sit illis hæreditas inter filios Israel.

63. Isti sunt numerati Mosis et Eleazar sacerdotis, qui numeraverunt filios Israel in campestribus Moab juxta Jordanem Jericho.

64. But among these there was not a man of them whom Moses and Aaron the priest numbered, when they numbered the children of Israel in the wilderness of Sinai:

65. For the Lord had said of them, They shall surely die in the wilderness. And there was not left a man of them, save Caleb the son of Jephunneh, and Joshua the son of Nun.

64. Inter istos autem non fuit quisquam de numeratis Mosis et Aharon sacerdotis qui numeraverant filios Israel in deserto Sinai.

65. Dixerat enim Jehova de illis, Moriendo morientur in deserto, et non fuit superstes ex eis quisquam, nisi Caleb filius Jephuneh, et Josue filius Nun.

1. *And it came to pass after the plague.* This is the second *census* which we read of having been made by Moses; nevertheless it is easy to perceive, from Exodus xxxviii., that it was at least the third; although it is more probable that either yearly, or at stated times, those who had arrived at the age of twenty gave in their names. Still the number of the people could not be thus obtained, unless there were also a comparison of the deaths. This, at any rate, is incontrovertible, that those who had grown up to manhood were three times numbered in the desert, for we gather thus much from the passage before us, since it is said in the fourth verse that this enrolment was made "as the Lord had commanded Moses, and the children of Israel, which went forth out of the land of Egypt;" from whence it is plain not only that they followed as their rule the custom established from the beginning, but that the *census* of the people was again taken, as it had been in the wilderness of Sinai. From hence again a probable conjecture may be made, that, from the time in which they came out from thence, nothing similar had taken place in the interval. For Moses there records how many talents were collected from the tribute of the people, and mentions their number, viz., 603,550;[1] and he adds afterwards, when they moved their camp from Mount Sinai, how the *census* was taken according to God's command; but I pass over this subject the more cursorily, as having been already spoken of elsewhere.[2]

[1] In the *Lat.* these numbers are misprinted, 600,550; in the *Fr.*, 650,300.

[2] On Numbers i., &c., vol. iii. pp. 437, *et seq.* *Fr.* substitutes for the last clause, "pource qu'il n'est point de grande importance;" because it is not of great importance.

Now let us see with what object God desired to have His people numbered before He led them into the possession of the promised land. In less than forty years the whole generation of an age for military service had perished: many had been carried off by premature deaths; nay, a single scourge had lately destroyed 24,000; who would not have thought that the people must have been diminished by a fourth? We must then account it a remarkable miracle, that their numbers should be found as great as they were before. It was a memorable proof of God's anger that only two of the 603,000 still survived; but that by continued generation the people were so renewed, as that, at the conclusion of the period, their posterity equalled their former number, was the work of God's inestimable grace. Thus, in that awful judgment wherewith God punished His sinful people, the truth of His promise still shone forth. It had been said to Abraham, "I will multiply thy seed as the stars of the heaven, and as the sand which is upon the sea-shore," (Gen. xxii. 17;) and it was by no means fitting that this blessing should be obscured at the time, when the other part of the promise was about to be fulfilled: "Unto thy seed will I give this land." (Gen. xii. 7.) For, whilst the people had been instructed by punishments to fear God, still they were not to lose the savour of His paternal favour. And thus does God always temper His judgments towards His Church, so as in the midst of His indignation to remember mercy, as Habakkuk says, (iii. 2.) This was the reason why the people was numbered immediately after the plague, in order that it might be more conspicuous that God had marvellously provided lest any diminution should appear after the recent loss of so many men.

8. *And the sons of Pallu; Eliab.* The curtailment which had occurred in the superior line is here introduced, either in exaltation of God's grace, because, notwithstanding so great a loss, the tribe of Reuben was still numerous; or else to mark the cause of its diminution, for it might otherwise have seemed strange that other tribes exceeded in numbers that one whose founder and parent was Jacob's first-born. But when he has narrated how the two sons of

Eliab had been destroyed with their company, he briefly adverts to the clemency of God towards the sons of Korah, in that He spared them. And surely this was no common exercise of mercy not only to preserve them uninjured from the calamity, but afterwards to raise up shoots from the accursed root, in whom His spiritual riches might shine forth for the general advantage of the Church: for we know what honourable mention is often made of this family; and it is probable that certain of them were the authors of some of the Psalms, and thus were endued with the Spirit of prophecy, when possibly at that time none of the priests was possessed of this gift. This is that profound abyss in the various and unequal judgments of God, which it becomes us to adore with sober humility. Meanwhile, in a single word, Moses hints at the reason why he repeats this same history, whereby the formidable mode of their death might be held up as a perpetual example: for the Hebrew word נס, *nes*, which is primarily a standard[1] or banner, is often used for some portentous thing, which strikes men's senses with astonishment, and at the same time fills their minds with fear.

19. *The sons of Judah were Er and Onan.* Since the tribe of Judah was so numerous, Moses magnifies the greatness of God's grace by this circumstance, that of the three sons which he begat, two perished in the land of Canaan, by whose loss he might have appeared to be condemned to perpetual sterility. But the climax of God's unparalleled mercy was this, that although two of his children were born of an incestuous connexion, they grew up into so great a people.

28. *The sons of Joseph after their families.* The comparison of the two tribes, which sprang from the same head, is worthy of notice. By the fact that Manasseh was the father of only one son,[2] the prophecy of Jacob, when he declared that the first-born should be inferior to his younger

[1] "Un mot Hebrieu qui signifie tant banniere, que mas de navire, ou une haute perche;" a Hebrew word which signifies a banner, as well as the mast of a ship, or a high pole.—*Fr.*

[2] There appears to be an oversight here: see Joshua xvii.

brother Ephraim, began already to receive its accomplishment. Nevertheless, God's blessing extended far and wide for the increase of his family, so that they exceeded the tribe of Reuben in number. But further, though the larger number of children (πολυτεκνία) in which the descendants of Ephraim were superior, was a kind of type of his promised fecundity, still the excellency and dignity, of which Jacob prophesied, was deferred to a distant period; since in this respect the tribe of Ephraim was inferior by about a third, whereas a more numerous issue had been promised him. Although, therefore, God had not spoken in vain, yet the fulfilment of His promise did not immediately appear.

In the tribe of Dan, however, the incredible power of God was put forth. He was contemptible among his brethren; and thence it was an extraordinary blessing accorded to him in the shape of an honourable degree and name, when Jacob declares that "Dan shall judge his people." (Gen. xlix. 16.) He is said to have begotten only one son; yet his posterity exceeds 64,000.

51. *These are the numbered of the children of Israel.* By this sum total, what I have above adverted to is more clearly shewn, that amidst so many losses, and especially after the terrible vengeance which God had recently executed, the race of Abraham was preserved in an incredible manner, so that the fulfilment of the promise might not be brought about only towards a small body of persons. Nature itself and reason would have suggested that a few only should enjoy the promised land; but if the inheritance had been restricted to a small number of men, God's promise would have lain, as it were, in obscurity and concealment. Yet within thirty-eight years, during which more than 603,000 men had fallen, God marvellously brought it to pass that the same number of persons should still remain, some 2500 only excepted. Assuredly they must be blind four times over, as it were, who do not behold in this bright mirror God's wonderful providence, and the faithfulness of His gratuitous adoption, and His steadfastness in keeping His promises. At the same time, that

which I have already referred to in Deuteronomy clearly appears, that those who survived, were strikingly admonished by this great loss, that they should not fall away at any time into superstition.

53. *Unto these the land shall be divided.* This must have had great influence towards encouraging believers, when they gave in their names before God, and professed that they were heirs of the land; since it was exactly the same as if they actually had it in their grasp, when God called them to its certain possession; for the demonstrative pronoun is used emphatically, lest they should suppose that they were to be put off any longer, and that what was promised them was still to be kept in store for their posterity. The actual fulfilment, therefore, and immediate presence of the thing is indicated, when God prescribes that the land was to be divided to those who were just numbered, and whose names appeared in the public registers. A proportionable mode of division is then enjoined, so that their share should be distributed to every tribe according to the number of their names. We now perceive that they were registered, and, so to speak,[1] *lustrated*, in order that they might more earnestly bestir themselves to take possession of the promised land.

57. *And these are they that were numbered of the Levites.* He treats separately of the tribe of Levi, which God had dissevered from the rest of the people; and of the sons of Levi, the last mentioned is Kohath, the founder of the sacerdotal family. Hence we may probably conjecture that the law of primogeniture was not regarded when God deigned to take the priests from thence. But why Moses should expressly state the name of his mother, contrary to the usual custom of Scripture, does not clearly appear; for it is not likely that he did this as a distinction to his own family, because he at the same time shews how he himself, as well as his children, was deprived of the honour (of the priest-

[1] *Lat.*, "Quasi lustratos." *Fr.*, "Comme receus de nouveau;" as it were received anew:—the allusion is, I need hardly say, to the Roman *lustrum*, or quinquennial census and readjustment of the classes of the people.

hood,)[1] in which certainly there is no appearance of ambition. It is more probable, if the word *daughter* is literally taken, that he did not conceal a disgraceful circumstance, in order to extol more highly the indulgence of God; for, in this case, Moses and Aaron sprang of an incestuous marriage, since Amram, their father, must have married his aunt, which natural modesty forbade. It will, then, be rather an ingenuous confession of family dishonour, than an ambitious boast. If we inquire how this could have been tolerated, the answer will readily suggest itself, that this license had so largely prevailed among the oriental nations, that no one deemed that to be illicit which was in such universal use. And this we shall presently see[2] to be expressly referred to, when God, by forbidding incestuous marriages, distinguishes His people from other nations. It will be no matter of surprise, then, that those who were not yet prohibited from doing so by the law of God, had followed the general custom.

60. *And unto Aaron was born Nadab.* Since two of Aaron's four sons were cut off by a sudden death, the dignity of the high-priesthood, which depended on the life of two persons, appeared to be endangered. And with this view Moses repeats the history already given, in order that God's wonderful providence might be more clearly perceived in the preservation of this order, with which the safety of the whole Church was connected. Unquestionably, unless other families had been much more prolific, the whole tribe of Levi would have consisted of very few persons; yet, if we come to compare them, their fecundity will be incredible, inasmuch as 23,000 are numbered, whereas the sacerdotal race issued from only two heads. But God exalts His Church to pre-eminence by ways and means unknown to men, in order that His power may be magnified in this weakness. Moreover, the cause of their death is again recorded, that the priests, being admonished by this warning, may not only more diligently beware of wilful sacrilege, but also of error and negligence.

[1] Added from *Fr.*

[2] The *Fr.* more correctly says, "Ce que nous avons veu ci dessus;" this we have seen above;—the table of prohibited degrees having been considered *ante*, vol. iii. p. 96, *et seq.*

63. *These are they that were numbered.* The former registration was made by Aaron. The difference between the two *census* is therefore specified, in order that Moses may take occasion to commemorate God's judgment, which can never be sufficiently considered, that of 600,000, only two were found who had survived to the term prescribed by God. If any should object that the greater part would have died naturally, since they had arrived at their thirtieth, fortieth, and even fiftieth year,[1] and thus would have been some eighty years old before the completion of the forty years, I admit that such is the case; but many had not yet reached their twenty-fourth year. Nor can we doubt but that not a few of them were younger than Caleb and Joshua, whom we know to have been not only alive and well, but even strong and vigorous for many years afterwards. At any rate, therefore, not old age, but God's vengeance, cut off half of them by an untimely death, as if He had openly put forth His hand from heaven and smitten them. It is not without reason, then, that Moses states that they were dead, as God had pronounced; not merely that by the punishment inflicted upon them he may inculcate upon us the fear of God, but also that we may learn to be aroused in earnest by His threats.

NUMBERS, CHAPTER XXVII.

1. Then came the daughters of Zelophehad, the son of Hepher, the son of Gilead, the son of Machir, the son of Manasseh, of the families of Manasseh the son of Joseph: and these *are* the names of his daughters, Mahlah, Noah, and Hoglah, and Milcah, and Tirzah.

2. And they stood before Moses, and before Eleazar the priest, and before the princes and all the congregation, *by* the door of the tabernacle of the congregation, saying,

3. Our father died in the wilderness, and he was not in the company

1. Accesserunt autem filiæ Salphaad, filii Hepher, filii Galaad, filii Machir, filii Manasse de familiis Manasse, filii Joseph: hæc verò sunt nomina filiarum ejus, Malhah, Noah, Hoglah, et Milchah, et Thirsah.

2. Hæ steterunt coram Mose et coram Eleazar sacerdote, et coram principibus atque universa congregatione ad ostium tabernaculi conventionis, dicendo:

3. Pater noster mortuus est in deserto, qui tamen non fuit in con-

[1] This sentence is omitted in the edit. of Geneva, 1563.

of them that gathered themselves together against the Lord in the company of Korah; but died in his own sin, and had no sons.

4. Why should the name of our father be done away from among his family, because he hath no son? Give unto us *therefore* a possession among the brethren of our father.

5. And Moses brought their cause before the Lord.

6. And the Lord spake unto Moses, saying,

7. The daughters of Zelophehad speak right: thou shalt surely give them a possession of an inheritance among their father's brethren: and thou shalt cause the inheritance of their father to pass unto them.

8. And thou shalt speak unto the children of Israel, saying, If a man die and have no son, then ye shall cause his inheritance to pass unto his daughter.

9. And if he have no daughter, then ye shall give his inheritance unto his brethren.

10. And if he have no brethren, then ye shall give his inheritance nuto his father's brethren.

11. And if his father have no brethren, then ye shall give his inheritance unto his kinsman that is next to him of his family, and he shall possess it: and it shall be unto the children of Israel a statute of judgment; as the Lord commanded Moses.

gregatione quæ congregata fuit adversus Jehovam, in congregatione Core: quia in peccato mortuus est, et filii non fuerunt ei.

4. Quare tolletur nomen patris nostri de medio familiæ suæ, propterea quod non sit ei filius? da nobis hæreditatem inter fratres patris nostri.

5. Retulit autem Moses causam earum coram Jehova.

6. Et respondit Jehova ad Mosen, dicendo:

7. Rectum filiæ Salphaad loquuntur: dando dabis eis possessionem hæreditatis in medio fratrum patris sui, et transferes hæreditatem patris earum ad eas.

8. Ad filios autem Israel loqueris, dicendo, Quum quis mortuus fuerit, et filius non fuerit illi, tum transferetis hæreditatem ejus ad filiam ipsius.

9. Quod si non fuerit ei filia, tunc dabitis hæreditatem ejus fratribus ipsius.

10. Si vero non fuerint ei fratres, tunc dabitis hæreditatem ejus fratribus patris ipsius.

11. Quod si non fuerint fratres patri ipsius, tunc dabitis hæreditatem ejus propinquiori illi de familia ipsius, hæreditatemque accipiet illam: erit autem istud filiis Israel in statutum judicii, quemadmodum præcepit Jehova Mosi.

1. *Then came the daughters of Zelophehad.* A narrative is here introduced respecting the daughters of Zelophehad, of the family of Machir, who demanded to be admitted to a share of its inheritance; and the decision of this question might have been difficult, unless all doubt had been removed by the sentence of God Himself. For, since in the law no name is given to women, it would seem that no account of them was to be taken in the division of the land. And, in fact, God laid down this as the general rule; but a special exception is here made, *i.e.*, that whenever a family shall be destitute of male heirs, females should succeed, for the preservation of the name. I am aware that this is a point

which is open to dispute, since there are obvious arguments both for and against it, but let the decree that God pronounced suffice for us.

Although (the daughters of Zelophehad) plead before Moses for their own private advantage, still the discussion arose from a good principle; inasmuch as they would not have been so anxious about the succession, if God's promise had not been just as much a matter of certainty to them as if they were at this moment demanding to be put in possession of it. They had not yet entered the land, nor were their enemies conquered; yet, relying on the testimony of Moses, they prosecute their suit as if the tranquil possession of their rights were to be accorded them that very day. And this must have had the effect of confirming the expectations of the whole people, when Moses consulted God as respecting a matter of importance, and pronounced by revelation that which was just and right; for the discussion, being openly moved before them all, must have given them encouragement, at least to imitate these women.

3. *Our father died in the wilderness.* The plea they allege is no contemptible one, *i.e.*, that their father died after God had called His people to the immediate possession of the promised land; for, if the question had been carried back to an earlier period, it might have originated many quarrels. This restriction with respect to time, therefore, aided their cause. In the second place, they plead that their father had committed no crime whereby he might have been excepted from the general allotment of the land; for in the conspiracy of Dathan and Abiram, they include by *synecdoche*, in my opinion, the other sins, whose punishment affected the posterity of the criminals. His private sin is, therefore, contrasted with public ignominy; for so I interpret what they say of his having "died in his own sin." And surely it is mere childish nonsense which the Jews[1] affirm of his having been the man who gathered sticks on the Sabbath-day, or one of the number of those who were

[1] *S. M.* refers to this Rabbinical gloss. R. Sal. Jarchi tells us: "R. Akiba says, that he collected the wood; but R. Simeon says that he was one of those who were contumacious."—Edit. Breihthaupt, *in loco*, p. 1243, and notes.

slain by the bite of the serpents; and it is unnatural, too, to refer it to the curse under which the whole human race is laid. They distinguish, then, his private sin from any public crime, which would have caused him to deserve to be disinherited, lest the condition of their father should be worse than that of any other person. At the same time, they hold fast to the principle which is dictated to us by the common feelings of religion, that death, as being the curse of God, is the wages of sin.

5. *And Moses brought their cause before the Lord.* It is probable either that there was a difference of opinion, or that the minds of the judges were in doubt, as respecting an obscure and uncertain point. At any rate, it was expedient that the law should be laid down by God, lest any future controversy should arise; for, if a sentence had been pronounced by human judgment on the matter before them, the obstinacy of many would not perhaps have been sufficiently set at rest. It is worth while to remark the pious modesty of Moses, who was not ashamed to confess his ignorance, until he had been instructed by the mouth of God. Although he had promulgated the law forty years before, still he was always ready to learn. Besides, there is no doubt but that God impelled him to inquire of Himself, whenever any serious matters were in question, until his doctrine was absolutely perfect. And, although God does not now deliver from heaven what is to be done, nevertheless rulers are reminded that they ought to have recourse to God in points of perplexity, in order that He may instruct them by the Spirit of wisdom; and assuredly they will not be without this, if they ask Him; since He is no less ready to listen to them, than He here shewed Himself to be to Moses.

8. *And thou shalt speak to the children of Israel.* This question was the occasion of the delivery of a law, which was to be a perpetual and general rule as to the right of inheritance. But, although God prefers the daughters to all other relatives, when there is no male issue, still, with this single exception of the first degree, He admits none but males to the succession, and thus preserves the usual order. And surely it would be very unjust to exclude a man's (natural)

heirs on account of their sex; but when it became necessary to pass from his own children to other kindred, the prerogative of the male line began to be established. I speak of the land of Canaan, in which not only the name of Abraham but also that of the twelve tribes was to be preserved, in order that the memory (of God's blessing)[1] might be more distinct and unclouded.

NUMBERS, CHAPTER XXXVI.

1. And the chief fathers of the families of the children of Gilead, the son of Machir, the son of Manasseh, of the families of the sons of Joseph, came near, and spake before Moses, and before the princes, the chief fathers of the children of Israel.

2. And they said, The Lord commanded my lord to give the land for an inheritance by lot to the children of Israel: and my lord was commanded by the Lord to give the inheritance of Zelophehad our brother unto his daughters.

3. And if they be married to any of the sons of the *other* tribes of the children of Israel, then shall their inheritance be taken from the inheritance of our fathers, and shall be put to the inheritance of the tribe whereunto they are received: so shall it be taken from the lot of our inheritance.

4. And when the jubilee of the children of Israel shall be, then shall their inheritance be put unto the inheritance of the tribe whereunto they are received; so shall their inheritance be taken away from the inheritance of the tribe of our fathers.

5. And Moses commanded the children of Israel according to the word of the Lord, saying, The tribe of the sons of Joseph hath said well.

6. This *is* the thing which the Lord doth command concerning the

1. Accesserunt verò principes patrum è familia filiorum Gilad filii Machir, filii Manasse de familiis filiorum Joseph, et loquuti sunt coram Mose, et coram principibus capitibus patrum filiorum Israel:

2. Ac dixerunt, Domino meo præcepit Jehova ut daret terram in possessionem sorte filiis Israel, etiam domino meo præceptum est à Jehova ut daret possessionem Salphaad fratris nostri filiabus ejus.

3. Quæ si alicui de filiis aliarum tribuum filiorum Israel dentur in uxores, minuetur hæreditas earum ab hæreditate patrum nostrorum, addeturque hæreditati tribus quibus nupserunt, et de sorte hæreditatis nostræ minuetur.

4. Quumque fuerit jubilæus filiis Israel, addetur hæreditas earum hæreditati tribus quibus nupserint: atque de hæreditate tribus patrum nostrorum detrahetur hæreditas earum.

5. Præcepit itaque Moses filiis Israel juxta sermonem Jehovæ, dicendo, Rectum tribus filiorum Joseph loquitur.

6. Hoc est quod præcepit Jehova de filiabus Salphaad, dicendo, Ut

[1] Added from *Fr.*

daughters of Zelophehad, saying, Let them marry to whom they think best: only to the family of the tribe of their father shall they marry:

placebit illis, sint in uxores, veruntamen familiæ tribus patris sui sint in uxores.

7. So shall not the inheritance of the children of Israel remove from tribe to tribe; for every one of the children of Israel shall keep himself to the inheritance of the tribe of his fathers.

7. Ne transferatur hæreditas filiorum Israel de tribu ad tribum: nam filii Israel singuli adhærebunt hæreditatibus patrum suorum.

8. And every daughter that possesseth an inheritance in any tribe of the children of Israel, shall be wife unto one of the family of the tribe of her father, that the children of Israel may enjoy every man the inheritance of his fathers.

8. Et omnis filia quæ possederit hæreditatem de tribubus filiorum Israel, uni de familia tribus patris sui erit in uxorem, ut possideant filii Israel singuli hæreditatem patrum suorum:

9. Neither shall the inheritance remove from *one* tribe to another tribe; but every one of the tribes of the children of Israel shall keep himself to his own inheritance.

9. Ne transferatur possessio de tribu ad tribum aliam: sed singuli ex tribubus filiorum Israel hæreditati suæ adhærebunt.

10. Even as the Lord commanded Moses, so did the daughters of Zelophehad:

10. Quemadmodum præceperat Jehova Mosi sic fecerunt filiæ Salphaad.

11. For Mahlah, Tirzah, and Hoglah, and Milcah, and Noah, the daughters of Zelophehad, were married unto their father's brothers' sons.

11. Nam Mahalah, Thirsah, et Hoglah, et Milcah, et Noah, filiæ Salphaad, filiis patruorum suorum fuerunt in uxores:

12. *And* they were married into the families of the sons of Manasseh the son of Joseph; and their inheritance remained in the tribe of the family of their father.

12. His qui erant de familia filiorum Manasse filii Joseph fuerunt in uxores, fuitque hæreditas earum tribui familiæ patris earum.

13. These *are* the commandments and the judgments which the Lord commanded, by the hand of Moses, unto the children of Israel in the plains of Moab, by Jordan *near* Jericho.

13. Ista sunt præcepta et judicia quæ præcepit Jehova per manum Mosis filiis Israel in campestribus Moab juxta Jordanem Jericho.

1. *And the chief fathers of the families.* It might appear strange that God had given an imperfect law with reference to succession, as if what will be now stated had not occurred to His mind until Moses was reminded by the chief men of the families (of Machir,)[1] that it was unjust that the inheritances should be alienated, which would have been the case if the daughters of Zelophehad had married into other

[1] Added from *Fr.*

tribes, whereas their portion had fallen in the lot of the tribe of Manasseh. For whatever fell into the hands of those of another tribe, was a diminution of that lot. As, therefore, God had lately made provision for preserving the rights of individuals, He now treats of the general advantage or loss. What, then, can be the meaning of the objection, that God only half considered what was right? In my opinion, He so arranged His replies, that only when inquired of He assigned to each one his rights. The daughters of Zelophehad come, and demand justice of Moses and the elders, and God complies with their prayers. Now the heads of the tribe come, and agitate the question respecting the loss they would incur by the alienation of the inheritances; and it is then provided that other tribes should not be enriched by their loss. In short, whereas God might have spontaneously anticipated this, He preferred to grant it at the request of those who asked nothing but what was just and equitable. For it cannot be said that in this case it happened, as it often does, that, whilst every one pertinaciously maintains his own cause, and is eager to advance his own interests, one question arises out of another; for, when God has taken cognizance of the case, He pronounces that both parties only demanded what was right. It follows, therefore, that God designedly withheld His decisions until they naturally arose out of the circumstances of the case. It is a common saying that the law makes no provision for those things which rarely occur.[1] Thus it would have been commonly supposed that this law was superfluous; and especially it would have detracted somewhat from the authority of his teaching, if Moses had treated of this trifling matter, had not circumstances led to it. In fine, God allowed Himself to be interrogated familiarly with respect to doubtful points of no primary importance, in order that posterity might recognise His reply as a proof of His fatherly indulgence. Meanwhile, let us bear in mind that if heavenly things are the subject of as much anxiety to us,

[1] "De his, quæ frequenter fieri solent, non quæ raro, leges fieri debent." l. 3. et sequentibus ff. de legib.; l. 3. Digest. si pars hæredit. petatur; l. 28 ff. de judiciis; l. ea quæ 64, de regul. juris.

as earthly things were to the children of Manasseh, the rule that we should observe will always be made clear to us.

2. *And they said, The Lord commanded my lord.* They here allege a kind of discrepancy, in that the tribes had had the land allotted to them agreeably to God's command, but now their lots would be thrown into confusion, when the inheritance should pass over to another tribe. They assume it, however, to be an acknowledged impossibility, that God should be inconsistent with Himself: hence it was necessary that an interpretation should be delivered in order to remove the legal contradiction (*ἀντινομίαν.*) The Law of God, say they, which ought to remain inviolable, enjoins that the land should be distributed by lot; how, then, will it accord that women should carry elsewhere the inheritance of their own tribe? Thus, in seeking a remedy for this evil, they submit themselves to God's governance, and reverently accept what He had prescribed. And further, they enlarge upon the absurdity which would arisen from hence; viz., that in the fiftieth year, when they were to return to their original lots, so much would be withdrawn from the portion of the tribe of Manasseh as the daughters of Zelophehad had taken away with them. Reasonably, therefore, do they demand that a decree should be given to reconcile the two former laws, which otherwise appeared to be at variance with each other.

5. *And Moses commanded the children of Israel.* The account here given is not identical with the previous one, that Moses referred the matter to God; yet the same thing is more briefly stated, viz., that Moses answered the people out of the mouth of God, from whence we infer, that God was consulted by him. Moreover, God not only decides in favour of the children of Manasseh, but approves of their appeal, in that they were contented with their allotment, and claim for themselves what could not be alienated without the violation of the Divine decree. From this particular occasion, a general law is laid down, that no woman, to whom an inheritance had fallen, was to marry out of her tribe, because she would defraud her own relatives of her marriage portion. In this way, however, a free permission to marry was accorded to females, provided they renounced their

paternal inheritance. The words, indeed, seem to be of wider application, *i e.*, that no man should marry a wife, except of his own kindred; but the meaning of the law is to be sought from the cause which led to its enactment. Moreover, there is no doubt but that promiscuons marriages are here forbidden, in so far as they confound the order of hereditary rights.

NUMBERS, CHAPTER XXXI.

1. And the Lord spake unto Moses, saying,	1. Et loquutus est Jehova ad Mosen, dicendo:
2. Avenge the children of Israel of the Midianites: afterwards shalt thou be gathered unto thy people.	2. Ulciscere ultionem filiorum Israel de Madianitis, postea aggregaberis ad populos tuos.
3. And Moses spake unto the people, saying, Arm some of yourselves unto the war, and let them go against the Midianites, and avenge the Lord of Midian.	3. Loquutus est itaque Moses ad populum, dicendo, Accingant se ex vobis viri ad bellum, et sint contra Madian, ut dent ultionem Jehovæ.
4. Of every tribe a thousand, throughout all the tribes of Israel, shall ye send to the war.	4. Mille de singulis tribubus, de omnibus tribubus Israel mittetis ad bellum.
5. So there were delivered out of the thousands of Israel, a thousand of *every* tribe, twelve thousand armed for war.	5. Et traditi sunt ex millibus Israel mille per singulas tribus, duodecim millia accincti ad militiam.
6. And Moses sent them to the war, a thousand of *every* tribe, them and Phinehas the son of Eleazar the priest, to the war, with the holy instruments, and the trumpets to blow in his hand.	6. Quos misit Moses, mille de singulis tribubus ad bellum: misit, inquam, illos et Phinees filium Eleazar sacerdotis ad bellum, et vasa sancta, et tubæ clangoris erant in manu ejus.
7. And they warred against the Midianites, as the Lord commanded Moses; and they slew all the males.	7. Et pugnaverunt contra Madian, quemadmodum præceperat Jehova Mosi, et occiderunt omnem masculum.
8. And they slew the kings of Midian, besides the rest of them that were slain; *namely*, Evi, and Rekem, and Zur, and Hur, and Reba, five kings of Midian: Balaam also the son of Beor they slew with the sword.	8. Reges quoque Madian occiderunt cum occisis eorum, Evi et Recem, et Sur, et Hur, et Reba, quinque reges Madian: et Balaam filium Beor occiderunt gladio.
9. And the children of Israel took *all* the women of Midian captives, and their little ones, and took the spoil of all their cattle, and all their flocks, and all their goods.	9. Abduxerunt autem captivas filii Israel uxores Madianitarum, et parvulos eorum, atque omnia jumenta eorum, omniaque pecora eorum, et omnem substantiam eorum prædati sunt.

10. And they burnt all their cities wherein they dwelt, and all their goodly castles with fire.

11. And they took all the spoil, and all the prey, *both* of men and of beasts.

12. And they brought the captives, and the prey, and the spoil, unto Moses, and Eleazar the priest, and unto the congregation of the children of Israel, unto the camp at the plains of Moab, which *are* by Jordan *near* Jericho.

13. And Moses and Eleazar the priest, and all the princes of the congregation, went forth to meet them without the camp.

10. Omnes quoque urbes eorum per habitationes eorum et omnes ædes combusserunt igni.

11. Tuleruntque omnia spolia, et omnem prædam, tam de hominibus quam de jumentis.

12. Et adduxerunt ad Mosen et Eleazar sacerdotem, et ad congregationem filiorum Israel, captivitatem, et prædam, et spolia ad castra ipsa in campestribus Moab, quæ sunt juxta Jordanem Jericho.

13. Egressi sunt ergo Moses et Eleazar sacerdos, et omnes principes congregationis in occursum eorum extra castra.

1. *And the Lord spake unto Moses.* Amongst the other prerogatives which God conferred upon His Church, this one is celebrated, that He armed the godly " to execute vengeance upon the heathen,—to execute upon them the judgment that is written," (Ps. cxlix. 7-9:) and although the Spirit declares that this should happen under the kingdom of Christ, still He refers to ancient examples, one of which, well worthy of remembrance, is here recorded. The Midianites had organized a wicked conspiracy for the destruction of God's people: and God, in undertaking to punish this cruel act of theirs, gave a striking proof of His paternal favour towards the Israelites; whilst His grace is doubled by His constituting them the ministers of His judgment. This passage, therefore, shews us how anxious God was for the welfare of His elect people, when He so set Himself against their enemies, as if He would make common cause in all respects with them. At the same time we must observe this additional favour towards them, that although the Israelites themselves were not without blame, He still deigned to appoint them as judges of the Midianites. Inasmuch, however, as He everywhere prohibits His people from indulging the lust of vengeance, we must not forget the distinction between men's vengeance and His own. He would have His servants, by patiently bearing injuries, overcome evil with good; while, at the same time, He by no means abdicates His own power, but still reserves to Himself the right of in-

flicting punishment. Nay, Paul, desiring to exhort believers to long-suffering, recalls them to the principle, that God takes upon Himself the office of avenging.[1] Since, then, God is at liberty to execute vengeance, not only by Himself, but also by His ministers, as we have already seen, these two things are not inconsistent with each other, that the passions of the godly are laid under restraint by the Word, that they should not, when injured, seek for vengeance, or retaliate the evils they have received, and still that they are the just and legitimate executioners of God's vengeance, when the sword is put into their hands. It remains, that whosoever is called to this office, should punish crime with honest zeal, as the minister of God, and not as acting in his own private cause. God here intrusted the office of vengeance upon His people, but by no means in order that they might indulge the lust of their nature: for their feeling ought to have been this, that they should have been ready to pardon the Midianites,[2] and still that they should heartily bestir themselves to inflict punishment upon them.

That, whilst God so severely judged the Midianites, He spared the Moabites, was for the sake of Lot, who was the founder of their race. But I have already frequently reminded my readers that, when God's judgments surpass our understanding, we should, in sober humility, give glory to His secret, and to us incomprehensible, wisdom: for those who, in this respect, seek to know more than is fitting, elevate themselves too high, in order to plunge with headlong audacity into a profound abyss, in which, at length, all their senses must be overwhelmed. Why was He not at liberty to remit the punishment of the Moabites, and at the same time to repay to the Midianites the recompense which was their due? Besides, it was only for a time that he pardoned the Moabites, until their obstinacy should render them inexcusable, after they had not only abused His forbearance,

[1] The reference here, both in *Lat.* and *Fr.*, is to Rom. xiii. 4, though I presume it ought to be to Rom. xii. 19,—the former citation being transferred to what follows.

[2] Added in *Fr.*, "s'il les eust voulu laisser impunis:" if He had been willing to leave them unpunished.

but tyrannically afflicted their brethren, by whom they had been treated with kindness.

Moreover, God desired, whilst Moses was still alive, again to testify by this final act His love towards His people, in order that they might more cheerfully advance to the possession of the promised land: for this was no feeble encouragement, when they saw that God spontaneously put Himself forward to avenge them. At the same time it was expedient for Moses that, at the very moment of his death, he should feel, by a fresh instance, what care God took for the welfare of the people. For he was able joyfully to leave them in God's keeping, whose hand he had so recently seen put forth to fulfil to the utmost His gracious purposes towards them. To the same effect were the words, "Thou shalt be gathered unto thy people," which were undoubtedly spoken as a consolation in death. It was also a reason for making haste; for if the death of the holy Prophet had been waited for, perhaps the Israelites would not have dared to attack, with arms in their hands, a peaceful nation, from whom there was no peril or inconvenience impending. But so great was the authority of Moses over them, that they were more ready to obey his bidding than that of any other person.

Although it is said indifferently of the reprobate as well as believers, that they are gathered or congregated to their fathers by death, still this expression shews that men are born for immortality; for it would not be appropriate to say this of the brute animals, whose death is their final destruction, inasmuch as they are without the hope of another life.

3. *And Moses spake unto the people.* There is no doubt but that Moses delivered the commands which he had received from God; although, therefore, it is stated[1] that only ten thousand went forth to the war, yet the facts themselves demonstrate that the number, as well as the mode of warfare, was prescribed by God. And assuredly it would have been inconsiderate of Moses to attack so great a people with so small a band; and thus he would have

[1] "Combien doncques qu'il n'y est rien exprimé d'avantage, sinon que, &c;" although, therefore, nothing more is stated than that, &c.—*Fr.*

deservedly incurred the penalty of his rashness, if he had attempted it of his own accord; still, when God's command had preceded, he happily concluded the matter, which had been properly and rightly undertaken. Nor can it be questioned but that God desired by this test to prove the faith of His people. For, according to human apprehension, it was folly to endanger themselves without cause; and the objection was obvious that it was by no means advisable, when six hundred thousand men were at hand, to restrict to so few the office of waging such a perilous war. Just, therefore, as God afterwards destroyed the great army of the Midianites by only four hundred men under the guidance of Gideon, so also under the hand of Moses He sent forth only a single thousand from every tribe for the destruction of that nation. The tribe of Zebulon alone could have furnished five times as many soldiers as God took from the whole people. Thus, then, they proved their faith, when, in reliance on the aid of God alone, they did not hesitate boldly to rush forward against their enemies. And the event itself more fully illustrated God's grace than as if they had fought with all their forces, for then it would have been believed that the Midianites were overwhelmed by the infinite multitude of men. As, therefore, the people testified their obedience by prompt compliance, so they experienced in the result that there is nothing better than to submit ourselves to God, and to leave the prospect of success so completely in His hand, as that our confidence may depend solely upon Him.

Lest either of the tribes should boast itself against the others, they were each of them commanded to give the same number of soldiers. Moreover, Phinehas was sent with them, not so much that he might engage personally with the enemy, or be their General, as that he might rule and control their minds as God's messenger and interpreter. They were to be kept in the fear of God, and to be elevated to the expectation of victory, and therefore God's priest was their leader, so that the war might be a holy one; and the same was the object of the silver trumpets, with which, in obedience to the Law, as we have elsewhere seen,[1] the Levites were accustomed to sound, that it might be manifest that their battles were not fought without the will and authority of heaven. Amongst "the holy instruments," some commentators, in my opinion rightly, include the Ark of the Covenant.

7. *And they warred against the Midianites.* It was a signal example of obedience, that 12,000 men did not refuse to engage in a war which was full of danger, when it was reasonable for them to object that it was not right for them to be exposed to butchery, as it were, whilst the people sat idly in the camp, who by their great numbers and with little trouble would have routed and overcome the enemy. It was therefore no common proof of piety, that they obeyed God's command, and sought for no pretext to cover their cowardice. God, too, shewed by the result that He did not rashly expose His servants to danger; for it is in His power to rescue those whom He takes under His protection, from a hundred deaths. From hence also we are taught that there is no surer means of safety than to follow whither He calls. What Moses afterwards adds, tends to render praise to their perseverance, with one exception. They were right in killing all the males, even to the kings, whom Moses relates to have been slain in the general slaughter; and especially that they inflicted punishment on Balaam, who by his cunning and his snares, had endeavoured to destroy the people of God. They were right, too, in spoiling the whole land; nor did they act with less propriety and discretion in razing all the cities and towns, which might have been a temptation to the timid and inactive to take up their abode there; for, as we have seen before, all hindrances were to be taken away, so that the people might advance freely and without incumbrance into the land of Canaan; else, when there was an opportunity of repose, many would have willingly foregone the promised inheritance. Hence the cities were consumed by fire, lest they should afford any hold for those who were willing to stay. Thus far the selected soldiers faithfully performed their duty: in one respect they failed, in that, under the impulse either of avarice or lust,

[1] See *ante*, on Numbers x. 2, vol. ii. p. 104.

they preserved the women alive: on which point we shall see more presently.

11. *And they took all the spoil.* It was a sign both of their disinterestedness and modesty, that they brought the booty, which they had taken in the ardour of battle, to Moses and Eleazar; nor was it a mere empty and pompous ceremony, as many boastingly parade the wealth which they desire to keep to themselves; but their intention was, to acquiesce in the determination of Moses as to its distribution. For, when Moses soon afterwards allots half of it to the people, they are so far from rebelling against his decision, that they do not even murmur. It is clear, then, that in this respect they were no less submissive than they had been when, at the outset, they took up arms, and boldly went forth to battle, whilst the rest were quietly reposing out of the reach of the darts.

14. And Moses was wroth with the officers of the host, *with* the captains over thousands, and captains over hundreds, which came from the battle.

15. And Moses said unto them, Have ye saved all the women alive?

16. Behold, these caused the children of Israel, through the counsel of Balaam, to commit trespass against the Lord in the matter of Peor, and there was a plague among the congregation of the Lord.

17. Now therefore kill every male among the little ones, and kill every woman that hath known man by lying with him.

18. But all the women-children, that have not known a man by lying with him, keep alive for yourselves.

19. And do ye abide without the camp seven days: whosoever hath killed any person, and whosoever hath touched any slain, purify *both* yourselves and your captives on the third day, and on the seventh day.

20. And purify all *your* raiment, and all that is made of skins, and all work of goats' *hair*, and all things made of wood.

21. And Eleazar the priest said

14. Iratusque est Moses contra præfectos exercitus, tribunos et centuriones qui revertebantur de expeditione belli.

15. Et dixit eis Moses, Reservastisne omnes mulieres?

16. Ecce, ipsæ fuerunt filiis Israel, consilio Balaam ad tradendum in prævaricationem contra Jehovam in negotio Phogor, et fuit plaga in congregatione Jehovæ.

17. Nunc ergo occidite omnes mares in parvulis, et omnem mulierem quæ cognoverit virum concubitu masculi, occidite.

18. Omnes autem parvulas inter mulieres, quæ non cognoverint concubitum masculi, servate vivas vobis.

19. Vos vero manete extra castra septem diebus: omnis qui occiderit aliquem, quicunque item tetigerit occisum, purificabitis vos die tertia et die septima, vos et præda vestra.

20. Omne quoque vestimentum, et omnem supellectilem pelliceam, et omne opus è pilis caprarum, et omne vas lineum purificabitis.

21. Et dixit Eleazar sacerdos ad

unto the men of war which went to the battle, This *is* the ordinance of the law which the Lord commanded Moses;	milites qui iverant ad bellum, Hoc est statutum legis quod præceperat Jehova Mosi.
22. Only the gold, and the silver, the brass, the iron, the tin, and the lead,	22. Profecto aurum, et argentum, æs, ferrum, stannum, et plumbum, et quicquid ingreditur ignem, transire facietis per ignem, et mundabitur;
23. Every thing that may abide the fire, ye shall make *it* go through the fire, and it shall be clean; nevertheless it shall be purified with the water of separation: and all that abideth not the fire ye shall make go through the water.	23. Veruntamen aqua expiationis purificabitur, quicquid autem non ingreditur ignem, transire facietis per aquam.
24. And ye shall wash your clothes on the seventh day, and ye shall be clean, and afterward ye shall come into the camp.	24. Lavabitis præterea vestimenta vestra die septima, et mundi eritis, et postea intrabitis castra.

14. *And Moses was wroth with the officers.* A successful issue usually obtains pardon for any errors in performance, nay, in a manner covers them, so that they are not taken into account; but, although the army brought with it many causes of congratulation, still Moses does not forbear from severely reproving their single fault. By this example we are taught that, whilst we give praise to virtuous actions, we are not to approve of anything which deserves reprehension. The anger of Moses might appear to us inhumane, when he severely reproves his soldiers because they had not treated the female sex with the greatest cruelty; but it is not our business to canvass the judgments of God, before whose tribunal we must all hereafter stand. Although, therefore, they may be repugnant to our own feelings, still we must rest assured that, even where they may seem to be excessive, He nevertheless tempers the most severe punishments with the most perfect equity; yea, that although He may for a time overlook, or at any rate not so severely punish, the same sin in the Moabites which He sorely avenged upon the Midianites, there is still a most just cause for this distinction, although it may be hidden in His own breast. It is not our part to murmur against Him, lest He should absolve Himself by condemning our blasphemous audacity and temerity.

The Israelites sinned, in that, when they were only the ministers of God's vengeance, it rested not in their own discretion to relax any part of it. And this is worthy of observation, that those who are armed with the sword, must not go out of the way on either side one tittle, but faithfully execute whatever God prescribes. By the praise which is given to the anger of Moses, the imagination of the Stoics is refuted, with whom indifference[1] (ἀπάθεια) is the highest of virtues. But rather are we to labour that all our affections should proceed from a good motive, and that they should be kept under such restraint, that they may contain no ebullition of carnal passion, but that spiritual zeal may preside in them. Moses, however, gives the reason why the women were no more to be spared than the men, viz., because they had prostituted themselves in order to lay deadly snares for the Israelites. As regards the little ones, the same reason did not affect them, inasmuch as they were guilty of no crime ; yet is it not doubtful but that God justly desired that the very name of this wicked and irrecoverable nation should be utterly blotted out ; just as He afterwards gave over to destruction the nations of Canaan, together with their offspring. The question, however, arises by what means the women, who "had not known a man," were to be distinguished from virgins. The Jews, according to their custom, invent a fable[2] in reply, whereas it is probable that the decision was only come to on the ground of their age.

19. *And do ye abide without the camp seven days.* We have elsewhere seen,[3] that, if any one had touched a dead body, he was accounted unclean. Moses, by now extending the ceremony of expiation to lawful homicide, intimates how carefully we ought to abstain from shedding human blood. It was required of the Israelites that they should strenuously advance through the midst of carnage ; but, inasmuch as it is in a manner contrary to the order of nature that men

[1] "De n'avoir nulle passion ;" to be without any passion.—*Fr.*

[2] "(Eleazar) made them pass before the plate, (*i.e.*, the golden plate engraved like a signet, Ex. xxviii. 36,) and the face of her who was suited for marriage grew yellow as a crocus."—See R. Sal. Jarchi, *in loco.* Ed. Breithaupt. p. 1270.

[3] See *antè*, on Numbers xix. 11, vol. ii. p. 42.

should be killed by men, as if they were raging against their own bowels, God would have some vestiges of humanity preserved even in just punishments, so as to put a restraint upon all cruelty in the abstract. Nor is it without cause that Scripture, even in commending heroic bravery, uses this form of expression, that "they have polluted their hands with blood," who have slain any of their enemies, *i.e.*, in order that we may abhor all acts of homicide, as being repugnant to the preservation of the human race. Although, therefore, the Israelites had slain the Midianites not only justly, but by God's command, still, lest they should accustom themselves to the indiscriminate shedding of blood, they are commanded to purify themselves on the third and the seventh day, before they returned to the camp, so that their pollution should not infect the people. The reason for purifying the booty was different, viz., because the uncleanness of their vessels indicated how detestable was this people, whose very utensils, until they were purified either by fire or water, defiled every one by the mere touch. Lest, however, the soldiers should refuse to obey, or should comply unwillingly, Eleazar reminds them that nothing more was required of them than the observance of an old injunction. Nor is it to be doubted but that Moses designedly resigned the office of teaching to his nephew, because the interpretation of the law was hereafter to be sought from the mouth of the priest.

25. And the Lord spake unto Moses, saying,

26. Take the sum of the prey that was taken, *both* of man and of beast, thou, and Eleazar the priest, and the chief fathers of the congregation;

27. And divide the prey into two parts, between them that took the war upon them, who went out to battle, and between all the congregation;

28. And levy a tribute unto the Lord of the men of war which went out to battle: one soul of five hundred, *both* of the persons, and of the beeves, and of the asses, and of the sheep:

25. Loquutus est deinde Jehova ad Mosen, dicendo:

26. Cape summam prædæ captivitatis, tam de hominibus quam de jumentis, tu et Eleazar sacerdos, et capita patrum congregationis.

27. Et partieris in duas partes prædam, inter bellatores qui egressi sunt ad pugnam, et inter universam congregationem.

28. Tollesque censum Jehovæ à viris bellatoribus qui egressi sunt ad militiam, unam animam de quingentis, ex hominibus, et ex bobus, et ex asinis, et ex pecudibus.

29. Take *it* of their half, and give *it* unto Eleazar the priest, *for* an heave-offering of the Lord.

30. And of the children of Israel's half, thou shalt take one portion of fifty, of the persons, of the beeves, of the asses, and of the flocks, of all manner of beasts, and give them unto the Levites, which keep the charge of the tabernacle of the Lord.

31. And Moses and Eleazar the priest did as the Lord commanded Moses.

32. And the booty, *being* the rest of the prey which the men of war had caught, was six hundred thousand, and seventy thousand, and five thousand sheep,

33. And threescore and twelve thousand beeves,

34. And threescore and one thousand asses,

35. And thirty and two thousand persons in all, of women that had not known man by lying with him.

36. And the half, *which was* the portion of them that went out to war, was in number three hundred thousand, and seven and thirty thousand and five hundred sheep:

37. And the Lord's tribute of the sheep was six hundred and threescore and fifteen.

38. And the beeves *were* thirty and six thousand, of which the Lord's tribute *was* threescore and twelve.

39. And the asses *were* thirty thousand and five hundred, of which the Lord's tribute *was* threescore and one.

40. And the persons *were* sixteen thousand, of which the Lord's tribute *was* thirty and two persons.

41. And Moses gave the tribute, *which was* the Lord's heave-offering, unto Eleazar the priest; as the Lord commanded Moses.

42. And of the children of Israel's half, which Moses divided from the men that warred,

43. (Now the half *that pertained unto* the congregation was three

29. De media parte illorum capietis: et dabitis Eleazaro sacerdoti oblationem Jehovæ.

30. Et de media parte filiorum Israel capies unam portionem ex quinquaginta, ex hominibus, ex bobus, ex asinis, et ex pecoribus, id est ex omni jumento: et dabis illa Levitis custodientibus custodiam tabernaculi Jehovæ.

31. Et fecit Moses et Eleazar sacerdos quemadmodum præceperat Jehova Mosi.

32. Et fuit præda, residuum scilicet prædæ quam prædati sunt milites, ovium sexcenta septuaginta quinque millia,

33. Et bovum septuaginta duo millia,

34. Et asinorum unum et sexaginta millia,

35. Et animarum hominis è mulieribus quæ non cognoverant coitum masculi: omnium, inquam, animarum, duo et triginta millia.

36. Fuit autem dimidia pars, portio eorum, qui egressi fuerant ad militiam, numerus ovium trecenta triginta septem millia et quingentæ.

37. Fuit verò census pro Jehova, ex ovibus sexcentæ septuagintaquinque.

38. Et bovum, sex et triginta millia: et census eorum Jehovæ, duo et septuaginta.

39. Et asinorum triginta millia et quingenti: census autem eorum Jehovæ unus et sexaginta:

40. Et animarum hominum sedecim millia: census verò eorum Jehovæ, duæ et triginta animæ.

41. Deditque Moses censum oblationis Jehovæ ipsi Eleazar sacerdoti, quemadmodum præceperat Jehova Mosi.

42. Et de dimidia parte filiorum Israel, quam deduxerit Moses à viris que militaverant:

43. Fuit autem dimidia pars congregationis de ovibus, trecenta et

hundred thousand, and thirty thousand, *and* seven thousand and five hundred sheep,

44. And thirty and six thousand beeves,

45. And thirty thousand asses and five hundred,

46. And sixteen thousand persons,)

47. Even of the children of Israel's half, Moses took one portion of fifty, *both* of man and of beast, and gave them unto the Levites, which kept the charge of the tabernacle of the Lord; as the Lord commanded Moses.

triginta septem millia et quingentæ.

44. Et bovum sex et triginta millia.

45. Et asinorum triginta millia et quingenti.

46. Et animarum hominum sedecim millia.

47. De dimidia, inquam, parte filiorum Israel tulit Moses portionem unam è quinquaginta ex hominibus et ex jumentis, et dedit eam Levitis custodientibus custodiam tabernaculi Jehovæ, quemadmodum præceperat Jehova Mosi.

25. *And the Lord spake unto Moses.* A most equitable distribution of the booty is here described, in which the law of proportion was so well observed that, whilst the soldiers were not defrauded of the reward of their labour, at the same time some advantage accrued to the rest of the people in whose name the war was carried on. The share of the multitude was indeed small, for the same proportion was awarded to the 12,000 as to the remaining 600,000. But, since the booty had been already won by the soldiers in right of their victory, it ought not to have been a cause of complaint to the people who had not borne arms, that they received an honorary gift, although it might be of little value. And assuredly it would have been a shame that those who remained in the camp should be altogether without any part of the spoil, as if they had been convicted of cowardice, whereas it did not depend on themselves that they had not taken part with their brethren in the conquest of the enemy. For it was from no want of courage that they had escaped the burden and the perils of war, but they had modestly allowed the general glory to be appropriated by a few, because it had so pleased God. But, whilst it was just that some of the fruits of the victory should be communicated to all, so it was no less right that the fuller and more liberal reward should be received by those who had borne the whole brunt of the war.

It appears to some that David pursued the same rule, when he distributed the spoil equally amongst his followers who had gone down to the battle, and those who had stood by the baggage. (1 Sam. xxx. 24.) In my opinion, however, what David then decided was very different; for if the portion of those who remained with the baggage had been equal with that of those who were actually engaged, it would have been far more advantageous to remain out of the reach of the weapons. For, when a battle is fought, only a few men out of a large army are generally left with the baggage, and thus half the booty would have accrued to a few idlers. The partition, therefore, which is there mentioned, must have been an equal distribution to each individual; and very justly did David enjoin that those who remained stationed in the camp should have a full share of the spoil, lest[1] the condition of those should be dissimilar who were under the operation of the same rule. But in this case the actual warriors are justly rewarded above those who quietly attended to their own domestic cares.

28. *And levy a tribute unto the Lord.* God now requires a tribute, or holy oblation, out of the spoil from both parties, but in unequal portions, the people paying ten times more than the soldiers. There was a twofold reason and object for this tribute; for it was not fair that the Levites alone should be sent away empty, as if their condition were worse than that of the rest, because they were occupied in the service of God, and in taking care of the holy things. But the part which He assigns to them, God commands to be offered to Himself, that men may not only regard equity amongst each other, but that religion may stand in the foremost place; for nothing can be more unreasonable than that the rights of men should be maintained inviolate, whilst God Himself is overlooked. In order, then, to testify their piety, the offering was enjoined, as if God claimed for Himself the glory of the victory in taking this fiftieth and five-hundredth portion. But, inasmuch as He has no want of anything, having full satisfaction in Himself alone, the Le-

[1] The *Fr.* gives a different turn to the sentence, "veu que tous à la verité guerroyoyent;" seeing that in truth all were alike engaged in the war.

vites are substituted in His stead, that they may receive some reward for their ministry.

Again, we perceive that God dealt more liberally with the soldiers than with the rest of the multitude; nor is this a matter of surprise, for, since He had laid a greater burden upon them, it was just that they should be enriched by more fruits of the victory, for He heaps blessings upon blessings according to His pleasure.

From this distribution we also gather that it depends upon His ordinance that some should be richer than others; for, if there were no such thing as property, there would be no test of justice and integrity.

37. *And the Lord's tribute of the sheep.* The greatness of the victory is shewn by the result, since such an abundance of cattle could only have been collected from a wide and populous country. It is probable that it was not very fertile, and consequently only live stock, and not corn and wine, are enumerated as amongst their wealth.. Still, we may conjecture that it was famous for pastures, since barren mountains could not have fed so many oxen, and goats, and sheep, and camels; besides, it is most evident, from the number of young women, that the men who were slain were more in number than their conquerors who had been sent to the battle; for suppose they each of them had an unmarried daughter, they would have almost three times outnumbered the 12,000 Israelites. Hence, again, it is manifest that the victory was effected by Divine power. It may, however, seem strange that, although the nation was almost destroyed, nevertheless their posterity existed some little time afterwards, as if new Midianites had been begotten from the ashes of their sires. For it was not a very long time that elapsed between this slaughter and the time of Gideon, when they again dared voluntarily to attack the Israelites, and in reliance on their multitude, to rush into the very heart of Canaan; nay, they had already brought all the neighbouring nations into subjection. How this could have happened, since the Scriptures do not inform us, it only remains for us to make the conjecture, that many of them, as is often the case in a season of confusion, fled elsewhere. and soon afterwards returned into the land, which

was now unoccupied. For the sudden irruption of the Israelites was like a storm which soon passed away; nor was flight a difficult thing for this unsettled and wandering nation. It might also have been the case, that many immigrants from various quarters flowed into the land, when stripped of its inhabitants; or even that the Israelites, having performed their work but slackly, sounded the recall sooner than they ought, and that God afterwards punished their remissness. At any rate, we are taught by this example that the wicked sprout up like foul and noxious weeds, so that, though often cut down, they soon cover the ground again.

48. And the officers which *were* over thousands of the host, the captains of thousands, and captains of hundreds, came near unto Moses:

48. Et accesserunt ad Mosen præfecti militum militiæ, tribuni et centuriones.

49. And they said unto Moses, Thy servants have taken the sum of the men of war which *are* under our charge, and there lacketh not one man of us.

49. Dixeruntque ad Mosen, Servi tui levarunt (*vel,* subduxerunt,) summam virorum bellatorum qui sunt in manu nostra, et non defuit in nobis quisquam.

50. We have therefore brought an oblation for the Lord, what every man hath gotten, of jewels of gold, chains, and bracelets, rings, ear-rings, and tablets, to make an atonement for our souls before the Lord.

50. Propterea obtulimus oblationem Jehovæ quisque quod invenit, vasa aurea, brachiale, et ornamentum manus, annulum in aurem, et subligaculum fœmineum, ad expiandum animas nostras coram Jehova.

51. And Moses and Eleazar the priest took the gold of them, *even* all wrought jewels.

51. Et accepit Moses et Eleazar sacerdos aurum ab illis, omnia vasa operis.

52. And all the gold of the offering that they offered up to the Lord, of the captains of thousands, and of the captains of hundreds, was sixteen thousand seven hundred and fifty shekels.

52. Fuitque omne aurum oblationis quod obtulerunt Jehovæ, sedecim millia, septingenti et quinquaginta sicli, à tribunis et centurionibus.

53. (*For* the men of war had taken spoil, every man for himself.)

53. (Viri namque exercitus prædati fuerant quisque sibi.)

54. And Moses and Eleazar the priest took the gold of the captains of thousands and of hundreds, and brought it into the tabernacle of the congregation, *for* a memorial for the children of Israel before the Lord.

54. Accepit inquam Moses et Eleazar sacerdos aurum à tribunis et centurionibus, et intulit illud in tabernaculum conventionis, in memoriam filiis Israel coram Jehova.

48. *And the officers which were over the thousands.* We have here an example of signal gratitude, that the leaders of the army, when they saw that none of their men were lost, consecrated their spoils of gold and silver to the Lord.

By the offering of the first-fruits, they had already sufficiently testified their piety and obedience; nor, indeed, after they had faithfully complied with God's command, could anything more have been expected from them; hence does their liberality deserve so much the more praise, when they lay themselves under the obligation of a new and extraordinary vow. At the same time, Moses magnifies God's special blessing in bringing them all back safely to a man from this great battle. Surely, since their spoils must have been driven from many villages, it was strange that some few of them at least had not been slain in their very passage from one place to another. Hence, therefore, it was more than ever manifest that the war was thus successfully concluded under the guidance of God, who had protected the 12,000 men. Hence the incredible goodness of God towards His people is here celebrated, as well as the pious profession of the officers, when it is expressly stated that, having mustered their forces, they had found them all safe, so that there could be no doubt nor question about the grace of God. In acknowledgment, therefore, of His wondrous power in the preservation of the soldiers, they offer as the price of their redemption whatever gold and silver they had taken among the spoils. Moses records the sum, so that it may more clearly appear that, in the performance of this act of homage, it was no trifling amount of gain that they despised, for its amount is more than 10,500 *livres* of French money.[1]

But what becomes of the soldiers? whilst these vows are being paid for their safety, they quietly enjoy their plunder: for there is an implied comparison here, when Moses, after having praised the centurions and tribunes, presently adds the exception, that "the spoil which each man had taken was his own." It is, indeed, amazing that the soldiers, as if they had conquered by themselves, and for themselves alone, should have been so ill-conditioned and mean, as not to imitate this laudable example. And, in truth, it often happens, that the multitude indulges its meanness without

[1] 16,750 shekels. *C.'s* calculations are, as far as I have observed, rarely accurate. The equivalent for the shekel in French money, which he professed to adopt, was somewhat more than 14 sous, or 14-20ths of the franc or livre. See *ante*, vol. i. p. 483, and vol. iii. p. 416.

shame, as well because it is ignorant of what true nobility is, as because the crowd conceals the disgrace. Meanwhile, those in office are reminded to take care, that the higher the dignity may be to which they are called, the more eminent should their virtues be.

51. *And Moses and Eleazar the priest took the gold.* It was fitting that this should be added, lest any should suppose that Eleazar made a profit by the liberality of others. Moses, therefore, relates, that whatever gold was offered, was faithfully laid up as an ornament for the sanctuary. When it is said, " for a memorial for the children of Israel," it may be taken either actively or passively; viz., either that the gift may be a monument of their gratitude, or that it might conciliate favour for the people in the eyes of God; as if that offering of expiation brought before God, and represented, all those who thus professed themselves to be preserved by His grace. I prefer the latter sense myself, *i.e.*, that this memorial was set before His eyes, in order that God might hereafter also be favourable to His people.

NUMBERS, CHAPTER XXXII.

1. Now the children of Reuben and the children of Gad had a very great multitude of cattle; and when they saw the land of Jazer, and the land of Gilead, that, behold, the place *was* a place for cattle;

1. Peculium verò multum erat filiis Ruben, et filiis Gad multum admodum: qui viderunt terram Jaazer et terram Galaad, et ecce, locus ille erat locus peculii.

2. The children of Gad and the children of Reuben, came and spake unto Moses, and to Eleazar the priest, and unto the princes of the congregation, saying,

2. Venerunt igitur filii Gad et filii Ruben, et dixerunt ad Mosen et Eleazar sacerdotem, et ad principes congregationis, dicendo:

3. Ataroth, and Dibon, and Jazer, and Nimrah, and Heshbon, and Elealeh, and Shebam, and Nebo, and Beon,

3. Ataroth, et Dibon, et Jaazer, et Nimrah, et Heshbon, et Elalech, et Sebam, et Nebo, et Bebon:

4. *Even* the country which the Lord smote before the congregation of Israel, *is* a land for cattle, and thy servants have cattle:

4. Terra quam percussit Jehova ad congregationem Israel, terra peculii est, et servis tuis est peculium.

5. Wherefore, said they, if we have found grace in thy sight, let this land be given unto thy servants for a possession, *and* bring us not over Jordan.

5. Dixerunt, inquam, si invenimus gratiam in oculis tuis, detur terra hæc servis tuis in possessionem: ne transire nos facias Jordanem.

6. And Moses said unto the children of Gad, and to the children of Reuben, Shall your brethren go to war, and shall ye sit here?

6. Respondit autem Moses filiis Gad, et Ruben, Num fratres vestri ingredientur pugnam, et vos manebitis hic?

7. And wherefore discourage ye the heart of the children of Israel from going over into the land which the Lord hath given them?

7. Et quare frangetis cor filiorum Israel, ne transeant ad terram quam dedit eis Jehova?

8. Thus did your fathers, when I sent them from Kadesh-barnea to see the land.

8. Sic fecerunt patres vestri quando misi eos de Cades-barnea ut viderent terram istam.

9. For when they went up unto the valley of Eshcol, and saw the land, they discouraged the heart of the children of Israel, that they should not go into the land which the Lord had given them.

9. Ascenderunt namque usque ad vallem Eschol, videruntque terram, postea fregerunt cor filiorum Israel, ne ingrederentur terram quam dederat eis Jehova.

10. And the Lord's anger was kindled the same time, and he sware, saying,

10. Unde irata excandescentia Jehovæ in die illa, juravit dicendo:

11. Surely none of the men that came up out of Egypt, from twenty years old and upward, shall see the land which I sware unto Abraham, unto Isaac, and unto Jacob, because they have not wholly followed me:

11. Si videbunt homines qui ascenderunt ex Ægypto, a filio viginti annorum et supra, terram de qua juravi Abraham, Isaac et Jacob: quia non compleverunt ire post me:

12. Save Caleb the son of Jephunneh the Kenezite, and Joshua the son of Nun: for they have wholly followed the Lord.

12. Præter Caleb filium Jephune Cenezæum, et Josue filium Nun, quia compleverunt ire post Jehovam.

13. And the Lord's anger was kindled against Israel, and he made them wander in the wilderness forty years, until all the generation that had done evil in the sight of the Lord was consumed.

13. Et irata est excandescentia Jehovæ in Israelem, vagarique fecit eos in deserto quadraginta annis, donec consumeretur tota illa generatio quæ fecerat malum in oculis Jehovæ.

14. And, behold, ye are risen up in your fathers' stead, an increase of sinful men, to augment yet the fierce anger of the Lord toward Israel.

14. Ecce autem surrexistis pro patribus vestris, accessio hominum sceleratorum, ut adderetis adhuc ad iram excandescentiæ Jehovæ contra Israelem.

15. For if ye turn away from after him, he will yet again leave them in the wilderness; and ye shall destroy all this people.

15. Si aversi fueritis ut non eatis post eum, tum addet adhuc deserere illum ipsum in deserto, et perdetis universum populum hunc.

1. *Now the children of Reuben and the children of Gad.* In this narrative we behold, as in a glass, that whilst each individual is but too attentive to his own private interests, he forgets what is just and right. Those, indeed, who seek their own advantage, do not reflect that they are doing injury to others; but it is impossible for them to avoid seek-

ing more than is their due, and preferring themselves to others; and thus they sin against that rule of charity, that we should not seek our own. The sons of Gad and Reuben, who had a great quantity of cattle, see a tract of rich and fertile land; self-interest takes possession of them, so that it does not occur to them that they were under an obligation to their brethren not to covet for themselves anything peculiar, or separate from them. Nevertheless, there was a specious pretext for this, whereby their eyes were blinded, viz., that nothing was taken away from the others, but rather that so much addition was made; for by these means the whole country on the other side of Jordan continued to be theirs; and, besides, they were rather relieved of an inconvenience than exposed to a loss; since the progress of their expedition would be less difficult, if the body of persons, who were charged with the cattle, should stay there, and thus should cease to be an incumbrance to the army, which would be in lighter condition for advancing. Their association, however, for the war had been established by God, and bound them by an indissoluble tie not to desert the rest of the people: whilst it was also a solemn duty (*religio*) imposed upon them not to alter the bounds of the inheritance promised by God. The land of Canaan was assigned to the whole race of Abraham, in which they were to be enclosed, and to inhabit it as a peculiar world. The tribes of Gad and Reuben now transgress those limits, and, at the same time disunite themselves from the body of the Church, as if they desired to be emancipated from God. Hence ought we to be the more on our guard, lest we should go astray after our own lusts. And when Moses says, that they *saw*, or considered, the land, let us learn to beware lest our eyes, by unlawful looks, should lead us into snares, and blind our minds; and thus that our senses should be so deceived by the envenomed sweetness, as that reason and equity should be utterly overthrown.

The Hebrew word,[1] which we have rendered *peculium*, signifies not only cattle and herds, but also flocks of sheep. Almost all the Israelites were indeed possessors of cattle; but we gather from the words of Moses, that these two

[1] מקנה, *mikneh.*

tribes were especially rich in them; perhaps, because the district which they inhabited in Egypt, being more suited for pasture, had invited them to apply themselves more earnestly to that mode of life, which was common to all, and had been handed down to them by their fathers; for it is not probable that they had thus surpassed the rest in this respect, during the course of their march.

2. *The children of Gad and the children of Reuben came.* Their request was apparently a reasonable one, that, since God had driven out the inhabitants of the land, and its fertility invited them to dwell there, the possession of these empty and deserted fields should not be denied them. Their modesty also was praiseworthy, in that they neither detach themselves from the people, nor seditiously and violently seize upon the places which were so suitable for them; but seek to obtain them by the permission of Moses and the elders, as if they submitted their cause to their decision. But as I have just said, their private interest had so laid hold of their minds, that the main point did not occur to them, viz., that the land of Canaan was set before them all, in order that they might dwell together there separate from heathen nations; and, again, that it was unjust for them not only to enjoy repose, whilst the others were fighting, but also to be settled in an assured and peaceable habitation, while the ten tribes were still advancing to the conquest of the promised land.

6. *And Moses said unto the children of Gad.* So sharp and severe a reproof shews us the greatness of the wrong: for neither did inconsiderate warmth carry away Moses into such violent anger, nor did he fall into error, so as to deliver his opinion on a point which he did not well understand. He knew, therefore, what the sons of Gad and Reuben asked; and hence he inveighed against them thus vehemently, because they desired to lacerate the body of the Church by this wicked severance. He begins by expostulating with them with regard to their sinful and unreasonable covetousness, in that they sought to indulge in idleness, when their brethren were about to march through a hostile land; for they were possessed of no rightful superiority, so as to

throw upon the others all the labours, perils, and burdens of the war. Since, therefore, God had imposed the same condition upon all,[1] it was not right that part of them should be exempted from it, as if by privilege. More severely, however, is their ingratitude and perverseness towards God chastised, than their injustice towards their brethren, whilst he alleges to their reproach, that thus the hearts of the children of Israel would be broken,[2] so that they would refuse to obey the call of God.

8. *Thus did your fathers.* He amplifies their crime by reference to their continued perverseness: for so far is the imitation of ungodly parents from being an excuse for their children, that it rather doubles their guilt. Thus also does Stephen allege against the Jews of his days, their persevering in the sins of their fathers; as if he had cried out against them, that they were "the bad eggs of bad birds." "Ye stiff-necked (he says) and uncircumcised in heart and ears, ye do always resist the Holy Ghost: as your fathers did, so do ye." (Acts vii. 51.) So also the Prophet, when he is exhorting their posterity to obedience, recalls these same circumstances to their memory: "Harden not your hearts, as in the provocation, and as in the day of temptation in the wilderness, when your fathers tempted me. Forty years long was I grieved with this generation," &c. (Ps. xcv. 8-10.) It is not without cause that Moses now complains that there was no end or limit to their impiety, whilst the sons inherited their fathers' iniquity, and ceased not to resist God: and, in order that the similarity and affinity of their crime may be more apparent, he reviews their history at some length. He does not, however compare the Reubenites and Gadites to the whole people, but to the ten spies, from whom the sedition arose, because, as far as in them lay, they turned aside the people from the right way. Secondly, he connects with this the punishment which ensued, that, at least, he might inspire them with

[1] "Que Dieu les avoit conjoints ensemble, afin que les uns teinssent compagnie aux autres;" that God had united them together, so that they should keep company with each other.—*Fr.*

[2] See Margin, *A.V.*, ver. 7, "*Heb.* break."

terror, since it was hardly to be expected that they would amend of their own accord. He reminds them, therefore, that, when God so severely dealt with their fathers, He had given them a signal proof that their descendants would not be unpunished, unless they were teachable and submissive. The expression is remarkable, "Because they fulfilled not after me;"[1] whereby he signifies that there is nothing praiseworthy in the most vigorous course, unless men persevere even to the goal. And, although this had happened forty years ago, still, inasmuch as the vengeance which God had threatened had been before their eyes even to that day, it behoved them to be just as much affected by it, as if they saw the hand of God still stretched forth. For, whenever any died in the desert, so often did God set His seal to His vengeance, lest it should be at any time buried in oblivion. [2]If, then, God had been so wroth with the multitude in general, how much less should the instigators themselves escape?

14. *And, behold, ye are risen up in your fathers' stead.* He signifies that, by their evil doings, they were "filling up the measure" of their fathers, as Jesus spoke of the Jews of His own time. In this sense he calls them an addition (*accessio,*) which word I take to mean a climax (*cumulus.*) For their translation is a poor one, who render it education, or offspring, or foster-children. With the Hebrews, תרבות,[3] *tarbuth,* is literally an increase, or multiplication; and thus is applied to usury. This passage, however, requires that it should be explained as a heap, as much as to say that a new body of persons were springing up afresh, who carried impiety to its very height. In a word, he intimates that fuel was added to the fire which was now smouldering, whereby a new flame was excited: for he says that they were furnishing materials for God's wrath, so that it should burst forth more and more against the whole people.

[1] See Margin, *A.V.*, ver. 11.

[2] "Or, il conclud du plus petit au plus grand;" he argues then from the less to the greater, that, &c.—*Fr.*

[3] תרבות is a noun heemantic, from רבה, to increase and multiply. The *V.* has "incrementa et alumni," as though the Latin translator thought the first word insufficient to express the whole meaning of the Hebrew noun.—*W.*

16. And they came near unto him, and said, We will build sheepfolds here for our cattle, and cities for our little ones;

17. But we ourselves will go ready armed before the children of Israel, until we have brought them unto their place: and our little ones shall dwell in the fenced cities, because of the inhabitants of the land.

18. We will not return unto our houses, until the children of Israel have inherited every man his inheritance:

19. For we will not inherit with them on yonder side Jordan, or forward; because our inheritance is fallen to us on this side Jordan eastward.

20. And Moses said unto them, If ye will do this thing, if ye will go armed before the Lord to war,

21. And will go all of you armed over Jordan before the Lord, until he hath driven out his enemies from before him,

22. And the land be subdued before the Lord; then afterward ye shall return, and be guiltless before the Lord, and before Israel; and this land shall be your possession before the Lord.

23. But if ye will not do so, behold, ye have sinned against the Lord: and be sure your sin will find you out.

24. Build you cities for your little ones, and folds for your sheep; and do that which hath proceeded out of your mouth.

25. And the children of Gad, and the children of Reuben, spake unto Moses, saying, Thy servants will do as my lord commandeth.

26. Our little ones, our wives, our flocks, and all our cattle, shall be there in the cities of Gilead;

27. But thy servants will pass over, every man armed for war, before the Lord to battle, as my lord saith.

16. Et accesserunt ad eum, ac dixerunt, Caulas pecudum ædificabimus peculio nostro hic, et urbes parvulis nostris:

17. Nos vero accincti erimus armis, festinantes ante filios Israel, donec introduxerimus eos ad locum suum: et manebunt parvuli nostri in urbibus munitis propter habitatores terræ.

18. Non revertemur ad domos nostras, donec possideant filii Israel quisque hæreditatem suam.

19. Non enim hæreditatem accipiemus cum eis trans Jordanem et ultra: quod evenerit hæreditas nostra nobis citra Jordanem ad Orientem.

20. Et dixit illis Moses, Si feceritis hoc, si accinxeritis vos armis coram Jehova ad bellum:

21. Et transierint ex vobis omnes accincti armis ipsum Jordanem ante Jehovam, donec expulerit inimicos suos à facie sua,

22. Et subjiciatur terra illa coram Jehova: postea revertemini, et eritis absoluti à Jehova, et Israele: eritque terra ista vobis in possessionem coram Jehova.

23. Quod si non feceritis ita, ecce, peccastis Jehovæ, et perpendite peccatum vestrum quod inveniet vos.

24. Ædificate vobis ergo civitates pro parvulis vestris, et caulas ovibus vestris, et quod egressum est ex ore vestro, facietis.

25. Et dixerunt filii Gad, et filii Reuben ad Mosen, dicendo: Servi tui facient quemadmodum dominus meus præcepit.

26. Parvuli nostri, uxores nostræ, pecora nostra, et omnia jumenta erunt ibi in urbibus Galaad.

27. Servi autem tui transibunt omnes accincti armis ad militiam coram Jehova ad bellum, quemadmodum dominus meus loquitur.

16. *And they came near unto him, and said.* It is probable that they returned after having held a consultation:

and now,—when they had considered what they ought to do, before promising what they had not previously thought of,—they assent to the decision of Moses, in accordance with their general opinion. From their reply itself we gather how usefully the severity of Moses had influenced their minds. If he had dealt with them with greater mildness and gentleness, his kindness would perhaps have been received with contempt. It was more profitable, therefore, that their stubborn hearts should be smitten with shame and fear, in order that they might lay aside their rebelliousness. Still, they do not altogether abandon their request, but devise a middle course, whereby, whilst they do not forsake their brethren, they may still occupy the land. They promise, then, to accompany them throughout the whole expedition, and to unite with them in the war; nay, to be the first to undergo danger, and expose themselves to the attacks of the enemy, provided a settled abode should be granted them for their families and their herds. Thus they would be exempt from guilt, since the rest would not be held back by their bad example, nor the strength of the people for carrying on the war be diminished; in one respect only they would have the advantage, that, by depositing their wives and children in a peaceful spot, they would have the opportunity of improving their domestic finances.

20. *And Moses said unto them.* Moses might seem to err on the side of excessive good-nature, in that he extends the boundaries prescribed by God, in complying with their wish. For, since their inheritance had been promised them in the land of Canaan, they ought to have been contented with that as their abode; nor was it allowable for Moses to make any alteration in the Divine decree. There is also another thing no less inconsistent, that in a point of so much perplexity, Moses does not, as usual, consult God, but gives an immediate answer, which indirectly overthrows the previous ordinance of God. And, in truth, their desire was by no means excusable, since it would have never entered their minds, if they had borne in memory the covenant of God, and had been satisfied with His goodness: since it cannot be but that the flesh should be constantly running riot, unless kept

under restraint by the calling of God. But God, who knows how to bring light out of darkness, not only pardoned their error, but takes occasion also to extend His liberality. Thus the land of Bashan, and its neighbourhood, were added to the former boundaries. At the same time, however, He shewed on the other hand how much better it would have been for them to have been kept together, so that they might have mutually protected each other, and dwelt securely in their appointed habitation. And, after the lapse of a long period, the Reubenites and Gadites learnt from experience that they had been too hasty in wishing for the land which they obtained ; nevertheless, through God's indulgence, that which might justly have been injurious to them, turned out for their advantage.

We may gather, however, from the result, that Moses was guilty of no rashness in his interference with the ordinance of God, both because he commands that which he now determines to be ratified and maintained after his death ; and when, in the book of Joshua, it is recorded that the several tribes had their inheritance assigned to them, this country beyond Jordan is excepted, as having been granted by Moses to the tribes of Reuben and Gad and half of Manasseh. Hence it is evident that his decision was approved by God. Moreover, since he is there often honoured with the title of "servant of God," we are taught that nothing was done by him in this matter without the authority of God, and the guidance of His Spirit. Neither is it at random that he here so often makes use of God's name, but rather does he thus imply that whatever he does is suggested by Him.

23. *But if ye will not do so.* He makes a solemn protestation that they will deal wickedly, if they break their promise : and at the same time denounces punishment against them, as if he were summoning them before the tribunal of God. But, although he speaks conditionally of that particular engagement, whereby the two tribes had voluntarily bound themselves, still we may derive from his words the general doctrine, that, unless we abide by our promises, God will always be the avenger of fraud and

treachery. The expression, "Sin will find you out," is more emphatic than as if he had simply said, You shall not escape God's hand; for the meaning of it is that vengeance is so connected with sin, that it cannot be severed from it. Thus, in Gen. iv. 7, it is said, "Sin lieth at the door," to lay hold at length of the guilty. For, such is our propensity to sin, that we too often find from experience that we are encouraged to audacity by God's forbearance, whilst we think that we have escaped, if He makes as though He saw us not for a time.

28. So concerning them Moses commanded Eleazar the priest, and Joshua the son of Nun, and the chief fathers of the tribes of the children of Israel:

29. And Moses said unto them, If the children of Gad, and the children of Reuben, will pass with you over Jordan, every man armed to battle, before the Lord, and the land shall be subdued before you; then ye shall give them the land of Gilead for a possession:

30. But if they will not pass over with you armed, they shall have possessions among you in the land of Canaan.

31. And the children of Gad, and the children of Reuben, answered, saying, As the Lord hath said unto thy servants, so will we do.

32. We will pass over armed before the Lord into the land of Canaan, that the possession of our inheritance on this side Jordan *may be* ours.

33. And Moses gave unto them, *even* to the children of Gad, and to the children of Reuben, and unto half the tribe of Manasseh the son of Joseph, the kingdom of Sihon king of the Amorites, and the kingdom of Og king of Bashan, the land, with the cities thereof in the coasts, *even* the cities of the country round about.

34. And the children of Gad built Dibon, and Ataroth, and Aroer,

35. And Atroth, Shophan, and Jaazer, and Jogbehah,

28. Et præcepit de eis Moses ipsi Eleazar sacerdoti, et Josue filio Nun, et principibus patrum tribuum filiorum Israel:

29. Et dixit illis, Si transierint filii Gad et filii Ruben vobiscum Jordanem, omnes accincti armis ad bellum coram Jehova, et subjecta fuerit terra coram vobis, dabitis eis terram Galaad in possessionem:

30. Quod si non transierint accincti armis vobiscum, tum possessionem habebunt in medio vestri in terræ Chenaan.

31. Et responderunt filii Gad et Ruben, dicendo: Quod dixit Jehova servis tuis, sic faciemus.

32. Nos transibimus accincti armis coram Jehova in terram Chenaan, ut vobiscum sit possessio hæreditatis nostræ citra Jordanem.

33. Dedit itaque illis Moses, filiis Gad, et filiis Ruben, et dimidiæ tribui Manasse filii Joseph, regnum Sihon regis Amorrhæi, et regnum Og regis Basan, terram cum urbibus suis, cum terminis, urbes terræ per circuitum.

34. Et ædificaverunt filii Gad Dibon, et Ataroth, et Aroer,

35. Et Atroth, Sopham, et Jaazer, et Jogbehal,

36. And Beth-nimrah, and Beth-haran, fenced cities; and folds for sheep.

37. And the children of Reuben built Heshbon, and Elealeh, and Kirjathaim,

38. And Nebo, and Baal-meon, (their names being changed,) and Shibmah: and gave other names unto the cities which they builded.

39. And the children of Machir the son of Manasseh went to Gilead, and took it, and dispossessed the Amorite which *was* in it.

40. And Moses gave Gilead unto Machir the son of Manasseh; and he dwelt therein.

41. And Jair the son of Manasseh went and took the small towns thereof, and called them Havoth-jair.

42. And Nobah went and took Kenath, and the villages thereof, and called it Nobah, after his own name.

36. Et Beth-nimrah, et Beth-haran, urbes munitas et caulas ovium.

37. Filii vero Ruben ædificaverunt Hesbon, et Eleale, et Ciriathaim,

38. Et Nebo, et Baal-meon versis nominibus, et Sibmah: et vocaverunt nominibus nomina urbium quas ædificaverant.

39. Perrexerunt autem filii Machir, filii Manasse in Galaad, acceperuntque eam, et expulerunt Amorrhæum qui erat in ea.

40. Itaque dedit Moses Galaad ipsi Machir filio Manasse, et habitavit in ea.

41. Jair præterea filius Manasse profectus erat, et acceperat vicos eorum, et vocavit eos Havoth-Jair.

42. Nobah similiter profectus erat, et ceperat Cenah et villas ejus: vocavitque eam Nobah secundum nomen suum.

28. *So concerning them Moses commanded.* Moses annexes these conditions to his decision, lest, when the Reubenites and their companions had performed their military tasks, they should be falsely alleged to have passed over Jordan for the purpose of seeking a new home; whilst at the same time, if they should deceive the other tribes, he provided that their cowardice and deceit should not profit them. In short, if they assisted their brethren in pursuance of their agreement, he commands that the territory, which he now grants them, should always remain theirs; but, if they departed from their promise, he would have them forced against their will to participate in the common allotment. For he does not assign them this portion in the midst of Canaan as a reward for their inertness, in case they should stay behind; but signifies that they should be forcibly and authoritatively carried onwards, so as to be subject to their brethren under all circumstances; since it was not lawful for them to consult their own separate interests.

In laying down rules for the division of the land, as if it were soon to happen, he encourages the minds of all to confidence, so that they should more cheerfully hasten to pass over; as if the victory were not only already in their hands, but that the fruits of it were soon to be enjoyed.

33. *And Moses gave unto them.* We must understand that Moses *gave* it in such sort, as that, relying on God's command, he laid down an inviolable law. For, although it is not expressly stated that God interposed His authority, still His subsequent approbation fully assures us of it. So also, although no mention is made of Eleazar and the elders, still it is certain that they were not passed over, but that they were united with him in the decision; especially since the case had been brought before them by the sons of Gad and Reuben, (ver. 2.) There is only an implied contrast between the old covenant which God had made with Abraham, and this new and special privilege, wherewith He condescended to enrich His people.

At first only the two tribes had been named; half the tribe of Manasseh is now added, inasmuch as the descendants of Machir, and Jair, and Nobah, who were all of the family of Manasseh, had seized upon certain cities, and men. The rendering which some give, as if they[1] had obtained these victories after Moses had permitted the Reubenites and Gadites to inhabit this side of Jordan, does not appear to me suitable; but rather the reason is given why that portion is excepted, which came to the sons of Manasseh, viz., because they were not to be defrauded of the lands which they had separately acquired. Nor is it probable, that, when the country beyond Jordan had been given to others, they afterwards made their incursion so as to appropriate what did not belong to them. The order of the narrative does not make this necessary; for it is common with the Hebrews to transpose the order of occurrences, especially when something before omitted is incidentally added to give a reason for what is done. If, however, any should prefer to believe that they were attracted by the advantage that presented itself, I will not pertinaciously contend the point.

But how does it accord that cities are said to be *built*

[1] *C.* translates the verbs in ver. 41 in the pluperfect tense, "Jair, the son of Manasseh, *had* gone and taken, &c."

which were still standing undestroyed? for we have already seen that the people who had taken them, were dwelling in them. I reply that, inasmuch as it seldom happens that cities are taken without the walls being destroyed, it is not unreasonable that the restoration of these should be called *building.* It was necessary that the cities should be fortified lest the unarmed multitude[2] should be exposed to the assaults of every enemy. To this end they repaired what had been thrown down, and thus in a manner renewed the cities which were a mass of ruins.

A Repetition of the same History.

DEUTERONOMY, CHAPTER III.

12. And this land, *which* we possessed at that time, from Aroer, which *is* by the river Arnon, and half mount Gilead, and the cities thereof, gave I unto the Reubenites, and to the Gadites.

13. And the rest of Gilead, and all Bashan, *being* the kingdom of Og, gave I unto the half-tribe of Manasseh; all the region of Argob, with all Bashan, which was called the land of giants.

14. Jair the son of Manasseh took all the country of Argob, unto the coasts of Geshuri and Maachathi, and called them after his own name, Bashan-havoth-jair, unto this day.

15. And I gave Gilead unto Machir.

16. And unto the Reubenites, and unto the Gadites, I gave from Gilead even unto the river Arnon, half the valley, and the border, even unto the river Jabbok, *which is* the border of the children of Ammon;

17. The plain also, and Jordan, and the coast *thereof,* from Chinnereth even unto the sea of the plain, *even* the salt sea, under Ashdoth-pisgah eastward.

12. Et hanc terram possedimus eo tempore ab Aroer, quæ sita erat ad torrentem Arnon: et dimidium montis Galaad, et urbes ejus dedi Rubenitis et Gaditis.

13. Residuum vero Galaad, et universam Basan regni Og dedi dimidiæ tribui Manasse, et omnem regionem Argob, totam Basan quæ vocabatur terra gigantum.

14. Jair filius Manasse cepit omnem regionem Argob usque ad terminum Gesuri et Maachathi: et vocavit eas secundum nomen suum Basan Havoth Jair usque ad diem istam.

15. Porro ipsi Machir dedi Galaad:

16. Rubenitis vero et Gaditis dedi Galaad, usque ad torrentem Arnon, medium torrentis, et terminum: et usque ad Jabboc torrentem terminum filiorum Ammon:

17. Et planitiem, et Jordanem, et terminum a Chinnereth usque ad mare planitiei, mare salis, sub effusionibus aquarum collis ad orientem.

[2] "La troupe des femmes et des petits enfans;" the multitude of women and little children.—*Fr.*

18. And I commanded you at that time, saying, The Lord your God hath given you this land to possess it: ye shall pass over armed before your brethren the children of Israel, all *that are* meet for the war.

19. But your wives, and your little ones, and your cattle, (*for* I know that ye have much cattle,) shall abide in your cities which I have given you;

20. Until the Lord have given rest unto your brethren, as well as unto you, and *until* they also possess the land which the Lord your God hath given them beyond Jordan: and *then* shall ye return every man unto his possession, which I have given you.

18. Præcepique vobis eo tempore dicendo, Jehova Deus vester dedit vobis terram istam, ut possideatis eam, accincti armis transibitis ante fratres vestros filios Israel, quotquot robusti estis.

19. Tantummodo uxores vestræ, et parvuli vestri, et pecudes vestræ (novi quod pecora multa sint vobis) remanebunt in urbibus vestris quas dedi vobis:

20. Donec requiem dederit Jehova fratribus vestris sicut vobis, et possideant ipsi etiam terram, quam Jehova Deus vester dat eis trans Jordanem: tunc revertemini singuli ad possessionem suam quam dedi vobis.

12. *And this land, which we possessed at that time.* In this passage Moses confirms his decision, that the possession of the country beyond Jordan should be insured to the Reubenites and Gadites, and half the tribe of Manasseh. For, since it had fallen to them exceptionally, the matter might be brought into controversy with posterity. Lest, then, any should disturb them, he again declares that they were the rightful possessors of that district. Moreover, inasmuch as the very gift of it might be called in question, since it was situated outside the bounds of the inheritance promised by God, Moses anticipates this objection also, asserting that God had not in vain given it to be possessed by His people. Hence it follows that the right of inhabiting it was conferred upon them. Lest, then, so unequal a partition should be made a subject of contention, he marks out their boundaries on every side, as though he set up the authority of God as a wall and rampart against any who should presume to invade it.

With reference to the names of the places, the Dead Sea is called the Sea of Salt, and the Lake of Genesera or Gennesareth, Chinnereth. As to the "outpourings of the hill," translators are not agreed; for some consider Ashdoth-Pisgah to be the proper name of a city.[1] I prefer, however,

[1] אשדת הפסגה. *A. V.*, "Ashdoth-Pisgah;" *marg.*, "The springs of Pisgah, *or*, of the hill." The *LXX.* in like manner only substitutes Greek

to take the word "outpourings" (*effusionum*) appellatively, not for fountains and streams, but for the root (of the hill) where the ground by a gentle descent seems in a manner to pour itself forth. We shall presently see that Pisgah was one of the summits of Mount Abarim.

18. *And I commanded you at that time.* This address is directed only to those to whom an inheritance was given on the other side of Jordan; but Moses declares that he had introduced an agreement that the two tribes and a half should not enjoy their possession until they had accompanied their brethren in the subjugation of the land of Canaan. He says, therefore, that he had given them a place, not where they were at once to settle themselves, but where they might deposit their wives and cattle, until the whole people were peaceably established in their land.

DEUTERONOMY, CHAPTER IV.

41. Then Moses severed three cities on this side Jordan, toward the sun-rising;

42. That the slayer might flee thither, which should kill his neighbour unawares, and hated him not in times past; and that, fleeing unto one of these cities, he might live:

43. *Namely,* Bezer in the wilderness, in the plain country of the Reubenites; and Ramoth in Gilead, of the Gadites; and Golan in Bashan, of the Manassites.

41. Tunc separavit Moses tres urbes trans Jordanem ad exortum solis:

42. Ut fugeret illuc homicida qui occidisset proximum suum nesciens, (*vel,* per errorem, *vel,* per incogitantiam,) quem non odisset ab heri et nudiustertius: ut fugeret ad unam ex urbibus istis, et viveret.

43. Bezer in deserto, in terra planitiei a Rubenitis: Ramoth Galaad a Gaditis, et Golan in Basan a Manasse.

God had destined, as we have before seen,[1] six cities for refuge, in case any one had killed a man, provided he could prove his innocence before the judges. As to the three

letters for the Hebrew, treating both words as proper names. But when the same words occur at the close of the next chapter, our translators have placed their previous marginal translation in their text, and the *LXX.* instead of Φασγὰ have τὴν λαξευτήν, as though פסגה were an appellative, from פסג, to cut. In construing אשרת as a noun, from אשר, and rendering it *effusions*, *C.* followed *S.M.*, as also in putting the *hill* for Pisgah. Our translators and Luther have agreed in rendering the former word *springs*, when it occurs in Joshua x. 40, and xii. 8; whilst the *LXX.* and Diodati have treated it as a proper name in both those texts.—*W.*

[1] See *ante,* on Numb. xxxv. 10-34; vol. iii. pp. 62, *et seq.*

which He had appointed on the other side of Jordan, Moses records that he had faithfully performed what God had commanded. Hence it appears that, although he could not immediately comply with God's command to its full extent, still he did not wait until the three other cities could be added; but that, as far as circumstances permitted, he discharged his duty. Hence let us learn that, even when we cannot at once entirely carry out what God commands us to do, we are still to be by no means idle. For nothing but sheer laziness stands in our way, unless we speedily commence at God's command what it is His will to finish and accomplish by the hands of others.

NUMBERS, CHAPTER XXXIII.

1. These *are* the journeys of the children of Israel, which went forth out of the land of Egypt with their armies, under the hand of Moses and Aaron.

2. And Moses wrote their goings out according to their journeys by the commandment of the Lord: and these *are* their journeys according to their goings out.

3. And they departed from Rameses in the first month, on the fifteenth day of the first month; on the morrow after the passover the children of Israel went out with an high hand in the sight of all the Egyptians.

4. (For the Egyptians buried all *their* first-born, which the Lord had smitten among them: upon their gods also the Lord executed judgments.)

5. And the children of Israel removed from Rameses, and pitched in Succoth.

6. And they departed from Succoth, and pitched in Etham, which *is* in the edge of the wilderness.

7. And they removed from Etham, and turned again unto Pi-hahiroth, which *is* before Baal-zephon: and they pitched before Migdol.

1. Istæ sunt profectiones filiorum Israel, qui egressi sunt e terra Egypti, per exercitus suos, per manum Mosis et Aharon.

2. Scripsit autem Moses egressus eorum per profectiones eorum juxta sermonem Jehovæ: istæ, inquam, sunt profectiones eorum per egressus eorum.

3. Profecti sunt igitur Ramesse mense primo, decimaquinta die mensis primi, postera die Phase egressi sunt filii Israel in manu excelsa in oculis omnium Egyptiorum.

4. (Egyptii autem interim sepeliebant quos percusserat Jehova ex eis, omnem primogenitum et in diis eorum fecerat Jehova judicia.)

5. Profecti sunt, inquam, filii Israel e Ramesse, et castrametati sunt in Suchoth.

6. Profecti autem de Suchoth, castrametati sunt in Etham, quæ est in extremo deserti.

7. Et profecti de Etham, reversi sunt in Phi-hahiroth, qui est ante Baal-sephon, et castrametati sunt ante Migdol.

8. And they departed from before Pi-hahiroth, and passed through the midst of the sea into the wilderness, and went three days' journey in the wilderness of Etham, and pitched in Marah.

9. And they removed from Marah, and came unto Elim: and in Elim *were* twelve fountains of water, and threescore and ten palm-trees; and they pitched there.

10. And they removed from Elim, and encamped by the Red Sea.

11. And they removed from the Red Sea, and encamped in the wilderness of Sin.

12. And they took their journey out of the wilderness of Sin, and encamped in Dophkah.

13. And they departed from Dophkah, and encamped in Alush.

14. And they removed from Alush, and encamped at Rephidim, where was no water for the people to drink.

15. And they departed from Rephidim, and pitched in the wilderness of Sinai.

16. And they removed from the desert of Sinai, and pitched at Kibroth-hattaavah.

17. And they departed from Kibroth-hattaavah, and encamped at Hazeroth.

18. And they departed from Hazeroth, and pitched in Rithmah.

19. And they departed from Rithmah, and pitched at Rimmon-parez.

20. And they departed from Rimmon-parez, and pitched in Libnah.

21. And they removed from Libnah, and pitched at Rissah.

22. And they journeyed from Rissah, and pitched in Kehelathah.

23. And they went from Kehelathah, and pitched in mount Shapher.

24. And they removed from mount Shapher, and encamped in Haradah.

25. And they removed from Haradah, and pitched in Makheloth.

26. And they removed from Makheloth, and encamped at Tahath.

8. Profecti vero de Phi-hahiroth, transierunt per medium maris in desertum: et ambulaverunt viam trium dierum per desertum Etham, et castrametati sunt in Marah.

9. Profecti vero de Marah venerunt in Elim: in Elim vero erant duodecim fontes aquarum, et septuaginta palmæ, et castrametati sunt illic.

10. Et profecti ex Elim, castrametati sunt juxta mare Suph.

11. Profecti autem e mari Suph, castrametati sunt in deserto Sin.

12. Et profecti e deserto Sin, castrametati sunt in Dopheah.

13. Profecti autem e Dopheah, castrametati sunt in Alus.

14. Et profecti ex Alus, castrametati sunt in Rephidim, ubi non erant aquæ populo ad bibendum.

15. Ideo profecti e Rephidim, castrametati sunt in deserto Sinai.

16. Profecti autem e deserto Sinai, castrametati sunt in Cibroth-Hathaavah.

17. Et profecti ex Cibroth-Hathaavah, castrametati sunt in Haseroth.

18. Et profecti de Haseroth, castrametati sunt in Rithmah.

19. Profecti vero de Rithmah, castrametati sunt in Rimmon Peres.

20. Et profecti e Rimmon Peres, castrametati sunt in Libnah.

21. Profecti vero e Libnah, castrametati sunt in Rissah.

22. Et profecti e Rissah, castrametati sunt in Ceheloth.

23. Profecti item e Ceheloth, castrametati sunt in monte Sepher.

24. Profecti quoque e monte Sepher, castrametati sunt in Haradah.

25. Et profecti sunt e Haradah, et castrametati sunt in Macheloth.

26. Et profecti e Macheloth, castrametati sunt in Thahath.

27. And they departed from Tahath, and pitched at Tarah.
28. And they removed from Tarah, and pitched in Mithcah.
29. And they went from Mithcah, and pitched in Hashmonah.
30. And they departed from Hashmonah, and encamped at Moseroth.
31. And they departed from Moseroth, and pitched in Bene-jaakan.
32. And they removed from Bene-jaakan, and encamped at Hor-hagidgad.
33. And they went from Hor-hagidgad, and pitched in Jotbathah.
34. And they removed from Jotbathah, and encamped at Ebronah.
35. And they departed from Ebronah, and encamped at Ezion-gaber.
36. And they removed from Ezion-gaber, and pitched in the wilderness of Zin, which *is* Kadesh.
37. And they removed from Kadesh, and pitched in mount Hor, in the edge of the land of Edom.
38. And Aaron the priest went up into mount Hor, at the commandment of the Lord, and died there, in the fortieth year after the children of Israel were come out of the land of Egypt, in the first *day* of the fifth month.
39. And Aaron *was* an hundred and twenty and three years old when he died in mount Hor.
40. And king Arad the Canaanite, which dwelt in the south in the land of Canaan, heard of the coming of the children of Israel.
41. And they departed from mount Hor, and pitched in Zalmonah.
42. And they departed from Zalmonah, and pitched in Punon.
43. And they departed from Punon, and pitched in Oboth.
44. And they departed from Oboth, and pitched in Ije-abarim, in the border of Moab.
45. And they departed from Iim, and pitched in Dibon-gad.
46. And they removed from Di-

27. Profecti autem e Thahath, castrametati sunt in Tharah.
28. Profecti quoque e Tharah, castrametati sunt in Micheah.
29. Profecti item e Micheah, castrametati sunt in Hasmonah.
30. Et profecti sunt de Hasmonah, et castrametati sunt in Moseroth.
31. Et profecti de Moseroth, castrametati sunt in Bene-jaacan.
32. Profectique e Bene-jaacan, castrametati sunt in Hor Gilgad.
33. Et profecti de Hor Gilgad, castrametati sunt in Jothathah.
34. Et profecti de Jothathah, castrametati sunt in Abronah.
35. Profecti vero ex Abronah, castrametati sunt in Esion-gaber.
36. Et profecti ex Esion-gaber, castrametati sunt in deserto Sin, quod est Cades.
37. Et profecti sunt e Cades, et castrametati sunt in Hor monte, in extremo terræ Edom.
38. Ascendit autem Aharon sacerdos in Hor montem juxta sermonem Jehovæ, et mortuus est anno quadragesimo ex quo egressi sunt filii Israel e terra Egypti mense quinto, primo die mensis.
39. Eratque Aharon natus centum et viginti tres annos quando mortuus est in Hor monte.
40. Audivit autem Chenaanæus rex Arad (is vero habitabat in meridie, in terra Chenaan quum ingrederentur filii Israel.)
41. Et profecti de Hor monte, castrametati sunt in Salmonah.
42. Profecti vero ex Salmonah, castrametati sunt in Punon.
43. Profecti e Punon, castrametati sunt in Oboth.
44. Profecti item ex Oboth, castrametati sunt in Ije-haabarim in termino Moab.
45. Et profecti ex Ilim, castrametati sunt in Dibon-gad.
46. Profecti item ex Dibon-gad,

bon-gad, and encamped in Almon-diblathaim.

47. And they removed from Almon-diblathaim, and pitched in the mountains of Abarim, before Nebo.

48. And they departed from the mountains of Abarim, and pitched in the plains of Moab, by Jordan *near* Jericho.

49. And they pitched by Jordan, from Beth-jesimoth *even* unto Abel-shittim, in the plains of Moab.

50. And the Lord spake unto Moses in the plains of Moab, by Jordan *near* Jericho, saying,

51. Speak unto the children of Israel, and say unto them, When ye are passed over Jordan into the land of Canaan;

52. Then ye shall drive out all the inhabitants of the land from before you, . . .

53. And ye shall dispossess *the inhabitants of* the land, and dwell therein: for I have given you the land to possess it.

54. And ye shall divide the land by lot for an inheritance among your families; *and* to the more ye shall give the more inheritance, and to the fewer ye shall give the less inheritance: every man's *inheritance* shall be in the place where his lot falleth; according to the tribes of your fathers ye shall inherit.

55. But if ye will not drive out the inhabitants of the land from before you; then it shall come to pass, that those which ye let remain of them *shall be* pricks in your eyes, and thorns in your sides, and shall vex you in the land wherein ye dwell.

56. Moreover, it shall come to pass, *that* I shall do unto you, as I thought to do unto them.

castrametati sunt in Almon-diblathaim.

47. Profecti præterea ex Almon-diblathaim, castrametati sunt in montibus Abarim ante Nebo.

48. Et profecti e montibus Abarim, castrametati sunt in campestribus Moab, juxta Jordanem Jericho.

49. Tandem castrametati sunt juxta Jordanem a Beth-jesimoth usque ad Abel-sittim in campestribus Moab.

50. Loquutus est autem Jehova ad Mosen in campestribus Moab, juxta Jordanem Jericho, dicendo:

51. Alloquere filios Israel, et dicas eis, Quum transieritis Jordanem ad terram Chenaan.

52. Expellite omnes habitatores terræ a facie vestra, . . .

53. Expelletis, inquam, habitatores terræ, et habitabitis in ea, vobis enim dedi terram, ut eam possideatis.

54. Possidebitis autem terram illam per sortem, per familias vestras: pluribus multiplicabitis hæreditatem eorum, et paucioribus diminuatis hæreditatem eorum: in loco in quo egredietur illi sors, erit illis: per tribus patrum vestrorum hæreditatem capietis.

55. Quod si non expuleritis habitatores terræ a facie vestra, tum erit ut quos reliqueritis ex eis, sint in cultros in oculis vestris, et in spinas lateribus vestris, et affligent vos super terram in qua vos habitabitis.

56. Evenietque ut quemadmodum cogitavi facere illis, faciam vobis.

1. *These are the journeys of the children of Israel.* Moses had not previously enumerated all the stations in which the people had encamped, but scarcely more than those in which something memorable had occurred, especially after the passage of the Red Sea; because it was of great importance

that the actual localities should be set, as it were, before their eyes, until they were not only rescued from impending death by God's amazing power, but a way unto life was opened to them through death and the lowest deep. In fact, in one passage he has as good as told us that he omitted certain stations, where he records that the people "journeyed from the wilderness of Sin, after their journeys, according to the commandment of the Lord," to Rephidim, (Ex. xvii. 1 ;) here, however, he more accurately states every place at which they stopped, as if he were painting a picture of their journey of forty years. His object in this is, first, that the remembrance of their deliverance, and so many accompanying blessings, might be more deeply impressed upon them, since local descriptions have no little effect in giving certainty to history; and, secondly, that they might be reminded by the names of the places, how often and in how many ways they had provoked God's anger against them; but especially that, now they were on the very threshold of the promised land, they might acknowledge that they had been kept back from it, and had been wandering by various tortuous routes, in consequence of their own depravity and stubbornness, until they had received the reward of their vile ingratitude. Whilst, at the same time, they might reflect that God had so tempered the severity of their punishment, that He still preserved and sustained the despisers of His grace, notwithstanding their iniquity and unworthiness; and also that He carried on to the children (of the transgressors) the covenant which He had made with Abraham.

It is not without reason that Moses premises that "these were the journeys of the children of Israel;" for, at the period when they came out of the land of Goshen, they were affected with no ordinary fear and anxiety, when they saw themselves buried, as it were, in the grave; for they were shut in on every side either by the sea or the defiles of two mountains, or by the army of Pharaoh. Having entered the desert, they had seven stations before they arrived at Mount Sinai, in which they must have perished a hundred times over by hunger and thirst, and a dearth of everything, unless God had marvellously succoured them. And although they might have completed their whole journey in so many days, even then their obstinate perversity began to subject them to delay. If the lack of bread and water beset them, they ought to have been more effectually stirred up by it to have recourse humbly to God. So little disposed, however, were they to that humility, which might have taught them to ask of God by prayer and supplication a remedy for their need, that they rather rebelled against Moses: and not only so, but they petulantly assailed God Himself with their impious taunts, as if He were a cruel executioner instead of their Redeemer. Hence, therefore, it came to pass that it was not before the fortieth day that they were at length brought to Mount Sinai. Scarcely had the Law been promulgated, and whilst the awful voice of God was still ringing in their ears, whereby He had bound them to Himself as His people, when, behold, suddenly a base, nay, a monstrous falling away into idolatry, whence it was not their own fault that, having rejected God's grace, and as far as depended upon themselves having annulled the promise, they did not perish miserably as they deserved. By this impediment they were again withheld from further progress. With the same obstinacy they constantly raged against God, and, though warned by many instances of punishment, never returned to a sound mind. The climax of their insane contumacy was, that when arrived at the borders of the promised land, they repudiated God's kindness, and exhorted each other to return, as if God were adverse to them, and His inestimable deliverance, which ought to have been a perpetual obligation to obedience, were utterly distasteful to them. The stations, which then follow, express in a more lively manner how,—like a ship which is driven away from its port by a tempest, and whirled round by various currents,—they were carried away from approaching the land, and wandered by circuitous courses: as if they deserved that God should thus lead them about in mockery. It will be well for us to keep our eyes on this design of Moses, in order that we may read the chapter with profit.

He calls the order of their marches journeys (*profectiones,*) in contradistinction to their stations: for they did not strike their camp unless the signal were given, *i.e.*, when the cloud left the sanctuary, and moved to another spot, as if God stretched forth His hand from heaven to direct their way: and hence it was more clearly apparent, that they were retained in the desert by His power.

3. *And they departed from Rameses.* I do not approve of their opinion, who think that the name of this city is used for the whole land of Goshen: since it is not reasonable that they should have set forth at the same time from various distant and remote places. And this would still less accord with what presently follows,[1] that they went forth in orderly array; though it might not be the case that they all mustered together in the city, because it is hardly credible that so great a multitude could be received within its walls, but that by the order of Moses and Aaron, they were all assembled in the neighbourhood of the city, so that they might be organized, lest in the confusion of their hurried march they should impede each other.

After having stated that they went out by "the high hand" of God, for the purpose of extolling still more His wonderful power, he adds that the Egyptians were witnesses and spectators of it: whence we conclude that they had at last yielded to God,[2] or were so thoroughly subdued, as not to dare to lift up a finger. Another circumstance is also added, viz., that the Egyptians were then burying all their first-born; by which words Moses does not mean to indicate that they forbore from hindering the departure of the Israelites,[3] because they were occupied with another matter; but rather signifies that, although they were exasperated by grief at the loss of their sons, still they lay stupified, as it were, since the power of God had enfeebled them, so that they had lost the ability to offer resistance.

When Moses says, that God "executed judgments" upon

[1] There seems to be an oversight here; he probably refers to ver. 1, "per exercitus suos."

[2] "Qu'ils ont quitté le combat pour ne plus resister à Dieu;" that they had abandoned the contest so as to resist God no longer.—*Fr.*

[3] The *Fr.* omits the negative here, and states the meaning of Moses to be, that the Egyptians forbore to hinder the departure of the Israelites, *not only* because they were preoccupied by the burial of their dead, but *also*, &c.

the gods of the Egyptians, it is with the object of recommending the true faith, lest the children of Israel should ever turn aside to the superstitions of the Gentiles, which, at the time of the deliverance, they had found to be mere delusions. For not only were Pharaoh and his troops overthrown, but their gods also put to shame, when they pretended to be the protectors of their land: and thus were all their superstitions refuted and convicted of error and folly. It is a silly imagination, that all the idols of Egypt fell down of themselves,[1] in order that the God of Israel might claim the glory of Deity for Himself alone. It is enough that God triumphed over the idols, when He effectively shewed that they had no power to aid their worshippers, and, at the same time, discovered the trickeries of the magicians. To this Isaiah appears to allude, when he says, "Behold, the Lord shall come into Egypt, and the idols of Egypt shall be moved at His presence," (Isa. xix. 1;) for he signifies that God will give such proofs of His power in Egypt, as shall demonstrate the vanity of all their errors, and overthrow all the superstitious fictions whereby the Israelites had been deceived.

8. *And they departed from before Pi-hahiroth.* He relates how the people marched forwards for three days; not so much in praise of their endurance, as in celebration of God's wonderful power, who sustained so great a multitude without water. For we must bear in mind, what I have elsewhere shewn, that from the passage of the Red Sea to Marah there was no water found; whence the impiety of the people was the more detestable, since they there burst forth into rebellion on account of the bitter taste of the water. On the other side, the incomparable mercy of God shone forth, in that He condescended to refresh these churlish and provok-

[1] De Lyra's gloss is: "Tunc enim idola Ægypti corruerunt, et comminuta sunt." Corn. à Lapide refers to his own note on Exod. xii. 12, which is as follows: "Hence it appears, says Caietanus, that Apis or Serapis, and all the other images of gods in Egypt are thrown down, and dashed to atoms on the Passover night, either by an earthquake, or by thunderbolts, as St. Jerome, after the Hebrews, asserts, 'Ad Fabiol. de 42 Mansion,' at the beginning. Artabanus, an old historian, in Eusebius, *lib.* 9, 'De præpar.' *cap. ult.*, tells us that this was the case; and Isaiah alludes to it, xix. 1. The Hebrews, moreover, have a tradition that the Egyptian idols, which were of stone, were then ground to powder; that those of wood were rotted or reduced to ashes, and those of metal melted and liquefied."

ing men in a pleasant and delightful station; for from their first encampment they were led on to Elim, where they found twelve fountains and seventy palm-trees. Moses passes briefly over the wilderness of Sin, as if nothing worthy of being recorded had occurred there; whereas the vile impiety of the people there betrayed itself, and the place was ennobled by a signal miracle, since the manna rained from heaven for the nourishment of the people, so that, the windows of heaven being opened, mortal man "did eat angels' food." He also briefly adverts to the want of water to drink at Rephidim: but he deemed it sufficient here to enumerate the stations, which might recall the various occurrences to the memory of the people. On the Graves of Concupiscence a memorial of God's punishment was inscribed; but since he simply gives a list of other places, without any record of events, we may gather, as I have above stated, that he had no other design than to set before the eyes of the people the peregrination in which they had been engaged for forty years. He, however, cursorily mentions the death of Aaron; because his life had been prolonged, by God's special blessing, for the good of the people, until the time approached when they were about to enter the promised land; since his authority was a useful and necessary restraint upon the ungovernable character of this headstrong people. At the same time the punishment inflicted upon the holy man should have reminded posterity that it was not without reason that their fathers had been so severely chastised, since they had not ceased to add sin to sin, when God had not spared even His own servant on account of a single transgression.

When he adds just afterwards, that the Canaanite then first heard of the coming the children of Israel, he indicates that God had put a veil over the eyes of their enemies, lest they should oppose them at an earlier period. For God so mitigated the severity of His judgment, that the exile of the Israelites was, at any rate, undisturbed, and free from outward molestation, as long as they had to wander in the desert.

50. *And the Lord spake unto Moses.* The end and de-

sign of God in willing that these nations should be expelled, I have elsewhere explained,[1] viz., lest they should adulterate the pure worship of God by their admixtures, should corrupt the people by their bad examples, and thus be pollutions to the Holy Land. But Moses now refers to another point, for, when about to speak of the division of the land, he begins by saying that it must be emptied of its inhabitants, that its free and full enjoyment may remain for the children of Israel. We must remark the connexion here, for else this passage would have been a supplement of the First Commandment, to which I have indeed appended the latter part of the verse: but, since God declares connectedly, "Ye shall dispossess the inhabitants of the land, and dwell therein, for I have given you the land to possess it," it would have been absurd that one clause should be disjoined from the other.

54. *And ye shall divide the land by lot.* The mode of division is also stated, that each should possess what fell to him by lot; and this was the best plan, for the several tribes would never have allowed themselves to be sent here or there at the option of men: and even if the arrangement had been left to the voices of the judges, they would rather have quarrelled with each other than determined what was right. But we must here take into consideration something deeper; viz., that by this method God gave certain proof that the children of Israel were the inheritors and masters of that land by His liberality and special blessing. And, in the first place, we must remember that, although men consider nothing more fortuitous than casting lots, still they are governed by God, as Solomon says. (Prov. xvi. 33.) God, therefore, commanded the people to cast lots, reserving to Himself the judgment as to those to whom they should fall. For how came it to pass that Zebulun obtained his portion on the sea-shore, except because it had been thus predicted by the Patriarch Jacob? Why did a district productive of the best corn fall to the tribe of Asher, unless because it had been pronounced by the same lips, that "Out of Asher his bread should be fat; and he should yield royal dainties"?

[1] See *ante*, vol. ii. p. 397, &c.

(Gen. xlix. 20.) By the same prophecy the tribe of Judah obtained an inheritance rich in vines, and abounding in the best of pastures. Thus the division of the land, by lot, clearly shewed that God had not formerly promised that land to Abraham in vain; because the proclamation of the gift by the mouth of Jacob was actually confirmed. The pious old man had been expelled from hence by famine; he was but a sojourner in Egypt, and twice an exile, and yet he assigns their portions to his descendants in the most authoritative manner, just as the father of a family might divide his few acres of land among his heirs. Yet God finally sealed what then might have seemed ridiculous. Hence it appears that things which, in the feebleness of our senses, we imagine to move at the blind impulse of chance, are directed by God's secret providence; and that His counsel always proceeds in such a regular course, that the end corresponds with the beginning. Again he recommends to them the law of proportion, so that, according to their numbers, a greater or a less allotment should be given to the several tribes. The allegory which some conceive to be indicated here, viz., that we obtain our heavenly inheritance by God's gratuitous good pleasure, as if by lot, although at first sight plausible, is easily refuted. Hebron was a part of the inheritance, but Caleb obtained it without casting lots: and a still more decided exception appears in the case of the tribe of Reuben, Gad, and half Manasseh, who, by the consent of the rest, and not by lot, acquired by privilege, as it were, all the territory that had been won on the other side of Jordan. Let my readers, therefore, learn to abstain from such conceits, lest they should often be obliged to confess with shame, that they have caught at an empty shadow.

55. *But if ye will not drive out.* We have elsewhere seen why God's wrath was so greatly aroused against those nations, that He desired them to be exterminated. Even in Abraham's time gross indulgence of sin had begun to prevail there, as we gather from God's word, when He said that "their iniquity was not yet full." After they had abused the forbearance of God Himself for 400 years, who will deny that their destruction was the just and reasonable reward of

their long obstinacy? Still, in cutting them off, God had regard to His elect people, in order that they might be separated from the heathen, and never turn aside to foreign superstitions. But the punishment which is here threatened the Israelites deserved twice over by their remissness, for they neither performed their duty in executing God's vengeance, and, as far as in them lay, they detracted from His grace. He had conferred upon them no common honour, when He appointed them to be His ministers for executing His judgments. It was therefore base supineness in them to be remiss on this point. But again, He had given them the whole land; when, then, they contented themselves with part of it, and neglected the rest, their perverse ingratitude betrayed itself by their indifference. Besides, they had wilfully entangled themselves in deadly nets, by mixing with heathen nations, from whom they had been separated by God, lest they should imitate their habits, and corrupt religious ceremonies. God, therefore, threatens that these nations shall be as prickles to pierce their eyes, and thorns in their sides. That this was fulfilled, the Book of Judges affords the clearest and most ample testimony, although, even to the days of David, this punishment was constantly in course of infliction upon their eyes and sides. Thus, also, is their untameable headstrongness proved, since such a solemn admonition had no effect in causing[1] them to go forwards, no less in the open punishment of iniquity, than in a course of victory and success.

NUMBERS, CHAPTER XXXIV.

1. And the Lord spake unto Moses, saying,
2. Command the children of Israel, and say unto them, When ye come into the land of Canaan, (this

1. Et loquutus est Jehova ad Mosen, dicendo:
2. Præcipe filiis Israel, et dicas eis, Quum intraveritis terram Chenaan (ista est terra quæ cadet vobis

[1] "Pour les faire marcher vertueusement parmi leur victoires, à punir les crimes dont ils estoyent juges;" to cause them to advance virtuously amidst their victories, in punishing the crimes of which they were the judges.—*Fr.*

is the land that shall fall unto you for an inheritance, *even* the land of Canaan, with the coasts thereof,)

in hæreditatem, terra Chenaan per terminos suos.)

3. Then your south quarter shall be from the wilderness of Zin, along by the coast of Edom, and your south border shall be the outmost coast of the salt sea eastward.

3. Erit vobis plaga meridiei à deserto Sin usque ad terminos Edom: erit inquam vobis terminus meridiei ab extremo maris salis ad orientem.

4. And your border shall turn from the south to the ascent of Akrabbim, and pass on to Zin: and the going forth thereof shall be from the south to Kadesh-barnea, and shall go on to Hazar-addar, and pass on to Azmon.

4. Et circuibit vobis iste terminus à Maale Acrabim, et transibit usque ad Sin: et erunt egressus ejus à meridie in Cades-Barnea, atque illinc egredietur ad villam Addar, et transibit usque ad Asmon.

5. And the border shall fetch a compass from Azmon unto the river of Egypt, and the goings out of it shall be at the sea.

5. Præterea circuibit terminus iste ab Asmon usque ad flumen Ægypti: et erunt illinc egressus ejus ad occidentem.

6. And *as for* the western border, ye shall even have the great sea for a border: this shall be your west border.

6. Terminum autem occidentalis erit vobis mare magnum, terminus, inquam, iste erit vobis terminus occidentalis.

7. And this shall be your north border: from the great sea ye shall point out for you mount Hor.

7. Iste vero erit vobis terminus aquilonaris, à mari magno describetis vobis Hor montem.

8. From mount Hor ye shall point out *your border* unto the entrance of Hamath; and the goings forth of the border shall be to Zedad.

8. Ab hoc monte describetis usque ad introitum Hamach: et erunt eggressus termini illius ad Sedad.

9. And the border shall go on to Ziphron, and the goings out of it shall be at Hazar-enan: this shall be your north border.

9. Et illinc egredietur terminus iste ad Ziphon, eruntque egressus ejus ad villam Enan: iste erit vobis terminus aquilonaris.

10. And ye shall point out your east border from Hazar-enan to Shepham.

10. Describetis præterea vobis terminum ad orientem, à villa Enan usque ad Sepham.

11. And the coast shall go down from Shepham to Riblah, on the east of Ain; and the border shall descend, and shall reach unto the side of the sea of Chinnereth eastward.

11. Et descendet iste terminus à Sepham usque ad Riblah ab oriente Ain: et descendet terminus iste, provenietque ad latus maris Cinnereth ad orientem.

12. And the border shall go down to Jordan, and the goings out of it shall be at the salt sea: this shall be your land, with the coasts thereof round about.

12. Et descendet iste terminus ad Jordanem, eruntque egressus ejus ad mare salis: ista erit vobis terra per terminos suos, per circuitum.

13. And Moses commanded the children of Israel, saying, This *is* the land which ye shall inherit by lot, which the Lord commanded to give unto the nine tribes, and to the half-tribe.

13. Præcepit autem Moses filiis Israel, dicendo: Hæc est terra quam possidebitis sorte, et quam præcepit Jehova dare novem tribubus, et dimidiæ tribui.

14. For the tribe of the children

14. Acceperunt enim tribus fili-

of Reuben, according to the house of their fathers, and the tribe of the children of Gad, according to the house of their fathers, have received *their inheritance*, and half the tribe of Manasseh have received their inheritance:

15. The two tribes and the half-tribe have received their inheritance on this side Jordan *near* Jericho eastward, toward the sun-rising.

16. And the Lord spake unto Moses, saying,

17. These *are* the names of the men which shall divide the land unto you; Eleazar the priest, and Joshua the son of Nun.

18. And ye shall take one prince of every tribe, to divide the land by inheritance.

19. And the names of the men *are* these: Of the tribe of Judah, Caleb, the son of Jephunneh.

20. And of the tribe of the children of Simeon, Shemuel the son of Ammihud.

21. Of the tribe of Benjamin, Elidad the son of Chislon.

22. And the prince of the tribe of the children of Dan, Bukki the son of Jogli.

23. The prince of the children of Joseph, for the tribe of the children of Manasseh, Hanniel the son of Ephod.

24. And the prince of the tribe of the children of Ephraim, Kemuel the son of Shiphtan.

25. And the prince of the tribe of the children of Zebulun, Elizaphan the son of Parnach.

26. And the prince of the tribe of the children of Issachar, Paltiel the son of Azzan.

27. And the prince of the tribe of the children of Asher, Ahihud the son of Shelomi.

28. And the prince of the tribe of the children of Naphtali, Pedahel the son of Ammihud.

29. These *are they* whom the Lord commanded to divide the inheritance unto the children of Israel in the land of Canaan.

orum Rubenitarum per domos patrum suorum, et tribus filiorum Gaditarum per domos patrum suorum, et dimidia tribus Manasse: acceperunt inquam hæreditatem suam:

15. Duæ tribus et dimidia acceperunt possessionem suam citra Jordanem Jericho ad orientem ad exortum solis.

16. Loquutus est præterea Jehova ad Mosen, dicendo:

17. Ista sunt nomina virorum qui possidendam vobis distribuent terram, Eleazar sacerdos, et Josue filius Nun.

18. Et principes singulos de qualibet tribu capietis ad possidendam terram.

19. Ista sunt nomina virorum: de tribu Jehudah, Caleb filius Jephune.

20. Et de tribu filiorum Simeon, Samuel filius Ammihud.

21. Et de tribu Benjamin, Elidad filius Chislon.

22. Et de tribu filiorum Dan, princeps Bucci filius Jogli.

23. De filiis Joseph, de tribu filiorum Manasse, princeps Huiel filius Ephod.

24. Et de tribu filiorum Ephraim, princeps Cemuel filius Siphtan.

25. Et de tribu filiorum Zabulon, princeps Elisaphan filius Parvach.

26. Et de tribu filiorum Issachar, princeps Paltiel filius Azzam.

27. Et de tribu filiorum Aser, princeps Ahihud filius Selomi.

28. Et de tribu filiorum Nephthali, princeps Pedahel filius Ammihud.

29. Isti sunt quibus præcepit Jehova, Ut distribuerent hæreditatem filiis Israel in terra Chenaan.

1. *And the Lord spake unto Moses.* God here undertakes the office of a prudent and careful father of a family, in fixing the boundaries of the land on every side, lest their right to possess it should ever be called in question. He begins on the southern side, where it must be observed that the district of Bashan is included in it, and all that the Israelites had acquired before their passage of the Jordan, so that this addition was approved of by God. He extends this part as far as the wilderness of Sin, and the borders of Edom, and brings it round from Kadesh-barnea to Addar, and the passage of Azmon, and, finally, to the stream which washes[1] the city of Rhinocorura, in the immediate vicinity of Egypt; for by "the river of Egypt" the Nile is by no means to be understood, the course of which was not at all in that direction. The southern boundary, therefore, was from the Mediterranean Sea towards Arabia. On the western side the land was washed by the Mediterranean Sea, which is here called "the Great Sea," in comparison with the Lake of Gennesareth, and the Salt Sea, by which name the *Lacus Asphaltites* is here meant. The beginning of the northern boundary was the promontory of Hor, for it would not accord to suppose that the mountain is here referred to in which Aaron died, and which was far away, and situated on the opposite side of the land. It extended from hence to Epiphania in Syria, which is called Hamath; for I agree with Jerome in thinking that there were two cities of this name, and it is undoubtedly probable that Antioch is called "Hamath the great" by the Prophet Amos (vi. 2,) in comparison with the lesser city here mentioned, the name of which was given it by that wicked and cruel tyrant (Antiochus) Epi-

[1] There has been much discussion amongst the commentators on this point. The conclusion to which Dr. Kitto comes, after due examination of the opposite theory, is, that "the river of Egypt," when mentioned as a boundary, cannot mean the Nile. "The present 'river of Egypt' (he adds) probably denotes a stream which formed the extreme boundary of the country eastward of the Nile, which Egypt, even in these early times, professed to claim, and which derived its name from that circumstance. It was probably not far from El-Arish, to which, under the name of Rhinocorura, it is expressly referred by the Septuagint. That it was a stream somewhere between the southern frontier of Palestine and the Nile we are deeply convinced."—Illustr. Com., *in loco.*

phanes; whether, however, the greater Antioch was formerly called Hamath and Riblah, as Jerome states, I leave undecided. It then passed on to Zedad and Ziphron, and its extremity was the village of Enan. The eastern boundary passed from thence through Shephan, Riblah, and Ain, until it reached the Lake of Gennesareth, a lake sufficiently well known, and here called the Sea of Chinnereth. Thus the eastern boundary pointed from Arabia in the direction of Persia, and Babylon was situated to the north-east of it.

13. *And Moses commanded the children of Israel.* Though this is a repetition, yet it is not a superfluous one; for he contrasts the new allotment of the nine tribes and a half with the former grant;[1] for the exception, which is immediately added, as to the lands beyond Jordan, given to the Reubenites, and Gadites, and half tribe of Manasseh, does not exclude them from their part of the promised inheritance—as if they were disinherited, and therefore banished beyond the boundaries prescribed by God—but only from being subject to the casting of lots, because they had by special privilege obtained from their brethren what would else have been included in the common inheritance. Not that this had been revealed from the beginning, but because God in His indulgence had complied with their request, whereby they enlarged the boundaries of the land. And assuredly it would have been absurd that no place should be given them among their brethren in the promised land, as if they were cast off from the family of Abraham. We have lately seen that this part, which seemed to be separated from the others, was included in the limits laid down by God. Moses, therefore, merely wished to declare that what remained was to be divided by lot.

16. *And the Lord spake unto Moses.* The question here arises, if the Israelites were to divide the land among themselves by lot, wherefore was the authority of the judges required, as if there was anything for them to decide? But if we consider what has been lately shewn, that reference was to be had, in the distribution of the land, to the numbers in

[1] "La donation qui avoit este desia faite de la region de Basan;" the grant which had been already made of the district of Bashan.—*Fr.*

every tribe, it was requisite for two purposes,—first, that God might shew by His decree the districts respectively assigned to them; and, secondly, that their dimensions might be proportionate to the number of their occupants. For the casting of lots was still necessary, because many would have been averse to the sea-coast, or would have preferred the centre of the land to its extremities, or would have been unwilling to be banished to the mountains; in short, they would have contended with each other beyond measure in murmurings and strife. On this account the lots were cast, by the decision of which God placed the several tribes in whatever position He pleased, although the judges, together with the High Priest and Joshua, had before divided the land into ten portions. But after it was declared in what district the several tribes were to dwell, as if God had there designated their abodes, the determination of men was again necessarily had recourse to, as to how far, and in what direction, the boundaries of the greater tribes were to extend; otherwise the lesser tribes would have refused to be cooped up in a less convenient position. And although the supreme authority was justly vested in Eleazar and Joshua, lest God should expose them to calumny and ill-will, He associated with them a council, in which also there was a prudent precaution against rivalry, for each of the twelve tribes contributed its judge to preside over the distribution, so that none might complain of being aggrieved. Moreover, inasmuch as it was of great importance that the possession, once established, should be secured to posterity, first of all the names of the princes are recorded, in order to give certainty to the history; and, secondly, as had been stated at the beginning of the chapter, so also it is repeated at the end that they were chosen by God, from whence the Israelites learnt that the boundaries then fixed could not be altered without overthrowing the authority of God Himself.

DEUTERONOMY, CHAPTER XXXI.

1. And Moses went and spake these words unto all Israel.

1. Abiit itaque Moses, et loquutus est verba ista ad universum Israelem.

2. And he said unto them, I *am* an hundred and twenty years old this day; I can no more go out and come in: also the Lord hath said unto me, Thou shalt not go over this Jordan.

3. The Lord thy God, he will go over before thee, *and* he will destroy these nations from before thee, and thou shalt possess them: *and* Joshua, he shall go over before thee, as the Lord hath said.

4. And the Lord shall do unto them as he did to Sihon and to Og, kings of the Amorites, and unto the land of them, whom he destroyed.

5. And the Lord shall give them up before your face, that ye may do unto them according unto all the commandments which I have commanded you.

6. Be strong and of a good courage, fear not, nor be afraid of them: for the Lord thy God, he *it is* that doth go with thee; he will not fail thee, nor forsake thee.

7. And Moses called unto Joshua, and said unto him in the sight of all Israel, Be strong, and of a good courage: for thou must go with this people unto the land which the Lord hath sworn unto their fathers to give them; and thou shalt cause them to inherit it.

8. And the Lord, he *it is* that doth go before thee; he will be with thee, he will not fail thee, neither forsake thee: fear not, neither be dismayed.

2. Dixitque eis, Centum et viginti annorum sum hodie, non possum ultra egredi et ingredi: præterea Jehova dixit ad me, Non transibis Jordanem istum.

3. Jehova Deus tuus ipse transiturus est ante te, ipse disperdet gentes istas à facie tua, possidebisque eas: Josua ipse transiturus est ante te, quemadmodum dixit Jehova.

4. Facietque Jehova illis quemadmodum fecit Sihon et Og, regibus Emorrhæi, et terræ eorum quos disperdidit.

5. Quum ergo dederit eos Jehova ante faciem vestram, tunc facietis eis omnino juxta præceptum quod præcepi vobis.

6. Estote fortes, et roborate vos, ne timeatis, neque paveatis à facie eorum: Jehova enim Deus tuus est qui pergit tecum, non deseret te, neque te derelinquet.

7. Vocavit ergo Moses Josua, et dixit illi in oculis totius Israelis, Esto fortis, et robora te: tu enim ingredieris cum populo isto terram quam juravit Jehova patribus eorum se daturum illis, et ipse sorte divides eam illis.

8. Jehova autem est qui præcessurus est te, ipse erit tecum: non te deseret, neque derelinquet te, ne timeas, neque paveas.

1. *And Moses went and spake these words.* By the word *went* he signifies that, having received the commands from God, he came to the people to report them. Hence we gather that they were warned in good time to beware, if they had been sensibly disposed. And it was necessary that the people should hear from his own mouth these addresses, which were by no means gratifying, as being full both of cruel threats and severe reproofs; for, if they had been delivered after his death, they would have straightway all exclaimed that they had been deceitfully devised by

some one else, and thus that his name was falsely attached to them.

Moreover, the peculiar time of their delivery did not a little avail to enhance their weight, so that the people should not only submit themselves with meekness and teachableness to his instruction at the moment, but also that it might remain hereafter deeply impressed upon their hearts. We know with what attention the last words of the dying are usually received; and Moses,[1] now ready to meet death at God's command, addressed the people as if bidding them finally farewell. To the credit and dignity belonging to his office as a Prophet, there was consequently added all the force and authority of a testamentary disposition.

As throughout his life he had been incredibly anxious for the people's welfare, so he now carries his more than paternal care still further. And assuredly it becomes all pious teachers to provide, as far as in them lies, that the fruit of their labours should survive them. Of this solicitude Peter sets himself before us as an example: "I think it meet (he says), as long as I am in this tabernacle, to stir you up by putting you in remembrance; moreover, I will endeavour that ye may be able after my decease to have these things always in remembrance." (2 Pet. i. 13, 15.)

2. *And he said unto them, I am an hundred and twenty years old.* Although Moses had been often proudly and disdainfully rejected, it could not but be the case, nevertheless, that his departure would both awaken the deepest sorrow, and inspire them with much alarm. By setting before them his age, therefore, he consoles their anxiety, and mitigates their grief; and also, by another reason, he represses their lamentations, *i.e.*, that God had fixed his term of life. He adduces it, then, as an alleviation, because both his death was more than mature, and he was no longer fitted in his extreme old age for enduring fatigue. Here, however, the question arises, why he should say that he was failing, and broken in strength, when we shall see a little

[1] "Ayant desia un pied levé et s'estant appresté à aller à la mort où Dieu l'appeloit;" having already one foot raised, and being ready to go to death whither God called him.—*Fr.*

further on that he retained his senses in their vigour even until his death? But the reply is obvious, that he would not have been useless in his old age, because his eyes were dim or his members tremulous, but because his age no longer allowed him to perform his usual duties. For he had been marvellously and preternaturally preserved up to that time; but, since he had now arrived at the end of his course, it was necessary that he should suddenly sink, and be deprived of his faculties.

"To go out, and come in," is equivalent to performing the functions of life: thus it is said in the Psalm, "Thou has known my going out and coming in."[1] (Ps. cxxi. 8.) And in this sense David is said to have gone out and come in, when he performed the duty intrusted to him by Saul. (1 Sam. xviii. 5.)

In the latter clause, where he refers to his exclusion from the land of Canaan, and his being prevented from entering it, he indirectly rebukes the people, for whose offence God had been wroth with himself and Aaron. Thus by this tacit reproof the Israelites were admonished to bear patiently the penalty of their ingratitude. At the same time, as he shews himself to be submissive to the divine decree, he bids them also acquiesce in it.

3. *The Lord thy God, he will go over.* By no ordinary consolation does he encourage their minds to renewed alacrity, because they should experience, even when he was dead, the unceasing favour of God. Hence we gather a lesson of especial usefulness, that whenever God raises up to us men endowed with excellent gifts, He is wont so to make use of their labours for a time, as still to retain others in His hand, and constantly to substitute others, unless our sins stand in the way. Hence it follows that the power of God is not to be tied to the illustrious qualities of men, as if their death was His destruction. It is true, indeed, that eminent men are rarely succeeded by their equals,[2] because our

[1] *C.* here quotes from memory: the words of the Psalm are, "The Lord shall preserve thy going out and coming in;" and so also in the other quotation, the actual words are, "And David went out whithersoever Saul sent him."

[2] "Pareils et de mesme calibre;" equal and of the same calibre.—*Fr.*

wickedness stifles the light of spiritual gifts, and, as far as it can, extinguishes them; still let this be deemed certain that, when God promotes our welfare by ministers of special eminence, He gives us a taste of His goodness, in order that we may expect its continuance; "because he forsakes not the work of his own hands." (Ps. cxxxviii. 8.) Moses says, therefore, that although he may be taken away by death, still God will undertake the office of their leader, or rather that He will continue to be their leader, as the Israelites had before experienced Him to be.

But he sustains their infirmity by another consolation also, pointing out Joshua as his successor; otherwise the people might have been ready to object that, if God was willing to go before them, why did He not manifest it by the election of a representative, by whose hand He might continue what He had begun by Moses. In this respect, therefore, he also shews that God's favour was by no means obscure, since Joshua was already chosen to sustain the care and burden of governing the people: for it is not by his own authority that he obtrudes Joshua and sets him over them, but he declares him to be called by God. Still, it is not a matter hitherto unknown which he puts before them, but only bids them remember what God had long ago revealed, as we have elsewhere seen.

4. *And the Lord shall do unto them.* He promises that, when they shall come into the land of Canaan, they shall be conquerors of all its nations: and this he confirms by experience; for, as God had delivered Sihon king of the Amorites, and Og king of Bashan, into their hands, so also He would give them the same success in subduing their other enemies. The world is indeed subject to many revolutions, but God still remains like Himself, not only because His counsel is never changed, but because His power is never diminished. By a *real* proof, therefore, as it is called, he encourages the expectations of the people, and at the same time exhorts them resolutely to execute God's command, viz., that they should purge the land of Canaan by the destruction of all its inhabitants. In appearance, indeed, this was fierce and cruel, to leave not even one alive;

but, since God had justly devoted them to extinction, it was not lawful for the Israelites to inquire what was to be done, but to abandon all discussion, and to obey God's command. In that they spared many, so much the worse was their remissness, since God had often prepared them to execute the vengeance which He had decreed.

6. *Be strong and of good courage.* After he had shewn that God would be with them, for their help, he exhorts the people to firmness and magnanimity. And surely this is one means of confirming our courage, to be assured that the assistance which God promises will suffice for us: so far is it from being the case, that our zeal and energy in acting aright is impaired, by our ascribing to the grace of God what foolish men attribute to their own free will. For those who are aroused to strenuous action in reliance on their own strength, do no more than cast themselves headlong in their senseless temerity and pride. Let us understand, then, that all exhortations are fleeting and ineffective, which are founded on anything else but simple confidence in the grace of God. Thus Moses assumes, as his ground of exhortation, that God will fight for the Israelites. It must, however, be observed that the people were animated to the perseverance of hope, when God declares that He will be their helper even to the end, by which lesson that impious hallucination is refuted, whereby the Popish theologians have fascinated the world. They deny that believers[1] can be certain of God's grace, except as to their present state. Thus do they hold faith in suspense, so that we may only believe for a day, and even from moment to moment, whilst we are in uncertainty as to what God will do with us on the morrow. Whereas, if faith corresponds with God's promises, and is, as it were, in harmony with them, it must needs extend itself to our whole life, nay, even beyond death itself; for God removes all doubt as to the future by these words, "I will not leave thee nor forsake thee."

[1] The dogmatical statement of this error is made in the decrees of the Council of Trent, *Sessio* vi. *cap.* ix. "Contra inanem hæreticorum fiduciam." It is controverted by *C.*, Instit. Book iii. ch. ii. § 40; in his "Antidote to the Council of Trent;" *C. Soc. Edit.*, p. 125, and elsewhere.

7. *And Moses called unto Joshua.* It hence appears that those, upon whom a public charge is conferred, have need of a twofold confirmation: for, after having addressed a general instruction to the whole people, he directs his discourse peculiarly to Joshua himself, as to one whose business it was to set an example of bravery to others, and whom severe contests awaited. Since, then, it is more difficult to lead all the rest than to follow a leader, it is necessary that he, who is set over many, should far excel them. But, inasmuch as no one can do anything of himself, we must seek of God whatever we want. Wherefore that, which Moses had enjoined upon the whole people, he now repeats to a single individual, because upon him the burden of ruling them was thrown. And this must be more carefully observed, because, in proportion to the degree of honour, in which a man is placed, so does he disdainfully look down upon all admonitions; whence it is the case that those, who are eminent in the world, carelessly reject the exhortations of God's servants. But Moses thoroughly overthrows all such fastidiousness, when he shews that all, who are in authority, should not only be instructed together with others, but even more urgently dealt with.

When Moses, in this place as well as above, forbids believers to give way to fear or dread, it must be observed that he would not have them so deprived of all feeling, as to be hardened into indifference to every danger, or to suppose, as some madmen do, that there is no such thing as bravery without stupidity, but only possessed of such confidence as may overcome all fears, which impede the course of their calling. Appropriately does the Apostle extend this lesson further, where he wishes to correct avarice, which arises from over-anxiety, whilst wretched men do not sufficiently reflect what it is to have God for their perpetual helper. (Heb. xiii. 5.)

NUMBERS, CHAPTER XXVII.

15. And Moses spake unto the Lord, saying,
16. Let the Lord, the God of the

15. Loquutus est igitur Moses ad Jehovam, dicendo:
16. Præficiat Jehova Deus spiri-

spirits of all flesh, set a man over the congregation,

17. Which may go out before them, and which may go in before them, and which may lead them out, and which may bring them in; that the congregation of the Lord be not as sheep which have no shepherd.

18. And the Lord said unto Moses, Take thee Joshua the son of Nun, a man in whom *is* the spirit, and lay thine hand upon him:

19. And set him before Eleazar the priest, and before all the congregation; and give him a charge in their sight.

20. And thou shalt put *some* of thine honour upon him, that all the congregation of the children of Israel may be obedient.

21. And he shall stand before Eleazar the priest, who shall ask *counsel* for him after the judgment of Urim before the Lord: at his word shall they go out, and at his word they shall come in, *both* he, and all the children of Israel with him, even all the congregation.

22. And Moses did as the Lord commanded him: and he took Joshua, and set him before Eleazar the priest, and before all the congregation.

23. And he laid his hands upon him, and gave him a charge; as the Lord commanded by the hand of Moses.

tuum omnis carnis, virum super congregationem:

17. Qui egrediatur ante eos, et qui ingrediatur ante eos, id est, qui educat eos, et introducat eos, ne sit congregatio Jehovæ velut pecudes quæ nullum habent pastorem.

18. Et dixit Jehova ad Mosen, Cape tibi Josue filium Nun, virum in quo est spiritus, et imponas manum tuam super eum.

19. Statuasque illum coram Eleazar sacerdote, et coram universa congregatione: et dabis illi mandata in oculis eorum.

20. Et pones de gloria tua super illum, ut audiant illum universa congregatio filiorum Israel.

21. Qui postea coram Eleazar stabit, et interrogabit eum de judicio Urim coram Jehova: ad verbum ejus egredientur ipse et omnes filii Israel cum eo, et tota congregatio.

22. Fecit ergo Moses quemadmodum præceperat ei Jehova: accepit namque Josua, et statuit illum coram Eleazar sacerdote, et coram universa congregatione.

23. Imposuitque manus super illum, ac dedit illi mandata quemadmodum dixerat Jehova per manum Mosis.

15. *And Moses spake.* Moses here sets forth not only God's providence in attending to the welfare of the people, but also his own zeal for them. Hence it appears how paternal was his affection for them, in that he not only performed his duty towards them faithfully and earnestly, and shunned no pains that it cost him, even to the end of his life, but he also makes provision for the future, and is anxious about a suitable successor, lest the people should remain without one, like a headless body. We perceive also his humility, when he does not arrogate the right of appointment to himself, nor on his own authority submit the matter to the election of the people, but establishes God as its sole arbiter. It was, in-

deed, permitted him to choose the officers, and this was a part of the political constitution ; but this was too difficult a task, to find by man's judgment one who should suffice for its performance ; and, consequently, it behoved that the power should be intrusted to God alone, who did not indeed refuse to undertake it. And this special reason had much force in so difficult a point, viz., that the people should receive their leader at His hand, in order that the supreme power should always remain vested in Himself. As, therefore, He had chosen Moses in an extraordinary manner, and had appointed him to be His representative, so He continued the same grace in the case of Joshua. Already, indeed, had He designated him ; but, out of modesty, Moses omits his name, and simply prays that God would provide for His people.

The title, with which he honours God, has reference to the matter in question. It is true, indeed, that God may be often called " the God of the spirits of all flesh," and for another reason, in chap. xvi. 22, Moses makes use of this expression ; but he now alludes to this attribute, as much as to say, that there must be some one ready, and as it were in His hand, who should be appointed, since He has the making of all men according to His own will. Men often are mistaken and deceived in their opinions, and, even although the Spirit of God may enlighten them, they go no further than to discern the peculiar endowment for which a person is eminent ; but God is not only the best judge of each man's ability and aptitude, nor does He only penetrate to the inmost recesses of every heart ; but He also fashions and refashions the men whom He chooses as His ministers, and supplies them with the faculties they require in order to be sufficient for bearing the burden. We gather from hence a useful lesson, *i.e.*, that, when we are deprived of good rulers, they should be sought from the Maker Himself, whose special gift the power of good government is. And on this ground Moses calls Him not only the Creator of men, but "of all flesh," and expressly refers to their " spirits."

When he compares the people to *sheep*, it is for the purpose of awakening compassion, so that God may be more disposed to appoint them a shepherd.

18. *And the Lord said unto Moses.* We here see that Joshua was given in answer to the prayers of Moses, which is not stated elsewhere. But, in order that he may obtain his dignity with the consent of all, he is honoured with a signal encomium: for, when God declares that the Spirit is in him, He does not merely intimate that he has a soul, but that he excels in the necessary gifts, such as intelligence. judgment, magnanimity, and skill in war; and the word "spirit" is used, in a different sense from that which it has just above, for that eminent and rare grace, which manifested itself in Joshua. For this metonymy[1] is a tolerably common figure in Scripture.

The solemn rite of his consecration by the imposition of hands follows, respecting which I have treated so fully elsewhere,[2] that it is now superfluous to say much upon it. It was in use before the giving of the Law, for thus the holy patriarchs blessed their sons. We have seen that the priests were inaugurated in their office, and that victims were offered to God, with this ceremony. The apostles followed this custom in the appointment of pastors. Moses, therefore, in order to testify publicly that Joshua was no longer his own master, but dedicated to God, and no longer to be regarded as a private individual, since he was called by God to the supreme command, laid his hands upon his head.

There was also another reason, viz., that, according to the requirements of the office intrusted to him, God would more and more enrich him (with His gifts;[3]) for there is nothing to prevent God from conferring richer endowments upon His servants according to the nature of their vocation, although they may have previously been eminent for spiritual gifts. Thus to Timothy, when he was appointed a pastor, new grace was given by the imposition of the hands of Paul, although he had before attained to no ordinary eminence. (2 Tim. i. 6.) To the same effect is what follows, that Moses should put

[1] "De mettre l'Esprit pour les dons qui en previennent;" to put *the Spirit* for the gifts which proceed from it.—*Fr.*

[2] See *ante* on Lev. viii. 10, vol. iii. p. 422.

[3] Added from *Fr.*

some of his glory[1] upon him, as if resigning his own dignity; for by the word *glory*, not only external splendour, but rather spiritual honour is signified, whereby God commands reverence towards His servants; not that he was stripped of his own virtues by transferring them to Joshua, but because, without diminution of his own gifts, he made the person who was about to be his successor his associate in their possession.

It was fitting that this should be done before all the people, that all might willingly receive him as presented to them by God.

The charge given to him partly tended to confirm the authority of Joshua, and partly to bind him more solemnly to discharge his duties; for, inasmuch as Moses commanded him what he was to do in the name of God, he exempted himself from all suspicion of temerity; and, on the other hand, by the introduction of this duly authorized engagement, Joshua must have been more and more encouraged to faith and diligence.

21. *And he shall stand before Eleazar the priest.* Joshua is here subordinated to the priest on one point, viz., to inquire of him by the Urim and Thummim: for, as we have seen before,[2] the dignity of the priesthood was exalted by this symbol, that the prince should consult God by the mouth of the priest, who, being clothed in the sacred Ephod, the emblems of which were the Urim and Thummim, gave replies as the interpreter of God Himself. This passage, then, shews that the rule of Joshua was not profane; as in all legitimate dominion religion ought surely to hold the first place; for, since all things depend upon God, it is absurd that they should be separated from His service.

משפט, *mishphat,* that is, judgment, is here used for a rule, or prescribed course of action, as if he were commanded to seek the Law[3] from the oracles of God, which the priest was to receive and deliver from Him, and that in perplexing matters he was to follow nothing else.

Moses adds, in conclusion, that he did what God had en-

[1] *A. V.*, "honour."

[2] See on Exod. xxviii. 4, vol. ii. p. 196.

[3] "Sa leçon;" his lesson.—*Fr.*

joined, so that all might be fully assured that God would rule, no less than before, in the person of Joshua.

A Repetition of the same History.

DEUTERONOMY, CHAPTER III.

21. And I commanded Joshua at that time, saying, Thine eyes have seen all that the Lord your God hath done unto these two kings: so shall the Lord do unto all the kingdoms whither thou passest.

22. Ye shall not fear them: for the Lord your God he shall fight for you.

23. And I besought the Lord at that time, saying,

24. O Lord God, thou hast begun to shew thy servant thy greatness, and thy mighty hand: for what God *is there* in heaven or in earth that can do according to thy works, and according to thy might?

25. I pray thee, let me go over and see the good land that *is* beyond Jordan, that goodly mountain, and Lebanon.

26. But the Lord was wroth with me for your sakes, and would not hear me: and the Lord said unto me, Let it suffice thee; speak no more unto me of this matter.

27. Get thee up into the top of Pisgah, and lift up thine eyes westward, and northward, and southward, and eastward, and behold *it* with thine eyes: for thou shalt not go over this Jordan.

28. But charge Joshua, and encourage him, and strengthen him: for he shall go over before this people, and he shall cause them to inherit the land which thou shalt see.

29. So we abode in the valley over against Beth-peor.

DEUT. IV. 21. Furthermore, the Lord was angry with me for your sakes, and sware that I should not go over Jordan, and that I should

21. Ipsi quoque Josua præcepi eo tempore, dicendo, Oculi tui viderunt quæcunque fecit Jehova Deus vester duobus regibus: sic facturus est Jehova omnibus regnis ad quæ tu pergis.

22. Ne timeatis eos, quia Jehova Deus vester ipse est qui pugnat pro vobis.

23. Rogaveram autem Jehovam tempore illo, dicendo:

24. Domine Jehova, tu cœpisti ostendere servo tuo magnitudinem tuam, et manum tuam validam. Quis enim Deus in cœlo, aut in terra, qui faciat secundum opera tua, et secundum fortitudines tuas?

25. Transeam quæso, et videam terram illam bonam, quæ est trans Jordanem, montem istum bonum et Libanum.

26. Iratus autem Jehova contra me propter vos, propterea non exaudivit me, sed dixit mihi, Sufficiat tibi, ne posthac addas verbum ad me super hac re.

27. Ascende verticem Pisgah, et leva oculos tuos ad occidentem, ad aquilonem, ad meridiem, et ad orientem, ac vide oculis tuis, non enim transibis Jordanem istum.

28. Præcipe autem Josuæ, et confirma eum, et robora eum, ipse enim transiturus est ante populum istum, et idem tradet illis terram possidendam, quam videbis.

29. Mansimus vero in valle e regione Beth-peor.

21. Jehova iratus fuit contra me propter verba vestra, juravitque quod non transirem Jordanem, neque ingrederer terram bonam, quam Je-

not go in unto that good land which the Lord thy God giveth thee *for* an inheritance;	hova Deus tuus dat tibi in hæreditatem.
22. But I must die in this land, I must not go over Jordan: but ye shall go over, and possess that good land.	22. Ego enim morior in hac terra, neque transeo Jordanem: vos autem transitis, ut possideatis terram istam bonam.

DEUT. III. 21. *And I commanded Joshua at that time.* He repeats what we have already seen, that he exhorted Joshua together with the whole people to prepare themselves to occupy the land with alacrity, relying as well upon God's promise, as upon the numerous proofs of His assistance, which were so many pledges of the future continuance of His grace.

23. *And I besought the Lord.*[1] Others have, "I besought;" but I have preferred using the pluperfect tense, because, in my opinion, Moses interrupts himself to shew why he had resigned his office to another, and did not rather declare that he would be their leader, as heretofore, and at the same time an example to the people of courage. He says, therefore, that when he had prayed that he might be permitted to enter the land, he received a refusal. For it is not probable that, after he had substituted Joshua for himself, he straightway conceived a desire, which was in direct opposition to it.

The drift of the prayer is that God, by granting him permission to enter the land, should thus fill up to the full the measure of His grace towards him: for he enumerates the blessings already vouchsafed to him, as the ground of his confidence in asking, and that God, who is not wont to forsake the work of His own hands, might carry on to the end the mercies He had begun. For this reason he says that the might of God had been shewn him; modestly hinting that it was natural to expect that he should be a partaker of the crowning blessing, in order that the end might correspond with the beginning. He also magnifies the power of God as proclaimed by the miracles; that so magnificent a work might not be interrupted. On the other hand, he speaks in commendation of the goodness of the land, and expressly shews that his desire to see it springs from earnest

[1] "I *had* besought, &c."—*Lat.*

piety; for I willingly subscribe to the opinion of those who understand Sion by the "goodly mountain;" for, with the exception of Lebanon, there was no other mountain so delectable in the land; whereas Lebanon, as if next to it in rank, is mentioned in the second place.

26. *But the Lord was wroth with me.* Some imagine that God was offended by such a longing as this; but Moses is rather giving the reason why he did not obtain what he sought, viz., because he had been already excluded from it. For, although he by no means enters into debate with God, as if he had been unjustly condemned for the faults of others, still he indirectly reflects upon the people, since it was well that they should be all reminded that the punishment which had been inflicted upon God's distinguished servant was incurred by the guilt of them all. We have elsewhere seen[1] how it was that the penalty of their common transgression was with justice imposed upon Moses.

Its mitigation then follows, when God commands him to get up into the top of Mount Abarim, which is here called Pisgah, and elsewhere Nebo, that he might nevertheless enjoy a sight of the promised land.

In conclusion, he more clearly explains why he exhorted Joshua, viz., because he was about to go over before the people; and in the last verse he assigns the reason of their delay, and why they remained so long in the valley near Mount Abarim; for it is precisely as if he had said that they were retained by the extension of God's hand, in order that they should not proceed any further until Joshua had been installed as his successor.

DEUT. IV. 21. *Furthermore, the Lord was angry with me.* He again records that it arose from the transgression of the people that he was not permitted to enter the land, not by way of expostulation, and much less in order to accuse God of cruelty, as if he had been improperly and unjustly substituted as a criminal in the place of others, but rather to magnify the goodness of God towards those whom He had treated with so much indulgence. For we must observe the comparison, that, whilst they were to enjoy the land, he

[1] See *antè*, on Deut. i. 37. p. 137.

was to be prevented from entering it. "I must die (he says) in this land" of Moab, whilst to you it is given to enjoy the promised inheritance. We perceive, therefore, that they are upbraided with their guilt in such a way that all the bitterness of the reproof is sweetened by the sense of God's mercy; nay, that by this sweetness they may be ravished into admiration, when they understand how mercifully that pardon is extended to them, which was denied to Moses.

The sense of the expression which I have rendered "for your words,"[1] might be "for your things," inasmuch as the Hebrews call men's affairs (*negotia*) דברים, *debarim*. Assuredly, although he had been impelled to sin by their rebellious clamours, he simply states that he was now punished on their account. If any should inquire why he lays the blame on them, whereas the actual offenders were most of them dead, the reply is obvious, that many of them were still surviving, and that it is no novelty that the children should be included with the fathers, when the whole body of a people has sinned.

DEUTERONOMY, CHAPTER XXXI.

14. And the Lord said unto Moses, Behold, thy days approach that thou must die: call Joshua, and present yourselves in the tabernacle of the congregation, that I may give him a charge. And Moses and Joshua went, and presented themselves in the tabernacle of the congregation.

15. And the Lord appeared in the tabernacle in a pillar of a cloud: and the pillar of the cloud stood over the door of the tabernacle.

16. And the Lord said unto Moses, Behold, thou shalt sleep with thy fathers; and this people will rise up, and go a whoring after the gods of the strangers of the land whither they go *to be* among them, and will forsake me, and break my covenant which I have made with them.

17. Then my anger shall be kindled against them in that day, and I will

14. Et dixit Jehova ad Mosen, Ecce, appropinquaverunt dies tui, ut moriaris: voca Josua, et state in tabernaculo conventionis, et præcipiam ei. Perrexit ergo Moses et Josua, steteruntque in tabernaculo conventionis.

15. Et apparuit Jehova in tabernaculo, in columna nubis, stetitque columna nubis super ostium tabernaculi.

16. Et dixit Jehova ad Mosen, Ecce, tu dormiturus es cum patribus tuis: postea surget populus iste, et fornicabitur post deos alienorum terræ ad quam pergit in medio ejus, et derelinquet me, irritumque faciet pactum meum quod pepigi cum eo.

17. Itaque irascetur vultus meus contra eum ipso die, ac derelinquam

[1] *A. V.*, "for your sakes;" (דברים.)

forsake them, and I will hide my face from them, and they shall be devoured, and many evils and troubles shall befall them; so that they will say in that day, Are not these evils come upon us, because our God *is* not among us?

eos, et abscondam faciem meam ab eis: et consumetur, et invenient eum mala multa, et angustiæ: dicetque in die illa, Nonne propterea quod non est Deus meus in medio mei invenerunt me mala hæc?

18. And I will surely hide my face in that day, for all the evils which they shall have wrought, in that they are turned unto other gods.

18. Ego verò abscondendo abscondam faciem meam in die illa, propter omne malum quod fecerit, quod converterit se ad deos alienos.

19. Now therefore write ye this song for you, and teach it the children of Israel: put it in their mouths, that this song may be a witness for me against the children of Israel.

19. Nunc itaque scribite vobis canticum istud, et doce illud filios Israelis: pone illud in ore eorum, ut sit mihi canticum istud in testem contra filios Israelis.

20. For when I shall have brought them into the land which I sware unto their fathers, that floweth with milk and honey, and they shall have eaten, and filled themselves, and waxen fat; then will they turn unto other gods, and serve them, and provoke me, and break my covenant.

20. Introducam enim eum in terram quam juravi patribus ejus, fluentem lacte et melle: comedet autem et saturabitur, impinguabitque se: tunc convertet se ad deos alienos, et colent eos, vilipendentque me, et irritum facient pactum meum.

21. And it shall come to pass, when many evils and troubles are befallen them, that this song shall testify against them as a witness; for it shall not be forgotten out of the mouths of their seed: for I know their imagination which they go about, even now, before I have brought them into the land which I sware.

21. Quum autem invenerint eum mala plurima, et angustiæ, tunc respondebit canticum istud in conspectu ejus in testem: non enim oblivioni tradetur ab ore seminis ejus, novi enim ingenium ejus, et quid ipse faciat hodie antequam introduxerim eum in terram de qua juravi.

22. Moses therefore wrote this song the same day, and taught it the children of Israel.

22. Scripsit itaque Moses canticum istud eo die, et docuit illud filios Israelis.

14. *And the Lord said unto Moses.* Joshua is now substituted in the place of Moses by a solemn ceremony, not only that he may be held in greater reverence by men, but also that he may be presented before God, and thus may acknowledge that he is dedicated to His service; for his being brought before the door of the tabernacle was a kind of consecration; and God also declares that He will give him a charge, which is equivalent to saying that He will instruct him in the performance of his duties. The appearance also of the glory of God in the cloud, was not less effectual for encouraging himself personally, than for giving public distinction to his high office. For he would

never have been recognised as the successor of Moses, unless this visible approbation of God had fastened the yoke upon the people.

16. *Behold, thou shalt sleep with thy fathers.* In order that Moses may labour more earnestly to retain the people in obedience to God, he is reminded of their indomitable perverseness. He had already sufficiently, and more than sufficiently, experienced how depraved and stubborn was the disposition of the Israelites, and how disobedient and contumacious they had been ; God now declares that they will be no better after his death ; nay, that they will indulge themselves in greater license in consequence of his absence from them. For it appears as if there was an antithesis implied between the words "lie down," and "rise up ;"[1] as if it were said, As soon as you have gone to rest, their insubordination shall break forth, as if they were released from all laws. Not, indeed, that this should take place immediately, for under Joshua they manifested some humility and submissiveness ; at any rate, the outward form of pure religion was then maintained, but soon afterwards they relapsed into their old habits. And perhaps this admonition was useful as a preventative, so that they should not fall away so soon.

Since now we understand the general object which God had in view, it will be well briefly to consider the words He employs. When it is said to Moses, "Thou shalt sleep with thy fathers," first of all the condition of the human race is stated, that Moses may not think it hard to depart from the world like all others, since he was born to this end. At the same time, the difference is indicated between the death of men and of the brute animals. Hence the best consolation is derived, for, if our death were total annihilation, we should not be said to sleep with our fathers.

Why the Spirit designates idolatry by the name of "whoring," we have seen elsewhere, as also why he calls all false

[1] See margin, *A. V.* "Il semble qu'il ait comparaison des choses opposees entre ces deux mots, que Moyse se couchera, et le peuple se levera ;" it seems that there is a comparison of two opposite things in these two expressions, that "Moses shall lie down," and "the people shall rise up."—*Fr.*

gods "strange," or "of the strangers," viz., because, as God chose to be served alone in Israel, so he had distinguished Himself by this title, that He was "the God of Israel." It is stated in aggravation of their crime, that they would not only be led away into the superstitions which they had learnt in Egypt, but would also pollute themselves with the defilements of Canaan, from which God had willed that it should be purged by their hand. These words, then, are to be read emphatically, The people shall go a whoring after the gods of the land whither they go, and indeed in the midst of it; for it was far more disgraceful to embrace those false gods, of which they were the conquerors and judges, than to invent for themselves fresh idols.

Another aggravation of their crime is also added, that they would desert the God by whom they had been adopted as children, and wickedly depart from His covenant. For they could not pretend ignorance, when they had been again and again so clearly and solemnly warned. Meanwhile let us learn from this passage, that whosoever turn away to superstitious worships are covenant breakers, and thus, that all their pretences are vain, who profess that they worship the supreme God together with idols.

17. *Then my anger shall be kindled against them.* By this denunciation of punishment, God undoubtedly desired to put a restraint upon the senselessness of the people; but since this was done without their profiting by it, there was another advantage in this lesson, viz., that, after having been seriously chastised according to their deserts, they should at length repent though it might be late. Otherwise these punishments would have been inflicted in vain; and it would have never suggested itself to their minds that they received the just recompence of their ingratitude and perfidiousness. This is indeed the first step of prudence, voluntarily to choose that which is right; but the second is to beware, when we have listened to admonition, and to make a stand against evil. But, if our minds are so blinded, that reproofs and threats profit us nothing, there is still a third, *i.e.*, that those who have been careless in prosperity should at length begin to perceive that they are smitten by God's hand, and thus

be driven to acknowledge their guilt. Although, therefore, the simple admonition, as long as it was not followed by its consequences, was despised by the Israelites; still, when they were further instructed by its result, and by experience, it produced its fruit; and the same is daily the case with ourselves. There is scarcely one in ten of the godly, who, as long as God postpones His punishments, anticipates His judgment, but those who are aroused from their torpor, seriously consider the threats which they had hitherto passed over with indifference, and, being brought under conviction, condemn themselves.

By the word אפי, *ephi*, I here rather understand His *face* than His *wrath*;[1] for the expression is more appropriate; and then he sets forth the effect of His wrath, viz., that, being deprived of His aid, they shall be overtaken by all sorts of evils, until they are consumed and perish. Moreover, He affirms that they should be brought into such straits as should extort from them the confession, that the miseries which they suffered were tokens of God's alienation from them. But He adds, that He would not then listen to their prayers. Hence are we taught that, as our happiness depends on God's paternal favour, so there is nothing worse for us than to be forsaken by Him, as if He regarded us with no further care; and the lesson we are to learn is, that there is nothing more desirable for us than that He should honour us with His countenance. We read respecting all His creatures, in Ps. civ. 29, that they *are troubled* when He *hides His face;* but here it is more clearly perceived that nothing can be imagined more miserable than we are, when "our iniquities have separated between us and our God, and our sins have hid his face from us, that he will not hear," as Isaiah says, (lix. 2.)

I have already stated, that the greatness of their miseries is expressed, when the people shall confess that they are thus grievously afflicted, because God is departed from them; for it was by no light punishments that they would be brought to this state of feeling, especially considering their

[1] *A. V.*, "Then my *anger* shall be kindled." *C.*, "Itaque irascetur *vultus* meus."

great hardness of heart and blind obstinacy. It follows then, that severe punishments are indicated, that should compel them, though unwillingly, to reflect on God's anger, which they had previously taken no account of. Still, this confession is not referred to as the fruit or sign of sincere repentance; for, if the sinner sincerely flies to God, God will be sure to meet him, since He is inclined to mercy. But in this place He declares that He will not be favourable to them, but will suffer them to pine away in their wretchedness, for God says of Himself that He will "hide His face from them," in the 18th verse, with a deeper meaning than just before, in that He will take no notice of their groans and lamentations, and by the very continuance of their punishments will show how greatly wroth with them He is.

19. *Now, therefore, write ye this song.* It seems absurd that a useless remedy should be applied to an incurable disease. Why does not God rather correct their wickedness, and by His Spirit mould their hearts to obedience, than pour forth words in vain into their deaf ears? Thus do proud and profane men mock at this mode of dealing with them, as if God, throwing away His labour, were deluding unhappy men. We must bear in mind, however, that the preaching of the word, although it is a savour of death to them that perish, is still a sacrifice of sweet savour to God; nor is it to be considered thrown away and ineffectual, when it convicts the ungodly more and more, and renders them altogether inexcusable. And God expressly declares that this would be the use of the song as "a witness" against those, from whose mouth it should proceed. To some, indeed, it was profitable unto salvation; for, when subdued by chastisement, they at length learnt from it that their iniquities were the source and cause of all their evils. For, however God may redouble the blows of His scourges, unbelievers, who are without instruction, reap no advantage from them. Thus, this song was the means of assisting the elect to seek after repentance, when they were smitten by the hand of God. Still, although the word of God should do nothing more than condemn its hearers to death, yet it would be

enough that it was a sweet savour to Himself. It seems by no means accordant with our reason that God should have given this command to Isaiah; "Go, and tell this people, Hear ye indeed, but understand not; and see ye indeed, but perceive not. Make the heart of this people fat, and make their ears heavy, and shut their eyes, lest they see with their eyes, and hear with their ears, and understand with their heart, and convert, and be healed," (Isa. vi. 9, 10;) but, with respect to the secret judgments of God, whereby all our senses must be overwhelmed, let sober-mindedness be our wisdom.

20. *But when I shall have brought them.* In other words, God again enlarges upon the atrociousness of their iniquity, in that, when He had dealt liberally with the Israelites, they would turn His benefits into occasions of perversity, since nothing can be more base than such ingratitude. He says, then, that He will perform to them, unworthy as they are, that which He has sworn, so that He might thus be faithful to His promises. He commends the fertility of the land, since this striking pledge of His indulgence should have attracted them by its sweetness to love so beneficent a Father in return. Hence, therefore, the perverseness of their nature is demonstrated, inasmuch as, when full, they would kick against Him, like horses which become intractable from high feeding. But, after having complained of their future rebellion, He again says, that when they shall have been brought into sore straits, and overwhelmed with miseries, this song would be "as a witness," as if they should proclaim in it their own condemnation.

When He says that He knew their disposition,[1] or what they forged within them, (for the word employed is יצר, *yetzer*, which is equivalent to figment, or imagination, and includes all the thoughts and feelings,) it is apparent that He was by no means unaware how ill He was bestowing His benefits upon such unworthy persons, but that He thus contended with their unworthiness, in order that His goodness might be the more conspicuous; and also that He desired

[1] *A. V.*, "Their imagination." "The thing forged in their heart."—Ainsworth. "Figmentum;" Taylor, from יצר, *fingere, formare.*

this instruction to be set before them, ungodly and hopeless as they were, which He knew they would despise, so as to render them all the more inexcusable by this test. But it may be objected, Why then did He not turn their hearts to better things? for thus do ungodly railers allow themselves to dispute with Him; but let us rather reflect on the words of Paul, "Nay but, O man, who art thou that repliest against God? Hath not the potter power over the clay, to make" of it vessels according to his own will? (Rom. ix. 20, 21.) And, "Who hath first given to him, and it shall be recompensed unto him again?" (*Ibid.* xi. 35.) So will it come to pass, that we shall exclaim with trembling, Oh, how deep are the judgments of God; how incomprehensible are His ways!

That God should judge from their former life what they would be hereafter, does not seem very logical; but these two clauses are to be taken connectedly, that God foresees that nothing else is to be expected from them, but that they would be carried away into sin by their unbridled lust; and secondly, that it had already been sufficiently manifested by their many iniquities how desperate was their obstinacy.

23. And he gave Joshua the son of Nun a charge, and said, Be strong, and of a good courage: for thou shalt bring the children of Israel into the land which I sware unto them: and I will be with thee.	23. Dein præcepit Josuæ filio Nun, ac dixit, Fortis esto, et roborare, quia tu introduces filios Israel in terram de qua juravi eis: et ego ero tecum.
24. And it came to pass when Moses had made an end of writing the words of this law in a book, until they were finished,	24. Quum autem fecisset finem Moses scribendi verba legis istius in libro, donec ea complerentur,
25. That Moses commanded the Levites, which bare the ark of the covenant of the Lord, saying,	25. Præcepit Moses Levitis portantibus Arcam fœderis Jehovæ, dicendo:
26. Take this book of the law, and put it in the side of the ark of the covenant of the Lord your God, that it may be there for a witness against thee.	26. Capite librum istum legis, et ponite eum in latere arcæ fœderis Jehovæ Dei vestri, sitque ibi contra te in testem.
27. For I know thy rebellion, and thy stiff neck: behold, while I am yet alive with you this day, ye have been rebellious against the Lord; and how much more after my death?	27. Ego enim novi rebellionem tuam, et cervicem tuam duram: ecce, adhuc me vivente vobiscum hodie rebelles estis Jehovæ, et quanto magis posteaquam mortuus fuero?

28. Gather unto me all the elders of your tribes, and your officers, that I may speak these words in their ears, and call heaven and earth to record against them.

29. For I know that after my death ye will utterly corrupt *yourselves*, and turn aside from the way which I have commanded you; and evil will befall you in the latter days; because ye will do evil in the sight of the Lord, to provoke him to anger through the work of your hands.

30. And Moses spake in the ears of all the congregation of Israel the words of this song, until they were ended.

28. Congregate ad me omnes seniores tribuum vestrarum, et præfectos vestros, ut loquar in auribus eorum verba ista, et antestor contra eos cœlum et terram.

29. Novi enim postquam mortuus fuero, corrumpendo corrumpetis vos et recedetis de via quam præcepi vobis, unde eveniet vobis malum in novissimis dierum, quum feceritis malum in oculis Jehovæ, irritando eum opere manuum vestrarum.

30. Itaque loquutus est Moses in auribus totius congregationis verba cantici hujus, donec ea complerentur.

23. *And he gave Joshua the son of Nun a charge.* The more difficult was the task of Joshua, the more needful was it that he should be encouraged to exert himself, and to beware of failure. For this reason his charge is repeated, although in his person all the others were at the same time confirmed. Moses grounds it on the promise of God, which has been so often mentioned; and says that Joshua had been chosen to complete the work of deliverance already begun; for it was hardly credible that the disciple should be not only superior to his master, but that a man of humble position should be elevated to the dignity from which the sovereign Prophet, and God's chief minister, had been degraded, unless this was done by the decree and ordinance of God. At the same time, however, he makes him more confident of the result of his calling, by promising him that God, who was the mover of this expedition, would be with him; for He has the power to accomplish every work to which He has appointed any one of us.

24. *And it came to pass, when Moses had made an end.* By "the words of this law," we must understand not only those which are embraced in this book, but in the other three also; and there is an implied antithesis between the two tables written by God's hand, and the exposition which was afterwards added, lest there should be any obscurity respecting God's will on account of the brevity with which

it was delivered. At the very beginning, indeed, God had set forth whatever it was useful for them to know, but it was His will that what He had briefly comprehended in the Decalogue should be more fully unfolded, and not only so, but that it should be also committed to writing, lest it should be forgotten. We know how inclined to vanity is the mind of man, nay, how wilfully it is led away into error by its levity; whilst it has other faults also, such as inquisitiveness, and audacity in invention, and the love of novelty. Thus religion would have been corrupted in a thousand ways, had not its rule been diligently written down for posterity. Moreover, since the books of Moses were for a long time buried through the carelessness of the people and the priests, what darkness of error would have overspread the minds of all, if nothing had been written down!

Since the two Tables were enclosed in the Ark of the Covenant, a place at the side was assigned to the interpretation, so that they might have no doubt but that it proceeded from the same Divine Author; and, since the Decalogue is repeated in these books, it was not at all necessary that the Ark should be opened; which was not lawful, because they might seek in the books of Moses the instruction which was hidden in the Tables. This, indeed, we must remember, that the volume was placed near the Ark in token of its dignity, so that, when it was taken from thence by the Levites, it might be listened to with greater reverence. When it is said, "That it may be there for a witness against thee," this is not addressed to the Levites alone, but relates generally to the whole people, though the general statement is directed to them as one member of the whole body. But further, although the application of its doctrine is manifold, still one point only is adverted to; for the Law was not written with the single object of being a witness to condemn the people, but to be the rule of a pious and holy life, and a testimony of God's favour. But, since he had to do with hard and proud minds, Moses declares that, whenever its doctrine shall be set forth, it will render their perverseness inexcusable.

27. *For I know thy rebellion.* The reason is given why he

passed over the utility of his doctrine, and only cited it as a witness against the Israelites in terms of severity and reproach, viz., because he had found them by experience to be of a "stiff neck," (of which expression I have spoken elsewhere,) and has no confidence that they will be more tractable hereafter. He argues from the less to the greater; for, if, while such a leader as theirs was alive, they were rebellious, they were likely to assume greater audacity when he was dead. For we know of what avail is the authority of a great and excellent person to restrain the licentiousness of a people. At the same time, Moses does not arrogate so much to himself as to say that the good condition of the people depended upon his presence, but, pointing out their danger, he seeks to render them more obedient after his death.

28. *Gather to me all the elders of your tribes.* Special reference is here made to the Song, which we gather from the last verse to have been alone recited. Moses, indeed, appears to contradict himself when he commands the elders and officers only to be called to listen, whereas he soon afterwards records that he read it to the whole people. But these two things are easily reconciled, when we remember the order which he was accustomed to observe in gathering the multitude together; for it is manifest from many passages that they were not called together promiscuously, but that the heads of tribes, and the princes of the people, each of them led their band; so that the assembling of the elders here mentioned, is so far from excluding the rest of the multitude, that it rather indicates that the whole people were gathered together by their tribes and classes. And this we may infer from the context, for assuredly he did not "call heaven and earth to record against" the officers only; and yet so he seems to signify. Under the leaders, therefore, the whole multitude is included.

The Song of Moses.

It was the perverse nature of the people which extorted from Moses that unmixed bitterness with which he again addresses them. Doubtless he would have desired to leave a pleasing and joyful recollection of himself, and therefore would willingly have exhorted them to the performance of their duties, either with blandness, or at any rate with placidity, but their stubbornness compelled him to testify his indignation in the severity of his address. Besides, he does not judge from conjecture what they would do, but expressly declares that he knew it for certain, unquestionably because the Spirit, in dictating the Song, had also informed him of it. He indicates their revolt by two words, *corrupting*, and *turning aside from the way;* but, inasmuch as in the first there is an ellipsis, for the active verb is used without any word for it to govern, some supply "the way of the Lord." I have, however, followed a different reading,[1] which seems more correct, for the signification of the word is rather passive than transitive. He points out the manner of their corruption, declaring that they will depart from the way which they had learned; for this was their perfect soundness, to obey God, and to follow the way which he shewed them. By forsaking the Law, then, they were corrupted. Moreover, Moses indirectly reproves their ingratitude, inasmuch as he had thrown away his labour upon such despisers of pious instruction. Thus he desires that this song should be recited by them, in order that, when afflicted and half-consumed by miseries, they might at last learn that God is a just avenger. And the advantage of this assurance was, that those, whose state was not altogether desperate, should at length return to their senses; whilst the reprobate should be more and more condemned.

[1] It is *S.M.* who has thought fit to fill out the Heb. idiom, by adding the words, "the way of the Lord." *A.V.* supplies *yourselves*, in its italics, as *C.* has done; but modern critics would not call this "following a different reading."—*W.*

We have elsewhere seen what it is to call heaven and earth to witness.[1]

DEUTERONOMY, CHAPTER XXXII.

1. Give ear, O ye heavens, and I will speak; and hear, O earth, the words of my mouth.

2 My doctrine shall drop as the rain, my speech shall distil as the dew; as the small rain upon the tender herb, and as the showers upon the grass:

3. Because I will publish the name of the Lord; ascribe ye greatness unto our God.

4. *He is* the Rock, his work *is* perfect; for all his ways *are* judgment: a God of truth, and without iniquity; just and right *is* he.

5. They have corrupted themselves; their spot *is* not *the spot* of his children: *they are* a perverse and crooked generation.

6. Do ye thus requite the Lord, O foolish people and unwise? *is* not he thy father *that* hath bought thee? hath he not made thee, and established thee?

7. Remember the days of old, consider the years of many generations: ask thy father, and he will shew thee; thy elders, and they will tell thee.

8. When the Most High divided to the nations their inheritance, when he separated the sons of Adam, he set the bounds of the people according to the number of the children of Israel:

9. For the Lord's portion *is* his people; Jacob *is* the lot of his inheritance.

1. Auscultate cœli, et loquar, et audiat terra eloquia oris mei.

2. Stillabit, ut pluvia, doctrina mea: stillabit ut ros eloquium meum, ut pluviæ gramen, et ut imber super herbam.

3. Quia nomen Jehovæ invocabo: date magnitudinem Deo nostro.

4. Dei perfectum est opus: omnes enim viæ ejus judicium: Deus veritas, et non est iniquitas, justus et rectus est.

5. Corrupit sese illi, non filii ejus, macula eorum, generatio prava et perversa.

6. Jehovæ retribuitis istud populc stulte et insipiens: nonne ipse est pater tuus qui acquisivit te, ipse fecit te, et præparavit te?

7. Memento dierum seculi, intellige annos generationis et generationis, interroga patrem tuum, annuntiabit tibi: senes tuos, et dicent tibi.

8. Quando hæreditates distribuit Excelsus gentibus, quando separavit filios hominum, statuit terminos populorum pro numero filiorum Israelis.

9. Pars enim Jehovæ populus ejus, Jacob sors hæreditatis ejus.

1. *Give ear, O ye heavens.* Moses commences in a strain of magnificence, lest the people should disdain this song with their usual pride, or even reject it altogether, being exasperated by its severe censures and reproaches. For we well

[1] See on Deut. iv. 26, vol. iii. p. 269.

know how the world naturally longs to be flattered, and that no strain can be gratifying to it unless it tickles and soothes the ear with praise. But Moses here not only inveighs bitterly against the vices of the people, but with the utmost possible vehemence stigmatizes their perverse nature, their utterly corrupt morals, their obstinate ingratitude, and incorrigible contumacy. Moreover, he desired that these accusations, whereby he rendered their name detestable, should daily echo from their tongues; and thus they became still more offensive. It was, therefore, requisite that their impatience should be bridled, as it were, in order that they might patiently and humbly receive these just reproofs, however severe they might be. If, therefore, they should repudiate this song, or should turn a deaf ear to it, he declares at the outset that heaven and earth would be witnesses of their prodigious obtuseness; nay, he turns and addresses himself to heaven and earth, and thus signifies that it was worthy of the attention of all creatures, even although they were without intelligence or feeling. For it is a hyperbolical mode of expression, when he assigns the faculty of hearing, and being instructed, to the senseless elements; just as Isaiah, when he would intimate that he found none to give heed to him amongst the whole people, in like manner appeals to the heavens and the earth, and even summons them to bear witness to the prodigious iniquity, that there should be less of intelligence amongst the whole people than in oxen and asses. (Isa. i. 2, 3.) For it is but a meagre exposition, which some give of these words, that they are used, by metonymy, for angels and men.[1]

2. *My doctrine shall drop as the rain.* Some, as I think improperly, here resolve the future tense into the optative mood,[2] for in this splendid eulogium he rather celebrates, in order to commend his doctrine, the fruitfulness[3] which is actually imparted to it by the Holy Spirit, than asks for it to be given to him; and my readers must at once perceive

[1] See *ante*, on Deut. iv. 26, vol. iii. p. 269, and note.

[2] So the *LXX.*, *V.*, Vatablus, Junius, and others. Ainsworth combines the two, and says, "*shall drop*, or *let it drop*, as being a wish, and also a promise, that his doctrine should be profitable and effectual," &c.

[3] "L'eloquence."—*Fr.*

that such a request would have been by no means seasonable. He therefore compares his speech to rain or dew, as if he had said that, if only the people were like the soil in a state of softness and preparation, he would deliver doctrine to them which would irrigate them unto abundant fruitfulness.

Although this expression refers especially, and κατ' ἐξοχὴν to the Song, still its force and propriety extends to all divine teaching; for God never speaks except to render men fruitful in good works, just as, by instilling succulency and vigour into the earth by means of rain, He makes it fertile for the production of fruit. But, like the rocks and stones, which imbibe no moisture from the most abundant rains, so many are hindered by their own perversity from being fertilized by spiritual irrigation. Wherefore Moses indirectly throws the blame upon the Israelites, if the doctrine of this Song should drop upon them in vain.

3. *Because I will publish the name of the Lord.* He signifies by these words that, if there were any spark of piety in the Israelites, it must be manifested by their welcoming this address, wherein the majesty of God shines forth. The first clause of the verse, therefore, stands last in order, since it is an assignment of a reason for the other. For when he exhorts them that they should ascribe to God the glory He deserves, he inculcates upon them obedience and attention, as if he had said that, unless they reverently submit themselves to his teaching, God would be defrauded of His due honour; and this he confirms by adding as a reason that he will sincerely and faithfully publish the name of God. For the word *invoke*[1] is not used here as in many other passages, but is equivalent to making a profession of God. Moses, then, declares himself to be His proclaimer, in order that, under cover of His most Holy name, he may awaken attention to his words.

4. . . . *His work is perfect.* Those who take these expressions generally, and without particular reference to this passage, not only obscure their meaning, but also lessen

[1] *Hebr.* אקרא. *A. V.*, "I will publish," from קרא, which is stated by Taylor to signify, in its first sense, "Vocare, advocare, convocare, invocare, clamare, exclamare, legere."—*Concord. in voce.*

the force of the doctrine they contain. Let us, then, understand that the perfection of God's works, the rectitude of His ways, etc., are contrasted with the rebellion of the people; for if there were anything[1] in God's works imperfect and ill arranged, if His mode of dealing were deficient in rectitude, if His truth were doubtful; if, in a word, there were anything wanting, then there would have been a natural excuse why the people should have sought for something better than they found in Him, since the desire of obtaining that which is best is deserving of no reprehension. Lest, then, the Israelites should offer any such pretext, Moses anticipates them. Before he begins to treat of the wicked ingratitude of the people, he lays down this principle, that they were not induced to transfer their affections elsewhere by any deficiency in God. The general statement is indeed true in itself, and may be applied to various purposes; but we must consider what the object of Moses here is, namely, to remove from the people every pretext for their impious and perfidious rebellion, and this in order that their amazing folly may be more apparent, when they forsake the fountain of living waters, and hew them out cisterns with holes in them, as God himself complains in Jerem. ii. 13. We perceive therefore, that every honourable distinction which is here attributed to God, brands the people with a corresponding mark of ignominy, in that they had knowingly and voluntarily deprived themselves of the plenitude of all good things, which might have been enjoyed by them had they not alienated themselves from God.

God's work is spoken of, not only with reference to the creation of the world, but to the whole course of His providence; as if it were said that nothing could be discovered in God's works which could be found fault with.

Now this perfection is not perceptible in every individual thing, for even vermin are God's creatures; and amongst men some are blind, some lame, some deaf, and others mutilated in one of their members; and many fruits also never arrive at maturity. Yet we plainly see that it is

[1] "Quelque chose de coupé ou mutilé, ou bien mal compassé et confus;" anything defective or mutilated, or even ill-contrived and confused.—*Fr.*

foolish and misplaced to bring forward such questions as these as objections to the perfection of God, here celebrated by Moses, inasmuch as the very defects and blemishes of our bodies tend to this object, that God's glory may be made manifest. (John ix. 3.)

The next statement, *that all his ways are right,*[1] conveys a similar truth; for it is well known that the word משפט, *mishphat,* is used for rectitude, and *works* and *ways* are synonymous.

The latter part of the verse is a confirmation of the former part, since Moses signifies in both that all who censure God may be clearly convicted of petulant impiety, since supreme justice shines forth in all His acts.

The words I have rendered, "God is truth," others construe with the genitive case, "a God of truth." Either is true, and agreeable to the usage of Scripture; but the apposition is more emphatic, which declares that God is not only true, but the Truth itself. At any rate, this applies to the persons who pay entire allegiance to the word of God, for their expectations shall never be frustrated. Thus the people are indirectly reproved for their unbelief, in that they deserted God, whose faithfulness was not only tried and proved, but who is the very fountain of truth.

Although what follows, that there is no iniquity in God, seems to some to have but little force, it is nevertheless of great importance; for we well know how often men are so absurd in their subterfuges, as in a manner to arraign God instead of themselves; and although they do not dare to accuse Him openly, still they do not hesitate to acquit themselves, and thus to cast direct obloquy upon Him. Elsewhere, therefore, God inquires by His Prophet, "what iniquity *the people* had found in Him?" (Jer. ii. 5,) and in another place expostulates with them, because He was loaded with their hatred and abuse, as if He dealt unjustly with such sinners. (Ezek. xviii. 25.) When, therefore, He vindicates Himself from such calumnies, it follows that no blame attaches itself to Him, but that the wickedness of those who turn away from Him is abundantly condemned.

[1] *A. V.*, "all his ways are judgment."

5. *They have corrupted themselves.* Moses now inveighs unhesitatingly against the perfidy of the people, and gives loose to the most unmeasured upbraidings; for if God be just and true, then it was plain enough that the Israelites were a depraved and perverse nation. This perverse nation, he says, has corrupted itself towards Him, namely Him, whom he has just lauded for His perfect justice and faithfulness; and he accuses them of having basely prostituted to every sort of sin the chastity which they had promised to God. There is no doubt but that they were sorely wounded by these epithets, and would have been transported with rage, had they not seen that God's incomparable servant, when he had now been called upon to die by God's command, spoke as it were from heaven. The voice, therefore, of the dying man restrained their pride, so that they did not now dare to oppose him as a mortal; and afterwards, when the condemnation had been assented to by public authority, and by general accord, they were less at liberty to vent their madness against it. He introduces, by way of anticipation, the statement that they were not His children; for else they might obviously have made the objection that the sacred race of Abraham, which God had adopted, should be dealt with less reproachfully. Moses, therefore, declares that they are not children, because they are a perverse nation. For although their adoption always stood firm, still its efficacy was restricted to the elect part of them, so that God, without breaking His covenant, might reject the general body. But to explain the matter more clearly, it must be borne in mind that the Spirit, on different grounds, at one time assigns the name of God's children to hypocrites, at another takes it away; for sometimes it is an aggravation of their criminality, when they are called the children of Abraham and Jacob as well as of God, an instance of which will soon occur. Here, however, in order that they may cease to glory without cause, they are said not to be children, because they are degenerate, and therefore disinherited by God, so as no longer to retain their honourable position. In this sense Moses declares that they are not children, as having cast off God from being their Father. It is added

that this was done with their spot (or disgrace;[1]) unless it be thought preferable to take it that they were corrupted by their spots, or by their sins, to which I willingly assent; although I do not reject the other sense, namely, that their alienation from God had rendered them ignominious, or that they had contracted the stain of disgrace by their faithlessness.

6. *Do ye thus requite the Lord.* In order to expose the ingratitude of the people to greater infamy, he now begins to commemorate the benefits whereby God had laid them under obligation to Himself: for the more liberally God deals with us, the more earnest ought to be the piety awakened in our hearts; nay, His goodness, as soon as we have tasted of it, ought to draw us at once to Him. Now God, although He has been always bountiful towards the whole human race, had, in a peculiar manner showered down an immense abundance of His bounty upon that people; this, then, Moses alleges, and shews how basely ungrateful they had been. He first expostulates with them interrogatively, asking them whether this was a fitting return for God's especial blessings; and then proceeds to enumerate them. He inquires of them, then, whether God was not their father, from the time when He had honoured them with the distinction of His adoption: and under this single head he comprehends many things, because from this source proceeded whatever blessings God had conferred upon them. Not, however, to examine every point with the accuracy it deserves, what more binding obligation could be imagined than that God should have chosen one nation for Himself out of the whole world, whose father He should be by special privilege? For, although all human beings, since they were created in the image of God, are sometimes called His children, still to be accounted His children was the special privilege of the sons of Abraham. And, in order to prove that this was not a natural, but an acquired dignity, Moses immediately afterwards explains in what way God was their Father: viz., that He purchased, made, and prepared them. The foundation and origin, then, was the gratuitous good pleasure of God, when He took them to be His own pecu-

[1] Added from the *Fr.*

culiar people. Elsewhere, indeed, His second purchase of them is mentioned, when He redeemed them from Egypt; here, however, Moses goes back farther, viz., to the covenant made with Abraham, whereby they were separated from other nations, as will presently more clearly appear. I reject, as not in harmony with the context, the translation which some give of the word קנה, *kanah*, i.e, *to possess*.[1]

In the same sense it is added, that they were *made* by God: which does not refer to the general creation, but only to the privilege of adoption, whereby they became God's new work, and in which another form was imparted to them; in which sense also He is called their framer, or Maker. Elsewhere, also, when the Prophet says, "Know ye that the Lord he is God: it is he that hath made us, and not we ourselves," (Ps. c. 3,) he undoubtedly magnifies that special prerogative, whereby God had distinguished the sons of Abraham above all other races. For, since the fall of Adam had brought disgrace upon all his posterity, God restores those, whom He separates as His own, so that their condition may be better than that of all other nations. At the same time it must be remarked, that this grace of renewal is effaced in many who have afterwards profaned it. Consequently the Church is called God's work and creation, in two senses, *i.e.*, generally with respect to its outward calling, and specially with respect to spiritual regeneration, as far as regards the elect; for the covenant of grace is common to hypocrites and true believers. On this ground all whom God gathers into His Church, are indiscriminately said to be renewed and regenerated: but the internal renovation belongs to believers only; whom Paul, therefore, calls God's "workmanship, created unto good works, which God hath prepared," &c. (Eph. ii. 10.) The same is the tendency of the third word, which may, however, be taken for to "establish;"[2] although I have preferred to follow the more received sense, viz, that God had prepared His people, as the artificer fashions and fits his work.

[1] *S. M.* has rendered this word *possessed*. *A.V.* agrees more nearly with *C.* in rendering it *bought*.—*W.*

[2] So in *A.V.*, which Ainsworth follows; but explains, "formed, fitted, and ordered, firm and stable, that thou mightest abide in his grace."

7. *Remember the days of old.* This is an explanation of the preceding verse, for Moses again shews how God had acquired this people, viz., because He had chosen to separate them from other nations according to His own good pleasure. But, since the Israelites might be inflated by their present superiority, they are reminded of their origin, and Moses commands them not to consider what they now are, but also from whence they had been taken, and with this view he says, Remember the old times; ask the elders, &c. For we know how men, when they do not reflect that whatever they have, proceeded from God, and is held, as it were, at will, are blinded by their dignity, so as not only to despise others, but also to exalt themselves against the Author of all good things. Moses, in order to subdue this arrogance, says that all peoples were alike under the hand and power of God, and thus that their diversity was not in their original nature, but derived from elsewhere, *i.e.*, from God's free choice. In the word בהנחל, *behanchel,* there is some ambiguity: for some translate it, When the Most High divided the earth to the nations; and, though I do not reject this, still I have preferred the meaning more in accordance with the context;[1] for Moses says the same thing twice over, and the second clause is the explanation of the first. He says, therefore, that God *distributed* the nations, as an inheritance is divided; and then this is more clearly repeated, when he mentions the separation of the sons of Adam. When, in the latter part of the verse, it is said, that He set bounds to the nations according to the number of the children of Israel, it is commonly explained that He set bounds to the nations in such sort, that the habitation of the sons of Abraham was secured to them. Some of the Hebrews take it in a more restricted sense, viz., that in the distribution of the world, so much was given to the seven nations of Canaan as should be sufficient for the children of Israel. In my opinion, however, his meaning is, that in the whole arrangement of the world, the object which God had in view was to

[1] Ver. 8. *C.*'s application of this expression, בהנחל, can scarcely be deemed admissible; for נחל does not mean to divide, unless with reference to an inheritance, or, at least, to property.—*W.*

provide for His elect people: for, although His bounty extended to all, still He had such regard for His own, that, chiefly on their account, His care also extended to others. The word *number* is expressly employed; as if Moses had said, that, however small a portion of the human race the posterity of Abraham might be, nevertheless that number was before God's eyes, when He ordered the state of the whole world; unless it be preferred to take the word מספר, *misphar*,[1] for a *ratio;* but it will not be unsuitable to the passage to understand it that this small body was so precious to God, that he arranged the whole distribution of the world with a view to their welfare. Some refer it to the calling of the Gentiles, as if Moses had said that the empire of the whole world was destined to the seed of Abraham, because it was to be propagated through all the regions of the world; but this is altogether erroneous, for nothing is here indicated but the distinction, formerly conferred upon one nation.[2]

9. *For the Lord's portion is his people.* This is the main point, that God was moved by nothing but His own good pleasure to make so much of this people, who had been derived from a common origin with all others: for when he says, that Jacob was the portion of Jehovah, and the lot of His inheritance, he does not mean that there was anything better in them than in others, but he assigns the reason why God preferred this one nation to the rest of mankind; viz., because He took it to Himself as His hereditary portion, which dignity depends upon His gratuitous election.

10. He found him in a desert land, and in the waste howling wilderness: he led him about, he instructed him, he kept him as the apple of his eye.

11. As an eagle stirreth up her nest, fluttereth over her young, spreadeth abroad her wings, taketh them, beareth them on her wings;

10. Invenit eum in terra deserti, et in vastitate horroris deserti: circunduxit eum, introduxit eum, custodivit eum, ut pupillam oculi sui.

11. Ut aquila quæ excitat nidum suum, super pullos suos cubat, expandit alas suas, assumit eum, portando super alas suas.

[1] A noun *hœmantic:* like our word *tale*, as used in Milton's time, and *account*, as still used, it may either mean a narrative, or an enumeration, or a number, which is the result of an enumeration.—*W.* I have not ventured to translate *C.'s* very ambiguous word *ratio.* In the *Fr.* it is "Façon ou regle."

[2] "La distinction du peuple eleu d'avec les autres nations, du temps qu'ils estoyent comme retranchez de l'Eglise;" the distinction of the elect people from the other nations, from the time when these last were, as it were, cut off from the Church."—*Fr.*

12. *So* the Lord alone did lead him, and *there was* no strange god with him.

12. Jehova solus deduxit eum, et non fuit cum illo deus alienigenæ.

13. He made him ride on the high places of the earth, that he might eat the increase of the fields; and he made him to suck honey out of the rock, and oil out of the flinty rock;

13. Equitare fecit eum super excelsa terræ, et comedit fructus agri, et fecit ut sugeret mel è petra, et oleum è silice petræ.

14. Butter of kine, and milk of sheep, with fat of lambs, and rams of the breed of Bashan, and goats, with the fat of kidneys of wheat; and thou didst drink the pure blood of the grape.

14. Butyrum bovis, et lac ovium, cum adipe agnorum, et arietes filios Basan, et hircos una cum adipe granorum tritici, et sanguinem uvæ bibisti rubicundum.

15. But Jeshurun waxed fat, and kicked: thou art waxen fat, thou art grown thick, thou art covered *with fatness:* then he forsook God *which* made him, and lightly esteemed the Rock of his salvation.

15. Et impinguatus est Rectus, et recalcitravit: impinguatus es, incrassatus es, operuisti: et dereliquit Deum qui fecit eum, ac despexit Deum salutem suam.

16. They provoked him to jealousy with strange *gods*, with abominations provoked they him to anger.

16. Provocaverunt eum ad zelum super extraneos, per abominationes irritaverunt eum.

17. They sacrificed unto devils, not to God; to gods whom they knew not, to new *gods that* came newly up, whom your fathers feared not.

17. Sacrificaverunt dæmoniis, non Deo, diis quos non noverant, novis qui de propinquo venerunt quos non timuerunt patres vestri.

18. Of the Rock *that* begat thee thou art unmindful, and hast forgotten God that formed thee.

18. Dei qui genuit te, oblitus es, oblitus es, inquam, Dei qui creavit te.

10. *He found him in a desert land.* If the intention of Moses had been to record all the instances of God's paternal kindness towards the people, he must have commenced from the time of Abraham; like the prophet who, when presenting a complete narrative in the Psalm, begins from that original covenant, which God had made with the fathers, (Ps. cv. 8;) and also introduces the benefits which He had conferred upon them, when they were but few in number, and strangers in the land, when they went from one nation to another, yet He suffered no man to do them wrong, and reproved kings for their sakes. (Ps. cv. 14.) But Moses, studying brevity, deemed it sufficient to bring forward a more recent and more notorious blessing; nay, he omits the early part of their deliverance, and only makes mention of the desert. He says, then, that God *found them in the de-*

sert; not because He then first began to take pity upon them, since they had been previously rescued from the tyranny of Pharaoh by His marvellous power, and had passed the Red Sea dry-shod, but because it was profitable for them to have set before their eyes how they had been extricated from the deep abyss of death, in order that they might more readily acknowledge this to have been, as it were, the beginning of their life. For what was that waste and barren desert, in which not a crumb of bread, nor a drop of water was to be found, but a grave to swallow up a thousand lives? and, therefore, it is further called "the devastation of horror."[1] The sum is, that it was a kind of type of resurrection, not from one death only, but from innumerable deaths, that the people should have escaped from it in safety. That they should have done so, even had their march through it been straight and speedy, could not have been the case without a miracle; but, inasmuch as they wandered therein for forty years, our minds can hardly comprehend a hundredth part of the miracles (which followed one upon the other.[2]) Thus the word "led about," is not superfluous, for God's power was far more conspicuous than as if they had flown swiftly through the air. I apply the same meaning to what follows, "he instructed him;" for some, in my opinion improperly, refer it to the Law,[3] whereas it rather relates to the teaching of experience. For there was manifold, and no ordinary instruction in all these acts of bounty and punishment, wherein God, as it were, put forth His hand, and manifested His glory.

Two similitudes follow, to express God's love, mingled with solicitude more than paternal. First, he says, that God no less anxiously protected them from all injury and annoyance than every one is wont to protect the pupil of his eye, which is the most tender part of the body, and against the injury of which the greatest precautions are taken. And David also, when requesting that he may be kept safe under the

[1] "The waste howling wilderness."—*A. V.* "Un lieu vague où il n'y avoit qu'horreur, ou hurlement;" a waste place, in which there was nothing but horror or howling.—*Fr.*

[2] Added from *Fr.*

[3] "He taught them the words of his law."—*Chaldee.*

special guardianship of God, uses the same expression. (Ps. xvii. 8.) Secondly, God compares Himself to an eagle, which not only fosters her young ones under her outspread wings, but also indulgently, and with maternal tenderness tempts them to fly. It would be unseasonable to enter here into more subtle philosophical discussions respecting the nature of the eagle. The Jews, who are wont to trifle hazardously with things they do not understand, have invented fables respecting this passage, which have no relation to the meaning of Moses, who unquestionably spoke of the eagle as he might of any other bird. Nor can it be doubted but that Christ, when He compares Himself to a hen, desired to express the same sedulous care. "How often (He says) would I have gathered thy children together, even as a hen gathereth her chickens under her wings, and ye would not!" (Matt. xxiii. 37.) If, however, any should choose to apply here, what Aristotle writes respecting the eagle, I would not stand in his way: although I do not think Moses had anything in his mind, beyond what the words naturally express. And, surely that which at once occurs to us ought to be sufficient for us, viz., that we ought to be ravished with just admiration of God's inestimable goodness and indulgence, when He condescends so to stoop to us as to protect us with His wings, like a bird, and, hovering before us, to instruct and accustom us to follow Him: in which latter words a more than maternal anxiety to teach us is represented.

12. *So the Lord alone did lead him.* This is spoken by anticipation, in order to take away every pretext from the Israelites, provided they should seek, according to their custom, to mingle their superstitions with the pure service of God. For, when they were bringing in, from all quarters, gods of various nations, this was the excuse they commonly made, that God was not thus despoiled of His due honour: and hence it came to pass, that they permitted themselves to heap together a multitude of false gods, whom they worshipped as their patrons. But Moses anticipates them, and declares that God, as having no need of external aid, had not associated with Himself any strange gods in His pre-

servation of the people. Hence it follows, that whatever gods the people introduced, they transferred to them the honour due to the one true God. Let us then learn from this passage, that, unless God be served without a rival, religion is altogether perverted by the impious admixture.

13. *He made him ride on the high places.* Theirs is but a frivolous imagination, who suppose that Judea was so called as being the navel or centre of the earth ;[1] it is more likely that it was called *high* in reference to Egypt ; and, indeed, it is by no means an unusual expression, that those who go into Egypt, are said to go down, and those who come into Judea to come up. Still I am rather disposed to think that by *height* he denotes its excellency ; inasmuch as that land, on account of its illustrious endowments, was, as it were, the most noble theatre in the world.

Moses celebrates its fertility, when he says that the people *sucked honey from the rock and oil from the stones :* for he means to indicate, that no part of it was unproductive, since they gathered honey from the rocks, and upon them also the olive grew. The same is the intention of the other figures, that they ate " butter of kine, and milk of sheep ;" by which he signifies that the land was full of rich pastures. By " fat of lambs," he undoubtedly means the plumpness of their flesh, because it was not lawful to eat their actual fat ; but it is not unusual to denote by this word any kind of richness, as soon afterwards he calls the best meal or flour, from which the more delicate kind of bread was made, " the fat of wheat." With respect to the wine, he magnifies God's liberality by the use of a poetic figure, when he says they *drank of the blood of the grape.* There is no doubt but that he alludes to its colour ; yet he takes occasion to extol more highly the beneficence of God, by intimating that, when the juice of the grapes is expressed, it is just as if their blood flowed forth for the nutriment of men. Since, then, the metaphor is taken from the redness of wine, I have not hesitated to translate the epithet חמר, *chamer*, at the

[1] " In summa parte orbis, quòd Terra Sancta sit in medio climate mundi."—Vatablus, in Poole's Synopsis.

end of the verse, *red.*[1] From many passages it appears to have been very delicious; and in Isaiah (xxvii. 2) the word חמר, *chamer*, is used for a vine of great preciousness and of exquisite flavour. Those who render it *pure*, have rather taken into consideration the fact, than the signification of the word.

15. *But Jeshurun*[2] *waxed fat.* Moses here severely censures the ingratitude of the people, because when filled with delicacies, they began to wax wanton against God; for, according to the vulgar proverb, satiety breeds violence; but this arises from men's detestable depravity, who ought rather to be inclined to humility and gentleness by the loving-kindness of God, since the more abundantly He supplies us with food, the more does He invite us to shew forth the affection that becomes children, inasmuch as He thus more closely and familiarly declares Himself to be our Father. Intolerable, then, is the impiety of profane persons, who increase in insolence against Him, when they have gorged themselves with an abundance of all good things. They are here compared to restive horses, which, if they are well fed, without exercise, kick under their rider, and are rendered almost intractable. By using the word "upright" for Israel, he ironically taunts them with having departed from rectitude, and, reminding them of the high dignity conferred upon them, more severely reproves their sin of unfaithfulness. For elsewhere[3] Israel is honoured with the same title without any evil imputation in respect to their calling; but here Moses reproachfully shews them how far they had departed from the pursuit of that piety, to the cultivation of which they had been called.

[1] It may either mean *red* or *effervescing;* it is not easy to see why *A. V.* renders it *pure.—W.*

[2] *Lat.*, "Rectus." See next note.

[3] This word ישרון, *yeshurun*, occurs only here, and in chap. xxxiii. 5, 26, and Isa. xliv. 2. Commentators appear to be by no means agreed as to its derivation or meaning,—variously rendering it, *the upright; the beloved; the fortunate; the abounding; the seer of God*, &c. Singularly enough, *C.* himself, in his Commentary on Isaiah, (*C. Soc. Edit.* vol. iii., p. 359,) gives the following contradictory opinion: "This designation is also bestowed upon that nation by Moses in his song: for although some render it in that passage Upright, and in this passage also, the old rendering is more suitable, "My beloved is grown fat." (Deut. xxxii. 15.)

16. *They provoked him to jealousy.* It is only figuratively that jealousy is attributed to God, who is free from all passions; but, since men never sufficiently reflect how great pollution they contract by their idolatries, it is necessary that the grossness of the sin should be expressed in such terms as this, implying that men do no less injury to God, when they transfer to others the honour due to Him, and that the offence is no lighter than as if a licentious woman should provoke her husband's mind to jealousy, and inflict a wound upon him by running after adulterers. This jealousy has reference to the sacred and spiritual marriage, whereby God had bound His people to Himself. The sum is, that the Israelites were as insulting to God by their superstitions as if they had designedly provoked Him.

In the next verse an amplification follows, viz., that they had transferred to devils the worship due to God alone. By the general consent of all nations God ought to be worshipped by sacrifices; for, although the Gentiles invented for themselves divers gods, still the persuasion continued to prevail, that this service was the peculiar prerogative of Deity. Nothing, then, could be more disgraceful or detestable than to rob God of His honour, and to offer it to demons. This, indeed, would never have been admitted by the Israelites, inasmuch as they pretended that their minor gods were their advocates with the supreme and only Creator of the world, and did not hesitate to account as rendered to Him whatever they shared among their idols. Here, however, He first of all repudiates all such mixtures whereby His holy name is unworthily profaned, and suffers Himself not to be associated with idols; and, secondly, by whatever titles they may dignify their idols, He declares all false gods to be demons. Hence it follows that the sacrifices made to them are infected with sacrilege. Both of these points are worthy of careful remark, viz., that God abominates all corruptions of His service; and also, that whatever names the world may invent for its gods, they are so many masks, under which the devil hides himself for the deception of the simple.

Furthermore, Moses reproves the folly of the Israelites in

having promiscuously devoted themselves to unknown gods; just as an adulterous woman might prostitute herself indiscriminately to all comers. When he says that they came *from near*,[1] it has reference to time, and is equivalent to saying that they had lately sprung up. Thirdly, it is said, that these gods were not honoured by their fathers; for thus their perverse love of novelty is proved against them, inasmuch as they had not been even led by imitation of their fathers, but in their restless innovation had procured for themselves new and unwonted gods. Not that the law of piety is founded on antiquity alone, as if it were sufficient to follow the customs handed down by our ancestors; for thus any of the religions of the Gentiles might be proved true, but because the genuine and faithful tradition of *their* fathers would be the sure and approved rule for the worship of God. For Moses assumes a higher principle, viz., that their fathers were truly and most unmistakably instructed who was the one and only God, in whom alone they ought to trust. Yet a distinction is here to be drawn between these holy fathers and the reprobate; for the imitation of their fathers, which here seems to be deemed praiseworthy, is elsewhere severely condemned, because the Jews were carried away, without discrimination, after the bad examples of their fathers. Moses, therefore, here refers to no other fathers than those who were in a position to hand down what they had learned from God Himself. The word *fear* often comprises, by synecdoche, the whole service of God, and sometimes is applied to outward ceremonies: the word שער, *sagnar*, however, is here used, which means properly to *stand in awe of*, or *to dread*;[2] but still in the same sense.

18. *Of the Rock*[3] *that begat thee.* He again aggravates the criminality of the people by referring to their ingratitude, inasmuch as they did not fall through ignorance,

[1] *A.V.*, "newly." *Lat.*, "è propinquo."

[2] In the editions of Geneva, 1563 and 1573, *C.* is made to say, that this word is equivalent to "*formare*, vel *pavere*;" the former being probably a misprint for *reformidare*.—*W*. The *Fr.* renders the words "Redouter, ou avoir peur."

[3] *Lat.*, "of the God," &c.

but wilfully stifled that knowledge of God, which ought to have shone brightly in all their hearts: for this is the effect of the reproach, that they were *unmindful of their Rock:* as much as to say, that they would never have given themselves up to their impious superstitions, unless they had cast into voluntary oblivion that God whom, by the most conspicuous proofs, they had experimentally found to be the foundation and support of their salvation.

19. And when the Lord saw *it,* he abhorred *them,* because of the provoking of his sons and of his daughters.

20. And he said, I will hide my face from them, I will see what their end *shall be:* for they *are* a very froward generation, children in whom *is* no faith.

21. They have moved me to jealousy with *that which is* not God; they have provoked me to anger with their vanities: and I will move them to jealousy with *those which are* not a people; I will provoke them to anger with a foolish nation.

22. For a fire is kindled in mine anger, and shall burn unto the lowest hell, and shall consume the earth with her increase, and set on fire the foundations of the mountains.

23. I will heap mischiefs upon them; I will spend mine arrows upon them.

24. *They shall be* burnt with hunger, and devoured with burning heat, and with bitter destruction: I will also send the teeth of beasts upon them, with the poison of serpents of the dust.

25. The sword without, and terror within, shall destroy both the young man and the virgin, the suckling *also,* with the man of gray hairs.

26. I said, I would scatter them into corners, I would make the remembrance of them to cease from among men:

27. Were it not that I feared the wrath of the enemy, lest their adversaries should behave themselves

19. Quum autem vidisset Jehova, exacerbatus est irritatione filiorum et filiarum suarum.

20. Et dixit, Abscondam faciem meam ab eis, Videbo quid in novissimo eorum: generatio enim perversitatum sunt: et filii in quibus nulla est fides.

21. Ipsi ad zelum provocaverunt me, in eo quod non est Deus, ad iracundiam me provocaverunt in vanitatibus suis: et ego ad zelum provocabo eos in eo qui non est populus: in gente stulta provocabo eos ad iram.

22. Ignis enim succendetur in excandescentia mea, et ardebit usque ad infernum inferiorem: devorabitque terram et fructum ejus, et inflammabit fundamenta montium.

23. Cumulabo super eos mala, sagittas meas consumam in eis.

24. Combusti erunt fame, et comesti ægritudine calida, et excisione amara: dentes quoque bestiarum immittam in eos cum veneno serpentium super terram.

25. Foris orbabit gladius, et in cubiculis erit terror: etiam juvenem, etiam virginem, lactentem cum viro sene.

26. Dicerem, Dispergam eos per angulos, cessare faciam ex hominibus memoriam eorum.

27. Nisi iram inimici timerem, ne forte alienos se ostentent hostes eorum: ne forte dicant, Manus nos-

strangely, *and* lest they should say, Our hand *is* high, and the Lord hath not done all this.	tra excelsa, neque Jehova operatus est omnia ista.

19. *And when the Lord saw it.* The *seeing* of God, which is mentioned here, has reference to His forbearance in judgment: as if it were said, that He does not act hastily, and is not alienated from His children, without having duly weighed their case; in the same way as it is said elsewhere: "Because the cry of Sodom is great, I will go down now and see whether" it is so, and "I will know." (Gen. xviii. 20, 21.) Assuredly God has no need to make any examination, since nothing escapes His eyes, however hidden it may be; but this going down and inquiring is contrasted with preposterous haste. Thus in this passage Moses shews that God was wroth, when he saw His sons and His daughters drawn away so faithlessly after their idols. Again, when he calls them God's children, he does not judge them to be so on account of their merits, but in reference to God's adoption, which, although it was cancelled as regarded themselves, still had the effect of aggravating the guilt of their ingratitude. And for the same reason that he had just said that God *saw* them, Moses introduces Him deliberating, as it were, that the time for punishing them might be perceived to be fully come. But we must notice the degrees; for God does not at once break forth into extreme severity, but is said to *hide His face,* that He might secretly consider what they would do: since this is a middle course between the manifest exhibition of His grace and favour, and the tokens of His wrath. God is, indeed, elsewhere said, in many passages, to hide His face, when He rejects men's prayers, and withdraws His aid; but here He assumes the character of a man who, when he sees that he produces no effect by acting,[1] goes aside to some place, from whence he may quietly contemplate the result. And thus God's weariness of them is expressed; for when He at length saw that His efforts to control them were thrown away, He abandoned the care of them. It is a false inference, which some draw from hence,

[1] "Voyant qu'il ne profite rien en advertissant son ami qu'il se pert;' seeing that he does not at all profit his friend by warning him against self-destruction.—*Fr.*

that men, when forsaken by God, recover themselves by the exercise of their own free-will; as if God sat calmly and inactively in a watch-tower expecting what they may do; inasmuch as this *hiding* of Himself has reference only to the outward manifestation of His grace. In a word, it is a similitude taken from the conduct of men, whereby God signifies that He is overcome with weariness, and will no more be the leader and guardian of the people, until it shall effectually appear that they are altogether intractable. And this is gathered from the reason, which is presently added, wherein He censures their froward nature and want of faith, as much as to say, that, after long trial, nothing remained for Him but to abandon them.

21. *They have moved me to jealousy.* He now proceeds further, viz., that God, after having withdrawn Himself for a time, would, at length be the open enemy of the people, so as to repay them in kind. And he points out the mode of this retaliation, that as they had insultingly brought into antagonism with God empty phantoms and vanities, so on His part, He would exalt against them barbarous and worthless nations. This similitude is also taken from jealous husbands, who, when they perceive themselves to be despised by their adulterous wives, avenge themselves by their own amours. Why God should attribute to Himself the feeling of jealousy has been explained under the Second Commandment; Moses now only shews that it would be a most equitable mode of revenge, that God should insult, by means of despised and ignoble nations, those apostates, who had made to themselves idols in disparagement of Him.

The fulfilment of this sentence was manifested from time to time, when they were tyrannically oppressed by the neighbouring nations. It is true, indeed, that the Egyptians, the Assyrians, and the Chaldeans were included among those people of nought and foolish nations, although they were pre-eminent in power and wealth, and famous for other splendid endowments; but it is no matter of surprise that, in comparison with that dignity which God had conferred upon the Israelites, all other nations should be accounted but refuse. The sum is, that God's vengeance was ready whereby He would punish the vanities of His people, inasmuch as He could create out of nothing the enemies by whom they should be reduced to nothing. There is much elegance in the allusion of Paul, in which he extends this sentence further, inasmuch as, when God introduced the Gentiles into His Church, He stirred up the Jews to jealousy, in order that they might be led to repentance by a sense of their ignominy. Surely the calling of the Gentiles was exactly as if He created shadows, whom he might prefer to His reprobate people. (Rom. x. 19.)

22. *For a fire is kindled in mine anger.* He confirms what went before, but more generally; for He compares His anger to a burning fire, which should penetrate to the deepest abysses, and should utterly consume their land, so as not to spare the very roots of the mountains. This metaphor is, indeed, of frequent occurrence; but here more is expressed by it than in other passages. In the same sense also it is presently added, that God would spend all his scourges and arrows upon them; since, when His implacable anger is once aroused, there are no bounds to His severity. The verb אספה, *aspheh,* may, however, also be taken for to *heap,* or to *superadd;*[1] but I willingly follow the more received interpretation, viz., that God will not omit anything to destroy them, as if He would apply to this purpose all weapons which were at hand.

24. *They shall be burnt with hunger.* He now descends to some particular modes of punishment, not, indeed, to enumerate them all, but only to adduce such specimens of them as to inspire the people with greater terror, inasmuch as mere generalities would not have sufficiently affected them. He mentions three especial scourges, pestilence, famine, and the sword, on which the prophets constantly dilate, when their object was to apply the Law to the actual use of the people, from whence it arose that they familiarly employ many of the expressions used by Moses. He introduces indeed other

[1] It will be seen that *C.* translates both the verbs in this verse, אספה *aspheh,* and אכלה, *acalleh,* by the same word, *consumam;* whilst *A.V.* renders the first *I will heap,* and the latter, *I will spend;* in accordance with the view of Ainsworth, Marckius, and Dathe.

punishments, which the prophets also mention ; but the sum of what he says is this, that the Israelites should feel that God was armed with all the punishments which were only too well known by experience, and by them would utterly destroy them.

First, he says, that they should be dried up, or rather roasted with hunger.[1] Instead of pestilence he uses the words *burning* (*uredinem*,) and *bitter destruction :* and before he speaks of the sword, declares that He would send forth *beasts* and *serpents*, so that on the one hand, open violence should assail them, and, on the other, secret wiles. Amos has also imitated this figure: "The day of the Lord (he says) is darkness and not light: as if a man did flee from a lion and a bear met him ; or went into the house, and leaned his hand on the wall, and a serpent bit him." (Amos v. 18, 19.)

To war, and the cruelty of enemies he adds another evil, viz., *terror :* and this is, indeed, an aggravation worse than death itself, when we tremble within with terror, for it would be better to be slain ten times over bravely fighting in battle, than to be consumed with constant fear, as by a lingering death.[2]

Let us learn, then, from this passage, that, whatever perils surround us, and whatever adversities, they are God's weapons, and that they do not occur by chance to this or that person, but are directed by His hand. Thus it is the case that He not only stirs up enemies against us, but fierce and noisome beasts also ; that He shuts up the heaven and the earth ; that He infects the atmosphere with deadly disease ; that, in a word, He draws forth from all the elements manifold means of destruction.

But if it be the fact, that the godly are involved in similar punishments, since they suffer from hunger and want,

[1] Professor Liebig has pointed out the dreadful fact, in singular confirmation of the expression here employed by Moses, that "when a person is starved to death, he is, in fact, slowly burnt, as, during the process of starvation, a slow combustion of the body takes place."

[2] Un accessoire pire que toutes les morts du monde, quand nous maigrissons et sommes minez de frayeur ;" an aggravation worse than all the deaths in the world, when we are wasted away, and preyed upon by fear. —*Fr.*

and are not exempt from any evil; for even Paul acknowledges that he had himself experienced what God here denounces against those that wickedly despise Him, for he says that he was *troubled without* with *fightings*, and *within* with *fears*, (2 Cor. vii. 5;) we must bear in mind that all adversities are in themselves signs of God's wrath, since they derive their origin from sin; but that through God's marvellous provision it comes to pass, that to believers they are exercises of their faith and proofs of their patience. Hence we often see God's children afflicted in common with the ungodly, but to a different end; though nevertheless all adversities are proofs of God's wrath against the reprobate. On this point I have spoken at greater length in treating of the curses of the Law.

26. *I said, I would scatter them.* God again represents Himself in the character of a man, as if He were meditating opposite determinations, and restrained His vehemence in consideration of the impediments He encountered. What it amounts to, however, is this, that God suspended His final judgment upon them for no other reason but because He had regard to His own glory, which would else have been subjected to the taunts of the Gentiles. Hence the Jews were reminded that, whereas they had deserved certain destruction, they were preserved on no other grounds but because God was unwilling to give the reins to the insolence of the Gentiles. The expression *wrath*, is here used for arrogant boasting, because in their prosperity ungodly and profane men burst forth into cruelty; unless it be preferred to render it simply *irritation*,[1] in which sense it is used in 2 Kings xxiii. Immediately afterwards it is explained, "lest the adversaries should behave themselves strangely." נכר, *nacar*, signifies sometimes to be strange, sometimes to put on a different face, sometimes to acknowledge. Thus I do not doubt but that Moses meant to express the arrogance of those who in a manner transform themselves that they may dazzle the eyes of the simple by their pomp and empty exaltation. If any approve of a different sense, *i.e.*, lest they

[1] *Hebr.*, כעס, *cagnas*, used in the plural number in 2 Kings xxiii. 26, and translated in *A.V. provocations;* margin, "*Heb.* angers."

should separate themselves from God, and arrogate to themselves what belongs to Him alone, I make no objection: and this, indeed, seems to agree with what follows,[1] "Our high hand, and not the Lord, has done this:" for when men indulge in such unbridled license, they go so far astray as to have nothing in common with God. Thus the judgment of God, which should have been conspicuous in these punishments, would have been put out of sight, when the enemies appropriated to themselves the glory of the people's destruction. Nevertheless the ungodly did not cease to pride themselves on their victories, (as God complains by Isaiah, and Habakkuk confirms;)[2] although their insolence was in some measure repressed, as long as there were some remnants of the elect people preserved.[3]

It is only figuratively that God says, He feared this insolence, which He might have easily remedied and restrained: but I have already stated, that He speaks after the manner of men, to shew the Israelites that they escaped rather on account of their enemies, than by their own merits. The question, however, arises, how such a consultation as this could have taken place after God had determined to *consume* them with the fire of His wrath;[4] I reply, that the *consumption* there indicated was not such as totally to annihilate the nation, so that no ruins should remain as witnesses of their former state; whereas He now speaks of the destruction, which should altogether blot out the name of the nation, as if it had never been chosen by God.

28. For they *are* a nation void of counsel, neither *is there any* understanding in them.	28. Gens enim perdita consiliis sunt, nec est illis intelligentia.
29. Oh that they were wise, *that* they understood this, *that* they would consider their latter end!	29. Si sapientes essent, intelligerent novissimum suum.
30. How should one chase a	30. Quomodo persequutus fuisset

[1] See Margin, *A. V.*

[2] The references in the original to both these passages are obviously incorrect; it is probable, however, that Marckius *in loco* supplies them aright, viz., Isa. x. 12, 13, &c. and Hab. i. 16, 17.

[3] "Quand il y est tousjours demeuré quelque reserve du peuple eleu;" since some remains of the elect people always existed.—*Fr.*

[4] See *ante* on ver 23.

thousand, and two put ten thousand to flight, except their Rock had sold them, and the Lord had shut them up?

unus mille, et duo fugassent decem millia, nisi quod Deus eorum vendisset eos, et Jehova tradidisset eos?

31. For their rock *is* not as our Rock, even our enemies themselves *being* judges.

31. Nam non est sicut Deus noster, Deus illorum: et inimici nostri sunt judices.

32. For their vine *is* of the vine of Sodom, and of the fields of Gomorrah: their grapes *are* grapes of gall, their clusters *are* bitter:

32. Ex vite enim Sodom est vitis eorum, et ex vitibus Emorrhæorum uvæ eorum, uvæ veneni, botri amaritudinum sunt eis.

33. Their wine *is* the poison of dragons, and the cruel venom of asps.

33. Venenum draconum, vinum eorum: et venenum aspidum crudele.

34. *Is* not this laid up in store with me, *and* sealed up among my treasures?

34. Nonne est reconditum apud me, obsignatum in thesauris meis?

35. To me *belongeth* vengeance and recompence: their foot shall slide in *due* time: for the day of their calamity *is* at hand, and the things that shall come upon them make haste.

35. Mea est ultio, et retributio, tempore nutabit pes eorum: quia propinquus est dies afflictionis eorum, et festinant quæ futura sunt eis.

36. For the Lord shall judge his people, and repent himself for his servants, when he seeth that *their* power is gone, and *there is* none shut up, or left.

36. Quia judicabit Jehova populum suum, et super servos suos pœnitebit ipsum, quum videbit quod abierit manus, et non sit clausus et derelictus.

28. *For they are a nation void of counsel.* The cause is assigned why God had almost blotted out altogether the memory of the people, viz., because their fatuity was incurable: for He does not merely indicate that their conduct was rash and inconsiderate, because they lacked reason and discretion: but that they could be by no means brought to their senses, and, in fact, that not one drop of sagacity existed in them. The proof of this immediately follows, viz., that the tokens of God's wrath were too clearly set before their eyes to escape their notice, unless they were utterly blind and stupid. The word לו, *lu,* which they render, "Would that"[1] (*utinam,*) denotes commiseration rather than desire; and therefore it may be properly translated, "Oh, if they understood," &c.

By the expression, "latter," their exceeding stupidity is censured: since not even by many and long experiences were they aroused to reflect on the causes of their calamities;

[1] So *S.M.* "O that."—*A.V.*

whereas length of time extorts some sense at last from the very dullest, and almost idiotic persons. It was, therefore, a sign of desperate stupidity that they were still without understanding after so many years; as if by experience itself they had grown callous, when they ought to have shaken off their lethargy, and to have bestirred themselves to earnest inquiry. Justly, then, does Moses reproach them with not having considered even at the latter end; for not once only, nor in a single year, but by constant inflictions of punishment during a long series of years, had they been instructed without profit.

30. *How should one chase a thousand.* Of all the many tokens of God's wrath, he selects one which was peculiarly striking; for as long as God was on their side, they had put to flight mighty armies, nor had they been supported by any multitude of forces. Now, when, though in great numbers, they are conquered by a few, this change plainly shews that they are deprived of God's aid, especially when a thousand, who were wont before, with a little band, to rout the greatest armies, gave way before ten men. Moses, therefore, condemns the stupidity of the people, in that it does not occur to their minds that they are rejected by God, when they are so easily overcome by a few enemies, whom they far exceed in numbers. Moses, however, goes still further, and says, that they were *sold* and *betrayed*;[1] inasmuch as God, having so often found them to be unworthy of His aid, not only deserted them, but made them subject to heathen nations, and, as it were, sold them to be their slaves. This threat is often repeated by the prophets: and Isaiah, desiring to awake in them a hope of deliverance, tells them that God would redeem the people whom He had sold.[2] But, in case any should object that it was no matter of wonder, if the uncertain chance of war should confer on others the victory which often, as a profane poet says,

[1] " Shut them up."—*A. V.*

[2] The reference is here generally to Isa. lii. Ver. 3, however, to which *C.* probably alludes, hardly bears out the statement in the text: " Ye have *sold yourselves* for nought, &c. The *Fr.* stands thus, " Isaie, en parlant du retour de la captivité de Babylone, dit que Dieu rachetera le peuple qu'il a vendu."

"Hovers between the two on doubtful wings,"[1]

Moses anticipates the objection by declaring that, unless the people should be deprived of God's aid, they could not be otherwise than successful. A comparison is therefore instituted between the true God and false gods: as though Moses had said that, where the God of hosts presides, the issue of war can never be doubtful. Hence it follows, that God's elect and peculiar people are exempted from the ordinary condition of nations, except in so far as it deserves to be rejected on the score of its ingratitude. He calls the unbelievers themselves to be the arbiters and witnesses of this, inasmuch as they had often experienced the formidable power of God, and knew assuredly that the God of Israel was unlike their idols. It is, then, just as if he had said, that this was conspicuous even to the blind, or were to cite as witnesses those who are blessed with no light from on high. In thus inviting unbelievers to be judges, it is not as if he supposed that they would pronounce what was true, and thoroughly understood by them, but because they must needs be convinced by experience: for, if any one had asked the heathen whether the supreme government and power of heaven and earth were in the hands of the One God of Israel, they never would have confessed that their idols were mere vanity. Still, however malignantly they might detract from God's glory, Moses does not hesitate to boast, even themselves being judges, that God had magnificently exerted His unconquered might; although he refers rather to the experience of facts themselves, than to their feelings. Other commentators extract a different meaning, viz., that although unbelievers might be victorious, still God remained unaffected by it: neither was his arm broken, because He permitted them to afflict the apostate Israelites:[2] the former exposition, however, is the more appropriate one.

[1] diuque
Inter utrumque volat dubiis Victoria pennis.
Ovid. Metam. viii. 11, 12.

[2] This is the view of *S.M.* "Although our enemies now be our judges, this they have not from their own gods, but from our God, who has delivered us into their hands."

32. *For their vine is of the vine of Sodom.* I think it was far from the intention of Moses, as some make it to be, to refer to the punishment which the Israelites deserved; but that he rather inveighs against their corrupted morals, and obstinate disposition. But metaphorically he calls them an offshoot from the vine of Sodom and Gomorrah, inasmuch as they resemble in their nature both those nations, as much as if they had sprung from them, just as grafts of the vine produce fruits similar to the stocks from which they are taken. God complains by Isaiah that, when He looked for good and sweet grapes from His vineyard, *it brought forth wild grapes.* (Isa. v. 2.) And also by Jeremiah that, when He had planted a trustworthy and genuine seed, it was turned into the branches of a strange vine, (Jer. ii. 22;) but Moses goes further here, that the people was not merely a degenerate vine, but poisonous, and producing nothing but what was deadly; and therefore he adds, not only that *their clusters* were *bitter,* but that their wine was *the poison of dragons and asps;* whereby he signifies that nothing worse or more abominable than that nation could be imagined.

34. *Is not this laid up in store with me?* Although some explain this verse as relating to their punishments, as if God asserted that various kinds of them were laid up with Him, which He could produce whenever He pleased, it is more correct to understand it of their crimes. We are well aware that the ungodly, when God stays His severity, promise themselves impunity, as if His forbearance were a kind of connivance. Unless, therefore, He straightway lifts up His hand to chastise them, they imagine that all recollection of their crimes has vanished from before Him; and consequently the prophets often remind hypocrites of the day of visitation, in order that they may not suppose that they have gained anything by the delay. For this reason Jeremiah says that "the sin of Judah is written with an iron pen and with the point of a diamond," (xvii. 1.) Moses employs a different figure, that, although God may not appear as an immediate avenger, still their sins are stored up in His treasures, and will be brought to light by Him at the fitting

season. Hence we gather the profitable lesson, that although God may make as though He saw not (*dissimulet*) for a time, still He does not forget the iniquities, the memory of which wretched men foolishly imagine to be blotted out, unless they are pursued by God's immediate vengeance.

35. *To me belongeth vengeance.* This passage is quoted to different purposes by Paul, and by the author[1] of the Epistle to the Hebrews, (Rom. xii. 19; Heb. x. 30;) for Paul, with a view of persuading believers to bear injuries patiently, admonishes them to "give place unto wrath," inasmuch as God declares vengeance to be His; but the author of the Epistle to the Hebrews, proclaiming that God will be the avenger of impiety, confirms his declaration by this testimony. Hence it is that part of the commentators suppose that punishment is here denounced against heathen nations because they have cruelly afflicted God's elect people. And, indeed, this appears to be the meaning of Paul's words, that injuries should be patiently endured, since God claims for Himself the office of Avenger; but there is nothing to prevent the same statement from being accommodated to different uses, and therefore Paul did not irrelevantly confirm his exhortation by this saying of Moses, although it literally refers to the internal chastisements of the Church. Besides, the apostles are not in the habit of quoting every word from the testimonies which they adduce, but briefly remind their readers to examine more closely the passages quoted. But, since God here joins the two things together, that He will punish the sins of His people, and at the same time be the avenger of their oppressions, there will be nothing absurd in saying that Paul, as it were, points his finger at this passage;[2] still, the simple explanation will be, that the general declaration is accommodated to a special case, in order that believers should bear their injuries patiently, and leave to God the office which He pronounces to apper-

[1] It is notorious that *C.* adopted the opinion of the Western Church in the third and fourth centuries, and did not admit St. Paul to be the author of the Epistle to the Hebrews: see the Argument to his Commentary, (*C. Soc. Edit.*,) p. xxvii. This discrepancy is noticed, *ibid*, p. 249, and in Mr. Owen's additional note, p. 394.

[2] "Sans l'alleguer au long;" without adducing it in full.—*Fr.*

tain to Himself. In my judgment, indeed, these words are connected with the preceding verse; for God pertinently confirms His statement, that He takes account of the number of men's sins, and has them stored among His treasures, by adding that the power and office of judging rests with Himself; inasmuch as these two things are contrary to each other, that He should be cognizant of whatever is done unrighteously and amiss, and still leave it unpunished. Not that it is opposed to God's justice to pardon sinners when they repent, but because this principle always continues firm, that God is the judge of the world, for the punishment of all iniquities. Thus the confidence of hypocrites is destroyed, who flatter themselves with the hope of impunity, unless they are overtaken by immediate punishment.

The clause which follows some interpreters pervert by supplying the relative, "in the time *in which* their foot shall slide;" whereas Moses simply concludes that they will fall in their due time, or that, although they may think they stand, their ruin or fall was not far off; and this is further confirmed by what he adds, viz., that their day of calamity was at hand. This statement, as I have before said, often occurs in the Prophets, that there is with God a fit time,[1] in which to punish the sins which He has appeared to overlook, and therefore His long-suffering detracts nothing from the judgment which He delays. In this doctrine there is a twofold moral; first, that those whom God spares for a time, should not give way to self-indulgence; and, secondly, that the prosperity of the wicked should not disturb the minds of believers, but that they should allow God to decide the time and the place of executing vengeance. Inasmuch, however, as God's delay renders hypocrites secure, so that they lull themselves to sleep in their vices, and, although they hear that they will have to render account of them, thoughtlessly indulge themselves during[2] their period of en-

[1] "Son temps et saison determinée;" his time and determined season.—*Fr.*

[2] "Usurâ."—*Lat.* "Ils ne laissent pas de se donner bon temps, suyvant le proverbe diabolique, Que le terme vaut l'argent;" they cease not to indulge themselves, according to the diabolical proverb, that the delay is worth the money.—*Fr.*

joyment, Moses declares that *the day is near,* and *makes haste;* for, if God does not openly alarm them, and reduce them to straits, they exult in their immunity. Hence those blasphemous sayings recorded by Isaiah, (v. 19,) "Let him make speed, and hasten his work that we may see it; and let the counsel of the Holy One draw nigh and come, that we may know it!" Meanwhile we must bear in mind the words of Habakkuk, (ii. 3,) "Though *the prophecy* tarry, wait for it; because it will surely come, it will not tarry."

36. *For the Lord shall judge his people.* Some connect this sentence with what precedes it, and thus take the word *judge* for to *punish,* and the Apostle in the Epistle to the Hebrews, seems to support their opinion, inasmuch as he proves by this testimony how fearful a thing it is "to fall into the hands of the living God." (Heb. x. 30, 31.) But there is no reason why the Apostle should not have accommodated to a different purpose what was set forth by Moses for the consolation of the godly, in order that believers might be the more heedful, the nearer they saw God to shew Himself as the Judge of His Church; unless it be perhaps preferred to construe the words of Moses thus: Although God should judge His people, yet at length He will be propitiated, or touched with repentance, so as to temper the vehemence of His anger. Whichever way we understand them will be of little difference in the main; for, after Moses has threatened the despisers of God, and the apostates, who desire to be accounted members of His household the Church, he now turns to the strangers and denounces against them that the cruelty which they have exercised towards the Israelites shall not be unpunished, because God will at length be mindful of His covenant, and will pardon His elect people. If you take the word *judge* for to *govern,* or to *undertake their cause,* the particle *for* must be rendered adversatively, as though it were said *nevertheless* or *but;* if we prefer the other sense, it will be equivalent to *although,* or *even though.* Doubtless the object of Moses is to encourage the hopes of the pious, who have profited by God's chastisement, by shewing that He will

mitigate His severity towards His elect people, and *in* His *wrath* will *remember mercy.* (Hab. iii. 2.) Thus, then, Moses here teaches the same thing which God afterwards more clearly unfolded to David: "If *thy* children forsake my law, . . . I will visit their transgressions with the rod of man, . . . nevertheless my loving-kindness will I not take away from them," &c.[1] (Ps. lxxxix. 30, 33; 2 Sam. vii. 14, 15.) For nothing is more fitted to sustain us in afflictions than when God promises that there shall be some limit to them, so that He will not utterly destroy those whom He has chosen. Whenever, therefore, the ills which we suffer tempt us to despair, let this lesson recur to our minds, that the punishments, wherewith God chastises His children, are temporary, since His promise will never fail that "his anger endureth but a moment," (Ps. xxx. 5,) whilst the flow of His mercy is continual. Hence, too, that lesson which is especially directed to the Church:[2] "For a moment I afflicted thee, but I will pursue my mercies towards thee for ever." (Isa. liv. 8.)

He here calls them His *servants,* not because they had deserved His pardon by their obedience, but because He condescends to acknowledge them as His own; for this honour has reference to His gratuitous election; as when David says, "I am thy servant, and the son of thine handmaid," (Ps. cxvi. 16,) he assuredly arrogates nothing peculiar to himself; but only boasts that he from the womb had been of God's family, just as slaves are born in the house of their masters. At the same time we must observe that, whenever God declares that He will be merciful to His servants, He only refers to those who heartily seek for reconciliation, and not to the reprobate, who are carried away to destruction by their desperate obstinacy. In short, to the end that God should repent of His severity, repentance is required on the part of sinners; as He teaches elsewhere: "Turn ye unto me, . . . and I will turn unto you." (Zech. i. 3.)

Instead of *shall repent,* some translate the word, *shall*

[1] *C.* evidently quoted from memory, and amalgamated the two citations.
[2] Here also the substance, and not the words of the passage, are given.

console himself.[1] Jerome, regarding the drift of the passage rather than the meaning of the word, translates it *shall have mercy.*

We must, however, remark the time which God prefixes for the exertion of His grace, viz., when all their power (*virtus*) shall have departed from them, and all shall be reduced to almost entire destruction ; for the word *hand* is used for *vigour* ;[2] as though it were said that God would be by no means content with a light chastisement, and consequently would not be appeased until they should have come to extremities. This circumstance is well worthy of notice, so that our hopes may not fail us even in the most severe afflictions of the Church ; but that we may be assured that although all may be in the worst state possible, still the due season of reparation will come even yet.

That none should remain behind, or *shut up or left,* is almost a proverbial phrase in Hebrew ; as when it is said, (1 Kings xiv. 10,) "I will cut off from Jeroboam, . . . him that is shut up and left in Israel," *i.e.*, as well in the city as in the country, or at home as abroad. And this is again repeated respecting the posterity of Ahab. (*Ibid.* xxi. 21.) And hence it is plain that they are mistaken[3] who explain this as referring to riches shut up in treasure-houses, and cattle dispersed through the fields. And this will be still more apparent from another passage in which the Prophet unquestionably referred to this, "The Lord saw the affliction of Israel, that it was very bitter ; for there was not any shut up, nor any left," and inasmuch as He had not determined to *blot out* His people, "he saved them by the hand of Jeroboam ;" as much as to say, that God, as He had promised, had pity upon His people in their extreme destitution. (2 Kings xiv. 26, 27.)

37. And he shall say, Where *are* their gods, *their* rock in whom they trusted;	37. Et dicet, Ubi sunt dii eorum, deus in quo sperabant?

[1] *LXX.* παρακληθήσεται. *V.* "miserebitur." Addition in *Fr.*, "Le mot de *repentir* s'accorde mieux au stile de l'Escriture;" the word *repent* accords best with the style of Scripture.

[2] *Vide* margin, *A. V.*

[3] This notion is attributed in Poole to "many of the Hebrews, and Malvenda."

38. Which did eat the fat of their sacrifices, *and* drank the wine of their drink-offerings? let them rise up and help you, *and* be your protection.	38. Qui adipem sacrificiorum illorum comedebant, et bibebant vinum libaminis illorum: surgant et opitulentur vobis, sit super vos absconsio.
39. See now that I, *even* I, *am* he, and *there is* no god with me: I kill and I make alive; I wound, and I heal: neither *is there any* that can deliver out of my hand.	39. Videte nunc quod ego, ego sum, et non sunt dii mecum: ego mori faciam, et vivere faciam: percutiam, et ego sanabo, et nemo est qui de manu mea eruat.
40. For I lift up my hand to heaven, and say, I live for ever.	40. Certè levabo ad cœlum manum meam, et dicam, Vivo ego in seculum.
41. If I whet my glittering sword, and mine hand take hold on judgment, I will render vengeance to mine enemies, and will reward them that hate me.	41. Si acuero aciem gladii mei, et arripuerit judicium manus mea, reddam ultionem hostibus meis, et odio habentibus me retribuam.
42. I will make mine arrows drunk with blood, and my sword shall devour flesh; *and that* with the blood of the slain, and of the captives, from the beginning of revenges upon the enemy.	42. Inebriabo sagittas meas sanguine, et gladius meus devorabit carnem, sanguine, inquam, occisorum et captivorum à capite in ultionibus inimici.
43. Rejoice, O ye nations, *with* his people; for he will avenge the blood of his servants, and will render vengeance to his adversaries, and will be merciful unto his land, *and* to his people.	43. Laudate Gentes populum ejus, quia sanguinem servorum suorum vindicabit, et vindictam reddet hostibus suis, et propitius erit terræ suæ, populo suo.

37. *And he shall say, Where are their gods?* Commentators are here at issue, for some continue the paragraph, as if Moses were reporting the boastings and insults of their enemies in the afflicted state of the Church; whilst others consider it to be a pious exultation, wherein the faithful will celebrate the deliverance of the Church. If we suppose the enemies to be here speaking, it will be inconsistent that the word "gods" should be used in the plural number: besides, what follows will proceed from their mistake and ignorance, that the Israelites "did eat the fat," which was not lawful for them even in their common food, and much less in the sacrifices wherein the fat was burnt. The other exposition, however, is that which I rather approve of, viz., that when the tables were turned, and God should have shewn Himself as the avenger of the unbelievers' cruel injustice,—God's children would be at liberty to upbraid them. The

word "he shall say,"[1] is used indefinitely for "It shall be said by any or all of God's children." Just, then, as unbelievers, when they see the saints afflicted, impudently ridicule their faith, so on the other side Moses, when God comes to the help of His Church, introduces the saints derisively inquiring, where are the gods of the Gentiles, and where are all their patrons? since all of them, as is well known, had their tutelary gods. Thus their impure and spurious sacrifices are satirized in which they ate the fat, and drank the libations of wine. In short, Moses intimates that, when God succours His people, their mouth is opened to sing the song of triumph to the glory of the true God, and to upbraid unbelievers with the false confidence whereby they are deceived.

39. *See now that I, even I, am he.* Those who attribute the preceding verses to the unbelievers, now introduce God speaking, as it were, abruptly, and asserting His glory, in rebuke of their blasphemies. But it is rather a confirmation of that holy boasting which He has just dictated to the believers, when God not only bids His people lift up their voices against the idols, but Himself comes forward to condemn the senselessness of the Gentiles; although the context clearly shews that He addresses Himself to the faithful. After, therefore, He has exhorted His people to despise the idols, He now adds that He supplies them with ample grounds of confidence in Himself. For when He bids them "look," He signifies that no obscure manifestation of His power is before their eyes, if they will only pay attention to it. The repetition of the pronoun *I* is emphatic, both to arouse the people from their sluggishness, and to keep their minds steadfast, lest they should waver as if in doubt. For we know that men's minds can hardly be drawn to the true knowledge of God, because they wind about by circuitous courses, so as not to direct themselves straight to Him. And again, when they do apprehend God, we are aware how easily they are drawn away from Him; since the vicissitudes of things becloud them, so that they wander

[1] This sentence is omitted in the *Fr.*, but implied in the translation, "On dira."

hither and thither in uncertainty. For this reason, when God has overthrown all fictitious deities, He declares that He always remains the same, whether He kills or makes alive, so that in the thick darkness of affliction believers may not cease to look to Him. Let us learn from this passage that God is defrauded of His right, unless He alone is pre-eminent, all idols being reduced to nothing; and also that our faith is then truly fixed in Him, and has firm roots, if, amidst the various changes which occur, it does not stagger or waver, but surmounts such obstacles, so as not to cease to hope in Him even when He seems to "slay" us, as Job says, (xiii. 15.) And surely nothing is more unreasonable than that our faith should look round upon all events so as to depend upon them; since God would have His promises to quicken us in death itself. The close of the verse may fitly be referred to their enemies, inasmuch as God declares that none can deliver them out of His hand.

40. *For*[1] *I lift up my hand to heaven.* Others render it, "When I shall have lifted up my hand," and read it connectedly with the foregoing verse, that God's power in destroying and preserving will be manifest, if He raises up His hand to heaven. I do not doubt, however, but that it is the beginning of a new sentence, and that God thus commences, in order to affirm more strongly what He immediately adds respecting the future destruction of their enemies. If, however, any prefer the adverb of time "when," I have no great objection to offer, provided these clauses are connected, "As soon as I shall have lifted up my hand to heaven, I will put to confusion the enemies of my Church."

To lift up the hand is explained in two ways; for some suppose it to be a manifestation of power, as men are wont, by the uplifting of their hand, to glory, when they are confident in their strength, and despise their enemies. Others, however, more correctly state it to be a form of adjuration God, who is exalted above all heavens, cannot, indeed, be literally said to lift His hand; but it is no new thing for Him to borrow modes of expression taken from men's common habits and customs, especially when He suddenly rises

[1] *Lat.*, certè; *Fr.*, car; *V.*, cum.

again to sublimity, after having appeared for a while to sink below the level of His greatness. Certainly the words which follow contain in them an oath, "I live for ever;" and hence it is probable[1] that the elevation of His hand was expressive of His taking the oath.

God swears by His life in a very different sense from men. Sometimes, indeed, He adopts our common modes of speaking, as when He is said to swear by His soul; but here, "I live," is tantamount to His swearing by Himself, or by His eternal essence.

41. *If I whet my glittering sword.* The conditional particle does not leave the matter doubtful, or in suspense, but must be resolved into an adverb of time; as though He had said, As soon as He should take up arms, the destruction of the enemies would be certain; not indeed that God wants arms for the overthrow of His enemies; just as when He adds directly afterwards, "When my hand shall have taken hold of judgment," He does not mean that it ever is taken away from Him, or escapes Him, but He thus designates its present and manifest operation.[2] Since, therefore, God, when He spares His enemies, seems, as it were, to have thrown aside His weapons, and to be at rest, having ceased to execute the office of judge, He declares that His arms shall be ready wherewith to destroy His enemies; and again, that then He will once more take upon Him the judgment which He had seemed to lay aside; in which words He indirectly animadverts upon the foolish security of those who conceive that His power is annihilated, unless He openly exerts it, and that the judgment which He postpones is altogether extinct.

42. *I will make my arrows drunk with blood.* In these words He describes a horrible massacre, as though He had said, There shall be no end to my vengeance, until the earth

[1] I hardly understand the hypothetical form in which this sentence is put, after what *C.* has already said on this point on Exod. vi. 8 (vol. i. p. 131,) and on Numb. xiv. 30 (*ante*, p. 81.) Perhaps he merely meant that the coincidence of the adjuration with the uplifting of the hand fixed the sense of the latter expression in this place.

[2] "C'est pour signifier un effet present et manifest, lequel n'estoit point apparu devant;" it is to signify a present and manifest effect, which had not appeared before.—*Fr.*

shall be full of blood and corpses. Elsewhere[1] also, God's sword is said to be "drunk with blood," as here His arrows, when His wrath proceeds to inflict great acts of carnage; and in the same sense it is here said to "devour flesh."

The second מדם, *midam*, some render, "on account of the blood;" and I admit that מ, *mem*, is sometimes the causal particle. They understand it, then, that this would be the just recompense of their cruelty, when the wicked, who had slain the Israelites, or led them away captive, should be cut off by God. But I do not see why the same word should be expounded in two different senses; and I have no doubt but that it is a repetition of the same thing, that God will make His "arrows drunk with blood;"[2] but He says, "the blood both of the slain and of the captives," since, when an army is put to the sword, some fall in the battle itself, whilst others, maimed and wounded, make an effort to escape.

The conclusion of the verse is twisted into various senses; some expound the word "head" by change of number, "heads," as though it were said, "I will cut off the heads of the enemies;" it would, however, be more plausible to apply it metaphorically to the leaders. But others translate it more correctly, "the beginning," not, indeed, with reference to time, but as though it were said, the flower, or best of the multitude, according to the common phrase, "from the first to the last." My interpretation of "the revenges of the enemy" is, not those which God will inflict upon His enemies, but such as are capital, or deadly, as though He had said that He would deal as an enemy with the wicked, so that there should be no place for mercy.[3]

43. *Rejoice, O ye nations, with his people.* The appositive

[1] Jer. xlvi. 10.

[2] Addition in *Fr.*, "pour confermer le propos avec plus grand vehemence;" to confirm the point in question with greater vehemence.

[3] מראש פרעות אויב. *A. V.*, "From the beginning of revenges upon the enemy." *S. M.*, "From the head of revenges of the enemy." *V.* and Luther, "Of the bare head of the enemies." *LXX.*, "From the head of the chief enemies." The word ראש is either the *head* of a body, or the *beginning* of an event. פרעות comes from a verb signifying to *deal out retribution*, and has therefore been taken by some to mean *revenge*, and by others to mean *chiefs* or *rulers*, whose office it is to avenge wrongs; there are, however, instances in which פרע is acknowledged to be the *hair of the head.*—*W.*

reading, which some prefer, "Praise him, O nations, His people," supplying the word "God," is constrained. For there is no incongruity in the notion that the Gentiles should celebrate the benefits which God has conferred upon His people; at any rate, it is more simple to take it thus, that so conspicuous was the favour of God towards the Israelites, that the knowledge and favour of it should diffuse itself far and wide, and be renowned even among the Gentiles. For Scripture thus magnifies some of the more memorable exertions of God's power, especially when reference is made to the redemption of the elect people, and commands His praise to be proclaimed among the nations, since it would be by no means fitting that it should be confined within the narrow limits of Judea. A question, however, occurs, because Paul seems to quote this passage differently; for he says, "Rejoice, ye Gentiles, with his people," (Rom. xv. 10;) and undoubtedly the word נקם, *nakam,* which Moses uses, also signifies to rejoice.[1] If we admit that Paul took this sentence from Moses, the same Spirit, who spoke both by Moses and Paul, is the best interpreter of His own words; nor will it be inconsistent that the Gentiles should rejoice at the felicity of God's people. But it may have been the case that Paul did not take this testimony from any particular place, but from the general teaching of Scripture. At any rate, the dignity of the people is celebrated on the ground that God esteems their blood precious, and will deem their persecutors His own adversaries.

The word כפר, *caphar,* at the end of the verse, some render to *expiate,* others, to *be propitious,* which is the rendering I have preferred, although I do not reject the former meaning. The verb כפר, *caphar,* signifies that an expiation is made with sacrifice to appease God; and it is probable that Moses alludes to the legal mode of reconciliation; nevertheless, in my judgment, he means that God will restore His land and people to His favour.

44. And Moses came and spake all the words of this song in the ears of the people, he and Hoshea the son of Nun.	44. Venit autem Moses, et recitavit omnia verba cantici istius in auribus populi, ipse et Josue filius Nun:

[1] It would scarcely be conceded now that נקם ever means to rejoice.—*W.*

45. And Moses made an end of speaking all these words to all Israel:

46. And he said unto them, Set your hearts unto all the words which I testify among you this day, which ye shall command your children to observe to do, all the words of this law.

47. For it *is* not a vain thing for you; because it *is* your life: and through this thing ye shall prolong *your* days in the land whither ye go over Jordan to possess it.

48. And the Lord spake unto Moses that self-same day, saying,

49. Get thee up into this mountain Abarim, *unto* mount Nebo, which *is* in the land of Moab, that *is* over against Jericho, and behold the land of Canaan, which I give unto the children of Israel for a possession;

50. And die in the mount whither thou goest up, and be gathered unto thy people; as Aaron thy brother died in mount Hor, and was gathered unto his people:

51. Because ye trespassed against me among the children of Israel at the waters of Meribah-Kadesh, in the wilderness of Zin; because ye sanctified me not in the midst of the children of Israel.

52. Yet thou shalt see the land before *thee;* but thou shalt not go thither unto the land which I give the children of Israel.

45. Et finivit Moses recitare omnia verba ista ad universum Israelem:

46. Dixitque illis, Adjicite cor vestrum ad omnia verba quæ ego testificor adversum vos hodie, ut præcipiatis ea filiis vestris, ut custodiant, et faciant omnia verba legis istius.

47. Non enim verbum hoc inane à vobis, sed est vita vestra, et per hoc verbum prolongabitis dies super terram ad quam possidendam vos transitis Jordanem.

48. Loquutusque est Jehova ad Mosen eo ipso die, dicendo:

49. Ascende in montem Abarim istum, montem Neboh, qui est in terra Moab, et qui est è regione Jericho, et vide terram Chenaan, quam ego do filiis Israel in hæreditatem.

50. Et morere in monte ad quem ascendis, et congregare ad populos tuos, quemadmodum mortuus est Aharon frater tuus in Hor monte, et congregatus est ad populos suos.

51. Et quòd prævaricati estis me in medio filiorum Israelis ad aquas jurgii Cades deserti Sin, eò quod non sanctificastis me in medio filiorum Israelis:

52. E regione quidem videbis terram, sed illuc non ingredieris ad terram illam quam do filiis Israelis.

A Repetition of the same History.

NUMB. XXVII. 12-14. And the Lord said unto Moses, Get thee up into this mount Abarim, and see the land which I have given unto the children of Israel.

13. And when thou hast seen it, thou also shalt be gathered unto thy people, as Aaron thy brother was gathered.

14. For ye rebelled against my commandment in the desert of Zin, in the strife of the congregation, to

12. Dixit Jehova ad Mosen, Ascende in montem istum Abarim: et vide terram quam dedi filiis Israel.

13. Ubi videris eam, aggregaberis ad populos tuos tu quoque, sicut aggregatus est Aharon frater tuus.

14. Quandoquidem rebelles fuistis ori meo in deserto Sin, in jurgio congregationis, ut sanctificaretis me

sanctify me at the water before their eyes: that *is* the water of Meribah in Kadesh, in the wilderness of Zin.

in aquis coram oculis eorum. Istæ sunt aquæ jurgii Cades in deserto Sin.

DEUT. XXXII. 44. *And Moses came and spake.* It is not without reason that Moses again records that he repeated this Song before the people; because it thence appears how far from all ambition he was, in that he did not fear, at the very close of his life, to irritate all their minds, so as to render the memory of his name hateful; and besides, his authority was sanctioned by the silence and submissiveness of the people, when they suffered themselves to be thus severely dealt with. For, such was their general refractoriness, that they never would have listened to him, had not the secret inspiration of the Spirit interposed to subdue them.

He associates with himself Joshua, whom he undoubtedly desired to furnish with equal authority, and, what is worthy of observation, he bids them be attentive to the threatenings and reprehensions, in order to obtain reverence for the law. For we often see that bare doctrine is cold and nerveless, unless the sluggishness, which as it were stifles men's minds, is sharply stimulated; lest, then, the teaching of the Law should be despised or forgotten, or, from being but languidly received, should gradually be obliterated from their minds, he as it were spurs them up by the vehemence of this Song, and commands that their posterity should be instructed in it, in order that their attention may be aroused by its menaces. In the next verse (47) he recommends to them zeal in the observance of the Law on the score of its profitableness; for translators render it improperly, as it seems to me, "Lest it should be an empty word to you," or, "It is not an empty word, such as you should despise." Jerome's translation is better—"The precepts are not given you in vain;" for Moses simply intimates that the Law was not given in vain, so as to end in fruitlessness; and consequently they were to beware lest they should frustrate God's purpose, who desired to do them good. רק, *rek,* therefore, is used as the converse of "fruitful," as more clearly appears from the confirmation immediately added, that they "might prolong their days in the promised land." The Law, then, is said not to be vain, because it is fruitful unto salvation. In what way it is also deadly, and has no inherent efficacy, I have already shewn.[1] It is indeed true that the Law, as being the sure rule of righteousness, does not deceptively promise salvation to men; but, since there is no one who actually performs what God requires, through the *accidental* guilt of men, life is turned into death; but, when all are plunged beneath the curse, a new remedy supervenes, and by God's gratuitous pardon they are so reconciled to Him, as that their obedience, such as it is, becomes acceptable.

48. *And the Lord spake unto Moses.* We infer that this is not recorded in its regular order, because it is certain that Moses was warned of his approaching death before the Song was composed; and this the second passage, which I have here appended, expressly confirms; for he says that, before he substituted Joshua for himself, the place was pointed out to him in which he was to die. It is, however, by no means unusual for the order of narration to be inverted.

We may here perceive a singular specimen of faith and obedience. All naturally fly from death, so that no one hastens towards it of his own accord. He would never, therefore, have voluntarily entered the tomb, unless relying on the hope of a better life. We have already seen a similar instance in the case of Aaron: although the resurrection was not then so clearly revealed as it now is by the Gospel, nor had Christ appeared, who is the first-fruits of them that rise again. Wherefore, though our carnal sense may be averse from death, let our faith prevail to overcome all its terrors: even as Paul teaches that God's children, although they desire not "to be unclothed," still long to be "clothed upon, that mortality may be swallowed up of life." (2 Cor. v. 4.) This, however, was remarkable obedience, to prepare himself no less willingly for death than as if he had been invited to some joyful banquet. Thus it is plain that these holy men had so consecrated themselves to God, that they were ready to live or to die, according to His pleasure.

Mount Abarim seems to have obtained its name from its

[1] See especially, "On the use of the Law," vol. iii. 196.

angles or sides, because it was divided[1] into many hills; as it is called also Nebo in this place, and elsewhere by divers other names. Others think it is named from a *passage;* but the other opinion is more probable, since it is called in the plural number Abarim, that is, heights, or summits, or interstices, which were situated on opposite heights.

Although we shall presently see that there was another reason why God desired to withdraw His servant from the sight of men, still we must take notice of the consolation, which is here referred to, that the pain of his death was alleviated by the permission to behold the land of Canaan. For this reason he is commanded to get up into the top of the mountain; for, although he would have been satisfied with the mere promise of God, even had he been deprived of this blessing, still it had no slight additional effect in enabling him more cheerfully to leave the people on the threshold of their inheritance. For faith does not altogether deprive God's children of human feelings; but our heavenly Father in His indulgence has compassion on their infirmity. Thus, as it was a cause of sorrow to Moses to be withheld from entering the land, he was supported by a seasonable remedy, that he might not be hindered in his course by this impediment.

51. *Because ye trespassed against me.* We perceive from his punishment how necessary to Moses was such a token of favour.[2] For death in itself would not have been so bitter, but the cause, which is again alleged, grievously wounded the mind of the holy man, in that he saw himself to be excluded in God's just vengeance from the common inheritance on account of his own guilt, which is more afflictive to the pious than a hundred, nay, innumerable deaths. Hence those mournful complaints of David and Hezekiah, and

[1] It seems that Abarim is the general name of a range of mountains; and as Moses is said in one text to die in Mount Nebo, and in the present, (viz., Deut xxxiv. 1,) on the top of Pisgah, we must infer that Nebo was a mountain in the range of Abarim, and that Pisgah was the most elevated and commanding peak of that mountain."—Illustr. Com.

Abarim, from עבר, *gnabar,* to pass over; translated by Taylor *vada, transitus, latera.*

[2] "Que nous avons veu;" as we have seen.—*Fr.*

others elsewhere, when their life is taken from them by an angry God: "the grave cannot praise thee, death cannot celebrate thee: they that go down into the pit cannot hope for thy truth." (Isa. xxxviii. 18; Ps. vi. 5; Ps. cxv. 17.) Surely it was not so formidable a thing for them to die, but that they would have calmly and cheerfully departed from the world when their time came; but what they deprecated was the awful judgment of God, at the thoughts of which they were alarmed. The same grief might have overwhelmed the mind of Moses, had it not been alleviated.

But since none, however eminent, have been altogether exempt from temporal punishments, let us learn to bear them patiently. God did not spare Moses; what wonder if our condition is no better than his? Moreover, in the opinion of men it was a trifling offence, for the sake of which he was so severely chastised; for, carried away by indignation, he had been so irritated against the people that he had attributed less power to God than was due to Him. Now, those errors, into which we fall through thoughtless impetuosity, are more easily pardoned; but hence it is manifest how precious to God is His glory, when He does not suffer it to be obscured with impunity even by inadvertence. At the same time, also, we are taught that nothing is more irrational than to assume to ourselves the judgment respecting sins, and to weigh them in our own balance, when God is their only legitimate assessor.

But, although He declares that Moses and Aaron revolted, and were rebellious "to His mouth,"[1] still, lest it should be thought that they studiously refused credence to God's word, a kind of qualification is added, viz., that they did not *sanctify* God in the midst, or *before the eyes*, of the children of Israel. Hence it is plain that they were only condemned for the excessive violence of their passion, whereby they did not uphold God's glory before the people with sufficient energy.

As to the rest, it may be looked for under Numbers xx.

[1] Numb. xxvii. 14. "Against my commandment."—*A. V.*

DEUTERONOMY, CHAPTER XXXIII.

1. And this *is* the blessing wherewith Moses the man of God blessed the children of Israel before his death.

2. And he said, The Lord came from Sinai, and rose up from Seir unto them; he shined forth from mount Paran, and he came with ten thousands of saints: from his right hand *went* a fiery law for them.

3. Yea, he loved the people; all his saints *are* in thy hand: and they sat down at thy feet; *every one* shall receive of thy words.

4. Moses commanded us a law, *even* the inheritance of the congregation of Jacob.

5. And he was king in Jeshurun, when the heads of the people *and* the tribes of Israel were gathered together.

6. Let Reuben live, and not die; and let *not* his men be few.

7. And this *is the blessing* of Judah: and he said, Hear, Lord, the voice of Judah, and bring him unto his people: let his hands be sufficient for him; and be thou an help *to him* from his enemies.

1. Hæc autem benedictio qua benedixit Moses vir Dei filiis Israel in morte sua.

2. Et dixit, Jehova e Sinai prodiit, et ortus est e Seir ipsis, illuxit e monte Pharam, et venit cum decem millibus sanctitatis: a dextra ejus ignea lex illis:

3. Utique diligit populos, omnes sancti in manibus tuis, et ipsi adhæserunt pedibus tuis, ut sumerent ex eloquiis tuis.

4. Legem præcepit nobis Moses in hæreditatem cœtus Israel.

5. Et fuit in Recto rex, in colligendis capitibus populi, simulque tribubus Israel.

6. Vivat Ruben, et non moriatur, et (*vel,* quamvis) sit parvus numero.

7. Hoc etiam Judæ, et dixit, Audi Jehova vocem Jehuda, et ad populum suum duc eum, manus ejus sufficiat ei, dum auxilio fueris contra hostes ejus.

1. *And this is the blessing.* The bitterness of the Song was seasoned,[1] as it were, by this palliative, wherein Moses left a testimony with respect to God's future and perpetual grace, as if depositing an inestimable treasure in the hands of the people. For, as God, after the deliverance of His people, and the giving of the Law, renewed the covenant which Jacob had testified of and proclaimed, so Moses was, as it were, their second father, to ratify anew its blessings, lest the memory of them should ever be lost.

In order to beget confidence in his benedictions, he commences by magnifying his vocation before he proceeds to them; for, although the word *benediction* is equivalent to a prayer for success, yet must it be borne in mind that Moses

[1] "Ceste benediction a este comme du sucre," &c.; this blessing was like sugar, &c.—*Fr.*

does not here pray in the ordinary manner, like a private person, in such a way as fathers are wont to offer supplications for their children; but that, in the spirit of prophecy, he sets forth the blessings which were to be expected from God. This, then, is the reason why he extols the dignity and glory of his office as ruler in such lofty terms, viz., that the twelve tribes of Israel may be thoroughly assured that God is the author of these blessings. For the same reason he calls himself "the man of God:" that the people may receive what he is about to say as if it proceeded from God, whose undoubted minister he is. Nor is the circumstance of time without its weight—"before his death," or, "in his death," which adds to the prophecy the force of a testament.

2. *And he said, The Lord came from Sinai.*[1] In these words he reminds them that he is setting before them a confirmation of the covenant, which God had made with them in His Law, and that it is nothing different from it; for this connexion was of exceeding efficacy in establishing the certainty of the blessings, provided only the Law was duly honoured; for nothing was better adapted to confirm the grace of God than the majesty which was displayed in the promulgation of the Law. Some, as I conceive improperly, translate it,—"God comes to Sinai," whereas Moses rather means that He came from thence, when His brightness was made manifest. By way of ornament, the same thing is repeated with respect to Seir and Paran; and, since these three words are synonymous, therefore to *go forth*, to *rise up*, and to *come*, also represent the same thing, viz., that manifestation of the divine glory which should have ravished into admiration the minds of all; as though he had said that his blessings were to be received with the same reverence, as that which God had procured for His Law, when His face was conspicuously displayed on Mount Sinai. The Prophet Habakkuk (iii. 3) has imitated this figure, though with a different object, viz., that the people might confidently rely upon his power, which had formerly been manifested to the fathers in visible brightness.

[1] *Lat.*, "*Went* from Sinai."

By "ten thousands of sanctity,"[1] I do not understand, as many do, the faithful, but the angels, by whom God was accompanied as by a royal retinue; for God also commanded the ark to be placed between the Cherubim, in order to shew that the heavenly hosts were around Him. So in Isaiah, (vi. 6,) the Seraphim surround His throne; and Daniel says that he saw "ten thousand times ten thousand," (vii. 10;) thus designating an infinite multitude, as does Moses also by "ten thousand." It is probable that both Paul and Stephen derived from this passage their statement that the Law was "ordained by Angels in the hand of a mediator," (Gal. iii. 19; Acts vii. 53;) for its authority was greatly confirmed by its having so many witnesses (*obsignatores.*)

The Law is placed at *His right hand*, not only as a sceptre or mark of dignity, but as His power or rule of government; for He did not merely shew Himself as a king, but also made known how He would preside over them.[2] The Law is called *fiery*, in order to inspire terror and to enforce humility upon them all; although I am not adverse to the opinion that Moses alludes in this epithet to the outward signs of fire and flame, of which he spoke in Exodus xx. But, since the word דת, *dath*, means any statute or edict, some restrict it to the prohibition that none should more closely approach the mountain. In my own mind, however, there is no doubt but that it designates all the doctrine whereby God's dominion is maintained.

3. *Yea, he loved the people.*[3] If it be preferred to apply this to the Gentiles, the sentence must be thus resolved, "Although He loves all human beings, still His saints are honoured with His peculiar favour, in that He watches over their safety;" but it is more correct to expound it as referring only to the children of Abraham, whom He calls "peoples,"

[1] *A. V.*, "Ten thousands of saints. Ainsworth: "Heb., *of sanctity; meaning, spirits of sanctity;* which Jonathan in his Thargum expoundeth *holy angels:* —— so we by grace in Christ are come to ten thousands of angels. Heb. xii. 22."

[2] "Comme il vouloit presider, et estre honoré de son peuple;" how He would preside, and be honoured by His people.—*Fr.*

[3] *Lat.*, "the peoples."

because, on account of the multitude into which they had grown, in their several tribes, they might be reckoned as so many nations. And since the particle אַף, *aph*,[1] signifies prolongation of time, like *adhuc* in Latin, the following sense will be very satisfactory, that, Although the descendants of Abraham were divided into various races, and might therefore seem to be no longer a single family, nevertheless God still continued to regard them all with affection, and their numbers and divisions did not prevent Him from accounting them to be a single body. The sum is, that God's favour towards them was not extinguished, either by the progress of time, or the increase of the people; but that it was constantly extended to the race of Abraham, however far or widely it might be spread.

It must, however, be observed, that in proof of His love, it is presently added, that they were *in the hand* of God. Hence we infer that, from the time that God has embraced us with His favour, He is the sure guardian of our safety; whence also arises the firm assurance of eternal life. The change of person, from the third to the second, throws no obscurity on the meaning. Since many hypocrites were mixed up with the faithful—for the Church of God has always been like a threshing-floor[2]—Moses restricts this special grace of God to those who willingly submit themselves to Him, and with pious teachableness embrace His instruction, by which sign he distinguishes between the true children of God, and those spurious or degenerate ones, who falsely assume the name. Where my translation is, "They cleaved to thy feet," others render the words, "They were struck at thy feet," but in my judgment constrainedly. Others extract from it a useful piece of instruction, that "they were subdued by God's chastisements, so as to render Him obedience;" but the metaphor is rather taken from disciples, who, according to the common usage of the Hebrew language, are said to sit at their master's feet, in order to attend more diligently. And this is confirmed by the con-

[1] *A. V.*, "yea."

[2] In the *Fr.* this expression is thus explained,—"où les grains de blé sont cachez sous la paille;" where the grains of wheat are hidden beneath the straw.

text, for the faithful are said to have attached themselves to God's feet, that they might *receive of His words, i. e.*, profit by His instruction.

4. *Moses commanded us a law.* What he had declared respecting the glory of God, and the excellency of the Law, he now applies to his own person, since it was his purpose, as I have said, to establish the authority of his own ministry. In order, therefore, to prove the certainty of his mission, he boasts that he was appointed by God to be the teacher of the people, and that not for a brief period, but throughout all ages; for by the word "inheritance," the perpetuity of the Law is signified. He then claims for himself the royal supremacy, not because he had ruled after the manner of kings, but that the dignity of this high office might add weight to his words. He says that "the heads of the people and the tribes were gathered together," with reference to their unhappy disorganization, which was tending to their destruction, as much as to say that, under his guidance, and by his exertions, the state of the people was re-established.

He begins with Reuben, the first-born, and so far removes or mitigates the ignominy of that condemnation wherewith he had been branded by his father Jacob, as only to stop short of restoring him to his place of honour. For the holy Patriarch had pronounced a severe sentence, namely, that Reuben should be "as unstable as water, and should not excel." (Gen. xlix. 4.) Lest, therefore, the whole of his posterity should be discouraged, or should be rejected by the other tribes, he abates the severity of his disinheritance, as if to pardon the condemned. In short, he assigns to the family of Reuben a place among the sons of Jacob, lest despair should drive them to headlong ruin. The second clause admits of two contrary meanings. Literally it is, "Let him be small in number;" and, in fact, this tribe was not of the more numerous ones. Since, however, it occupied a middle place, and surpassed several of the others, some repeat the negative, "Let him not die, nor let him be few in number."[1] But it appears more probable that an abatement is made

[1] *A. V.*, "and let *not* his men be few.

from the rank to which his primogeniture entitled the family of Reuben, and thus that some remainder of dishonour was introduced into the promise of grace. And, in fact, not only the tribe of Judah, but those of Simeon, Issachar, Zebulun, Dan, and Naphthali, surpassed it in size. Thus the qualification will be by no means inappropriate, that, although Reuben was to be reckoned among the people of God, still he should not altogether recover his dignity.

7. *And this* is the blessing *of Judah.*[1] Jerome has faithfully given the sense, "This is the blessing," although it is not actually expressed.

It might at first sight appear inconsistent that some abatement should be made from the splendid and abundant blessings which had been promised to the tribe of Judah. This, however, is by no means the case; for the inviolable decree respecting the supremacy of Judah is not thus altered; but Moses merely reminds them how difficult of accomplishment it would be. Jacob had declared, as if speaking of a peaceful dominion, that his "brethren should praise" him, that his "father's children should bow down before" him; that "the sceptre should not depart from Judah, nor a lawgiver from between his feet," (Gen. xlix. 8, 10;) but, inasmuch as this dignity lay dormant for a long time, and it was necessary that it should contend with many tedious obstacles before it finally manifested itself, Moses consequently speaks in more limited terms. Still, he seems to have referred not merely to the earlier period, but to the various calamities whereby the kingdom of David was not only apparently diminished, but destroyed; and especially to the melancholy interruption of it which arose from the Babylonish captivity. The sum is, that the prosperity of which Jacob prophesied was not to be so conspicuous in the tribe of Judah, as that all things were to be expected to be joyous and successful, but rather that those, to whom the supreme power as well as wealth was promised, would be exposed to many evils, so that they should be reduced to extremities, and be greatly in want of the help of God. He therefore betakes himself to prayer, and by his example admonishes not that

[1] And this also of Judah.

tribe only, but the others also, to implore the faithfulness of God in their overwhelming difficulties. And this lesson applies to ourselves also, in order that we may be the more aroused to prayer and supplication, the more Satan is urgent for the destruction of Christ's kingdom. At the same time, what I have stated must be observed, namely, that the promise remains firm, since it is not in vain that Moses places all the tribes under the dominion of Judah, when he petitions that he may be *brought unto his people,* nor promises in vain that God will be at hand to help him, so that he may prevail against his enemies.

8. And of Levi he said, *Let* thy Thummim and thy Urim *be* with thy holy one, whom thou didst prove at Massah, *and with* whom thou didst strive at the waters of Meribah;

8. Ad Levi vero dixit: Perfectiones tuæ et splendores tui fuerunt viro misericordi tuo, quem tentasti in Masa: et contendere fecisti eum ad aquas Meriba.

9. Who said unto his father, and to his mother, I have not seen him; neither did he acknowledge his brethren, nor knew his own children: for they have observed thy word, and kept thy covenant.

9. Qui dixit patri suo et matri suæ, Non vidi eum: et fratres suos non agnovit, et filios suos non cognovit: nam custodierunt eloquium tuum, et pactum tuum servarunt.

10. They shall teach Jacob thy judgments, and Israel thy law: they shall put incense before thee, and whole burnt-sacrifice upon thine altar.

10. Docebunt judicia tua ipsum Jacob, et legem tuam Israelem: ponent suffitum in nares tuas: et holocaustum super altare tuum.

11. Bless, Lord, his substance, and accept the work of his hands: smite through the loins of them that rise against him, and of them that hate him, that they rise not again.

11. Benedic Jehova substantiæ ejus, et in opere manuum ejus complaceas tibi: transfige lumbos inimicorum ejus, et odio habentium eum: ne resurgant.

12. *And* of Benjamin he said, The beloved of the Lord shall dwell in safety by him; *and the Lord* shall cover him all the day long, and he shall dwell between his shoulders.

12. Ad Benjamin dixit, Dilectus Jehovæ habitabit confidenter juxta illum, tegens illum tota die, et inter humeros ejus habitabit.

13. And of Joseph he said, Blessed of the Lord *be* his land, for the precious things of heaven, for the dew, and for the deep that coucheth beneath,

13. Ad Joseph vero dixit, Benedicta a Jehova terra ejus ab excellentia cœli, ob rorem, et ob voraginem cubantem deorsum.

14. And for the precious fruits *brought forth* by the sun, and for the precious things put forth by the moon.

14. Et ob præstantiam proventuum solis, et ob præstantiam fructuum lunæ:

15. And for the chief things of the ancient mountains, and for the precious things of the lasting hills,

15. Et ob præstantiam cacuminis montium antiquorum, et ob præstantiam collium perpetuorum.

16. And for the precious things of the earth, and fulness thereof, and *for* the good-will of him that dwelt in the bush: let *the blessing* come upon the head of Joseph, and upon the top of the head of him *that was* separated from his brethren.

17. His glory *is like* the firstling of his bullock, and his horns *are like* the horns of unicorns: with them he shall push the people together to the ends of the earth; and they *are* the ten thousands of Ephraim, and they *are* the thousands of Manasseh.

16. Et ob præstantiam terræ, et ob plenitudinem ejus: et beneplacitum habitatoris rubi veniat super caput Joseph, et super verticem separati a fratribus suis.

17. Primogeniti bovis ejus decor erit ei, et cornua unicornis cornua ejus: ipsis populos cornupetes simul usque ad fines terræ. Atque hæc sunt decem millia Ephraim, et ista millia Manasse.

8. *And of Levi he said.* This qualification, or modification of the harsher sentence of Jacob was introduced not only for the sake of the tribe of Levi, but rather of the whole people. Jacob had said, "Simeon and Levi are brethren: instruments of cruelty are in their habitations. O my soul, come not thou into their secret; unto their assembly, my tongue,[1] be not thou united," (Gen. xlix. 5, 6.) Assuredly their descendants might have been discouraged, or at least might have been regarded contemptuously, when a patriarch, and the founder of their race, had thus abominated them. God, however, afterwards consecrated this tribe to Himself, so that their sanctity might be communicated to the other tribes; which could not be the case unless their previous opprobrium were removed.

But if any contentious person had objected to this blessing, as if Moses were too much disposed to favour his own tribe, such a suspicion could not justly be harboured against him; first, because he, who now makes such honourable mention of the tribe of Levi, was also the proclaimer of their ignominy; and on many other occasions had not spared his own family, but, whenever it was requisite, had freely inveighed against their vices; and, secondly, he now commends nothing in the Levites except the new dignity, which it had pleased God to confer upon them. On this point, indeed, he ought to have been least of all suspected, inasmuch as he had degraded his own sons, and had exalted the

[1] *A. V.*, "Mine honour." See *C.* on Gen. xlix., *C. Soc. Edit.*, vol. ii. p. 447.

posterity of Aaron alone to the highest place of honour. Now, therefore, he has no other object but that the dignity of the priesthood should not be depreciated on account of the sins of men, and thus their religion itself be despised. For we all know how disposed people are to lay charges against the persons of men which may derogate from the sacredness of their office. Assuredly, if Levi had not been purged from that disgrace which he had incurred, the priesthood would have been altogether deprived of reverence; and thus God's worship would have been very lightly esteemed. Now, however, when God sanctifies this family to himself, He, as it were, restores it entirely; and hence it is apparent that its punishment was only temporary, since Moses had no intention of retracting what the Spirit had dictated to holy Jacob. Nor does he, indeed, advance anything of himself; but the same Spirit removes the ignominy, which might have disgraced the tribe of Levi, inasmuch as it had only been imposed upon it for a time. We have already seen elsewhere that what Jacob prophesied respecting the dispersion of this family, resulted in its honour; since God posted the Levites in all directions like sentinels, that through their means purity of doctrine might be fostered amongst the whole people. They were, therefore, scattered in such a manner as that their punishment might be productive of benefit. We must, therefore, conclude, that Moses spoke not to gratify his brethren, but made honourable mention of the priesthood, lest those, whom God had chosen as His ministers, should be treated with contempt. And, doubtless, the subsequent grace of their calling should have blotted out the recollection of their previous infamy. Thus Christ, when He would restore Peter to the office of an apostle, cancels his triple denial, by thrice setting him over His sheep. (John xxi. 17.)

The address, which follows, must be applied to God; for some translate it improperly, "The Urim and Thummim shall be with thee," as if Moses were addressing the tribe of Levi. In order, therefore, to avoid ambiguity, it will be well to translate it *of* Levi, rather than *to* Levi; and ל, *lamed*, is often used in this sense. Thus, with the purpose of increasing the authenticity of the benediction, Moses addresses God Himself, as if citing Him as a witness, or referring his injunctions to God's tribunal.

Although in Hebrew the words Urim and Thummim[1] are here used, which were principal parts of the sacred Ephod, I have not hesitated to translate them as common nouns: for it is unquestionable that by these symbols were denoted, *the knowledge of the Law* which is the only light of our souls, and *integrity of life.* The sum, however, is that the honour of the priesthood was deposited with Aaron, whom he calls *the man of God's clemency,* or, *the meek.* Jerome, as usual, renders it the *holy,* but improperly; for[2] חסיד, *chasid,* signifies *mild,* or *humane;* and this epithet is constantly applied to the children of God, in order that we may learn to imitate that Father of mercy, who "maketh his sun to rise upon the evil and the good."

What follows, viz., that God tried him at Massah, I conceive to be added by way of exception; for I have no doubt but that Moses magnifies God's mercy by this allusion, in that He had dignified Aaron with so great an honour, notwithstanding his having been overcome by impatience, and having fallen. Still it must be remarked that, in reference to the people, the zeal of Aaron is recorded as praiseworthy; as much as to say, that the sin of Aaron flowed from the fountain of virtue, since it was from holy indignation that he fell into the passion of impatience, when he could not endure that the people should rebel against God. Unless perhaps it be preferred to understand these words by way of apostrophe to the people, "Thou didst try, thou didst provoke him to contention, or didst quarrel with him." But the context will run better, if we understand that God then had a controversy with Aaron; inasmuch as, although overcome by the trial, he still gave no despicable proof of his

[1] *C.'s* criticism will be better understood here by giving his version in English:

Ver. 8., "But to Levi he said, Thy perfections and splendours were to Thy merciful man, whom Thou didst try in Massah, and madest him to contend at the waters of Meribah."

[2] *A. V.,* "Holy one." It cannot be reasonably said that this word is not used for *holy,* as well as for *merciful.*—*W.*

piety, and from that time forward did not cease to execute his office with sedulity.

9. *Who said unto his father and his mother.* In the person of Aaron an example is set before all the Levites for their imitation. And, first, he is said to have renounced his own flesh and blood, in order that he might be more disencumbered for obeying God; and in fact it is necessary that all the pastors of the Church should put off their earthly affections, which would otherwise often keep them back from devoting themselves entirely to God. Aaron, then, is said to have bid farewell to all his family, that he might be at liberty to lay himself out for God. Christ now requires the same thing of His disciples, that sons should forget their fathers, and fathers their sons, and husbands their wives, lest anything should retard their course, and prevent them from earnestly advancing through life and death to the end to which they are called. (Matt. x. 37.)

Moses afterwards, by using the plural number, embraces the whole Levitical order; and hence we may infer that what had preceded is not to be confined in its application to a single individual. But when he says that they "guarded (*custodisse*) the word of God, and kept his covenant," he does not refer to mere ordinary obedience, but to the peculiar care of preserving that which was intrusted to their charge. It is true that in like manner all believers are said to keep the Law, when they zealously devote themselves to live a holy life; but special allusion is here made to the office of teaching. The Levites, therefore, are called guardians of the Law, and keepers of it, as being *νομοφύλακες*, since with them was deposited the treasure of Divine instruction, as is more clearly set forth in the next verse, "They shall teach Jacob, &c." If any should prefer that this observing of the Law should be understood of their life and habits, as though it were said, that the Levites should surpass others in the examples they gave, I do not contend the point, though it seems to me that the second clause is explanatory, and that it more familiarly sets forth what was spoken with some little obscurity, pointing out the way in which the Law is to be observed, viz., by their being the teachers and masters of the people. We must, however, remark the method they are to adopt in teaching; for they are not permitted to introduce their own inventions, or to frame a rule of life out of their own heads; but they are commanded to seek in the Law itself what they are to teach, and to interpret it honestly and faithfully. And this condition was inserted in order that whosoever should desire to be successors in the honour should be mindful of their vocation, and faithfully devote themselves to the office of teaching. Thus, when in a corrupt state of the Church, priests, who had nothing of this sort about them, paraded their mere empty title; their silly vaunt is refuted by Malachi: "My covenant (he says) was with *Levi* of life and peace; . . . *for* the law of truth was in his mouth, and . . . the priest's lips should keep knowledge, and they should seek the law at his mouth, . . . but ye have corrupted *my* covenant," (Mal. ii. 5, 6, 7, 8.) Let us learn, then, from this passage, that whosoever claims for himself the primacy in the Church must be repudiated, unless he manifests himself to be a faithful teacher.

The third part of the priest's office follows, viz., that he should apply himself to the performance of the religious services; for God had disencumbered them from the labours of agriculture and other earthly business, that they might be more entirely at liberty for the duties of teaching and sacrifice; and, although this latter might appear to be but an humble occupation, still, if we regard it aright, it was no common honour that they should be mediators and intercessors for the reconciliation of the people to God; for even the very least of the Levites had something to do with making atonement.

Under the words "incense and whole burnt-sacrifice," the entire legal service is comprehended; and the incense is said to be put before the nose of God;[1] because the odour of this offering was grateful, and, as it were, sweet-smelling to Him, as we have elsewhere seen.

11. *Bless, Lord, his substance.* This supplication appears to have been intended tacitly to provide against the poverty

[1] Margin, *A. V.*, "*Heb.* at thy nose."

which awaited the Levites, if God had not supplied them with food from some other source besides the produce of the soil; for they were deprived of a share in the general inheritance, and God alone was their property. Lest, therefore, their condition should be painful to them, Moses offers them consolation, and bids them expect from God abundance for their support, whilst he promises that His blessing shall stand them in stead of the most redundant produce; as it is said in Psalm cxxxii. 15, "I will abundantly bless her provision, and satisfy her *priests*[1] with bread."

What follows, that "the work of his hands may be acceptable to God," may be either explained generally of the labour which is bestowed for the purpose of obtaining food, or of the service and ministry of the tabernacle; but, inasmuch as God engaged the Levites in sacred occupations, it seems indirectly to promise them that such exercises would be no less profitable to them than as if they were altogether occupied in the pursuit of gain. It was allowable for the rest to employ their industry for the advancement of their domestic interests, whilst the Levites, in order properly to perform their duties, were obliged to neglect their private affairs. Lest, then, they should be afraid of destitution, Moses reminds them that they might expect from God an earthly reward also for their spiritual labours.

The third point appears to be purposely introduced, that "God would smite through or transfix their enemies," because pious teachers are very much exposed to envy, and ill-will, and persecution; for the complaint which is made by Jeremiah, (xv. 10,) that he was "a man of strife," is applicable to all the prophets and ministers of God; since the world can hardly bear its affections to be slain by the spiritual sword of God's word, and hence many contentions arise. Besides, Satan, in order to render their doctrine contemptible, does not cease to harass them by whatever means he can, and to arm his bands to war against them; so that the pastors of the Church have need of God's special aid. This point, then, is peculiarly worthy of observation that, although

[1] *A. V.*, "poor." *C.'s* memory seems here to have failed him, and to have imported the word "priests" from the following verse.

many adversaries always threaten God's servants, besiege them, provoke them to conflict, in a word, are always plotting their destruction, still God's succour will be at hand, whereby they may be rendered invincible; as it was said to Jeremiah, "They shall fight against thee, but they shall not prevail against thee." (Jer. i. 19.)

The words I have translated "lest they rise again," others render "lest they rise against them;" and, although I do not reject this, still it seems to be less appropriate; for Moses did not wish to exempt the Levites from the annoyances of combat, but only to promise them victory, inasmuch as God would overwhelm and destroy their enemies.[1]

12. *And of Benjamin he said.* It is probable that Moses alludes to the inheritance which fell to the lot of the children of Benjamin; for the part of Jerusalem in which the temple stood was contained in it. Since, therefore, God assigned them a dwelling-place, in which He in a manner protected them, and cherished them beneath His wings, they are not without reason called His *beloved*, for this was no ordinary pledge of His love. To "dwell upon God,"[2] and "between his shoulders," is equivalent to reposing upon Him; a similitude taken from fathers who carry their children whilst yet they are small and tender. Others extract a different meaning, viz., that God would dwell upon the shoulders of Benjamin; but this is very unnatural.[3]

13. *And of Joseph he said.* Moses repeats some portions of the blessing of Jacob; nor with respect to any other tribe does he approach so closely to the words of the Patriarch. And, although the family of Joseph was already divided into two tribes or nations, still he begins by the head itself, and at the conclusion declares that what had been given to their fathers pertains to Ephraim and Manasseh. First, he celebrates the exceeding fertility of the land, in which the

[1] Addition in *Fr.*, "voire en sorte qu'ils demeurerent couchez tous plats;" that is to say, in such sort as they should remain altogether cast down.

[2] *A. V.*, "*by* God."

[3] It is, nevertheless, the exposition of the great majority of commentators, who suppose that by *shoulders* are figuratively meant *mountains*, or *coasts*.

descendants of Joseph were to dwell; and then ratifies his testimony by the authority of God. He promises them, then, that their land shall be fertile, from the best treasures of heaven; for מגד, *meged*, signifies whatever is best and most precious. I do not, therefore, approve of their translation, who render it *fruits*, although I know not whether Moses speaks of the excellency of the climate, or commends the beneficence of God; the latter, however, accords best with the context, in which he makes mention of the external means of fertility, viz., the dew, and the deep, by which word I understand the depth of the soil itself. In the next verse I admit that by the word מגד, *meged*, the choicest fruits are indicated, but without any change of its meaning. Others render it *delicacies*: others *sweet fruits*, on account of the peculiar excellency of the fruits. But I do not see why some translate the word גרש, *geresh*, "influence." It literally means *thrusting out*; and is used metaphorically for the fruit, which arises and breaks forth from the earth. But it is not very clear to me what fruits he speaks of respectively as "of the sun, and the moon;" for I cannot tell whether there are any grounds for assigning, as some do, to the sun the produce which springs from seed and the vintage; and to the moon, cucumbers and gourds; nor do I attempt to decide whether their idea is more correct who suppose the latter to be flowers or fruits which appear every month.

15. *And for the chief things of the ancient mountains.* In these words he shews that no part of the land would be barren. We know that the tops of mountains are generally arid and uncultivated, or at any rate bear nothing but trees that have no fruit. But Moses affirms that even there also there shall be the richest produce, for which reason, at least in my opinion, he calls the mountains *ancient*, and the hills *lasting*, as if being very highly renowned; for their antiquity is not praised, as if they were created before the rest of the world, but these mountains are honourably distinguished as the first-born, because God's blessing eminently rests upon them. Thus in the blessing of Jacob it is said, "unto the utmost bound of the everlasting hills,"

as much as to say, that no corner of these most celebrated mountains should be devoid of fertility. (Gen. xlix. 26.)

In the next verse he extends generally to the whole land what he had said of the mountains.

Those are wide of the meaning of Moses, who translate what follows: "On account of the good-will of the dweller in the bush the blessing shall come;" and *his* rendering is altogether barbarous who gives it, "On account of the piety," &c. My opinion is that the word רצון, *retzon*, is in the nominative case; for it is quite in accordance with the context that the "favour of God would come upon the head of Joseph;" for, after Moses had magnified His bounty, he now points out its source or cause, viz., that this extraordinary fertility was the result of God's gratuitous favour. The words of Jacob, "by the God of thy father," and "by the Almighty," exactly correspond with these; where also I have explained why Joseph was called a Nazarene among his brethren.[1]

God is called "the dweller in the bush" by *periphrasis*, with reference to the vision which was presented to Moses on Mount Sinai; for God then appeared a second time as the Redeemer and Father of His people; after having made His covenant with Abraham and Jacob. And this serves by way of confirmation; as if it were said, that the same God who had formerly blessed Joseph by the mouth of His servant Jacob, now repeated the same prophecy, in order to give fuller assurance of its truth.

17. *His glory is like the firstling.* Translators obscure the meaning by translating the word *firstling* in the nominative case. I have no doubt, however, but that he compares the glory of Joseph to the size of a very fine bullock, as if He had said, "His beauty is as of the most choice bullocks in his herds." At least it is very consistent that the word *firstling* should be used for *pre-eminent.* He says, then, that no more magnificent or glorious bullocks should be found in the land of Joseph than the people itself would be. And to

[1] *A. V.*, "Separated from his brethren." See on Gen. xlix. 26, *C. Soc. Edit.*, vol. ii. p. 470.

beauty he adds strength and vigour, so that they should be victorious over all their enemies.

At the end of the verse (as I have before stated,) he declares that what he had prophesied of Joseph should be common to the two families of Ephraim and Manasseh. At the same time he confirms the declaration of Jacob, whereby he had preferred Ephraim the younger to the elder. Manasseh, therefore, only reckons his thousands, but Ephraim his ten thousands, a proof of which fact God had given in the census which has been already recorded, in which the tribe of Ephraim was found to be the more numerous.

18. And of Zebulun he said, Rejoice, Zebulun, in thy going out; and, Issachar, in thy tents.

19. They shall call the people unto the mountain; there they shall offer sacrifices of righteousness: for they shall suck *of* the abundance of the seas, and *of* treasures hid in the sand.

20. And of Gad he said, Blessed *be* he that enlargeth Gad: he dwelleth as a lion, and teareth the arm with the crown of the head.

21. And he provided the first part for himself, because there, *in* a portion of the lawgiver, *was he* seated; and he came with the heads of the people, he executed the justice of the Lord, and his judgments with Israel.

22. And of Dan he said, Dan *is* a lion's whelp: he shall leap from Bashan.

23. And of Naphtali he said, O Naphtali, satisfied with favour, and full with the blessing of the Lord; possess thou the west and the south.

24. And of Asher he said, *Let* Asher *be* blessed with children; let him be acceptable to his brethren, and let him dip his foot in oil.

25. Thy shoes *shall be* iron and brass; and as thy days, *so shall* thy strength *be*.

18. Et ipsi Zebulon dixit, Lætare Zebulon quum egredieris, et Issachar in tabernaculis tuis.

19. Populos ad montem vocabunt: et illic sacrificabunt sacrificia justitiæ, quoniam affluentiam maris sugent, et tecti thesauri arenæ.

20. Et ad Gad dixit, Benedictus qui dilatare fecit Gad: sicut leo habitabit, et rapiet brachium atque verticem.

21. Et vidit principium sibi, quod illic portio legislatoris tecta, veniet autem cum principibus populi: justitiam Jehovæ faciet, et judicia ejus cum Israele.

22. Et ad Dan dixit, Dan ut catulus leonis saltabit è Basan.

23. Et Nephthali dixit, O Nephthali satur beneplacito, et plene benedictione Jehovæ, occidentem et meridiem posside.

24. Et Aser dixit, Benedictus præ filiis Aser, erit beneplacens fratribus suis, et tingens in oleo pedem suum.

25. Ferrum et æs, calceamenta tua (*vel*, feræ tuæ): et sicut dies tui fortitudo tua.

18. *And of Zebulun he said.* He compares two tribes with each other, which, although neighbours in position, were still very dissimilar; for the one being devoted to mercantile

pursuits, went forth frequently in various directions; the other took more delight in quietude and repose; and this their great variety of condition is indicated, when he bids Zebulun rejoice in its expeditions, and Issachar in its domestic repose. Moses thus confirms the prophecy of Jacob, who said that Zebulun should "dwell at the haven of the sea," so as to make voyages of traffic; whilst Issachar, as delighting more in repose, should be lazy and idle, so as to make no objections against paying tribute, in order to purchase peace. (Gen. xlix. 13-15.)

What follows I suppose to be added, as though Moses had said that their distant location should not prevent them from going up with the others to Jerusalem, for the purpose of performing their religious duties. For in that they were farther removed from the temple, their zeal in the legal service might have grown cold. Although, then, they dwelt in the utmost borders of the land, Moses says that they should nevertheless come to offer sacrifices to God. By the *peoples* some understand the other tribes, which does not appear at all consistent; and others, foreign nations, to which their commercial intercourse gave them access. My interpretation, however, is simply that, although the length of the journey should invite them to remain at home, still they should mutually exhort each other to betake themselves in large companies to the temple. The end of the verse may be the statement of a reason for this, as if it were said, that they will be more attentive to the service of God, because, being enriched by Him, they will be desirous to offer Him the praise. And assuredly it is a sign of gross ingratitude, when we are not stimulated by God's blessings to strive more earnestly to render thanks to Him, in proportion as He deals more liberally with us. At the same time, Moses shews that, in consideration of their great wealth, the expenses of the journey would be by no means onerous to them; for, although their country was not very fertile, still its position was most advantageous for the acquirement of riches. Thus when it is here said, "they shall suck of the abundance of the seas," an antithesis is to be understood between the fruits of the earth and the abundant revenues derived from merchandise. To the same effect, "the treasures hid in the sand" are spoken of. For the exposition given by some, that their treasures should be so great as that they should hide them in the sand; and by others, that the sands should there be so prolific in silver and gold; and by others, that they should collect what the sea should throw up, is poor and vapid. Whereas, therefore, others should grow rich from their lands, Moses says, by an elegant figure, that the sands of Zebulun should be filled with hidden treasures, on account of their foreign traffic.

20. *And of Gad he said.* In the blessing of the tribe of Gad, mention is only made of the hereditary portion, which it had obtained without casting of lots. He therefore celebrates the blessing of God, because He had accorded to the Gadites an ample dwelling-place; for the word "enlargeth" refers to the extent of their possession. But inasmuch as in that extremity of the land beyond Jordan, they were on a hostile border, he declares that they would be warlike, and hence compares them to a lion, which tears its prey sometimes from the head, and sometimes from the arm. Since, then, that position would not be so peaceful as any other region in the midst of Canaan, he declares that they should be safe and sound, through their own audacity. And although it is not a very pleasant condition to be harassed by constant wars, still, in such a disagreeable case, God's grace was not to be despised, which made them formidable to their enemies, and of great valour, whereby they might not only repel hostile invasions, but be willing of themselves to make predatory expeditions. If any should object that license for rapine was quite unsuitable for God's children, the solution is obvious, that reference is not here made to what was lawful, or what was desirable and praiseworthy, but that a consolation was offered them by way of protection against the incursions and annoyances of their enemies. Besides, the lust for booty is not made permissible, but praise is merely given to their courage in overcoming their enemies.

21. *And he provided the first part for himself.*[1] Others

[1] *Lat.*, "And he saw the beginning (*principium*) for himself," &c. *Heb.* וירא ראשית.

translate it not badly, *the first-fruits.* Jerome's rendering, *pre-eminence* (*principatum,*) however, is quite out of the question. The word *beginning* (*principium,*) however, is very suitable, for Moses thus signifies that the Gadites were beforehand in seeking a dwelling-place for themselves; for before possession of the land was accorded to the people, they asked for the kingdom of Sihon for themselves. It is afterwards added, in what way they were provident in choosing their abode, namely, because God suggested to them that Moses was at liberty to assign this portion to them. For it is called the "portion of the lawgiver," as being that respecting which Moses might lawfully decide, since he appropriated it to the Gadites, not by hazard, nor otherwise than by God's command. It is called the *hidden* portion,[1] as not having been included by God in His promise. The sum is, that although God's will was not yet revealed, with respect to this addition to the land, still they obtained it through His secret liberality. And Moses desires that his decision with regard to the Gadites remaining on this side Jordan should be thus confirmed, since disputes might have otherwise arisen, inasmuch as God's promise had assigned the boundaries of the whole people on the opposite bank. Theirs is a poor exposition who explain it that Moses was buried there; and those also violently wrest the words, who understand by "the lawgiver" the chiefs of the Amorites, and render the words "hidden portion," *the ceiled palaces;*[2] nor would they have been thus extravagant in their notions, if the natural meaning which I have given had occurred to them.

The other clause of the verse is added by way of qualification; for Moses shews that this advantageous provision was made for the children of Gad, on condition that they should accompany the other tribes, and not return home

[1] *A. V.*, "seated;" *marg.*, "*Heb.* ceiled." See next note.

[2] ספון. Part. pahul, ספן, *to hide.* *S. M.*, ("Pro legislatore) abscondendo." *C* learnt from the notes of *S. M.* that Rabbi Salomon expounds this clause, "He saw that in that land the legislator, Moses, would be buried," and that Aben-Ezra had interpreted סחוקק, *great*, and ספון, *a house with a dome-like roof*, and had then paraphrased the clause, as meaning, "there is the place suitable for the great and noble, who dwell in palaces."—*W.*

until the land of Canaan was at peace, and their enemies subdued. And we have already seen that, when they sought for themselves this location outside the land, in the kingdom of the Amorites, they were severely rebuked by Moses, until they promised that they would share the war with their brethren until its conclusion. This is what Moses means by "executing the justice of God, and his judgments with Israel;" not only because it was but just that they should share the war with their brethren, and assist them in obtaining possession of the land, but because God ordained that His just vengeance should be executed upon those heathen and wicked nations by the whole of Israel, and had chosen all the tribes generally to be the ministers of His judgment; as it is said, in Ps. cxlix. 7, 8, 9, that they were charged "to execute vengeance upon the heathen, . . . to bind their kings with chains, and their nobles with fetters of iron; to execute upon them the judgment written;" for it was no common honour to be appointed to be, as it were, the judges of the ungodly, so as to destroy them all, and thus to purify the land.

22. *And of Dan he said.* He foretells that the tribe of Dan, like that of Gad, should be warlike, not so much from voluntary disposition, as from necessity; for their love of war was not to be deemed praiseworthy, inasmuch as it is altogether contrary to humanity; but because the unscrupulousness of the enemies, by which that tribe was infested, compelled them to take up arms. He compares it to a lion impetuously leaping from Mount Bashan; and the particle of comparison must be understood here, for Mount Bashan was not situated in the territory of this tribe. But Moses means to say that they should be as ready for the combat as a lion, which, after it has issued from its den into the open plains, makes an attack upon every one that it meets.

23. *And of Naphtali he said.* He predicts that God would deal bountifully towards these two tribes; for to the first a fertile district would be allotted towards "the west and the south." What he declares respecting the tribe of Asher is not free from ambiguity; for he is said to be blessed, מבנים, *mibanim, i. e.*, either *with* children, or *above*

children. If we prefer the former meaning, his prolificness (πολυτεκνία) is celebrated, as though it were said, Asher shall be blessed with a numerous progeny. There may, however, be a comparison between this tribe and the others; and this might justly be made to its advantage, because it had a very fertile district allotted to it, and abounding in wheat of the best quality, as the blessing of Jacob testifies, "Out of Asher shall bread be fat, and he shall yield royal dainties." (Gen. xlix. 20.)

He adds that "Asher shall be acceptable to his brethren;" from whence we gather that his tribe should be of a placid disposition: and afterwards figuratively celebrates the abundance of his oil, and iron, and brass. For to "dip his foot in oil," is as much as to say that he should collect an abundant supply of oil; and that "his shoes should be iron and brass," is nothing more than that he should tread upon a soil full of these metals. It is to be readily inferred from hence, as from preceding passages, that the blessings, which are now mentioned, are not so much wishes or prayers, as prophecies; since without the spirit of prophecy Moses could never have divined what, or what sort of, territory was to be bestowed on the several tribes.

Commentators vary as to the latter words; for some render the word דבא, *daba, old age,* or, *grief,* as if there were a transposition of the letters,[1] and thus restrict the meaning of the word "days" to youth; but others more correctly suppose, that Asher was to be strong and vigorous through the whole course of his life. Since, therefore, years gradually debilitate men, Moses promises to the posterity of Asher that their vigour should be retained to the very end of life.

26. *There is* none like unto the God of Jeshurun, *who* rideth upon the heaven in thy help, and in his excellency on the sky.	26. Non est similis Deo recti, qui equitat super cœlos in auxilium tuum, et in magnificentia sua super nubes.
27. The eternal God *is thy* refuge,	27. Habitaculum est Deus æter-

[1] דבא, a word whose root does not occur in Hebrew. The *LXX.*, and the Chaldee paraphrast, and the Syriac, are unanimous in rendering it *strength;* but the *V.* has *old age,* and those critics, who maintain this to be its meaning, are driven to suppose that it is formed irregularly from דאב.—*W.*

and underneath *are* the everlasting arms: and he shall thrust out the enemy from before thee, and shall say, Destroy *them*.

nus: et subter brachia sempiterna, ejecit a facie tua inimicum, et dixit, Disperde.

28. Israel then shall dwell in safety alone: the fountain of Jacob *shall be* upon a land of corn and wine; also his heavens shall drop down dew.

28. Et habitabit Israel confidenter solus (*vel,* suus) oculus Jacob: in terra frumenti et vini, etiam cœli ejus stillabunt rorem.

29. Happy *art* thou, O Israel: who *is* like unto thee, O people saved by the Lord, the shield of thy help, and who *is* the sword of thy excellency! and thine enemies shall be found liars unto thee; and thou shalt tread upon their high places.

29. Beatus es o Israel, quis similis tibi popule qui servaris in Jehova scuto auxilii tui, et gladio excellentiæ tuæ? humiliabuntur inimici tui, et tu super excelsa eorum calcabis.

26. *There is none like unto the God.* Moses proceeds from the parts to the whole, and now comes to speak of the whole body, which consisted of the twelve families. All that he says tends to the same end, viz., that the people of Israel were happy as being taken by God under His faithful guardianship: for nothing is more to be desired with regard to our best interests, than that our welfare should be intrusted to the hand of God. But, since this inestimable blessing of being protected by the care of God is often but lightly prized, Moses exclaims in admiration, that there is none to be compared to the God of Israel. We know that all nations had their tutelary gods or patrons, and foolishly gloried in their respective idols; although they often found from experience, that whatever confidence they placed in them was vain and frivolous. Moses, therefore, separates from this imaginary multitude of false gods the God of Israel, like whom, he says, none can be anywhere found. He also extols His power, because He rides gloriously on the heavens and clouds, which is tantamount to all high things being subject to His dominion. But, whereas it would be of little profit to reflect on His infinite power except in its connexion with ourselves, Moses expressly reminds us that God is not strong for Himself, but in order that He may help His people.

27. *The eternal God is thy refuge.* This is just as if he had said that the Israelites were protected from above by the help of God, and also based, as it were, upon Him.

The beginning of the prayer corresponds with that other in Ps. xc. 1, "LORD, thou hast been our dwelling-place in all generations." The sum is, that although the Israelites might be exposed to many injuries, still there was secure repose for them under the shadow of God's wings; and assuredly unless the hand of God had been like a roof to protect them, they would have perished a thousand times over. But, inasmuch as it would not be sufficient for our heads to be in safety, the other point is also added, viz., that God's arms should be stretched forth to sustain them from beneath. He calls them "everlasting," because the security of the pious, who rely upon God, is never shaken: it is, therefore, just as though he represented God to be at the same time the foundation, and the roof, of their abode. Others translate it less correctly, "Thou shalt live under the arms of the Everlasting;" for an elegant distinction is drawn,[1] which, however, tends to the same point, when God it called קדם, *kedem,* and His arms עלם, *gnolam,* the first of which words has reference to the past, whilst in the other there is allusion to the future; as if he had said of God, that He was from the beginning, and that His power would endure unto the end.

He adduces experimental evidence of the above statements, inasmuch as God had[2] miraculously destroyed the enemies of His people; at the same time he specifies the manner in which this was done, viz., that He had said, Destroy, or blot out, or dissipate. And by this word he signifies that, although God had made use of the agency of the Israelites, still He only was the conqueror; since the Israelites prevailed not except at His bidding, and by His will.

28. *Israel then shall dwell in safety alone.*[3] The beginning of the verse is by no means obscure, for Moses promises in it to the elect people what all have naturally a great desire for, viz., peace or tranquillity; for he is said to *dwell*

[1] This sentence is omitted in the Latin edition of 1563 though given in substance in the French of 1564.

[2] It will be seen that *C.* translates the verbs here in the past tense; *A. V.* in the future: "he *shall* thrust out, &c."

[3] *Lat.*, "Israel *hath* dwelt," &c.

confidently *alone*, who fears no danger, whom no care harasses, and who needs no garrison, or defence. This, indeed, God never vouchsafed altogether to the Israelites, that they should inhabit their land in security and without the fear of enemies, inasmuch as their ingratitude did not allow of it; and therefore the prophets, in enumerating the blessings of Christ's kingdom, declare that every one should "dwell beneath his own vine, and his own fig-tree."

For "the *fountain* of Jacob," some have the word *eye*,[1] and suppose it to be used metaphorically for his vision; as though it were said, that the quiet and peaceful habitation referred to was to be expected by the people from the vision of their father Jacob. Others, however, more correctly read the words "fountain of Jacob," in apposition (with Israel,) inasmuch as all the tribes derived their origin from that one father. In this way the "fountain" will not be only the actual source; but the rivulet, or stream, which flows down from it.

In conclusion, Moses promises that the very sky of the Holy Land should be propitious, and benignant.

29. *Happy art thou, O Israel.* He again exclaims that happy is the people, whose salvation is in God; and surely this is the only true happiness; for unless we ascend to the first cause of Salvation, all salvations, so to speak, are but transitory. And, since God had honoured the Israelites alone with this privilege, their condition is here distinguished from the common lot of the whole human race. By the words *shield* and *sword* is meant a perfect defence, as much as to say, that no part of their armour was to be sought elsewhere.

DEUTERONOMY, CHAPTER XXXIV.

1. And Moses went up from the plains of Moab unto the mountain of Nebo, to the top of Pisgah, that

1. Ascendit ergo Moses è planitie Moab ad montem Nebo, in verticem collis qui est è regione Jericho, et

[1] עין. A *spring*, or an *eye* (from its weeping.) The *V.* with *S.M.* have taken it to mean *an eye* here. Luther, Diodati, and *A.V.* *a fountain*. *C.* saw in the notes of *S.M.* that Kimchi and the Chaldee paraphrast had taken the word literally to be *the eye*, and, by metaphor, the vision of Jacob.—*W.*

is over against Jericho: and the Lord shewed him all the land of Gilead, unto Dan,

ostendit illi Jehova omnem terram Gilaad usque Dan,

2. And all Naphtali, and the land of Ephraim, and Manasseh, and all the land of Judah, unto the utmost sea,

2. Et universam Nephthali, et terram Ephraim, et Manasse, et omnem terram Jehuda usque ad mare novissimum:

3. And the south, and the plain of the valley of Jericho, the city of palm trees, unto Zoar.

3. Et meridiem, et planitiem, vallem Jericho urbis palmarum, usque ad Soar.

4. And the Lord said unto him, This *is* the land which I sware unto Abraham, unto Isaac, and unto Jacob, saying, I will give it unto thy seed: I have caused thee to see *it* with thine eyes, but thou shalt not go over thither.

4. Et dixit ei Jehova, Hæc est terra de qua juravi Abrahæ, Isaac et Jacob, dicendo: Semini tuo dabo illam: videre te feci oculis tuis, at illuc non transibis.

5. So Moses the servant of the Lord, died there in the land of Moab, according to the word of the Lord.

5. Itaque mortuus est illic Moses servus Jehovæ in terra Moab, secundum mandatum Jehovæ.

6. And he buried him in a valley in the land of Moab, over against Beth-peor: but no man knoweth of his sepulchre unto this day.

6. Et sepelivit eum in Gai, in terra Moab, è regione Beth-peor: neque cognovit quisquam sepulchrum ejus usque ad diem hunc.

1. *And Moses went up from the plains of Moab.* It is not certain who wrote this chapter; unless we admit the probable conjecture of the ancients, that Joshua was its author. But since Eleazar the priest might have performed this office, it will be better to leave a matter of no very great importance undecided.

We have elsewhere said, that one part of mount Abarim was called Nebo, as another was called Pisgah, because they were distinct summits.

Now, the ascent of Moses was equivalent to a voluntary going forth to death: for he was not ignorant of what was to happen, but being called by God to die, he went to meet death of his own accord. Such willing submission proceeded from no other source than faith in God's grace, whereby alone all terror is mitigated, and set at rest, and the bitterness of death is sweetened. Doubtless to Moses, as to every one else, it must have been naturally an awful thing to die; but inasmuch as the testimony of God's grace is interposed, he does not hesitate to offer himself without alarm; and because he was firmly persuaded that the inheritance of the people would be there set before his eyes, he cheerfully ascended to the place from which he was to behold it. Already, indeed, by faith had he beheld the land, and the promise of God had been, as it were, a lively representation of it; but, since some remaining infirmities of the flesh still environ even the most holy persons, an ocular view of it was no slight consolation, in order to mitigate the bitterness of his punishment, when he knew that he was prevented from actually entering it by the just sentence of God.

When it is said, that God "shewed him all the land," it could not have been the case without a miracle. For, although history records that some have been endued with incredible powers of vision, so as to have been able to see further than the whole length of Canaan; there is still a peculiarity to be remarked in this case, that Moses distinctly examined every portion of it, as if he had been really on the spot. I allow, indeed, that Naphtali, and Ephraim, and Manasseh are mentioned by anticipation, but, nevertheless, the Holy Spirit would express that every part was shewn to Moses, as if they were close beneath his feet. Else the vision would have been but unsatisfactory and useless, if he had not been allowed to behold the future habitation of the people. And to the same effect is also what is afterwards added, that it was the land, which God sware to give unto His servants; for otherwise the desire of Moses would not have been satisfied, unless he had seen what a pleasant, fertile, and wealthy region the sons of Abraham were about to inhabit.

5. *So Moses the servant of the Lord died.* Since it was a mark of ignominy to die without the borders of the Holy Land, Moses is honoured with high eulogy, in order that the Israelites might learn the more to tremble at the judgment of God, who did not spare even His most illustrious servant. And it is expressly added, "according to the word (or mouth) of the Lord," lest they should despise the threatenings which were accomplished in so memorable a manner. For, if God spared not His own distinguished Prophet, but at length executed upon him what He had threatened, how should the ordinary multitude escape?

What follows, "he buried him," some render passively,

"he was buried;" and others transitively, "he buried himself;" but in both cases improperly; for, whilst they are afraid to assign this office to God, they labour to avoid an absurdity which does not exist; since it may be gathered from the end of the verse, that Moses was buried by divine means, for it is said that his sepulchre is unknown. It is likely that an effort to discover it was not omitted, or neglected to be made by the people; since it would have been barbarous for them not to discharge the last offices of humanity towards such, and so great a man. Since, therefore, no signs of his funeral, nor his body itself, were anywhere to be found, it might be inferred that he was hidden by God's determinate counsel; whilst it is superfluous to discuss in what manner God buried him, inasmuch as all the elements are under His control. It was enough, therefore, for Him to signify (*annuere*) to the earth, that it was to receive the body of the holy man into its bosom: nor was there any necessity to call in the assistance of angels, as some think, since the earth would have instantly obeyed the command of its Creator. From the Epistle of Jude (ver. 9) we learn that it was a matter of no slight importance that the sepulchre of Moses should be concealed from the eyes of men, for he informs us that a dispute arose respecting it between Michael the archangel, and Satan: and, although the cause of its concealment is not stated, still it appears to have been God's intention to prevent superstition; for it was usual with the Jews, and it is a custom for which Christ reproves them, to kill the prophets, and then to pay reverence to their tombs. (Luke xi. 47.) It would have, therefore, been probable that, in order to blot out the recollection of their ingratitude, they would have paid superstitious veneration to the holy prophet, and so have carried his corpse into the land, from which the sentence of God had excluded it. Timely precaution, then, was taken, lest in their inconsiderate zeal the people should attempt to subvert the decree of heaven.

7. And Moses *was* an hundred and twenty years old when he died: his eye was not dim, nor his natural force abated.

7. Moses autem natus erat centum et viginti annos quando mortuus est: non caligavit oculus ejus, neque aufugit vigor ejus.

8. And the children of Israel wept for Moses in the plains of Moab thirty days: so the days of weeping *and* mourning for Moses were ended.

8. Et fleverunt filii Israel Mosen in campestribus Moab triginta diebus, completique sunt dies fletus luctus Mosis.

9. And Joshua the son of Nun was full of the spirit of wisdom; for Moses had laid his hands upon him: and the children of Israel hearkened unto him, and did as the Lord commanded Moses.

9. Josua autem filius Nun repletus est spiritu sapientiæ, quoniam posuerat Moses manus suas super eum: parueruntque ei filii Israel, ac fecerunt quemadmodum præceperat Jehova Mosi.

10. And there arose not a prophet since in Israel like unto Moses, whom the Lord knew face to face;

10. Neque surrexit propheta ultra in Israele sicut Moses, quem nosset Jehova facie ad faciem.

11. In all the signs and the wonders which the Lord sent him to do in the land of Egypt to Pharaoh, and to all his servants, and to all his land,

11. In omnibus signis et portentis ad quæ facienda in terra Ægypti Pharaoni et servis ejus, et universæ terræ ejus, miserat eum Jehova.

12. And in all that mighty hand, and in all the great terror which Moses shewed in the sight of Israel.

12. Et in omni manu forti, et in omni terrore magno, quæ fecit Moses in oculis totius Israelis.

7. *And Moses was an hundred and twenty years old.* Again he celebrates a special favour of God, viz., that all the senses of Moses remained unimpaired to extreme old age, in order that he might be fit for the performance of his duties: for thus it was manifested how dear to God was the welfare of the people, for which He so carefully provided. Some, indeed, though very few, are found, who are capable of public government, even to their hundredth year. Already, however, at that period, the vigour of the whole human race had so diminished that, after their seventieth year, they dragged on their life in "labour and sorrow," as Moses himself bears witness. (Ps. xc. 10.) It was, consequently a conspicuous sign of the paternal favour, wherewith God regarded His people, that Moses should have been thus unusually preserved in vigour and strength. If the powers of Moses had failed him long before their entrance of the promised land, his debility would have been very inconvenient to the people: yet naturally he would not have been so long sufficient for the performance of his onerous duties. It follows, then, that when God did not suffer him to fail, He shewed wonderful consideration for the people's welfare. Mention is specially made of his eyes, by *synecdoche,* yet the sum of the matter is this, that he was neither

imbecile nor feeble, for neither were the faculties of his mind exhausted, nor his body dried up.

It needs not that I expound at any length, what is added respecting the solemn mourning, because I have elsewhere shewn,[1] that the ancients were particular in their attention to the performance of funeral rites, on account of their faith not being as yet so elevated from the measure of revelation they had received, as to be easily able to forego those external aids to it, for which there is not the same necessity under the Gospel. It is natural to man to mourn for the dead; and, besides, this mourning was justly instituted in consequence of the loss which the Church had sustained; but a ceremony is here recorded, which was brought to an end with the fulfilment of the shadows of the Law. Our dead are, therefore, now to be buried in such a manner as that our grief may be restrained by the hope of resurrection so clearly revealed by the coming of Christ.

9. *And Joshua the son of Nun.* It is again shewn how perseveringly God provided for the welfare of the people. We have already seen how, at the request of Moses, Joshua was chosen to succeed him. Now, when he is about to take upon him his office, "the spirit of wisdom" was imparted to him, that it might be effectually manifested that he was appointed by God. He had been, indeed, previously endowed with excellent gifts, but he was now much more splendidly adorned with the ensigns of dignity, in order that his calling by God might be more certainly proved; for thus is God wont to furnish those, whom He calls, with capacity for action. The imposition of hands was also subjoined, which was no empty symbol of God's grace. But inasmuch as I have already fully spoken of these things, I now only lightly touch upon them.

10. *And there arose not a prophet.* This eulogy seems to have been added, that the children of Abraham might place dependence on Moses until the manifestation of Christ; for although prophets were from time to time raised up, still it was fitting that the superiority should remain with Moses, lest they should decline in the smallest degree from the rule

[1] See on Lev. xxi. 1, vol. ii. p. 228.

of the Law. It must be concluded, therefore, that Moses was here placed in a position of supremacy, so as to be superior to all the prophets; as also Malachi (iv. 4) exhorts the ancient people, in order that they may continue obedient to the law of Moses. Two signs of his excellency are here recorded, namely, his familiar acquaintance with God, and the glory of his miracles. We have elsewhere seen that, by this prerogative, Moses was distinguished from the other prophets, that God spake to him face to face. For, although Jacob makes the same declaration respecting himself, still we know that God was more intimately revealed afterwards to Moses; not indeed that He beheld His glory in its perfection, but because, in comparison with others, he went beyond them all. As regards miracles, though they were wrought by others, still none of them came near to Moses in their performance.

END OF COMMENTARIES ON THE FOUR LAST BOOKS
OF MOSES, IN THE FORM OF
A HARMONY.

INDEX

OF HEBREW WORDS EXPLAINED.

INDEX

OF PASSAGES REFERRED TO, QUOTED, OR EXPLAINED.

GENERAL INDEX

TO THE FOUR LAST BOOKS OF THE PENTATEUCH.

A

D

H

I

N

O

P.

T

U

V

W

X

Y

Z

INDEX

OF THE CHAPTERS AND VERSES OF THE FOUR LAST BOOKS OF THE PENTATEUCH, SHEWING WHERE THE EXPOSITION OF THEM WILL BE FOUND.

NUMBERS.

DEUTERONOMY.

www.ingramcontent.com/pod-product-compliance
Lightning Source LLC
Chambersburg PA
CBHW051856090426
42811CB00003B/353

* 9 7 9 8 3 8 5 2 0 9 9 1 0 *